IDENTITY AND TERRITORIAL AUTONOMY IN PLURAL SOCIETIES

Editors

William Safran
University of Colorado, Boulder

Ramón Máiz
University of Santiago de Compostela

FRANK CASS
LONDON • PORTLAND, OR.

First published in 2000 in Great Britain by
FRANK CASS PUBLISHERS
Newbury House, 900 Eastern Avenue, London IG2 7HH

and in the United States of America by
FRANK CASS PUBLISHERS
c/o ISBS, 5804 N.E. Hassalo Street
Portland, Oregon 97213-3644

Website www.frankcass.com

British Library Cataloguing in Publication Data
Identity and territorial autonomy in plural societies. –
(Nationalism and ethnicity; no. 3)
1. Nationalism 2. National characteristics 3. Autonomy
4. Pluralism (Social science)
I. Safran, William II. Máiz Suárez, Ramón
320.5'4'089
ISBN 0 7146 5027 7 (cloth)

Library of Congress Cataloging-in-Publication Data:
Identity and territorial autonomy in plural societies / editors,
William Safran, Ramón Máiz.
    p. cm. – (Nationalism and ethnicity, ISSN 1462-9755)
    "First appeared in a special issue of Nationalism & ethnic politics
    (ISSN 1353-7113), Vol. 5, Nos. 3 & 4 (Autumn/Winter 1999)" – T.p. verso.
Includes bibliographical references and index.
ISBN 0-7146-5027-7 (cloth) – ISBN 0-7146-8083-4 (paper)
1. Nationalism. 2. Ethnicity – Political aspects. 3. Autonomy.
I. Safran, William. II. Máiz Suárez, Ramón. III. Series
JC312.I34 2000
321.02'3–dc21   99-087437

This group of studies first appeared in a special issue of Nationalism & Ethnic Politics
[ISSN 1353-7113] Vol.5, Nos. 3&4 (Autumn /Winter 1999) published by Frank Cass.

Printed in Great Britain by
Antony Rowe Ltd., Chippenham, Wilts.

Contents

Introduction

WILLIAM SAFRAN

The character of the nation has in recent years been the object of renewed discussion. Three or four decades ago, the 'nation-state' was considered the ideal type and the end product of political development towards which newly independent states were, or should be, striving; but subsequently it came to be challenged by a number of events. In the Third World, notably in sub-Saharan Africa, the applicability of the notion of a causal chain of independence – state building – nation building – democracy (with the attendant expectation of economic prosperity), which was accepted almost as a political law of nature, was put in doubt as the overwhelming majority of ethnic groups refused to dissolve into enlarged and internally undifferentiated political communities. In Europe, the nation-state was gradually demystified, and its image was tarnished by the oppressive and often barbaric behavior of advanced industrial countries, notably during the authoritarian interlude from the 1920s to the end of World War II. After the war, the superior claims of the nation-state were called into question as the various European countries proved unable to ensure peace and promote reconciliation and reconstruction on an individual national basis and had to band together under a supranational framework that culminated in the European Union.

With the founding of the Soviet Union and the post-war communization of east-central Europe, traditional nationalist ideology was believed to have been eclipsed by a transnational and transethnic class consciousness. That consciousness, however, had for the most part been politically engineered and institutionally (and undemocratically) enforced; and in the end it turned out to be ephemeral. With the implosion of the Soviet Union and the disintegration of the Communist system, the post-Soviet states of east-central Europe recovered their pre-Soviet (and/or pre-Nazi) sovereignties and, in so doing, seemed determined to revert to a traditional nationalism. But this proved to be difficult, for these 'successor' states found themselves with ethnic subcommunities that refused to give up their collective identities and demanded a degree of cultural, if not necessarily political, autonomy. There were two notable exceptions: Poland and Slovenia – the former having acquired a significant degree of national homogeneity as a result of 'ethnic cleansing', expulsions, and boundary shifts; and the latter having been left with a relatively insignificant number of ethnic minorities after the breakup of Yugoslavia.

A more recent challenge to the homogeneous nation-state came with the migration of massive numbers of people from one country to another, whether voluntarily, in search of better economic opportunities, or forcibly, as a result of expulsion or of flight from political oppression. In short, it had to be acknowledged that in most countries, state and nation were no longer congruent. The growing ethnocultural complexity of many modern societies has led academicians and politicians to re-examine the assumptions of nationalism and the meaning and evolution of forms of collective identity and to take up the problem of how to combine pluralism and sociopolitical stability – more specifically, how to ensure the preservation of both subnational identities and national unity.

The contributions that follow attempt to deal with these questions both by means of broad-ranged comparative-theoretical approaches and more precisely focused case studies. The former address themselves to the various meanings of autonomy and nationalism, to the variable forms of subnational governments, and to the role they play in reflecting collective identities; the latter exemplify experiences in Western Europe, Eastern Europe, Asia, Africa, and North America. Some of these experiences are presented in considerable detail.

The initial essay by the present writer attempts to compare territorial and non-territorial approaches to autonomy (as alternatives to both cultural homogenization and separatism) and the way they relate to one another. It also deals with the reasons for the different institutional and policy choices, including criteria of entitlement, and their consequences both for the ethnic minority and the dominant majority (or 'host' polity), both with respect to system stability and democratic and other values. Finally, it discusses the relationship between autonomy and interstate relations.

The contribution by Ramón Máiz provides a discussion of the complex relationship between democracy and nationalism – specifically, of the extent to which the definition of the nation as an indivisible unit and, indeed, the very notion of citizenship, is challenged by multiethnic society. Máiz calls for a more subtle approach to 'sovereignty' than has been provided by the Jacobin dogma of the nation-state. He stresses the importance of culture in the interpretation of political and social realities – an interpretation that is difficult to imagine without some form of autonomy. In his discussion of democracy and liberty, he points to the connection between individual rights and group rights, and he calls into question the traditional liberal assumption about the coextensiveness of cultural and political domains and the democratic nature of a society that seeks to homogenize an ethnoculturally diverse population. He examines various

approaches to constitutional engineering, and, making a strong plea for
pluralism as a political value in itself, he lays out a blueprint for a federal
arrangement that combines the preservation of cultural pluralism with
political unity – in other words, that makes possible both self-government
and shared rule.

Luis Moreno explores the relationship between local, national, and
intermediate forms of government and administration. He discusses the
impact of the information revolution, globalization, migration, and the
development of transnationalism and supranationality upon traditional
definitions of sovereignty. Supranational approaches lead to new
competences that are, for instance, reflected in the 'subsidiarity principle' of
the European Union. These developments lead to new approaches to
problem-solving and, in so doing, reinforce local and other subnational
identities. Such identities must not be considered parochial; rather, they are
forms of 'cosmopolitan localism'.

The experiences of Spain have been dealt with in a separate subsection,
not only because the contributions are based on a colloquium held in
Santiago de Compostela but, more important, because these experiences are
particularly interesting since the end of the Franco regime and the return of
Spain to the western model of constitutional democracy have also meant the
reinstitution of ethnic pluralism and the relegitimation of the claims of
subnational communities with their unique cultures – an effort that has led,
in turn, to a quasi-federal approach to accommodating strong provincial
sentiments without destroying the coherence of the Spanish state.

The four contributions are related; yet they approach the Spanish
situation from somewhat different perspectives. In a discussion rich in
historical detail, Justo Beramendi attempts to account for the apparent
coexistence of both 'national' unitary sentiments and strong regional
identities by reference, on the one hand, to relatively early political (but
'pre-national') consolidation and, on the other hand, to the fact that the state
that was built was weak and socio-economically underdeveloped. Francesco
Llera focuses on the Basque case, concentrating on the competition between
two strategies for achieving self-government, namely, party politics and
violence. In that effort, he refers to the memory of past oppression of the
Basques, which accounts for much of their present-day resort to violence.
Llera furnishes interesting survey data on public attitudes and political
mobilization as well as electoral data, which reflect a continuing tension
between anti-system activism and peaceful adaptation to the Spanish state
in response to institutional accommodation to autonomist demands. Xosé-
Manoel Nuñez, while stressing the minority nationalisms of the Basque
country, Catalonia, and Galicia, extends his discussion by analysing the
specific identities of 'non-ethnic' regions and the political means by which

these have been expressed. Antón Losada discusses the case of Galicia specifically. He explains the post-Franco development of regional autonomy, which occurred in several phases. He offers a detailed examination of the law that set up the *Autonomía* model, which provided for variable jurisdictions – national, provincial, and shared. Losada also analyses the legislative and other institutions and the political parties and personalities that have influenced their functioning. The study contains important data on public opinion as well as on the economic impact of autonomy, which has created an opportunity structure for both the growth of national solidarity and the consolidation of subnational identity.

The remaining contributions consider cases of individual countries on four continents. The Yugoslav situation exemplifies the irruption of traditional nationalist fever culminating in ethnocidal policies. Steven Majstorovic, focusing on the most recent conflict over Kosovo, provides a detailed background of that province's relationship to Serbia. Unlike so many political scientists, who ignore history because it is regarded as myth based on faulty memory, he recalls the past; in so doing, he tries not to take sides in apportioning blame. At the end, he introduces scenarios for a 'least worst' (*sic*) approach, which include combinations of territorial and personal autonomy, functional partition, dual citizenship, and consociational structures, in part in the context of a 'soft' (Serbian or Albanian) sovereignty, all to be guaranteed, in the short run, by NATO and legitimated by the international community. Such approaches might serve as a model for Macedonia and perhaps other conflict-ridden multiethnic areas.

Swarna Rajagopalan's contribution explores the relationship between collective identity and space and between rival identities and the conflict over space. She admits that territorial claims, including a quest for some form of autonomy, often reflect other grievances; in India, however, the demarcation units, rather than merely corresponding to a subcommunity's linguistic identity (as had been envisaged earlier) or history, are constitutional artefacts in so far as they are dependent on the will of the decision makers of the country as a whole. One reason for that is that subunits are themselves internally fragmented; another is that, unlike the US federal system, the federation of India has been based not on the delegation of jurisdictions from below to a national government but (as in the case of unitary systems) on the apportionment of 'original' political powers from above. Such apportionment was based on a variety of rationales – language (which was to become more important later on), religion, national security, administrative convenience, and (to a lesser extent) history. These criteria did not fully apply to Pakistan and Sri Lanka. In the construction of the former, the ethnicity and history of the component parts played a crucial role. The latter country was originally envisaged as a federal state, but its redefinition as a unitary state, with districts rather than ethnolinguistic regions as the basic components, led the Tamils to react by rejecting the notion of a transethnic 'national' identity and by making exaggerated claims for the extent of their community, thereby provoking a hostile counter-reaction on the part of the Sinhalese community. The three-country study points to a reciprocal causality between the actions of the state on the one hand, and the development of ethnocommunal identity and the territorial autonomy claims derived from that identity on the other hand. At the end, Rajagopalan offers several possible approaches to resolving the conflict between autonomy demands and national political unity.

Dennis Thomson's contribution on selected Indian tribes in Canada is a study in contrast. Unlike ethnic minorities in other countries, many of the tribes have been interested primarily in the maintenance of their way of life. Some have attempted to obtain from the government whatever economic help has been available; others have tended to reject those benefits that have threatened to infringe upon their culture, preferring cultural isolation. Most of them have been living on the margins of society at large rather than as fully integrated members of it, to the extent that has been feasible in face of physical encroachment by predatory outsiders and the economic modernization of the country. Some of the tribes have lobbied the national or provincial government, but that has not been easy, in view of the uncertain legal position of the Indian tribes. The economic and cultural conditions in their 'reserves' and their relationship with the government at various levels are traced chronologically and described in some detail. Canadian pluralism, according to Thomson, has been a socioeconomic (i.e., interest-group) pluralism but not an ethnocultural one – except, of course, for the recognition of the two 'constituent' communities, the Anglo and the Québécois, and their respective languages. That explains why accommodation of the tribes has stopped short of territorially based autonomy. Although the treaties made with the governments representing the European settlers in Canada officially conveyed the impression that the Indians were a sovereign nation, and hence a full negotiating partner, the Europeans in fact never regarded them as such. Although the Indians have considered themselves a nation, they have been interested, not in 'sovereignty' or even territorial autonomy in the strict formal sense, but in selective functional autonomy.

Shaheen Mozaffar and James Scarritt provide a detailed discussion of ethnic diversity in Africa. They question the feasibility of territorial autonomy for ethnic groups because ethnicity is only one of many markers of collective identity, the others being religion, language, territoriality, socioeconomic condition, and so on. They argue that ethnic identity is not fixed, but rather that it is a social construction of the state; and that where it is used as a basis of political mobilization it is done for instrumental purposes, i.e., for getting benefits from the state. Territorial autonomy is rejected also because it would lead to secession and the creation of hundreds of small, economically unviable mini-states. Most important, such autonomy would not solve the ethnic problem since the majority of areas where ethnic groups are heavily concentrated have their own minorities, who might demand autonomy in turn. Moreover, a political legitimation of ethnic claims is impossible to obtain within existing borders, because many ethnic communities spill over into neighbouring countries. The analysis is tightly reasoned; yet it is heavily informed by the 'anti-ethnic' ideology often found among American scholars of African political development. Taking the United States as their models, whether explicitly or implicitly, and convinced that ethnic consciousness is less 'rational' than concrete (i.e., economic) interest, they consider the quest for territorial autonomy to be based on 'reflexive primordialism' and therefore as reactionary. They insist that most ethnic minorities in sub-Saharan Africa do not pursue political autonomy, territorial or other; rather, they are 'communal contenders' competing with each other for relative advantage, in a way that may not involve the state – or may involve it primarily in so far as it provides payoffs to claimants based on the effectiveness with which they are organized. The authors' position is reflected in the fact that autonomy is thought of in terms of a negative prototype – that of apartheid – and in the belief that the territorial configurations of African states, the result of European imperialism, should now be accepted as *faits accomplis*. Curiously, the authors do not discuss functional or personal autonomy as alternatives to territorial autonomy.

Finally, the contribution by Caroline Hartzell and Donald Rothchild looks at the problem of autonomy from an international and cross-national perspective. The authors refer, *inter alia*, to the multiple, and often contradictory, causes of ethnic conflict: the domination of society as a whole by a single ethnic group (or its élite) to the detriment of rival groups (or their élites); the existence of a weak state that undermines the confidence of minorities by its inability to provide benefits across the ethnic spectrum or to maintain itself against the claims and counter-claims of ethnic groups; or, conversely, the existence of an excessively strong state that lords it over one or another ethnic group. The basic problem is how to prevent, or end, ethnic conflict – that is, how to reconcile state control and political unity with the desire of subcommunities for a modicum of self-determination. The authors examine 35 cases of civil war, for the most part in ethnically divided societies, and, being concerned with internal stability rather than nation-building or state maintenance for its own sake, they tend to be fairly positively inclined towards autonomy arrangements. They posit a variety of arrangements for autonomy, from federalism to local self-government to functional autonomy; and the weight of the evidence they marshal, although not conclusive in view of continuing ethnic wars, suggests a significant correlation between some form of territorial autonomy and regime stability.

The findings, interpretations, and propositions presented here are suggestive rather than categorical. Given the uncertainties that continue to prevail in Yugoslavia, and in Kosovo in particular, after the end of the recent NATO military intervention in the region, analyses are bound to be provisional and any scenarios can be only hypothetical. In India, ethnic pluralism is, on the one hand, politically divisive and, on the other hand, a way of defining the country's nature and even its *raison d'être*; in addition, it serves as an indicator of its commitment to democracy. In Africa, the expectations of democratization have not yet been convincingly fulfilled, and workable alternatives to ethnic autonomy have not yet been found; and in Canada, uncertainty continues to prevail about the prospects of independence of Québec, and about what contagion such independence might produce on the indigenous or 'aboriginal' communities and their own claims of autonomy. In the international arena as a whole, conflicts continue between ethnic (or religious) majorities and minorities and between the latter and the state, and these make generalizations difficult and predictions hazardous. Yet it is hoped that the chapters that follow will contribute to further debate about the meanings of identity and autonomy and the relationship between them.

I. COMPARATIVE APPROACHES

Spatial and Functional Dimensions of Autonomy: Cross-national and Theoretical Perspectives

WILLIAM SAFRAN

Problems of Terminology

A scholar attempting to deal with the theme defined by the title of this paper is faced with a number of difficulties. In the first place, there has been a widespread terminological confusion: self-government and autonomy are often used interchangeably, and autonomy has undergone incessant conceptual stretching. Thus in a book on autonomy that appeared two decades years ago, the term was used variously, not to refer to self-government, but as a synonym for pluralism, diversity, ethnically concentrated neighbourhoods, ethnonationalist movements, ethnic minority sentiments, and even the fight against discrimination.[1] In the view of some scholars, 'self-determination' goes beyond mere self-government, in that it refers to the principle that a community 'simply because it considers itself to be a separate national group, is uniquely and exclusively qualified to determine its own political status, including, should it so desire, the right to its own state'.[2]

An additional problem is the fact that, while there are numerous instances of self-government of territorially concentrated minorities, usually reflected in federalism or similar 'decentralist' approaches, there are relatively few examples of self-government of geographically dispersed minorities. Such minorities, usually (and often misleadingly) referred to as diasporas, have generally been objects of discrimination, expulsion, extermination, and occasionally even special protection; but they have seldom been accorded autonomy.[3] That has been the case despite the fact that autonomy of dispersed minorities is less threatening to the political integrity of the 'host' country than autonomy of concentrated minorities.

In many writings dealing with ethnic minorities and, specifically, with the problem of protecting their cultural rights, a distinction is made between territorial and non-territorial autonomy. The former refers to the granting of formal jurisdictional authority within a larger political entity defined as a

William Safran, University of Colorado, Boulder

state; the latter, to selective approaches to accommodation that I have called 'functional' autonomy, but that have been referred to elsewhere as examples of 'personal' autonomy[4] and 'institutional' autonomy.[5] There is considerable difference of opinion about, first, which kind of autonomy is more likely to prevent, or lead to, secession and which is to be avoided; second, which kind is more likely to satisfy the cultural claims of minorities; and, third, which minority is entitled to what kind of autonomy, and for what reason.

A clear distinction between territorial and other kinds of autonomy cannot be made, because all autonomies have a 'spatial' dimension. The idea of territoriality is suggested by the existence of networks of institutions – cultural, educational, social, commercial, and/or religious – that serve the particular needs of ethnic minorities. Churches, mosques, synagogues, cultural centres, commercial establishments and party and association headquarters all constitute physical magnets that serve the members of an ethnic community and together add up to a 'functional' territory. Where ethnic populations are widely scattered, autonomy can be only functional or (in Lapidoth's usage) 'personal'. Such autonomy implies selective self-management in educational and other activities mentioned above. The spatial dimension of such self-management is clearly evident when one speaks of ethnic city quarters, ghettos, gang 'turfs', Chinatowns, Harlems, barrios and Little Italies. Not all of these 'territories' are poor, and many of them have been established by the ethnic community itself. This is as true of most Chinatowns as of 'gated' communities for the rich, of urban enclaves of Hassidim, or of the normative orthodox Jewish communities who have created an eruv, an 'imaginary' physical boundary within which walking on the sabbath is permitted. It is also true of rural areas, such as Indian reservations and Amish rural districts.

In many cities, the influx of 'alien' populations has been so massive that it has resulted in a clustering of ethnically specific housing projects, specialty shops, voluntary societies and other institutions in selected neighbourhoods. This produces a degree of functional self-containment that has a territorial dimension in the sense that many activities take place within a limited space. These activities add up to 'autonomy' if they are voluntary and the state does not interfere. They add up to segregation if this clustering is externally enforced, if it is conditioned by economic necessity or if it serves as a protection against a hostile external society.[6]

Functional autonomy does not provide the jurisdictional boundaries that often serve to maintain the particular identity of ethnic minority communities. Under functional autonomy, such identity is nevertheless safeguarded in an urban or other spatial setting in the sense that the 'outside' world leaves the community more or less alone – in return for which the community does not threaten the political integrity of the state or the province. The network of ethnically specific institutions may compensate for the lack of legally defined subdivision of space associated with territorial autonomy. The impact of this functional space depends of course on the depth and intensity of the culture and thickness of the institutional network. These factors may be so important that they have an ethnogenic impact on residents in the area, whether or not they are 'categorically' members of the ethnic community. For example, assimilated bourgeois Jewish residents of Sarcelles, a working class town north of Paris with a heavy proportion of North African Jews, have been infected with a stronger Jewish collective consciousness than they had before.

The spatial character of ethnic institutions is reflected in the fact that the entry of individuals not belonging to the ethnic community tends to be regarded by it as an intrusion. This protectiveness is the obverse of the attitude of members of the ethnic majority, who regard the existence of the ethnic minority area as an encroachment or 'invasion' and as destroying the seamless continuity of *their* surroundings. One notes, for example, the frequent assertions of French or German citizens that a mosque does not quite fit into their town. In any case, the attempts by ethnic minorities to protect their 'turf' may be insufficient for maintaining their cultural uniqueness, especially if they are surrounded by a numerically strong majority whose culture is attractive and whose economy has a significant cooptive potential.

Practical functional autonomy may give a member of an ethnic minority the same cultural services that would be available in a legally defined autonomous territory. A Maghrebi Muslim immigrant in France may enjoy just as much protection for his religious and cultural rights in a functional autonomy setting where a network of institutional space exists. Under territorially defined autonomy, the cultural patrimony of minorities may be better protected against outside infringement; conversely, it may provide fewer cultural choices. The daughter of a Maghrebi Muslim immigrant might wish to escape and choose alternative (say, French) cultural options; but such choices would be more difficult if Maghrebi autonomy were too strictly defined.

The functional autonomies associated with Chinatowns or other ethnic urban preserves in big cities are usually *de facto* and not *de jure*, and can be taken away via urban renewal projects (or what cynics have called 'minority removal' projects) and a variety of city ordinances. But such a power is mostly theoretical; governments are not always strong enough to raze entire city districts. Territorial autonomy, because it is legally grounded, provides firmer protection against such intervention; but (unless we are speaking of selected federal systems) such autonomy, too, can be removed by national legislation. Territorial autonomy is sometimes preferred to functional or 'personal' autonomy because it creates an additional level of government, which may provide more regular, and better funded, ethnocultural services. Often, however, such services are of greater benefit to the ethnic élite (or ethnic entrepreneurs) than to the rank and file: the former have a vested interest in maintaining such autonomy, whereas the benefits of formal autonomy within administratively (over-)defined boundaries are uncertain. There may even be a disadvantage to members of ethnic minorities, insofar as they may be locked in to an ethnic minority situation which they would rather give up in order to 'exit' to the majority culture for the sake of economic benefits and upward mobility.

Who Deserves Ethnic Autonomy? The Question of Entitlement

The question normally asked in connection with the right to full political self-determination (secession) may also apply to the right to autonomy, namely: are ethnic minorities indiscriminately entitled to autonomy in terms of specific criteria? The number of 'deserving' candidates for autonomy is considerably reduced if they cannot answer positively one or more of the following questions:

- Are the members of the ethnic minority better off with autonomy or without it? Are the benefits cultural rather than economic, and what relative weights do members of the ethnic community attach to these benefits?
- Does the history of relations between the minority and majority suggest a pattern of political and/or economic discrimination so serious as to constitute a legitimate grievance that must be repaired?
- Is the threat posed by the majority to the maintenance of the minority culture under the existing system so serious that only some form of autonomy can alleviate that threat?
- Is the quality of the ethnic culture such as to be worth preserving, especially in comparison with one that might eclipse or replace it?
- Are the values of the ethnic culture compatible with other values that are transethnic, such as individual liberty, democracy, tolerance, social justice, peace, and equality?[7]
- Does the ethnic community have the institutional or economic means to profit from the autonomy it is offered?
- Does the provision of autonomy, or any other spatial arrangement or confinement, preserve the freedoms and the options of members of the ethnic minority that they already possess as individuals, or does it lock people into an identity that they might otherwise be tempted to abandon?

Affirmative answers to these questions suggest that some form of autonomy is necessary or desirable for the minority in question. It is to be recommended in a situation where the nationalism of a state with an ethnically mixed population is based on an illiberal and exclusivist nativism that provides little if any cultural space for minorities, has contempt for their culture, discriminates against them or oppresses them. It is to be avoided if the definition of membership in the political community is based on civic rather than organic-ascriptive nationalism, and where civil society is strong enough to make room for the expression of the cultures of minorities who may freely organize along ethnically specific lines in the context of a permissive and, where necessary, a supportive state. Autonomy is also to be avoided if it is likely to lead to a reinforcement of a subsystem political culture that is less tolerant, less open, and less democratic than that of society as a whole. Under a juridically (and more or less rigidly) defined territorial autonomy, Northern Italy ('Padania') would probably gain more than it would lose: it would retain more of its wealth while retaining existing democratic patterns and individual liberties. Conversely, an autonomous Mezzogiorno, while assuring greater power for traditional élites and more freedom to the Mafia, would be detrimental to the individual inhabitant, who would lose the economic aid coming from the North and who might also lose some of the constitutional protections provided by the Italian state. It is an open question whether the ethnic Albanians in Kosovo would gain greater individual freedom under formal territorial autonomy than they possessed before the recent war in Yugoslavia.

A number of analytic paradigms may serve to answer the questions posed above.

The Institutionalist Approach. The very existence of autonomy acts as a spur to the preservation and expansion of the collective responsibilities of a minority, even if these have become less relevant over time. If the demand for self-determination is the consequence of nationalism, and if nationalism is the ideology of 'an imagined political community',[8] that imagination soars and becomes reified as locally based ethnic institutions take shape that foster contact with similar institutions outside the country.

The 'Culturalist' Explanation. Minorities marked by a civic and 'participatory' culture are more likely to demand greater involvement in decisions affecting their own fate than those marked by a parochial and 'subject' culture. It is unclear, however, whether a civic orientation leads members of a minority to demand more meaningful participatory structures for their community or for themselves as members of the *civic nation* or the *ethnic group*. It is equally unclear in what way political culture is influenced by patterns of autonomy. For example, if Maghrebis in France were given significant autonomy in running an educational system, would they be tempted to invite Algerian educators who might spread ideas counter to French republican ideology? Or, on the contrary, would their French civic nationalism develop to the point where secular values replace their religious ones and the interest in cultural autonomy would wane?

Rational Choice. Functional autonomy may be a more flexible, more useful, and less dangerous approach than territorial autonomy, especially where the ethnic minority population is thinly dispersed, and therefore a more rational option for both the state and the minority. Even where population concentration appears to warrant micro-partitions, the territorial autonomy thus gained may make economic transactions less efficient, thereby neutralizing the minority's cultural gains by economic losses. Moreover, the creation of territorial micro-units in ethnically homogeneous areas may be based on the assumption (as in the cantons and half-cantons of Switzerland) that this homogeneity will remain unaltered.[9] This assumption has been called into question by population shifts, as, for example, in Belgium, Britain, and Israel. Territorially based autonomy becomes increasingly questionable as a consequence of migrations of diverse minority groups into conurbations in industralized democracies.

Considerations of rationality, therefore, argue for communal or 'personal autonomy'.[10] To be sure, this leaves open the question of how inclusive such autonomy should be, how far it should it extend, and how free members of a minority group should be to decide whether, and to what extent, to avail themselves of that autonomy. For instance, they may decide to partake of the language aspect of that autonomy, but not the religious, or vice versa, their decision depending on their rational calculation of cultural, economic, and social advantages for themselves and their families. Sometimes such options are not easily available to individual members of an ethnic or religious group. In order for the community's autonomy to be maintained, it needs a critical mass of members; and in order to secure it, individuals may be confined (by family and other social pressures) within the minority culture in such a way that they cannot easily get out: tribal scarring, tattooing, bodily mutilation or the inculcating of inferiority syndromes are often permanent and make it impossible for an individual to abandon his minority identity.[11] The question of what is the best *collective* choice becomes even more complicated: the costs and benefits of autonomy – political participation, cultural payoffs or psychic satisfactions, as against inferior education, jobs or chances of upward social mobility and a growing hostility on the part of the majority – are not the same for the ethnic minority élite and for the ethnic rank-and-file, even assuming that the latter were undifferentiated.

The criterion of rationality is often associated with that of legitimacy. Thus the French would not consider Basque, Catalan, or Breton demands for autonomy legitimate, because it is an article of the Jacobin faith that France is a country that is democratic; that it is 'one and indivisible'; that it treats all individuals equally regardless of their origins; and that sufficient opportunities exist to pursue ethnic cultural interests within a free society. In view of this, it is argued, autonomy would only reinforce 'primordial' collective identities; it would be retrogressive and for that reason lack legitimacy. Spain does not have a Jacobin ideology, and the existence of Catalan and Galician identities combines easily enough with membership in the Spanish nation. For that reason, Catalonia appears to be satisfied with autonomy instead of total independence. Moreover, in its present position, Catalonia functions as a 'kingmaker' for Spain as a whole while protecting its cultural autonomy.

The question of the rationality of the quest for autonomy is more complex in the case of Corsica. Given the history of that island – including the fact that Napoleon was born there and the fact that at least a third of its inhabitants are immigrants from the mainland or from North Africa – formal national independence is highly unlikely. Under the French decentralization laws of the 1980s, Corsica attained a considerable degree of self-government in selected areas. Yet most Corsicans want *more* autonomy in order to express their Corsican identity (*corsitude*). However, the values of *corsitude* (expressed in traditional economic pursuits, affective social relátions, and ascriptive approaches to problem-solving) may clash with values of *francité*, which include free and fair elections, freedom of association, *laïcité* (secularity), and the rule of law; and there is some doubt whether these values could maintain themselves adequately and protect Corsican residents against clan rule without French national 'overlordship' (*tutelle*).[12] Moreover, there is the infusion of considerable economic aid from the mainland government; and the question arises whether Corsicans could handle autonomy if it implies the obligation to make independent economic policy decisions.[13]

An ethnic community's claim to autonomy is often expressed in terms of 'legitimate rights'. Exactly what does legitimacy mean when one speaks of the rights of Palestinians in the Middle East, Kosovars in Yugoslavia, or Algerian immigrants in France? Is the claim of Palestinians legitimated by agreement of the major powers, by popular vote, or by improvements with respect to democracy, liberty, or prosperity? Amitai Etzioni has spoken of 'the evils of self-determination'.[14] He may have exaggerated; nevertheless, self-determination, or autonomy, may have more negative than positive consequences: there may be less democracy, liberty, or prosperity than prevailed before autonomy. As citizens of the successor state of Poland, many people enjoyed less individual freedom and less democracy, and some minorities less economic prosperity, than they had as citizens of the Austria-Hungarian monarchy. It is true that Kurds in Iraq enjoy neither democracy nor individual liberty; but there is no way of telling whether they would enjoy more of these things under conditions of autonomy within that country or, for that matter, as citizens of an independent Kurdistan. The same uncertainty applies to Chechnya, which does not have an indigenous democratic tradition.

For the Bantustans of South Africa, autonomy was no substitute for complete sovereignty, because it was accompanied by as much misery, and as little democracy, as had existed before, except that this time, the misery was administered more directly by their own people. Complete political independence, however, is not necessarily an improvement over one or another form of autonomy, because it might not bring about democracy. For Kosovars, Magyars, Bosnian Muslims, as well as Croats and Serbs (under numerical minority status), autonomy, however limited within an integral Yugoslavia, was arguably preferable to the condition they fell under after the break-up of Yugoslavia. Economic conditions, individual liberties, and the possibilities of democratic participation were better for the Slovaks and the inhabitants of White Russia when they enjoyed limited autonomy, respectively, as part of a semi-federal Czechoslovakia and the Soviet Union, than they came to be in an independent Slovakia and Belarus.

Whether all minorities are entitled to one or another form of autonomy is open to question. One scholar[15] argues that most aboriginal groups, for example, are too small, too isolated, too weak economically and perhaps culturally too 'backward' to benefit from any kind of autonomy, and therefore should not be accommodated. But cultural backwardness or superiority is often in the eye of the beholder; thus, Parisian bourgeois intellectuals tended to denigrate Breton and other ethnoregional minority cultures in the Hexagon in the interest of promoting 'national' integration.

Another criterion of entitlement is the size of the ethnic community. There is a strong incentive for a state to accommodate a large ethnic minority, because it may disrupt the political system if that is not done. But the argument has an obverse side: it is less risky to accommodate smaller communities, regardless of their economic or cultural 'readiness', because they represent little danger to the system, whereas any meaningful cultural autonomy granted a larger group gives it a base from which to escalate and politicize its demands.

This brings us to a third criterion: the risk that a grant of (functional as well as territorial) autonomy poses for the values or the security of the state.

Autonomous educational institutions for Maghrebi schoolchildren in France would undermine elements of the republican value system (such as *laïcité* and the principle of gender equality) and the authority of the state if the institutions in question taught the supremacy of *sharia* law. Similarly, autonomy granted to minorities practising polygamy would undermine the existing social order of society at large.

Still another criterion is the circumstance surrounding the presence of a minority in a given territory. The international community (which accepts as nearly sacrosanct the principle of the territorial integrity of states) is more supportive of one or another form of autonomy for ethnic minorities if they are indigenous to the area and find themselves in a political entity through no choice of their own, as a result of conquest or boundary changes. In the view of some observers, only involuntary minorities have the right to 'jurisdictional (i.e., territorial) cultural autonomy', whereas voluntary minorities (e.g., immigrants) may have a justified claim only to functional or institutional autonomy, such as schools or social services.[16] This distinction is perhaps too rigid, for the differences between indigenous and settler minorities, or involuntary and voluntary ones, is not always clear. Which of these labels applies to most of the Arabs in Israel, to Jews in Poland, to Muslims or Eastern Orthodox Christians in Kosovo, to the Protestants in Northern Ireland? The criterion is confusing because the status of 'original' inhabitant depends on the historic time-frame one uses for reckoning such status, and because many who have immigrated have done so under some constraint (e.g., political refugees, expellees, and victims of population transfers).

One of the criteria for determining an ethnic or religious minority's entitlement to autonomy is the political and socioeconomic context of the country as a whole. In the ideal Jacobin democracy, where membership in the political community is defined by an implied social contract and where every person enjoys equality as an individual, ethnic autonomy is unnecessary since most, if not all, ethnically specific needs can be fulfilled under existing conditions because the state permits or facilitates such fulfillment. Ergo, ethnically based territorial autonomy should be granted not to Corsicans or Bretons in France, Swedes in Finland, South Tyroleans in Italy, Pomak Muslims in Bulgaria, or Magyars in Romania. Although not all of these countries have a fully 'civic' (as opposed to 'ethnic') definition of membership in the political community, they at least have sufficiently democratic structures and reasonably free civil societies.

In many multiethnic societies, particularly in the Third World, such democracies do not exist. Therefore another criterion is introduced – that of political correctness. 'Nation-building' is widely regarded as a progressive enterprise both by indigenous fighters for independence from colonial overlords and by Western political scientists, especially scholars of political development. Such a process, of course, in most cases requires the submerging of ethnic minorities into larger sociopolitical units.[17] According to this logic, the demand by ethnic communities in sub-Saharan Africa for territorial autonomy is illegitimate from a democratic perspective, because it interferes with 'nation-building' and is therefore, by definition, retrogressive. For these reasons, Western political scientists have pushed for neither territorial nor 'functional' autonomy for ethnic minorities; instead, they have put their emphasis on individual human rights, out of a sort of Jacobin (or American liberal) conviction that such rights tend to be incompatible with group rights. But many states grant neither ethnic minority group rights nor individual rights; in those cases, the international community does not interfere on the grounds of the principle of non-interference in the internal affairs of sovereign states. But neither the international community nor Western intellectuals are consistent. They seem to apply their principles on the basis of selective criteria. Among these are what Allan Buchanan has called 'saltwater' and 'pigmentation'. Under the 'saltwater' test, colonies separated from their mother country by an ocean requiring, if not separation, at least territorial autonomy; under the 'pigmentation' test, claimants for secession or at least autonomy have increased legitimacy if they are 'of a different colour from those from whom they wish to secede'.[18] The assumption is, of course, that minority communities in Africa and Asia had been particularly victimized by colonial rule because of the colour of their skin; and a further assumption is that these tests should not be applied to ethnic subcommunities who stake claims for autonomy against the newly independent state.

There is an additional criterion that is essentially ideological: autonomy should be granted where it serves justice and human dignity, and is therefore 'progressive', and should be withheld where it promotes injustice. Under this criterion, it is widely argued that autonomy should be given to Palestinian Arabs because they would gain more individual freedom and democracy than they have under Israeli rule; but it should not be actively promoted for the Kurds, given their lack of democratic traditions and their penchant for terrorism. But these criteria are not consistently applied. Promoting autonomy for Kurds in Turkey and Iraq, Tibetans in China, East Timorese in Indonesia, or Chiapas Indians in Mexico might offend the rulers of states where the minorities are located and might not be in accord with the national interests of countries wishing to maintain friendly relations with those states.

Autonomy, Governability, and Stability

In some cases, a multiethnic state may be too small to afford having its sovereignty divided on a territorial basis; such as Israel, Lebanon, Cyprus,

Fiji, and Georgia, the maintenance of whose territorial integrity might be possible only if it were guaranteed by some sort of collective security agreement. Georgia, for instance, has an Abkhazian, an Ossetian and several Slavic communities; if each of them were given territorial autonomy, that country would be hopelessly fragmented, and its independence (unlike that of multiethnic Switzerland) is too fragile to survive this fragmentation. If the major ethnic minority, the Abkhazian, were given territorial autonomy, it would be necessary for this to be 'functionally' subdivided between the Christian Orthodox and the Muslim Abkhazians.

The decision whether to grant autonomy to an ethnic subcommunity or dependent territory also revolves around the effect of that autonomy on the granting country. The granting of 'home rule', to Greenland (which Lapidoth cites as one of the post-World War II success stories),[19] was a matter of convenience for Denmark, just as in the case of Britain's granting of dominion status to selective colonies under the Statute of Westminster of 1931. In both cases the colonies were too far away to be governed effectively from the centre; moreover, the achievement of sovereignty, which was envisaged as the ultimate aim of home rule, would not threaten the existence of Great Britain. South Tyrolean (quasi-territorial or functional) autonomy is no longer likely to be used by Austrians for irredentist claims, in part because both Austria and Italy now belong to the same supranational system under which traditional 'nation-state' sovereignties are increasingly called into question. There is little danger that ethnoregional minorities in China will secede, given the overwhelming cultural and political dominance of the Han majority; therefore, the Chinese central authorities can afford to grant functional autonomy for *practical* reasons to ethnic communities in selected provinces (except for Tibetans), especially in education (and even resort to affirmative action, as they have done for Uygurs and others in Xinjiang province).[20] There is equally little danger of minorities in France, such as the Bretons, Basques or Alsatians, seceding to form independent states, irrespective of that country's *ideological* constraints against granting meaningful territorial autonomy. The most the French government has been able to do is to delegate selective administrative and policy making powers to regions under decentralization – but there remains the *tutelle* of the central government, under which the delegated power can easily be retrieved.

Whether extending the existing functional autonomy of Arabs within Israel (e.g., in education, religion, and personal status law) would transform them into a 'fifth column' is a matter of controversy. Granting territorial autonomy to Palestinian Arabs, however, does represent a danger to the existence of Israel. Palestinian territorial autonomy is regarded by the Palestinian Authority (and virtually all the countries supporting that autonomy) not as a definitive status but as a transitional stage towards independent statehood;[21] and there is good reason to believe that a Palestinian state would serve as a staging area for destabilizing Israel and threatening its physical security.[22] Similarly, the Albanian Kosovars are not likely to be satisfied with autonomy under Serbian sovereignty, and they will undoubtedly try to join Albania as soon as feasible. Yet the Kosovars, once they have detached themselves from Serbia, do not threaten to destroy the rest of that country.

The granting of autonomy to an ethnic minority is also undesirable if it is disruptive and interferes in the political or economic development of the political system as a whole. It may even be dangerous where the minority is geographically contiguous with, or likely to get strong support from, an ethnic 'homeland' that is autocratic or expansionist and could serve as a springboard for mischief-making. Finally, it is undesirable if the state is too weak – where its sovereignty is not firmly established and the legitimacy of its central government is open to challenge. This applied to the enlarged kingdom of Romania after World War I, which, owing to contested boundaries and a lack of a democratically oriented élite, was so weak that it could ill afford to grant autonomy to its minorities. Today, such a situation applies to post-communist Slovakia, which, since its secession from the Czechoslovak Republic, is still too preoccupied with consolidating its independence and firming up its national identity to grant meaningful autonomy to its Magyar and Roma minorities. This is equally true of Latvia and Estonia in relation to their Russian minorities.

Expectations, Risks, and Perverse Consequences

There are instances of 'success': the Aland Islanders in Finland; the South Tyroleans in Italy; Baltic states after World War I, selectively (e.g., Memel in Lithuania); and after World War II, the Slovenes in Austria; Greenland; the Catalans in Spain; and the Netherlands and Belgium, with their various approaches to local options for minorities.[23] The most recent instance is Hong Kong, where (at the time of writing) autonomy has meant more democracy and freedom than in the rest of China. But such positive results do not always obtain, whether the autonomy is territorial or functional, because the factors making for success are not always present, such as reciprocal accommodation, geographical distance from the mother country, and common political values.

The provision of territorial autonomy for Québec has contributed greatly to the revaluation of francophone culture. Its further extension, however, may have a ripple effect: it may encourage the Native American minority in that province (or future independent state) to seek its own autonomy. It will thereby interfere in the creation of a culturally homogeneous francophone Québec society – a major Québécois goal – and in the end destabilize self-determination for Québec itself. Palestinian autonomy, while liberating some of the West Bank Arabs from Israeli overlordship, has already been marked by constrictions of freedoms of expression and by police brutality. Kosovar autonomy may have a negative contagion effect on Macedonians; it is doubtful, moreover, whether the Kosovars, left to their own devices, would institute greater democracy or individual freedom than they now have. Granting autonomy to Abkhazians and Ossetians, in weakening Georgia, would make it more dependent on Russia and undermine its own independence. In the cultural domain, it would mean the legitimation of the languages of these minorities, so that Russian would become the sole accepted superordinate language, a situation that would undermine the prestige of Georgian.[24]

Having recently recovered its political independence, Lithuania, like its northern Baltic neighbours, is still preoccupied with reaffirming its national identity, and is probably not strong enough to grant any kind of autonomy to the 300,000 Poles in Vilnius. What will happen if the Lithuanians refuse to do this in the future (assuming, of course, that Polish ethnocultural identity is still significant)? There could be pressure from Poland; this would stop short of a replay of the Pilsudski invasion of the early 1920s, but it would be culturally and psychologically important, because it would encourage cultural nationalism among the Vilnius Poles that might ultimately assume a political dimension. Alternatively, it might encourage the Polish minority to look to Russia and incite it to exert political and economic pressure, which would undermine Lithuanian independence.

It cannot be assumed that formal territorial autonomy provides a better protection of ethnic identities or cultures than does functional or personal autonomy. The autonomy of the 'West Bank', whether or not it culminates in an independent state, is unlikely to safeguard the specific identity of the Arabs in that region. For the 'Palestinian' patina of that identity may be replaced by a Jordanian, or perhaps Syrian, one and be subsumed under the identity of '*umma 'al 'arabiyya*'.

The relationship between autonomy and language is even more controversial. The territorial approach to Scotland and Wales that has existed in Britain has not been enough to protect the Scots Gaelic and Welsh languages, nor has Ireland's independence served to revive the meaningful use of the Irish language. Perhaps independence came too late to Ireland; and perhaps the impact of the English language was too strong for Ireland as well as Scotland and Wales to resist. In Tito's Yugoslavia, the existence of territorial autonomy for the Serbs, Croats, and Bosnians in their own federal provinces did not *ipso facto* sharpen whatever distinctions existed between the Serb and Croat elements of Serbo-Croatian; on the contrary, ideologically impregnated intellectuals in all these provinces often spoke of the 'Yugoslav' language. In the Soviet Union, the autonomous territorial status of Jews in Birobidjan was not enough to promote the use of the nominally official Yiddish language there. Conversely, Yiddish maintained itself extremely well for generations in several Eastern European countries despite the lack of territorial autonomy for its speakers. Similarly, the two Norwegian languages have not fused into one despite the unitary character of the Norwegian state.

It is apparent from the discussion above that formal political autonomy is not always *sufficient* to guarantee meaningful self-government or even the preservation of ethnocultural distinctiveness. Conversely, territorial autonomy is not always *necessary* to safeguard ethnocultural identity. The Chinese in Malaysia and elsewhere in south-east Asia, the Armenians and Greeks in Asia Minor and the Jews in Poland and elsewhere in eastern Europe were able to preserve their identities, in part because the cultures of the majorities in their respective 'host' countries were not more attractive than their own.

States v Minority Communities: Incentives and Constraints

Why are some states more forthcoming than others in granting autonomy to minorities? What is the context in which autonomy claims are made, granted, or refused? What are the benefits and risks for the minority and for the state?

Developmental Aspects. Both the nature of the a minority's demands for autonomy and the degree of readiness of a state to grant it depend on the shape of the minority group and the evolution of the state. If the state is strong, it is in a better position to afford to grant autonomy to its minorities; but if it is weak, it may be unable to refuse it. The case of Czechoslovakia in the inter-war period is instructive: On the one hand, the imperatives of belated state-building tempted the Czechs to be unresponsive to demands by non-Czech minorities for cultural autonomy; on the other hand, the Czechs' commitment to democracy caused them to pay greater attention to the post-World War I minorities' provisions of the peace treaties and the League of Nations than was the case with other successor states. However, the Czechs could afford to maintain that position only as long as Germany, Czechoslovakia's major neighbour, was relatively weak. But the moment Germany, under Hitler, became strong, and encouraged the Sudeten Germans to escalate their demands, the Czech government could not longer resist them.

Both the Polish-Lithuanian kingdom and the Ottoman Empire were weak states; the former permitted the existence of the 'Council of the Four Lands' (the system of Jewish functional autonomy) and the latter the institution of the *millet* (ethnoreligious communal autonomy). In neither case, however, was there a danger of anti-state mobilization and hence, of separatism – in part because the minorities had no political ambitions, and in part because they were too dispersed geographically to unite into coherent communities able to assume responsibilities for activities normally associated with sovereign states, such as foreign affairs and territorial management.

A major reason for the inability of certain dispersed minorities to gain significant cultural autonomy in modern times is the absence of an ethnically unifying élite (Kurds, Gypsies, Sami, Inuit); or of an élite whose political aspirations were sufficiently developed (Jews and Armenians before the twentieth century). The gradual development of such an élite has been one of the *consequences* of the institutionalization of ethnic cultural autonomy, however limited.

Another developmental factor is the nature of the polity. A common assumption, shared by French Jacobins and American liberals, has been that in liberal democratic countries, both constitutionally guaranteed individual rights and socioeconomic pluralism based on voluntary associations not only make demands for ethnic autonomy irrelevant but, equally important, are adversely affected by such demands.[25] Experience suggests, however, that ethnic group rights can be associated comfortably with individual rights and that authoritarian political systems (e.g., the Soviet Union, Nazi Germany, Franco Spain, Vichy France, and Communist China) that deny group rights deny individual rights as well.[26] The lack of success of the Volga Germans and Jews in gaining autonomy in the Soviet Union and the failed attempts of the Kurds in the Middle East must be attributed in large measure to the location of these communities within societies ruled by dictatorial governments that have feared the impact of pluralism.

Geography. The geographic location of the ethnic minority has been a crucial factor. It has been particularly important in an assessment of the risks incurred by a state in granting autonomy: these risks are multiplied when ethnic 'brethren' are located in contiguous countries. This applied in the past to the Sudeten Germans, and it applies today to Serb minorities in Bosnia and Croatia, a significant element of whom have pursued irredentist goals. It may apply equally to other ethnic minorities, for example the Druze in Israel, the Tamils in Sri Lanka, and the Russians in Baltic countries. The Israelis have worried that autonomy structures might be used by 'external' Druzes, especially in Lebanon and Syria, working on behalf of the Syrian government to mobilize Israeli Druzes for subversive activities against Israel. A physical attachment of the Tamils to India is out of the question; however, the fear persists among the Sinhalese that territorially based autonomy might tempt India to exert a neo-colonial influence over the island. Formal territorial autonomy for the Russians in the Baltic republics is out of the question in view of their geographic dispersal within these republics; but even functional or personal autonomy is viewed as dangerous, given Russia's gigantic and contiguous presence.

Owing to the geographical proximity of a country that is relatively strong and is dominated by ethnic confrères, there is a fear in all these cases that even limited self-determination would encourage irredentism and escalate to secession. Conversely, the possibility of secession might be an incentive for the 'host' society to make cultural autonomy, and life in general, sufficiently attractive for the minority so that it will not be tempted to secede – and, by derivation, might serve to democratize the host society as well. At present, the political and economic backwardness of Romania provides little incentive for the inhabitants of Moldova to become part of the Romanian 'homeland'. Conversely, the Magyars of Transylvania and Slovakia might well be tempted to opt for a reattachment to Hungary unless the governments of their host countries become more democratic and more prosperous.

Remaining Questions

The foregoing discussion leads us to pose a number of questions.

1. Is local autonomy a means of emphasizing and institutionalizing the collective identity of a minority in the context of the political entity in which it lives, or does it serve as a locus, a part of a network, for regular contacts with coethnics outside the state and hence as a means of fortifying the links with other communities of the dispersed 'nation'?

This question is difficult to answer. Ethnicity can be defined exclusively neither by a specific cultural content nor by a purely subjective feeling of (collective) identity, but rather by an interplay between ethnic communities and the state. Such an interplay includes the spheres of action assigned to the former by the latter. However, we are not clear about the implications of such autonomy for the relationships between the ethnic communities dispersed in various countries. Thus the grant of autonomy to an ethnic minority within a state defines or redefines the character and consciousness of that minority and helps to restructure its collective identity. On the one hand, the minority gains more freedom to relate to ethnic cohorts outside the host country; on the other, its autonomous status ties it institutionally to the host polity and differentiates it from ethnic cohorts in other countries who do not possess that autonomy. Differential definitions have applied to the following:

- Armenians as an ethnic minority (in the USA); as a nationality with its own territorial base (in the former Soviet Union); as members of one or another church (in France);
- Chinese as a constituent 'nation' with formal political rights (Singapore); as an 'ethnic group' benefiting from affirmative action policies (USA); as individuals with no special status (France);
- Jews as an ethnic community (USA); as a nationality without territorial base (the Soviet Union); as a race (Nazi Germany); and as individual members of a religion (France).

2. Does autonomy for a minority blunt the dynamic of political mobilization, or does it serve as a 'trigger' for further demands, and ultimately, for secession?[27] More specifically, to what extent can functional autonomy be contained within the subpolitical sphere? Will the grant of selective functional autonomy accommodate the cultural concerns of ethnic minorities and make them more loyal to the state, create an ethnic Trojan horse or sharpen ethnic consciousness and lead to a political escalation of ethnicity either because 'the appetite grows with the eating', or because institutions determine behaviour? The answer depends upon the kinds of functions involved. It is difficult to see how the maintenance of autonomously managed hospitals can impinge on concerns going beyond health. Ethnoculturally or ethnoreligiously specific educational establishments, however, are a different matter. Unless religion is purely spiritual or language is merely a neutral vehicle without a unique cultural baggage, educational curricula disseminate collective memories, myths, and social norms that may be at variance with those of the majority.

3. What is the impact of foreign pressures, initiatives, guarantees, or other interventions on the institution and functioning of self-government of minorities?

4. To what extent is the grant of selective self-rule to minorities merely a form of 'buck-passing' by national governments?

5. What are the consequences of self-determination? To what extent are the efficacy and the political outcomes of self-determination influenced by ethnographic, sociological, and demographic factors, e.g., the birthrate; by the cultural developmental phase of the minority in question; by the nature of the ethnic minority élite; and by exogenous factors, e.g., powerful states

or the international community? The political consequences of grants of selective autonomy to ethnonational communities (e.g., Sami, Gypsies) and certain religious minorities (e.g., Amish, Copts, Jews, Parsees), have been modest, for some or all of the following reasons: they are insufficiently concentrated to form the cohesive structures for the kinds of transactional patterns needed for political autonomy; they do not have political agendas; and they do not have the support of outside parties who might exploit the minorities' autonomy for their own ends.

6. Is ethnic self-determination integrative or disintegrative? It depends on what is meant by self-determination, on the socioeconomic and political context, on the degree of dispersal of the minorities in question, and on the criteria according to which the state is defined.

The rights of minorities have been a subject of discussion at least from the beginning of the nineteenth century, when the Napoleonic empire collapsed and the traditional dynastic state began to be replaced by the so-called 'nation-state'. Thus, at the Congress of Vienna in 1815, the rights of ethnic minorities were considered, but little was done in cases where it was unfeasible for them to set up their own state. The accommodation of minorities – short of political independence – was imposed particularly on relatively weak states. Thus at the Treaty of Berlin in 1876, a provision was inserted that included the protection of the 'traditional rights and liberties' enjoyed by the religious community of Mount Athos in Greece; and the Bulgarian constitution of 1878 contained guarantees for the country's Greek and Turkish minorities.[28] Here a word of caution is in order. Treaties and constitutional provisions may sometimes be taken too seriously by academicians – as if they were indicators of the situation in practice.[29]

7. What is the connection between selective functional autonomy and self-government? Functional autonomy is transformed into self-government if the function has a significant territorial dimension; serves to foster a unique political consciousness and political value system, especially one that is at variance with that of the majority; and is protected juridically from penetration or arrogation by the national or central authority.

It should be noted that the existence of an autonomous ethnically specific school system is not the same as 'self-government'. But there is a relationship, which varies according to the context, including the nature of the curriculum and the degree to which the 'national' political values are shared by the members of the minority and the extent to which the ethnic school system inculcates these values in its pupils. In the former Soviet Union, there was little danger that ethnic educational autonomy would lead to separatism, in part because education was '(ethno)national' only in form and not substance; and in part because ethnic political expression, like all forms of expression, was severely limited. In contrast, ethnic educational autonomy for the German minority in the Sudetenland posed a much greater danger to the unity of the Czechoslovak state, because Germany was a powerful neighbour and because the content of education was increasingly suffused with irredentist aspirations.

8. Does the state have an obligation to grant any form of self-determination, cultural or other, to minorities? To what extent should such an obligation be based on the democratic imperative, on the special obligation to a minority that was brought into the country against its will, or on international treaty obligations?

9. Under what conditions can local functional autonomy based on cultural identity lead to the construction of a political identity whose values are no longer congruent with those of the state? For many years, the identity of Arabs in Israel was neither Israeli nor Palestinian; rather, it was based on *hamulas*, or patrilineal clans. The institution of representative councils to deal with education and other matters of concern to the Arab minority led to the expansion of links to councils in other localities within and beyond the borders of Israel, and subsequently to the growth of a Palestinian political identity focused on the transformation and, indeed, the destruction of the state. In short, the institutionalized grant of functional autonomy escalated to demands for territorially based self-determination.[30]

The institutionalization of cultural self-determination, especially in the case of diaspora communities, facilitates ongoing relationships with the 'home' country and makes possible cultural infusions from that country. Such infusions do not necessarily lead to separatism, especially in the case of minorities that are widely dispersed within the interior of a particular 'host' country; but – in a worst-case scenario – they may lead to the creation of a counter-culture that may destabilize a society, undermine 'national' values and norms and, in some cases, threaten the stability, if not the very existence, of the state. The following might be cited as possible examples: Islamic fundamentalist control of the curriculum in Maghrebi private schools in France; Mafia behavioural codes among selected Italian-Americans; Tong rule in Chinatowns; Nazi control of schools of the German minority in pre-war Sudetenland; Hamas control of Arab educational and social institutions in Israel; and communist influence in Chinese schools in various Southeast Asian countries.

10. What should be the ethnic reach of functional (or 'personal') autonomy, and how inclusive should it be? If autonomy is too rigidly formalized, it may transform indifferent or reluctant members of such communities into 'captive ethnics' and ghettoize them. If a member of a minority group has

the option of choosing between ethnically specific and general education, and a significant number (for whatever reason) choose the latter, the ethnic autonomy arrangement may be undermined; conversely, if there is no such option and members of an ethnic minority are automatically encompassed by the minority-specific arrangement, the result may be a 're-ethnification' of a community whose members were in process of cultural assimilation.

11. Does the granting of cultural autonomy strengthen or weaken the links of a minority community to its fellow minority members outside the state? The answer depends in part upon the cultural content of that autonomy. To the extent that Jewish culture was based on secular Yiddishism, the fact that such a culture was gradually disappearing in Western countries weakened the links between Jews in the Soviet Union and in the capitalist world. Despite the institution of a separate alphabet for the Moldavian language (to distinguish it from Romanian), the fact that Romania and Moldavia shared a communist ideology should have brought the two communities closer together; however, as long as a totalitarian Soviet Union existed and insisted on the integrity of its territory, irredentism was out of the question.

12. What purpose does autonomy serve? And *cui bono?* In (pre-1989) Yugoslavia, what was called 'communal self-government' meant that local statutes were adopted by the inhabitants of the communes, in which representatives of minorities figured heavily. Such self-rule referred, of course, to schools where the minority language was the medium of instruction. But it referred also to the use of minority idioms in economic self-management, including the organization of production and the regulation of workplace relations.[31] The primary aim of self-management was not the preservation of the minority culture as an end in itself but the maintenance of the national economic system and the building of socialism. One must take into account the majority's fears of what functional autonomy for minorities, no matter how selective, might portend for itself and for the state dominated by it – the fear of escalation in political claims, or, falling short of that, of domination by the ethnic minority of certain aspects of national life. This fear is especially pronounced where the minority has a high natural growth rate (e.g., Albanians in Kosovo, Arabs in Israel, Catholics in Ulster); is perceived as being more advanced or more enterprising than the majority (Magyars in Slovakia, Tamils in Sri Lanka, Ibos in Nigeria, Chinese in Malaysia); and is concentrated in a region that borders a country dominated by ethnic fellow-members of the minority.

The preceding discussion tempts us to put forth the following hypotheses:

- Selective functional autonomy tends to be conducive to the maintenance of transethnic political unity when the national economic and political systems are open enough to permit entry of members of ethnic communities; when there exists a significant network of pluralistic non-ethnic transactions; when the social structure of the ethnic community is itself complex enough to encourage ethnically cross-cutting relationships; and when 'national' élite management structures exist in which the participation of ethnic élites is institutionalized.
- The threat of autonomy structures leading to secession is credible only under limited conditions, viz.: if the network of non-political transactions is sufficiently institutionalized to be capable of functional expansion towards more 'political' activities; if the clientele served by ethnic institutions is large and concentrated enough to have a spatial dimension; if a large part of the ethnic community is concentrated near the border of a 'homeland' state, and if the political and economic conditions in that 'homeland' are considered sufficiently enticing (or insufficiently forbidding) for the ethnic minority to change its political loyalty. These conditions appear to apply in particular to a number of former communist countries in Eastern Europe, e.g., Macedonia, where the two million inhabitants include 500,000 Albanians, i.e., 25 per cent of the population, having a high rate of natural increase; Yugoslavia, where the Albanians of Kosovo and the Magyars of Vojvodina constitute a considerable element of the regional population, an element strongly attracted to the idea of joining a neighbouring country. In both countries, the state is weak, and neither the economy nor the political system is attractive enough to provide an incentive for the minorities to identify fully with the 'host' society.

Conclusion

What are the prospects for the self-government of subordinated minorities today? One scholar has argued that there are conditions today that foster greater tolerance towards ethnic minorities and a greater readiness on the part of national governments to grant them autonomy. The growing interdependence of states in economic matters has raised the question of whether *national* sovereignty is truly possible; in view of the fact that the traditional nations have turned increasingly to transnational and supranational solutions, 'demands for the autonomy of ethnic minorities no longer seem so threatening'.[32] In addition, it is often argued that the demand for ethnic autonomy has become legitimated by international and regional conventions that affirm the right of minorities to the protection of their languages, religions, and traditions.[33]

But such arguments need to be re-examined, and it may be suggested that the 1990s are not a particularly auspicious time for the claims of minorities. It is precisely the 'transnationalization' of economic activities and the permeability of national cultures to extranational influences that – in the eyes of the majority population of 'host' countries – threaten national identity and political integrity. The affirmations of the legitimacy of minority claims on the part of the United Nations, the Council of Europe, and the European Union have been 'balanced' (and in part nullified, at least until the recent NATO intervention in Yugslavia) by the even greater emphasis on the rights of members of minorities *as individuals*, the principle of non-discrimination against them, the goal of their integration into the majority culture, and the repeated affirmations of existing political sovereignties and of the principle of non-intervention in the internal affairs of member countries.[34] In any case, the declarations of United Nations and other international bodies lack operational validity, given their weaknesses. In the 1920s, the minorities provisions of the League of Nations *vis-à-vis* the successor states were honoured more in the breach than the observance; minority demands in several of these countries today are likely to meet a similar fate. This is seen especially in the behaviour of the formerly communist Eastern European countries. Having regained their independence after more than four decades of subordination, they are not very eager to share any elements of their sovereignty.

Clearly, a state that is self-confident and strong – whether because of effective central governing structures, attractive political values and output that have a transethnic appeal, or sufficient military power to ward off threats from neighbouring countries – can be more generous in accommodating itself to minorities' demands for cultural autonomy than a state that is afflicted by political or economic weaknesses. Such autonomy might extend to the following institutions and activities:

- ethnic or religious schools and universities, which are involved in curricular matters and whose diplomas have national and extranational validity;
- language academies, with the power of setting language norms;
- religious councils, which set norms for rites of passage, and which resolve disputes;
- trade unions, mutual societies, and philanthropies;
- ethnically or religiously specific personal-status laws and jurisdictions within (and perhaps across) state lines;
- tribunals for the settlement of intra-minority civil disputes;
- contracts, in selective areas, between an ethnic minority and the 'host' state or with governments or ethnic communities outside the state.

These forms of autonomy imply the existence of institutions that are to some extent analogous to voluntary, non-governmental organizations that operate on both sides of an international boundary.[35]

The different kinds of functional autonomy are not equally appropriate in all situations and at all times. This is particularly the case with respect to religion and education. Several centuries ago in Western countries, and a few generations ago in many other parts of the world, the grant of autonomy to minority communities in educational matters constituted no danger to the political integrity of the state, because education was not concerned with the shaping of a collective political consciousness or with political mobilization. Today, however, education, and the language in which it is provided, is one the most important instruments of the state in this matter, and ethnolinguistic particularism is viewed as a threat to 'nation-building'. Conversely, while in most modern societies, marked by a highly secular culture, the delegation of powers in religious matters no longer poses a serious threat to political unity and stability, such delegation may be dangerous in societies in which religion is highly politicized and the teachings associated with it are not congruent with the political values of the state.

Whatever these differences, the granting of autonomy is contingent upon the acceptance by minorities, both inside and outside the state, of the legitimacy of the state and its existing international boundaries. Given this acceptance, it is possible in most cases to accommodate both the needs of a stable democracy and the preservation of the ethnocultural identities of minorities.

NOTES

1. Raymond L. Hall (ed.), *Ethnic Autonomy – Comparative Dynamics* (New York: Pergamon, 1979), pp.xi–xii and *passim*.
2. Walker Connor, 'The Political Significance of Ethnonationalism within Western Europe', in Abdul Said and Luiz R. Simmons (eds), *Ethnicity in an International Context*. (New Brunswick: Transaction Books, 1976), pp.111–2.
3. See William Safran, 'Diasporas in Modern Societies: Myths of Homeland and Return', *Diaspora*, Vol.1, No.1 (1991), pp.83–99.
4. Ruth Lapidoth, *Autonomy: Flexible Solutions to Ethnic Conflicts* (Washington, DC: US Institute of Peace Press, 1996).
5. Evelyn Kallen, 'Ethnicity and Self-Determination: A Paradigm', in Donald Clark and Robert Williamson (eds), *Self-Determination: International Perspectives*. (London: Macmillan, 1996), pp.113–23.
6. For a general discussion of these points focused on case studies of selected cities, see Curtis C. Roseman, Hans-Dieter Laux, and Gunther Thieme (eds), *Ethnicity: Geographic Perspectives on Ethnic Change in Modern Cities* (Lanham, MD, and London: Rowman & Littlefield, 1996).
7. This question is based on, and extended from, the criteria cited by Allan Buchanan, 'Self-Determination and the Right to Secede', *Journal of International Affairs* (special issue on

Rethinking Nationalism and Sovereignty), Vol.45, No.2 (Winter 1992), pp.347–65.

8. Benedict Anderson, *Imagined Communities: Reflections on the Origins and Spread of Nationalism*, 2nd ed. (London: Verso, 1991), p.6.

9. John McGarry and Brendan O'Leary (eds), *The Politics of Ethnic Conflict Regulation* (London: Routledge, 1993), pp.31f.

10. See Ruth Lapidoth, 'Autonomy: Potential and Limitations', *International Journal of Group Rights*, Vol.1, No.4 (1994), p.280.

11. John Waterbury, 'Avoiding the Iron Cage of Legislated Identity', in Wolfgang Danspeckgruber and Arthur Watts (eds), *Self-Determination and Self-Administration* (Boulder, CO, and London: Lynne Rienner, 1997), pp.375–87.

12. On gangland slayings and extortion rackets in Corsica, see Marlise Simons, 'The Ugly Face Behind Corsican Nationalism's Mask', *New York Times*, 13 Feb. 1998.

13. Jean-Louis Andreani, 'Une "économie identitaire" à la base d'un nouveau contrat social', *Le Monde*, 12 March 1998.

14. Amitai Etzioni, 'The Evils of Self-Determination', *Foreign Policy*, No.3 (Winter 1992), pp.21–35.

15. Guntram F.A. Werther, *Self-Determination in Western Democracies: Aboriginal Politics in a Comparative Perspective* (Westport, CT: Greenwood Press, 1992), p.26.

16. Kallen, pp.120–1.

17. Walker Connor, 'Nation-Building or Nation-Destroying?' *World Politics*, No.24 (April 1972), pp.319–55.

18. Allan Buchanan, p.349.

19. Lapidoth, *Autonomy*, p.143ff..

20. Barry Sautman, 'Preferential Policies for Ethnic Minorities in China: The Case of Xinjiang', in William Safran (ed.), *Nationalism and Ethnoregional Minorities in China* (London: Frank Cass, 1998), pp.86–118.

21. Lapidoth, *Autonomy*, p.157.

22. Yassir Arafat and other Palestinian leaders have in effect frequently asserted that Palestinian autonomy would be used to 'liberate' the rest of Palestine, including Israel.

23. Some of these instances are cited by Lapidoth, in *Autonomy*, pp.93–6.

24. See James Brooke, 'Ethnic Chaos in the Caucasus', *International Herald Tribune*, 4 Oct. 1991.

25. See Robert A. Dahl, *Polyarchy* (New Haven, CT: Yale University Press, 1971), p.108.

26. See William Safran, 'Ethnicity and Pluralism: Comparative and Theoretical Perspectives', *Canadian Review of Studies in Nationalism*, Vol.18, Nos.1–2 (1991), pp.5, 7.

27. See Paul R. Brass, *Ethnicity and Nationalism* (Newbury Park, CA: Sage, 1991), pp.270.

28. Hurst Hannum, *Autonomy, Sovereignty, and Self-Determination* (Philadelphia: University of Pennsylvania Press, 1990), p.51.

29. This tendency is particularly noticeable among specialists in public and international law. See, for example, Hannum, *Autonomy*, p.51 fn., p.63ff, who cites selected Koranic passages and provisions in the constitutions of Islamic states to suggest that minorities are *in reality* accorded protections and rights.

30. Davida Wood, 'Politics of Identity in a Palestinian Village in Israel', in Kay B. Warren (ed.), *The Violence Within: Cultural and Political Opposition in Divided Nations* (Boulder, CO: Westview, 1993), pp.97–120.

31. See Ernest Petrica, 'Minority Rights in Yugoslav Municipal Statutes', in William F. Mackey and Albert Verdoodt (eds), *The Multinational Society* (Rowley, MA: Newbury House, 1975), pp.120–4.

32. Richard W. Sterling, 'Ethnic Separatism in the International System', in Raymond Hall, *Ethnic Autonomy*, p.410.

33. E.g., the writings of Yoram Dinstein and Hurst Hannum.

34. See James Fawcett, *The International Protection of Minorities*. Report no. 41 (London: Minority Rights Group, 1979), pp.4–19.

35. For a useful discussion, see Jack D. Forbes, 'Limited Authority Cross-Boundary Sub-States', *Plural Societies*, No.15 (1984), pp.255–64.

Democracy, Federalism and Nationalism in Multinational States

RAMÓN MÁIZ

The 1990s have turned out to be extraordinarily rich for the study of nationalism, both in the area of political experience as well as in the realm of theoretical elaboration. The logic of democracy and the logic of nationalism have on occasion shown themselves to be in open conflict, while in other cases they are at the very least not completely in agreement, demonstrating significant imbalances in Eastern Europe and in some Western European states as well as Canada. At times this gap between the two political logics has derived from internal nationalist problems that question the traditional centralism of the nation-state. On other occasions it arises from the increasingly multiethnic nature of societies due to the presence of immigrant minorities that demand a political statute of recognition of their differences. The case to be examined here is of special relevance: *multinational states*, that is, states that contain one or more national minorities coexisting with a national majority that has historically been the backbone of the state. The nation/state equation, inherited from the nineteenth century, has become problematic due to crises in traditionally unitary nation-states (Spain, England, Italy), in federal or quasi-federal ones (Canada, Belgium), and the rise of new independent states that implemented compulsory policies of nationalization after their authoritarian regimes broke down (the former Yugoslavia and Soviet Union). This has forced a reexamination of the conditions that could make possible the harmonious and democratic coexistence of several nationalities within one state.

All of these events have given rise to rich and complex institutional and regulatory experiences, revealing the limits to traditional policies of assimilation, ethnic regulation and accommodation. New inroads have also been made into reformulating the classic structures of federalism and consociationalism, giving flexibility to the solutions and classic models of political decentralization and self-government. In addition, this laboratory of experiences has resulted in more elaborate arguments, not only of an empirical or comparative tendency but also normative, strongly influenced

Ramón Máiz, Universidad de Santiago de Compostela

by the pressing political problems of all these countries. Thus, when considering national problems from the perspective of encouraging democracy, we have again found that it makes little sense to separate the analysis of what is and its causal explanations from the analysis of what should be and its philosophical-political and moral fundamentals.

Given these new experiences and theoretical developments, we are at an excellent juncture to proceed to reevaluate the set of problems posed by self-government, political decentralization and the production/recognition of collective political identities. Taken from the perspective that here concerns us – multinational states – it demands a point of departure that overcomes the mutual misunderstanding that has until now been characteristic of the various fields of study directly involved in this question. First of all, then, it will be necessary to make close connections between three fields of analysis that have so far been foreign to each other, developing themselves in compartmentalized fashion and working at separate tables. We are referring to the political theory of democracy, the comparative institutional studies of federalism, and the analysis of nationalist mobilization. Secondly, it will be no less important to place alongside each other *positive* analyses and empirically oriented theories, and the most novel contributions that have taken place within *normative* theory in the fields of federalism, nationalism and democracy. As they develop their research programmes, hypotheses and questions, normative theories need the analysis of nationalist mobilization and the constructive efficacy of institutions that sociology and political science offer, while the empirical theories cannot ignore the normative world of recognized values, free choice agreements and democracy.

In effect, the three fields cited have experienced recent novel and interesting developments, both in the empirical-positive realm and in the normative one, allowing for a much deeper and unprejudiced discussion of the problems that contemporary multinational states pose. Something has taken place in this field of study, which seems to indicate that we are moving slowly towards a perspective finally capable of overcoming the limited traditional duality of nationalism and statism, heads and tails of the same obsolete and reductionist vision of the problem.

Thus the theory of democracy has revealed the insufficiencies of both the self-satisfied polyarchic minima as well as the participative euphoria of the 1970s. It has generated a revision, which, parting from processes of deliberation and the moral resources and constitutive efficacy of institutions, points towards a viewpoint that is not merely 'expressive' of democratic politics, but is also constructive or, so to speak, 'performative' concerning preferences, interests and identities. Studies of federalism, in turn, have gone beyond the classical model of legal-formal and taxonomic analyses, in order to examine the dynamic and open processes of flexible self-regulation, centring on the interaction between cooperation and competition, actors and institutions. Finally, recent studies of nationalism have overcome the traditional primordial or organic model of the nation – according to which the nation was defined objectively on the basis of a series of diacritical features of race, culture, language, or religion – in order to present it as the open and indeterminate result of a process of national construction which is politically generated from ethnicity itself by organizational, discursive and institutional mobilization.

In the following pages we will examine briefly certain arguments derived from these theoretical contributions and from contemporary political experiences, with the reasonable conviction that they may contribute to the renewal of normative and institutional analysis of multinational states, thus in turn facilitating their complex democratic viability.

Democratic Values and Multinational States

The very existence of multinational states brings into the foreground an issue that had been prematurely considered as resolved by considering them as 'nation-states': the prior definition of the *demos*, the agreement on the territorial basis for the legitimacy of political power. In effect, if the criteria for the democratic process presuppose the legitimacy of the unit upon which it develops, the justification for identifying the 'people' with the 'nation' logically precedes the procedural requirements for a democracy.[1] A democracy cannot exist without a prior agreement on the the political power's area of territorial validity: 'The very definition of a democracy involves agreement by the citizens of a territory, however specified, on the procedures to be used to generate a government that can make legitimate claims on their obedience.'[2] The democratic rationale itself is ultimately founded on a factual element, not a rational one.[3] And the *popular sovereignty* that dictates the constituent power ('We the people...') points us to *national sovereignty*, by which the people must see themselves as the nation (*une et indivisible*) which surrounds itself with a state, in turn reinforcing its substantive unity and homogeneity.[4] The purportedly self-evident national state implies that the nation, which is taken as an underlying assumption of democracy, becomes intellectually opaque.[5] This opacity disappears in multinational states, where the *demos* turns out to be composed of various *demoi*, who do not accept as legitimate a political power which they challenge as foreign and imposed. This occurs because the state, in spite of possessing overall democratic legitimacy for its institutions, does not recognize the right of *demoi* to develop their own culture, to protect their own economic interests, or, in sum, to develop some degree of self-government. The issue of which territorial unit is the appropriate one for making certain decisions, to infuse them with a double level of procedural and territorial legitimacy, is an area that is traditionally left unexamined in the political theory of democracy.

However, there are two relevant contemporary issues in the normative debate concerning multinational states. Not only are the *people* presented as forming several nations, but in addition these nations redefine the people as the particularity of its citizens. That is, the concept of *citizenship* is reformulated in a drastic manner, since the singular individual is now within the 'decision-making context' that his or her specific nationality provides. This context of a shared culture and language, of a political will to coexist and a common project, favours citizen trust, participation and autonomy at 'regional' level. It thus constitutes a central dimension of the complex, plural citizenship of multinational states.

Now this redefinition of the territorial legitimacy of political power and citizenship within multinational states implies, in turn, a reformulation of the traditional principles and values that rule democratic nation-states, as elaborated by the liberal tradition as self-evidently mononational. We will examine this briefly.

First of all, it becomes clear that the traditional concept of *freedom* is insufficient, since in its liberal formulation it is postulated unilaterally as 'individual freedom', which resists or completely opposes the recognition of collective or group rights. In effect, freedom was translated above all as *freedom of choice*, by which every individual citizen chooses how to live his or her life, following criteria and beliefs that are irreducibly personal in regard to their conception of what is 'good'. But freedom also implies *autonomy* – that is, the capacity to revise and criticize one's own prior preferences, ends and beliefs, in order to change one's idea of the good life in the light of new information, experiences or deliberation.[6]

We cannot ignore the fact that both dimensions of liberty – the choice and revision of one's own ends and beliefs – require not only freedom of information but also tolerant education that respects other lifestyles. Furthermore, they require the availability, in a real sense within anyone's grasp, of other values and cultures that are different from one's own. In sum, liberty demands a plural environment that is as rich as possible, facilitating contrast, comparison and the possibility of choice and revision of one's own lifestyle.

In addition, if freedom implies choice and autonomy, liberal society should provide not only the availability of options, but also attend to the sources that give meaning to the individual's options. The cultural environment of one's own language, traditions and history often provides citizens with 'meaningful ways of life'[7] in all economic, social, educational and other human activities. In fact, the *national identity* is built upon a set of 'myths, memories, values, and symbols'.[8] Citizens make choices based on preinterpretations of the value of certain practices, values and attitudes. They do this from a context of choice that gives them a prior horizon of meaning, given in turn by one's own culture, language, historical tradition and mythical-symbolical complex – a shared vocabulary of tradition and convention. This is precisely what nationality provides: a cultural context for preinterpretation of reality.

Access to autonomy is thus a culturally mediated access. The choices and criteria for selection take place, not from the abstract rational view of a supposed 'radical chooser', but from the specific standpoint provided by the original national culture. The citizen is always a 'contextual individual',[9] a 'strong evaluator'.[10] People combine individuality and sociability and choice/revision of their own ends according to a contextually and culturally based prior understanding. Choices, and in turn freedom, become contingent upon one's own set of socially acquired evaluations that serve as the initial criterion for personal evaluation.

However, contextualized choices and autonomy do not imply a strictly *communitarian* reading of these cultural and national contexts of decision making. That is, the nation as a decision-making context does not presuppose a substantive agreement on a collective idea of the good life or of goodness, nor does it require a collective consensus on 'shared understandings' or 'shared values'. Rather, 'the roots of unity in national communities are outside the normative sphere'.[11]

In this way, the right to one's own culture becomes inseparable from the value of liberty, since it can only be realized in its double aspect of choice and autonomy in a context that provides an initial and revisable reading of the available options and of the citizen's previous criteria for selection. The problem lies in the fact that liberals have traditionally theorized this level following the assumption that cultural and political borders essentially coincide. Thus, within a state considered by definition as self-evidently mononational, there would only be one culture that provides individuals with a social context for choices and so, not unexpectedly, most liberals are 'banal' nationalists.[12] If this is problematic in national states due to surviving elements of some differentiated culture or large numbers of immigrants, it becomes entirely unsustainable in the case of multinational states. In effect, in the latter case, the various nationalities constitute different contexts of choice and thus of freedom for citizens, and as such ought to be recognized and respected. Otherwise, universalistic citizenship – the undeniable carrier of equality and justice – will also bring with it a partial democratic deficit.

From a strictly liberal viewpoint one's own national culture cannot be renounced, but at the same time political and cultural limits do not coincide (as the latter are territorially delimited within the multinational states). It thus becomes necessary to substitute the traditional policies of 'eliminating differences' by integration and assimilation, with regulations that are more in tune with liberal principles themselves, 'managing differences' by federalization or consociationalism, or other forms of self-government and national rights.[13]

This redefinition of freedom also determines certain substantive effects on the value of *participation* in multinational states. Since citizens want to be governed by institutions that function within a culture that they can understand and make sense of and that are as transparent as possible in their meaning, self-government of a national area favours increased involvement and participation of citizens. Benjamin Constant's dilemma of the *liberté des modernes*, apathy and closed privacy, abstaining from voting, and so on, all constitute serious problems of motivation within the concepts of citizenship, of state neutrality and of John Rawls's 'overlapping consensus'. Yet in relations that provide mutual recognition and a sense of purpose lie one of the key elements for generating confidence in institutions.[14] In a complex universe where face-to-face relationships have disappeared, democratic *trust* in other citizens and in institutions, which is essential to democratic life, is powerfully strengthened by the presence of these 'imagined communities' we call nations.[15]

From the perspective of a quantitative and qualitative increase in participation, multinational states with democratic institutions provide a dual aspect to citizen participation. Most importantly, self-government allows political decentralization which then locates the seat of power closer to the *demoi*, so that territorially specific problems can be taken care of with greater efficacy, while increasing the opportunities for those in government to be controlled and for the people to participate politically. But there is also a second arena of national import, which allows for shared responsibility and participation in the overall governing of the state. Peaceful coexistence, pluralist diversity, collaboration, and solidarity are all strengthened in the political realm through the existence of a second representative chamber set up territorially, along with institutions for coordination and cooperative federalism, participation in international politics, and other activities.

Thus the reconsideration of freedom in a multinational setting in turn yields reasonably significant results in the area of *equality*, and first of all in legal equality of all citizens before the law and the institutions. The unitary classical perspective implied understanding equality as non-discrimination and equality of opportunity, thus over-universalizing citizenship according to certain majoritarian criteria that made it impossible to allow for national minorities' group rights. In this sense, from a homogenizing and unitary model of equality, which also generated beneficial effects such as the correction of inequalities, the recognition of group or minority rights was perceived as creating unacceptable inequalities for a liberal mindset.

But as we have said, the national cultural context becomes essential to freedom, so that equality needs to be reformulated in order to recognize and accommodate differences, even though this might cause a certain asymmetry in citizens' rights. To treat in a like fashion those who are not alike is, in fact, to maintain inequality. Authentic equality would allow an accommodation of differences and protection of the precarious cultural-national contexts of minorities, since the majority culture/nation does not have serious problems in surviving and developing in a multinational state. The members of internal nationalities are, from a strictly democratic perspective, in a situation of clear disadvantage. The outcome of policies of 'benign neglect', which permit the market's 'invisible hand' to determine the fate of differences, will mean the definite erosion or even loss of the cultural heritage that constitutes the nationalities' specific context of choice and the collective explanation of their freedom. From the standpoint of equality, the existence of cultural rights and self-government for national minorities is justified by their fairness from a liberal point of view. Cultural self-government protects both the decision-making context upon which freedom depends and the unchosen inequality of belonging to a cultural minority that is threatened by extinction due to the hegemonic culture of the state.

But this democratic inclusion of cultural equality implies, in turn, strict limits on national and cultural rights, and on policies for the positive regulation of difference. From the liberal standpoint, equality generally requires, as a broad principle, 'external protections', but it should not imply 'internal restrictions', to use Kymlicka's terminology.[16] That is, equality justifies measures that tend to defend the group's culture *vis-à-vis* the negative impact caused by external decisions of the state's dominant majority. But it cannot allow measures that tend to discourage internal dissension or the free re-evaluation of myths, values and symbols, which would ban pluralism from the midst of the national minority's culture, forcing instead a dogmatic interpretation, which might require sacrificing 'autonomy' for 'authenticity'.[17]

This implies a difficult equilibrium within multinational states, full of hard cases where conflicts arise between collective or nationally based group rights and the generic rights of individually based citizenship, between majorities and minorities, both in the state and within the internal nationalities. Democratic theory must never allow a substantive erosion of citizens' individual or group rights, even if hypothetically justified to protect the rights of a majority in its own territorial context. If the protection of national minorities' group rights is justified as the defence of a decision-making context that provides autonomy, it would make no sense to allow a measure that restricts an individual's free exercise of autonomy.

From the perspective of equality that here concerns us, it is necessary to introduce a second and decisive dimension which affects those consequences derived from it, either by strengthening or weakening them: material equality. In other words, the protection of national rights within a multinational state must be congruent with individual and collective political rights and guarantees, but also with 'real freedom for all', avoiding any sort of exclusion from political or cultural life due to a lack of economic resources. This is realized by the right of access to some form of culture provided through participation in an egalitarian public educational system, the right to a minimum wage or 'basic income',[18] social security, public education and health care guaranteed by the welfare state. If multinational states with democratic institutions are to recognize the right to self-government and carry out accommodation policies based on the reasons cited, this recognition must also be compatible with a defence of the welfare state for the whole spectrum of citizens, seeking 'non-dominated diversity' while fighting unequal development and territorial dependency.[19] This in turn leads us to two key dimensions of solidarity: the so-called interclass one built on a progressive tax system, and the *interterritorial* one, set up as compensation mechanisms that correct economic inequality, along with the integrative function of the social rights of citizenship. By extension this requires an additional dimension, the reinforcing of the value of intercommunity *solidarity* within multinational states.

In effect, the recognition of the existence of nations within the state itself and the guarantee of self-government for them, through decentralized structures of a federal or consociational sort, bring to the foreground the nature of the links between the different territorial units – the ties that bind. The nation-state tended to solve these problems by tight identity links, equating political borders with cultural ones and generating a sort of nation-state 'ethnic community' that was the basis for a special package of moral obligations for the entire group of nationals.[20] The existence of various national contexts within one state is the foundation for the decisive identity links that legitimate the self-government of these nationalities, but it does not resolve the question of the links between them, the ties that bind them together.

The mere existence of a territorially legitimate multinational state – a decentralized political structure that attends to demands for cultural differentiation and self-government – along with certain rules of the game accepted by all the communities through overlapping consensus

(*Verfassungspatriotismus*) is in itself insufficient to produce the substantive solidarity that is necessary for interterritorial equality and the correction of unequal development. In order to cement the transfer of income and territorial equilibrium something additional is necessary. On the one hand, this additional approach should not go against the requirements of the liberal theory of democracy (which presupposes a substantive consensus on political values but is compatible with pluralism), and on the other hand, it should not go against a multinational state's democratic institutions by implying an oppressive concept of a the nation-state hegemonized by a national majority. So far there has been little progress in answering the question of what reasons there are for several nations to remain within one same state, conciliating their differences and maintaining solidarity. The solution to this decisive problem constitutes, no doubt, a task to be carried out by the contemporary multinational states, and everything points towards proceeding in the construction of a shared political identity. This must be an identity composed of non-antagonistic sub-identities, weaving together a moral, political, and mythical-symbolic narrative of tolerance built upon the explicit basis of 'deep diversity'.[21] It would link national differences with a variety of ways of belonging to the multinational state. This collective identity must be built beyond that which is merely cultural, involving explicit political and democratic structures, as an open, multicultural and participative project for the citizens within each nationality, generating simultaneously a liking for and trust in a common, egalitarian and just project for the future of the entire state. In sum, it would be a project for overlapping and non-antagonistic identities, mutually bound together, starting from the irrevocable richness of diversity and concluding in the configuration of a multinational state.

This deep diversity leads us nonetheless to a re-evaluation of *pluralism*. That is to say, beyond merely recognizing the fact that a society is plural, the postulate that diversity constitutes a fundamental democratic value for the citizenship of each nationality and for the entire multinational state needs to be defended.[22] In contrast with the individualist nature of the nation-state, the pluralism of a multinational state constitutes a complex entity that introduces an additional collective and nationality-based level. This type of pluralism is built upon the recognition and accommodation of a plurality of nations within the state. In the multinational state 'the fact of pluralism'[23] becomes a value as the comprehensive doctrines that citizens assume result from their freedom of choice and revision of ends and preferences. But an additional value would be the political pluralism of the various territorially-based national communities that seek or possess their own self-government and political will, and whose laws are on a par with state laws in areas of its own jurisdiction (since self-government and political decentralization imply the existence of the power to legislate).

At the same time, from their unique vantage point, these communities would participate in the broader common political project of solidarity and cooperation, guaranteed by the democratic institutions of the multinational state in permanent negotiation between actors and institutions. This richness of political diversity is lost when nationalist policies are implemented, whether they are policies of assimilation by the nation-state, imposed or self-imposed isolation, or secession by the internal nationalities that in turn become 'nationalizing states'.[24] The substitution of multiple and overlapping identities by mutually exclusive and non-negotiable identities is a less than optimal solution, constituting an irreparable loss from the perspective of pluralist coexistence. Furthermore, in no way does this constitute the natural and inevitable expression of all multinationality. Instead it is the outcome of a political process and discourse based on dichotomizing strategies, creating tension and polarization, forcing the citizens to choose or exclude, even though complementary and overlapping identities are feasible.[25]

The pluralism of a multinational state should also extend to reach within the national communities that form it. This is so, most of all, because individualist pluralism – the free adoption by each citizen of an idea of good, justice, religion, and other values – must be guaranteed within any democratic community. Thus the external protection of a national culture must never be extended to internal restrictions on individual freedom of thought, expression, culture or lifestyle for its citizens, since the contextual and cultural definition of the nation implies, as we noted, that it remains outside the normative sphere. In addition, pluralism within nationalities acquires another dimension as well, since nations, as we shall see, are not objective and natural phenomena. They do not exist in and for themselves, but instead constitute the outcome of complex processes of national construction. In consequence, the cultural definition of a nation must be completed by a *political* dimension that is concerned with the very process that gives life to it, that of debate, participation and mobilization. In this sense, from the perspective of the legitimate participants in the process of nation-building, the nation is composed of both its national majority culture and also its minority or minorities, as well as the irreducible plurality of singular individuals. Pluralism thus constitutes an internal cultural and political aspect of both the multinational state and the nations that exist within it. The multicultural plurality (the majority and the national minorities) and the political citizenry, in both individual and group dimensions, constitute two essential components of the nation from a democratic perspective.

Finally, multinational states place as a central value *constitutionalism*, which is often ignored when these issues are considered. The democratic institutions of the multinational state are characterized by values such as freedom, equality, participation, solidarity and pluralism, making obsolete the classical concept of *sovereignty* as the unlimited power of a people or nation, from or against the state.

In effect, there is no room for a sovereign in the democratic institutions of the multicultural state, since all powers are shared, guaranteed, and limited. Self-government, shared government and the separation of powers – *vertically* between legislative, judicial and executive powers, or *horizontally* between diverse communities and the state – all exclude by definition the existence of an absolute, original, and non-negotiable power. The central thesis that power resides in the people as *demos* and at the same time as *demoi* is not appropriately addressed in the unitary, vertical and non-negotiable nature of the concept of 'sovereignty'. This clearly converges with the very idea of the constitution as a limit to and ground for political power: if a constitutional democracy is a state without a sovereign, a democratically institutionalized multinational state is even more so. The constitution is seen as the guarantor of the rights of individuals as singular citizens and as members of a nationality. But it also becomes the guarantee of self-government for the various nationalities and of shared government in the broader context of the state. In this fashion, the constitutional *precommitment* becomes a fundamental factor for protection against both the centralizing and oppressive nation-state as well as the hypernationalism that may arise within minority nationalities, one that seeks to limit the individual rights of its citizens and the collective rights of minorities within it. *Verfassungstreue* (mere loyalty to a constitution) is insufficient to establish the necessary links that create shared coexistence in a multinational state. But such loyalty does constitute a *sine qua non* element: it becomes the legal framework for individual and collective rights to *self-rule* and *shared rule* for the equality of nationalities from a position of difference as well as for interterritorial solidarity between them.[26]

The superior formal rank of the constitution, as a supreme norm that overrides ordinary legislation, constitutes a central element guaranteeing multinational coexistence. This requires that the national communities should participate in the institution that controls the constitutionality of the laws and the protection of individual and collective rights. Such participation is essential in order to allow them representation in and interpretation of the constitution and the resolution of conflicts between the state and the nationalities. Without becoming an obstacle to the flexible resolution and negotiation of differences, the constitution thus becomes in democratic multinational states a guarantee of the territorial distribution of power and solidarity within a common project open to the choices of the participants and legitimated by them.

The normative redefinition of democratic values in a multinational state becomes a powerful democratic argument against problematic, in so far as they are anti-pluralistic, nationalist tendencies towards sovereignty and a nationalizing state. However, from its very assumptions this argument demands a revision of the terms that the classical discourse of nationalism uses: nation, culture, secession, mononational state, and so on.

The Logic of Monoculturalism and Nationalizing States

Often apparently insurmountable difficulties arise for the peaceful coexistence of several nationalities in a multinational state. They are the result of a multitude of factors that vary from country to country: specific historical traditions and experiences of grievance, social cleavages generating polarized party systems and electoral alignments, political cultures of hatred, inadequate constitutional frameworks, and assimilationist regulatory policies. It is worthwhile, however, to centre our attention on one of them which has shown itself to be especially influential, unaffected by the passage of time or by differences in political experiences or systems. We are referring to the intellectual conditions and political discourse of what Brubaker has labeled 'nationalizing states' or 'policies'.[27] In spite of substantial differences in the nationalisms that compete within a multinational state, we can detect a similar logic of nationalist discourse, whether by the nation-state and its majority nationality, or by internal nationalities with greater or lesser self-government powers centred on targeting the nation-state from below. This underlying logic may be labeled both as *expressive nationalism* and *exogenous ethnicity*.[28] It generates numerous difficulties and problems for voicing national demands within the context of democratic processes. It is also surprising to discover that this logic, which is ever present in nationalist discourses, becomes uncritically incorporated by certain researchers of nationalism, who thus contribute to the establishment of one of the most negative factors for accommodating democracy within multinational states.

We may summarize the argument of this underlying 'organic fallacy' logic as follows:

1. A prior *ethnicity*, which is objectively different based on a series of diacritical features (race, language, culture, traditions, territory, economy, symbols) sets the specific difference of the nation and generates an 'us-them' dualism.

2. This objective and given ethnicity produces a prepolitical set of *national interests*, of which the community becomes progressively conscious as its élites or intellectuals carry out a process of 'discovery' or 'rediscovery'.

3. The extension and diffusion of this consciousness of one's interests and differences determines a *collective political identity*, which is polarized and exclusive, creating the incentive to clarify the identity of the citizens, that is, to locate them on one side or the other of the us/them political-cultural limits.

4. This collective and conscious national subject is sooner or later carried into politics by one or more parties as a *nationalist movement*. By means of a complex formula of organizations such as cultural and educational associations, it attempts to broaden the national consciousness and to voice the demands of the entire nation, in order be perceived as constituting this national majority.

5. The resulting demands for self-government may include a broad range of decentralization formulas: autonomy, federalism, confederation. These tend, however, to be seen, *faute de mieux*, as mere intermediate steps of self-determination in a process leading to *secession*, in order to gain one's own independent state, thus fulfilling the classical principle of 'one nation, one state' ('every nation should become a state, every state should strive to become a nation-state').

This logic is based upon the assumption that the nation is an *exogenous* and *objective* fact, generated by each case's specific differential characteristics of ethnicity (language, culture, history and so on). The nationalist movements or parties *express*, that is, externalize and manifest this previous difference – the specific national interest – while extending their conception of these interests to the whole population. Finally, the institutions of self-government and especially of the state centre their focus on reinforcing ethnic differences, along with extending national consciousness and defending these interests.

Overshadowing other significant differences, this logic of discourse becomes applicable both to the internal nationalities of a multinational state, and to the nation-state. It only requires changing the sequence to 1-2-5-3-4 in order for the national state, understood as the institutionalization of a pre-existing ethnicity, to reinforce from above the cultural, economic, and administrative territoriality of the nation, lending support and incentive to nationalism in the party system. It is important to highlight that the logic of the argument is the same in both narratives: the nation is a fundamentally objective prior fact, a collective identity set around given differences, that expresses its interests through the demands of the nationalist parties. And the nation is reinforced institutionally in its ethnicity by the state that is sought or that already exists.

This *objective* concept of nation, however, implies that politics as a dual process of mobilization and institutionalization becomes entirely dependent on a supposed previously sutured identity, which in its basic features is already a social given. This derived and external nature of politics cannot be resolved by simply eliminating from among the objective elements that constitute a nation those factors which are most xenophobic or aggressive such as race or *lebensraum*. Yet this is the proposed 'solution' adopted by many contemporary nationalist movements, as well as by plenty of the positive or normative analyses of nationalism. In fact, even when the central element of the nation is redefined as the national language and culture, thus avoiding racial biology or the geographical determinism of a territory and vital space, the effects derived from it continue to be extremely problematic from the perspective of democracy and accommodation. Let us examine some of them.

If the nation is conceived as a *cultural nation*, it is essentially articulated around the language and culture of the majority, which then become hegemonic and expansionist, hand in hand with a strictly *monocultural* project that attempts to include the whole nation through 'normalization' policies. In consequence, it becomes very difficult or even impossible to guarantee that the key values of a democratic citizenry will be upheld if it has any substantial self-government powers. Most difficult to protect are the rights of individual citizens to critically assume –or not assume at all – the hegemonic, official version of the national culture. At the same time the rights of any internal minority group, whatever its origin, will become precarious since it will be treated as a residual element to be assimilated by the dominant national culture. Even more decisive is the fact that when the nation is defined objectively as monocultural, it becomes difficult to conceive of it as a democratic *political community*, that is, as a collective composed of singular individuals and members of the internal majority and minorities, who freely participate in a plural fashion in the definition of their own community, in recreating the appropriate set of myths, stories and symbols, and in voicing the internal and external political demands for self-government.

Several features of the objective monocultural definition of nation are problematic, both from the perspective of democratization and of multinational accommodation. First, the compartmentalization of politics into a merely vicarious status, dedicated to externally voicing demands, debilitates the constituent nature of the element of national will and consciousness as expressed democratically, which then opens the door for a nationalist élite to 'represent' the 'true' interests of the nation. Second, the depoliticization of the core of the nation weakens the democratic conception of it as an open, deliberative, and participative process in which individuals protected by both individual and group guarantees may decide the cultural, social and political configuration of their community, their project for future coexistence. Third, the democratic deficit of the objective monocultural definition of nation tends to encourage a dual identity that is polarized, excluding multiple or overlapping identities. Thus, a dichotomous us-them tension develops, which may even be transformed into friend/enemy tension between one's own community and other neighbouring nations or the multinational state. This creates obstacles to the negotiation and accommodation of an identity, and tends to predetermine that the final outcome and only possible solution is to doubt the principle of a multinational state and thus pursue secession and an independent state.

Even when secession is justifiable in cases where coexistence and mutual recognition have failed repeatedly, from a pluralist perspective it is still a shame to lose cultural, social, political and economic richness – in sum, the quality of democracy. In addition, processes of secession generally do not follow a self-evident natural logic of national demands for one's own state. Instead they follow a concrete dynamic that generates and broadly reproduces a scenario that denies any possibility for negotiation or accommodation of differences. Thus, for example, it has been shown that agreements deriving from negotiable positions encouraging coexistence are hard to defend strategically. The incentives that leaders experience in nationalist parties tend towards extreme demands that give them greater grass-roots popularity, thus generating a spiral or radicalization and intransigence that feeds on itself.[29]

We should look more closely at this last consequence of the monocultural definition of a nation. In fact, the underlying logic of this view not only predetermines a single normative solution (eventually softened for tactical purposes) which a priori writes off multinational democratic coexistence, seeking secession and an independent state. It also announces the arrival of, and constitutes the basis for, a state that ends up being 'ethnocratic' or 'nationalizing'.[30] If a nation is defined as monocultural, this implies that the state or self-government (autonomous, federal, confederal or independent) will constitute a state for and at the service of only one ethnic group, which must further the language, culture, demographic position, economic welfare and political domination of its institutions and public policies.

The characteristics of ethnocratic or nationalizing self-government or 'majoritarian nationalizing policies' may be listed briefly. Some are fully present, others partially, in the contemporary experiences of the independent states of Eastern Europe, but also in other unlikely places within the Western democracies, albeit to a lesser degree. They are:

1. The self-evident understanding that self-government is intended to serve the nationalizing policies that strengthen and deepen the differential

features of a monocultural nation. This leads to *de facto* or *de jure* monolinguistic policies and to a diffusion of mythical-symbolical narratives that exclude outsiders. In sum, it implies cultural policies of 'external protection' as well as 'internal restriction', excluding pluralism and internal multiculturalism.

2. An explicit or implicit distinction between 'authentic' national citizens and mere 'permanent residents', whose culture is seen as an anomaly or as residual in nature, thus determining either negative or positive incentives to abandon it or reduce it to the private realm, through policies of assimilation, normalization or acculturation.

3. Educational and media policies for reinforcing identity: mythical-historical narratives and literature of exclusion in textbooks, a monolinguistic territory through homogeneity, or research incentives that encourage differentiation.

4. Reforming the administration or the judicial power in order to encourage use of the official language.

In the contemporary analyses of nationalism two interesting types of substantive arguments have appeared to counter this extended monocultural and nationalizing logic. On *normative* grounds it has been argued that national identities 'are not cast in stone',[31] and that they are generated through an open process of debate and participation. The national culture, in turn, is as much recreated as it is received, so that the logic of authenticity must leave way for a 'polycentric nationalism' that is plural and democratic, allowing participative inclusion and accommodation.[32]

On a *sociopolitical* plane it has been argued that nations tend to be open processes, influenced by national mobilization and by interaction between actors and institutions, which are not merely expressions of mobilization but even directly inform it. It is nationalist movements – and, indeed, the entire citizenry (of the majority and minority, individuals from any position or origin) – which create the nations as social and political communities, not the monocultural nations who generate a movement to express themselves in purported unity and homogeneity. Thus a *constructivist* analysis that explains the political genesis of the nation becomes entirely necessary.[33] If institutions have a pivotal role in processes of national construction as they determine interests, forms of life and identities, if political identities are always to some extent in the making, the best argument against the logic of the nationalizing nation-state is the development of flexible and performative institutions for democratic accommodation. In this perspective, *multinational federalism* becomes a clearly plausible alternative.

The Democratic Institutionalization of Multinationality and Asymmetric Federalism

As a model for the territorial distribution of political power, federalism historically has provided a solution to the Hobbesian problem of order without requiring a sovereign, but instead relying on a *self-reinforcing* pact (*foedus*) of vertical-functional and horizontal-territorial division of powers. Now the federalism that is appropriate for a multinational state as discussed here, destined to 'hold together'[34] several nations within a democratically and territorially legitimate state, cannot be the federalism of mononational states. In fact, the expression 'asymmetric federalism' was forged to express principally the heterogeneity and dynamism of the processes and negotiations that link various nationalities and a central state, from a relational perspective of actors and institutions.[35]

In order to understand the implications of federalism in the sense expressed here, we must abandon the analysis of federal states as specific systems defined exclusively according to their exogenous effects, and also examine their endogenous political fundamentals. However, these fundamentals can hardly be discovered at present either in the philosophical field of generic federal principles ('autonomy', 'sovereignty', and 'the state') or in nineteenth-century nationalism ('self-determination', 'sovereignism'). Instead, a new examination of its *structure* needs to occur along 'neoinstitutionalist' lines, paying attention to the most *dynamic* aspects of the arena of actors, their interests and their strategies, as well as the dimension of institutions of self-government and their efficacy in conforming and constituting national interests and identities.

In this sense, the contemporary debate about federalism is characterized by progress in three areas, although the three clearly converge with what has been stated in the last pages. We shall proceed to examine them for purposes of argumentation:

1. The surrender of any theoretical presumption that a canonical and closed 'model' of the federal state is possible, and its replacement by a more modest perspective of institutional minima that allow a structure to earn the federal label.

2. A distinction between ideological *federalism* (the federalist principle) and *federation* (the federal principle) as a political system that responds less to a predetermined abstract institutional design, and more to the challenges and answers to a country's various specific social, political and economic problems.

3. Finally, the very terms of debate have moved away from the *structure* of the federation considered in a *static* perspective, and towards federation

as a *process*, to be analysed thus from an essentially dynamic standpoint, focused on negotiations and agreements.

Concerning the first aspect, defining institutional minima for a federal structure, two debates have recently been abandoned over the great concepts of 'state' and 'sovereignty': the confrontation since Calhoun over 'states' rights' and 'national federalism' in the United States, and the disquisitions about the differences between *Staatenbund* and *Bundesstaat* in Germany and Austria.

It is significant that there is a convergence of opinions between Europe and America concerning the minimum requirements for a federal structure or *federal matrix*.[36] This last concept relinquishes any pyramidal representation, with no loci of power, and is arranged as a horizontal distribution of *decision making* and policy implementation arenas in matters of exclusive or concurrent jurisdiction. This infuses federalism with great flexibility and political adaptability, in contrast with the traditional jurist's perspective of rigid and hierarchical divisions of power. Thus, for Max Weber, the minimum institutional criteria are: a state composed of territorially based units with administrative, legislative and political leadership powers; financial resources to carry out these commitments; the participation of the federated units in federal policies through a second chamber and local execution of federal laws; a rigid constitution as a strong guarantee in contrast to ordinary law; and a principally judicial mechanism for the resolution of conflicts.[37]

Lijphart, in turn, identifies five basic features: a written constitution that regulates the territorial distribution of powers; a bicameral parliament, with the second chamber representing the federated units; overrepresentation in this second chamber of the smallest units of the federation *vis-à-vis* the most populated ones; the participation of the federated units in amending the federal constitution; and political decentralization that is not merely administrative.[38]

The axis of minimum institutional requirements for federalism is limited by most scholars to:[39]

- *political decentralization*, which includes not only legislative power in certain areas along with the corresponding economic resources, but also the capacity for differentiated political leadership of the federated community *vis-à-vis* other communities and the whole federal state;

- *constitutional guarantees*, safeguarded by a judicial organ, so that in Ostrom's words a federal structure is presented principally as a 'constitutional choice reiterated to apply to many units of government where each is bound by enforceable rules of constitutional law'.[40]

- *multiplicity of constituencies* enabling the formation of different majorities at central and regional level with the possibility of different political choices.[41]

Multinational federalism is more a response to new demands for political decentralization of the state ('to *hold* together'), than to unification of dispersed elements ('to *come* together').[42] It implies a will to maintain a dynamic equilibrium around two poles, self-government and shared government, which is agreed upon and guaranteed by the constitutional process. This brings out the centrality of the constitutional moment, so that, as William Riker has stated, 'if we ignore the constitutional factor ... we lose the fundamental aspect of federalism'.[43] In sum, the political key to federalism is manifest in two aspects that must not be forgotten: *self- rule* and *shared rule*. They determine its usefulness as an alternative to the emerging nationalizing logic of multinational states.

However important the centrality of the written constitution as a guarantee, it cannot be a reason to ignore the dynamic dimension of federalism as an *open process*. In his classical response to Kenneth Wheare's thesis, and to the jurists in general, Carl Friedrich insisted on the need to abandon the traditional categories of 'state' and 'sovereignty', employed repeatedly until that time to explain federal political reality. Instead he proposed an unlikely conceptual distinction between state formations and those that do not enjoy that status, postulating the alternative of paying peremptory attention to the most lively and dynamic dimension of the *federalizing process*.[44] A federation is thus built upon the assumption that political institutions are more favourably established upon stable and guaranteed but open pacts and consensus, setting the rules of the game (*constitutional bargain*), than upon organic developments or the positivism of generic principles. The diverse variants of rational choice and public choice, as analytical approaches to the study of federalism, have all placed an emphasis on the agreements between actors as a result of the political and economic conditions of the environment.

Initial economic and fiscal studies of federalism, while principally applying a normative dimension to their analysis, were able to highlight the degree to which political decentralization encourages the appearance of competitive conditions in the supply of public goods and services. This gives credence to the idea that federalism is ahead of the centralized state in being able to satisfy the citizen's preferences, which in these initial models are considered given, complete and transitive.[45] Thus, the federal state is able to satisfy the preferences of a greater number of citizens precisely because it encourages different solutions from one state to another, assuming that these preferences are not distributed evenly among the population. This grants the federal system an ultimate superiority over the majoritarian democratic model.[46]

Its subsequent development followed especially through the research programme of *constitutional political economy*, which dedicated itself principally to the analysis of the effects of federalism. Through a lens that was broader than just politics and reached beyond the normative to the 'positive', it focused on providing a vision of federalism as a mechanism for controlling the interventionist discretion of the state, dissolving this monopoly. The traditional model of a federal state emphasizes the possibility of *exit* because of its low cost, which encourages 'voting with one's feet'. In contrast, James Buchanan's argument is based on a different motivational assumption in the federal implementation of efficacy criteria, referring instead to the position of the Leviathan interested in maximizing taxes. Thus, Geoffrey Brennan and Buchanan carry out a cost/benefit analysis that conceives of federalism as the dispersal of fiscal authority between several federal levels in competition with each other, thus limiting the taxation potential.[47] Federalism thus decreases the high mobility costs characteristic of a centralist state, blocking bureaucratization since it provides disincentives to fiscal pressure. In this fashion, interstate competition in search of greater fiscal resources and mobility between diverse federated units constitute two substantial axes of the federal model. In sum, greater efficiency is achieved by a plurality of federated units committed to competing with each other, which strengthens the cultural, political, and economic wealth of federal multinationalism.

Riker would eventually be the one to address the decisive question of the reproduction of federalism and its stability as a structure, using arguments that are of interest to us. In contrast with the behaviouralism of pluralist political theory, Riker outlines the stability of the U.S. political system using purely institutional factors, in such a manner that central to his analysis is the issue of federalism. Another researcher highlighted four decisive elements concerning the analysis of the *self-perpetuating* character of federal institutions: the requirement that political representatives reside in the state they represent; the variety of manners of electing a representative at the national level; the absence of power to dissolve the legislature; and the existence of strongly decentralized parties.[48]

In fact, the constitutionally-guaranteed territorial separation of powers is strengthened by the organizational decentralization of the parties, which avoids the establishment of a stable national leadership, thus blocking the formation of menacing majorities that might threaten the constitutional separation of powers. Since the legislators are elected according to rules established by their respective states, in electoral campaigns organized at a local level by the parties, and the president is unable to significantly influence the electoral outcome, there are few incentives to form centralized organizations at a federal level. As a result, the legislature defends the interests of the federated states against the 'national' state.

Conversely, the desire to win the presidency puts the brakes on local fragmentation, creating incentives for party coalitions at a federal level in order to compete in the election of the president. This decentralization/ centralization equilibrium is spurred on by the rules of the game, bringing us back to the central status of the constitution as the outcome of an agreement that provides advantages to those who enter into it. Although never expressly stated, the underlying argument in Riker's work is that the conforming capacity of institutions leads us in one sense or another to question the basic assumption of the rational choice model, not only regarding federalism but also regarding politics in general: the notion that preferences are given and complete. Both Kenneth Arrow and Riker himself pointed out that from the same preferences it is possible to arrive at different outcomes depending on the aggregation procedures and decision-making mechanisms used. In addition, analyses of institutions derived from economic theory will insist upon the fact that the success of collective decisions does not depend only on revealed preferences, but also on the capacity of the institutions to 'wash', purify, and even produce preferences. Institutions do matter, not so much in their capacity to restrict the actor's possible course of action in pursuing his or her interests, but most of all because institutions are able directly to determine the interests and actors present.

The analytical axis that traditional studies have stressed (federated states–federal states and dual federalism–national federalism) is now complicated by an additional level: the relationship between the federated states themselves, as a key level of the federal structure and processes. The substitution of hierarchy by competition, leaving aside the obsolete concepts of 'sovereignty' and 'state', implies an equal and non-hierarchical distribution of political power as a series of relations between equals, especially between the federated states themselves as a decisive level of analysis. All this highlights the usefulness of federalism in leading a multinational state to achieve solidarity through institutional arrangements.

For André Breton, federalism illustrates, or should illustrate if correctly formulated, the benefits of competition between institutions as such. This Canadian economist defends *competitive* federalism against the *cooperative* federalism of mononational states such as Germany, where 'collusion, conspiracy and conniving between administrators and those administered' occurs and in the end joint decision-making is done inefficiently, negating the political decentralization characteristic of federalism. Shared powers, whether vertically between different levels of government (federal state, federated states) or horizontally between similar levels of government (federated states), both give life to the federal process. Among the mechanisms that stimulate efficiency, Breton first of all lists the senate, as long as it is not constituted by proportional representation according to population. The federal senate would thus carry out three functions in a federal system: in a vertical competition sense, it introduces a confrontation between centre/periphery which highlights peripheral demands; in the horizontal competition sense it strengthens political equality, which creates pressure for economic equality, which is *sine qua non* for beneficial competition, requiring transfers that equalize the federated units; finally, the federal senate provides an arena for competition, avoiding restrictions on or lack of competition.

The ability of a second territorial chamber to function correctly would be determined by factors such as the index of representation of the federated units or the structure of the party system. Even more decisive than this institutional presence is the requirement that the federated states carry the weight of their own financial decisions, with the subsequent citizen accountability, and not be able to unload the costs of their own decisions onto other states. Territorial solidarity must not imply irresponsibility, creating non-competitive parasites, dependent on handouts.

This would have an extremely pernicious effect: a federated state that, with a permissive policy, increased its level of well-being through, say, industry and banking expansion in its territory, would then find part of its wealth transferred from its territory to others. Nonetheless, the allocation of resources would be ideal, as the companies would be located in the most adaptable areas. There would be a need for framework agreements in the federal arena to avoid externalities (a weakening of environmental protection measures or a worsening in the level of underdevelopment), and to avoid the *fiscal illusion* trap – an economy that parasitically depends upon handouts and circumvents making its citizens fiscally responsible – or the *race to the bottom*, degrading non-competitive conditions for the installation of industry and services. This need not imply a process of regulation at a higher level by the federal state, but rather might be implemented through *cooperative* federalism techniques.[49] Examining the actors realistically, Salmon has insisted that citizens do evaluate the services provided by diverse federated states, comparing services and using this evaluation when it comes time to vote.[50] The dimension of experimentation and innovation that is linked to territorial distribution of power would also derive from the *incentive scheme* of the federal competition logic.

Similarly, but from a neo-institutional standpoint of positivist constitutional theory, Weingast adds a third to Riker's two structural characteristics of federalism. Along with Riker's two levels of governmental organs – political decentralization with distribution of power between levels and a constitutional guarantee of this process – he envisages the dispersal of the loci of economic regulatory authority. Thus the so-called *market-preserving federalism,* along with political decentralization and constitutional guarantees, would be based on two additional conditions: that the capacity for regulating the economy not be monopolized by the federal state, and that the federated states not be able to create barriers to the goods and services offered by other states (federal or federated).[51] There are clear advantages: no monopolization of the global power to intervene in the economy, and competition between the federated units. In this way, only the economic restrictions which citizens are willing to pay for will survive in the mid-range; the states will compete for residents and economic activity using their respective public-policy instruments; and shared fiscal responsibility will imply financial controls – citizens, politicians and investors would be vigilant about how taxes are spent. In this manner federalism considerably decreases the danger of income-seeking in the public sector, avoiding the formation of the classical 'distribution coalitions', a parasite economy that is dependent upon subsidies and clientelist practices, such as exchanging votes for resources flowing from an external tax source.

If we empty these analyses of their neoliberal flavour, and retain the plausibility of their arguments, it is possible to postulate that *competitive* federalism may become, not a substitute as Weingast demands, but rather a complementary factor to *cooperative* federalism. In effect, cooperative federalism owes its existence to policies directed towards the public interest, and developed in close linkage with the welfare state.[52] Social policies involving scarce resources require cooperation, through joint decision-making and not merely coordination between different levels of federated and federal governments. Many scholars have pointed out the pertinence of cooperative techniques that limit fiscal autonomy, which tends to create a lack of solidarity between rich and poor states, encouraging unequal development. But the price to pay, the dark side of the undeniable efficacy and social sense of extreme cooperative federalism, has also been a part of historical experience. There are four problems to which our attention has been directed:

1. Deparliamentarization of the political realm by a 'federal state of governments', along with a neo-corporatist autonomy for bureaucrats and technocrats, thus giving birth to a sort of oligarchy of high civil servants;

2. An exorbitant requirement for consensus through decision-making mechanisms that require unanimity or qualified majorities, requirements which become incentives for broad coalitions that diffuse political responsibility, weakening the possibilities of democratic control, and worst of all, grievously eroding political pluralism;

3. The generating of *rent-seeking* in the public sector, with subsidy parasites and new forms of party clientelism;

4. Centralization and erosion of the self-government of the federated states, justified by the efficacy of global planning.

In sum, the four critical arguments point towards a similar global problem – the deficit of political and economic power in cooperative neocentralism. Competitive federalism would thus provide an element of scepticism in politics, while also reminding us of the need to avoid the collusion of interests in the political class, the unrestricted autonomy of bureaucracies *vis-à-vis* the citizen's interests, or the surrender of fiscal responsibility which links outflows to taxable income.

Nevertheless, cooperative techniques are fundamentally important in the case of asymmetric federalism, seen as an open and negotiable solution providing stability and harmonious coexistence in a multinational state, rather than a strategic prelude to secession. Asymmetric or territorial federalism is that in which federal units coincide broadly with the territorial location of the diverse national or regional groups existing in a state. It is distinguished from non-territorial federalism basically in the heterogeneity of its federated state powers and the central nature of its linguistic and educational regimes. But asymmetric federalism cannot in any fashion imply erosion of the interterritorial solidarity of the member states, which would then maintain or reinforce existing inequalities. The shared and cooperative dimension of federalism is central to the defence of the welfare state, providing mechanisms for social equality, stabilization, and the legitimacy of the multinational state as a project to achieve egalitarian coexistence.

Cultural and political asymmetry, as well as cooperation and competition, would thus become principles of a federal and democratic multinational state, as a plausible institutional alternative to the logic of nationalism, secession, and nationalizing states.

NOTES

1. 'Like the majority principle, the democratic process presupposes a unit. The criteria of the democratic process presuppose the rightfulness of the unit itself.' R. Dahl, *Democracy and its Critics* (New Haven, CT: Yale University Press, 1989), p.207.
2. J. Linz and A. Stepan, *Problems of Democratic Transition and Consolidation* (Baltimore, MD: Johns Hopkins, 1996) p.26.
3. G. Nodia, 'Nationalism and Democracy', in L. Diamond and Plattner (eds), *Nationalism, Ethnic Conflict and Democracy* (Baltimore, MD: Johns Hopkins, 1994), p.9.
4. R. Máiz, 'Los dos cuerpos del soberano: el debate siobre la soberanía popular y la soberanía nacional en la revolución Francesa', *Fundamentos* Vol.1, No.1, pp.176–214.
5. 'These obscurities not only enable nationhood to generate powerful political communities ... they make those communities seem natural.' M. Canovan, *Nationhood and Political Theory* (Cheltenham: Edward Elgar, 1996), p.2.
6. See M. Warren, 'Deliberative Democracy and Authority', *American Political Science Review*, Vol.90, No.1 (March 1996), pp.46–60; and R. Máiz, 'On Deliberation: Rethinking Democracy as Politics Itself', in E. Gellner (ed.), *Liberalism in Modern Times* (London: CEU, 1996) pp.145–71.
7. W. Kymlicka, *Multicultural Citizenship* (Oxford: Oxford University Press, 1995), p.76.
8. A.D. Smith, *The Ethnic Origin of Nations* (Cambridge: Cambridge University Press, 1986), p.15.
9. Y. Tamir, *Liberal Nationalism* (Princeton, NJ: Princeton University Press, 1993), p.33.
10. C. Taylor, *Philosophy and the Human Sciences* (Cambridge: Cambridge University Press, 1985). p.25.
11. Tamir, p.90.
12. 'Our nationalism is not presented as nationalism, which is dangerously irrational, surplus and alien ... our nationalism appears as "patriotism".' M. Billig, *Banal Nationalism* (London: Sage, 1995), p.55.
13. See J. McGarry and B. O'Leary, *The Politics of Ethnic Conflict Regulation* (London: Routledge, 1993), pp.1–41.
14 D. Miller, *On Nationality* (Oxford: Oxford University Press, 1995), pp.49–73.
15. B. Anderson, *Imagined Communities* (London: NLR, 1983), p.13.
16. Kymlicka, p.35.
17. C. Taylor, *Multiculturalism and The Politics of Recognition* (Princeton, NJ: Princeton University. Press, 1992), p.47.
18. P. Van Paris, *Real Freedom For All* (Oxford: Clarendon Press, 1996).
19. Huber, Ragin and Stephens, 'Democracy, Constitutional Structure and the Welfare State', *American Journal of Sociology*, Vol. 99, No. 3, pp.668–74.
20. Miller, p.23.
21. Taylor, *Multiculturalism*, p.23.
22. J. Raz, 'Multiculturalism: A Liberal Perspective', *Dissent*, Winter 1994, pp.67–78; G. Sartori, 'Pluralismo, multiculturalismio e estranei', *Rivista Italiana di Scienza Politica*, Vol. 27, No.3 (1997), pp.477–93.
23. J. Rawls, *Political Liberalism* (New York: Columbia University Press, 1993), p.65.
24. R. Brubaker, *Nationalism Reframed* (Cambridge: Cambridge University Press, 1996), pp.79–98.
25. J. Linz, 'Plurinazionalismo e Democrazia', *Rivista Italiana di Scienza Politica*, Vol.25, No.1 (1995), pp.21–50.
26. R. Dahl, *Democracy, Liberty and Equality* (Oslo: Norwegian University Press, 1986), pp.114–126.
27. Brubaker, p.43.
28. R. Máiz, 'Nacionalismo y Movilizacion Política', *Zona Abierta*, No.79 (1997), pp.167–217.
29. H. Meadwell, 'Transitions to Independence and Ethnic Nationalist Mobilization' in J. Booth and H. Meadwell (eds), *Politics and Rationality* (Cambridge: Cambridge University Press, 1993).
30. R. Stavenhagen, *Ethnic Conflicts and The Nation State* (London: Macmillan, 1996), p.47.

31. Miller, pp.43, 70.
32. Tamir, pp.32, 48.
33. R. Máiz, 'Dilemas del nacionalismo democrático', *Claves de Razón Práctica*, 1997, pp.32–8.
34. A. Stepan, 'Toward a New Comparative Analysis of Democracy and Federalism: Demos Constraining and Demos Enabling Federations', paper for panel 'Comparative Questions', International Political Science Association, XVII World Congress, Seoul 1997; Juan Linz, 'Democracy, Multinationalism and Federalism', working paper, CASS, Madrid, 1997.
35. F. Requejo, 'Pluralismo, democracia y federalismo', *Revista Internacional de Filosofía Política*, No.7 (1996), pp.93–120.
36. D. Elazar, *Exploring Federalism* (Tuscaloosa, AL: University of Alabama Press, 1987), p.37.
37. K. Weber, *Kriterien des Bundesstaates* (Vienna: Braumüller,1980).
38. A. Lijphart, *Democracies: Patterns of Majoritarian and Consensus Government in Twenty-One Countries* (New Haven, CT: Yale University Press, 1984).
39. W. Riker, *Federalism* (Boston, MA: Little, Brown,1964); R. Watts, *Comparing Federal Systems in the 1990s* (Kingston, Ontario: Queen's University, 1996).
40. V. Ostrom, *The Political Theory of a Compound Republic* (Blacksburg, VA., 1971), p.25.
41. B. Weingast, 'Constitutions as Governance Structures: The Political Foundations of Secure Markets', *Journal of Institutional and Theoretical Economics*, Vol.149, No.1 (1993), pp.286–311.
42. Stepan, 'Toward a New Comparative Analysis', p.4.
43. Riker, p.34. For Dahl federalism 'is a system in which some matters are exclusively within the competence of certain local units and are constitutionally beyond the scope of the authority of the national government; and where other matters are constitutionally outside the scope of the smaller units', Dahl, *Democracy, Liberty and Equality*, p 114. But that national forces must be structurally restrained from infringing on federal bargaining is only a necessary but not sufficient condition for durable federalism; regional temptations to renege on federal arrangements must be checked by the application of legal rules enforced by an independent judiciary. Bednar, Eskridge and Ferejohn, 'A Political Theory of Federalism', working paper, Stanford, CA, 1997.
44. C. J. Friedrich, *Trends of Federalism in Theory and Practice* (New York: Praeger, 1968).
45. See D.C. Mueller, 'Federalism', in *Constitutionnal Democracy* (Oxford: Oxford University Press, 1996), pp.77–93.
46. J. E. Lane and S. Ersson, *Political Institutions and Their Political Consequences* (Geneva, 1998).
47. James M. Buchanan and G. Tullock, *The Calculus of Consent* (Ann Arbor, MI: University of Michigan Press, 1962); Geoffrey Brennan and James M. Buchanan, *The Power to Tax* (Cambridge, MA: Harvard University Press, 1980); A. Breton, 'Towards a Theory of Competitive Federalism', *European Journal of Political Economy* No.3 (1987), pp.229–63.
48. Breton.
49. G. Brosio, *Equilibri Instabili. Politica ed Economia nell'evoluzione dei sistemi federali* (Torino: Bollati, 1994).
50. P. Salmon, 'Decentralisation as an Incentive Scheme', *Oxford Review of Economic Policy*, Vol.3, No.2 (1987), pp.24–43.
51. B. Weingast, 'Federalism Chinese Style', *World Politics*, No.48 (1995), pp.50–81.
52. G. Kisker, *Kooperation im Bundesstaat* (Tübingen: Meiner, 1971).

Local and Global:
Mesogovernments and Territorial Identities

LUIS MORENO

This article deals primarily with the interaction between the local and the global, the revival of territorial identities and the increasing incidence of the meso-level in contemporary life. The focus on territoriality should not be see as a neglect of other forms of societal identities also affected by globalization. However, our main area of analysis concerns identity and territory.

At the turn of the millenium, citizens face with some perplexity a situation of advanced modernity. They have discovered new horizons in the understanding of their own collective and individual life within a climate of uncertainty and rapid change. To a large extent, all these transformations have been made possible by the telecommunications revolution.

Nowadays, individuals and groups have immediate access to a wide range of endless data, information and news generated in the remotest corners in the earth. The integrated networks of personal computers, TV terminals, and web servers allow for reciprocal and fluid communication between the house or workplace and the multifaceted external world.[1] One consequence of these technological developments is a higher degree of democratization in the processes of dissemination and exchange of information.

A myriad of facts, including those related to cultures and collectivities all over the world, are now available to the general public. The 'digestion' of such avalanches of information increasingly conditions economic, political, and social activities. The restriction of information and representational images characteristic of power practices in the past has been progressively replaced by the efficient management of overwhelming masses of information produced swiftly and without restraint.

In parallel, the growing attachment of citizens to communities at local and meso-level is also noticeable, particularly in Europe. Such communities are of rather analogous socio-economic characteristics and are politically situated in a somewhat equidistant position between the nation state (or

Luis Moreno, Spanish National Research Council, Madrid

multinational state), and other transnational bodies and institutions (ASEAN, EU, GATT, G-7, IMF, NAFTA, NATO, WB, WTO). Territorial identities associated with these communities have provided new political underpinnings for citizens and groups.

The rebuilding of relationships between the inner and outer spheres of human existence is shaped by citizens' internalization of practicalities and values related to a global context affecting matters of everyday life. Identities are in the midst of such a process of redefinition, with crucial derivations for political culture, social mobilization, and political institutions. The most important factor in all aspects of globalization can be considered as the perceptual one.[2] Interpretations claiming that a blurring of local markers would follow the globalizing trends should nevertheless be qualified. In fact, we are witnessing a reinforcement of community identities at the sub-state level, a trend counteracting the simple assumption of a dehumanizing and undemocratic *Brave New World*.

Attachments to supranational identities should also be accounted for, as the process of Europeanization clearly shows. This multiplicity of identities is reflected in the way that electors cast their votes. Therefore, patterns of electoral behaviour should be regarded not only as the result of a combination of ideological offerings, party programmes and leadership, but also as the manifestation of 'tactical voting' depending on the territory related to the election in question (municipal, regional, national, supranational).

In the first section of this article a conceptual review of ideas and theoretical assumptions is presented. Ethnoterritoriality, collective identities and the territorial accommodation in plural societies are among the concepts analysed. In the second section, a reflection on the implications of globalization, the extension of market values and the relative loss of power and influence by the nation-state is put forward. The last section of this article focuses on the growing role played by those meso-level communities in Europe which have been able to make the general and the particular compatible. This development seems to be in line with a trend towards what can be labeled as a new *cosmopolitan localism*.

Premises and Concepts

At present, all-embracing and exclusive identities are openly questioned and have become problematic. While being corroded by the forces of globalization they are also subject to fragmentation, competition and overlapping elements of a multiple and diverse nature. The discontinuity and dislocation of social arrangements enable diverse identities, in particular territorial ones, to relate to each other in quite an unpredictable manner. In fact, identities are shared in various degrees by individuals and are subject to constant internalization by group members.[3]

A considerable problem arises in the process of establishing boundaries and degrees of citizens' self-identification and in the interpretation of the causes for political mobilization related to territorial identities. As pointed out earlier, a strengthening of meso-level identities goes hand in hand with a growing attachment to supranational levels of civic membership and institutional development. The apparent conflicts between supranational, state and local identities are to a considerable extent conciliated by means of the process of Europeanization.[4]

In this article we deal primarily with the concept of *ethnoterritoriality*, which refers to a dimension where conflicts and political mobilizations are developed and have as their chief social actors those ethnic groups which possess a geographical underpinning. Such a spatial reference is identifiable within the boundaries of a polity, usually of a compound or plural composition.[5]

In plural societies, individuals are tied to cultural reference groups which might be in competition among themselves.[6] This results in a multiplicity of dynamic and often shared sociopolitical identities, which are not necessarily expressed explicitly. Therefore, identity markers are malleable, and the intensity of their manifestation greatly depends upon contingent circumstances.[7]

The revival of ethnoterritorial political movements in the Western world has coincided with an increasing challenge to the centralist model of the unitary state. Within the European context, Spain offers a good example of how regional devolution and federalization seek to articulate a response to the *stimuli* of the diversity of society. This plurality comprises cultural/ethnic groups with differences of language, history and traditions, which can also be reflected in the party system.[8]

Citizens in multinational states in Europe incorporate, in variable proportions, both local/ethnoterritorial and state/national identities. The degree of internal consent and dissent in these plural polities has in the concept of *dual identity* a useful methodological tool for sociopolitical interpretations.[9]

Indeed, the quest for self-government by meso-level communities is in full accordance with the variable manifestation of such duality in citizens' self-identification: the more the primordial ethnoterritorial identity prevails upon modern state identity, the higher the demands for political autonomy. Conversely, the more characterized the state-national identity is, the less likely it would be for ethnoterritorial conflicts to appear. At the extreme, the complete absence of one of the two elements of dual identity would lead to a sociopolitical fracture in the multiethnic state, and demands for self-government would probably take the form of independence. In other words, when citizens in a sub-state community identify themselves in an exclusive manner, the institutional outcome of such antagonism will also tend to be exclusive.

This article sustains the view that ethnoterritorial cooperation and agreement may not only overcome conflicts and divergence within plural polities, but can also provide a deepening of democracy by favouring the participation of citizens at all possible levels of institutional life and political decision-making. Such developments usually fit better in multinational polities where internal ethnoterritorial and cultural diversity are politicized and where citizens share dual identities (state national and ethnoterritorial regional).

The social sciences have also been exposed to the effects of the information revolution. Changes generated by globalization have underlined the obsolescence of a good deal of their analytical, conceptual, and methodological tools. Let us remember, however, that during the last decades the contributions of some social scientists created no little confusion when reflecting on sociopolitical rights and territorial identities. Influential theories developed by North American social scientists have frequently concentrated on the description and prescription of social categories that have as referential contexts those of the United States and Canada. Some of these approaches – with universalistic pretensions – have impinged upon interpretations made by other academics around the world in a rather spurious manner.

Functional diffusionism, in particular, has persistently conveyed the idea that internal territorial differences within nation states would disappear with the extension of liberal democracy and industrial capitalism. As communication in political, economic and cultural matters increased, the peoples of different regions would develop a new common identity, which would transcend their differences.[10] Society would become 'modernized' by means of élite-initiated policies aimed at achieving social standardization (e.g., a common language and citizenship). As a consequence, the cultural identities of ethnic groups and minorities would be replaced by a set of class-orientated conflicts, or conflicts among interest groups. Thus, modernization was regarded to have brought about the idea of an all-embracing state national identity rooted in both cultural and civic axes. History has repeatedly falsified such analyses.[11]

Likewise, it has been argued that political accommodation to secure political and institutional stability in multiethnic societies or polyarchies is almost impossible. Furthermore, attempts made to achieve such a goal are bound to result in either the break-up of the state or the consolidation of a type of hegemonic authoritarianism for the control of the state's unity.[12]

Contemporary liberal thinkers have greatly revitalized the debate regarding individual and collective rights. Most of them can be labelled 'liberal nationalists'.[13] Some have argued persuasively for the case of multiculturalism and the politics of recognition for minorities.[14] However, some of their normative analyses insist upon the unfeasibility of accommodating ethnonational groups within federations – as the case of Quebec and Canada would illustrate.[15]

Representatives of the 'American' school of comparative politics had been convinced that the processes of periphery migrations into the urbanized core areas would eliminate the old local ascriptive identities in favour of new associative links of a functional nature. Some of these theses, advanced, *inter alia*, by Talcott Parsons and Karl Deutsch, were often accepted uncritically and rather dogmatically. Thus, many North American social scientists have adopted the view that universal progress requires a kind of assimilationist integration, which implies inclusive social systems and the practices of detribalization.[16]

The refutation of these theories and the analysis of complex political developments have stimulated social scientists to elaborate new frameworks for the understanding and explanation of contemporary social life. *Neo-institutionalism* can be regarded as an approach aimed at a conceptual and analytical *aggiornamento* carried out mainly by North American academics. There are three main variants within this school of thought: sociological, rational choice and historical. All three share the view that institutions shape the preferences and objectives of social actors in their decision-making processes. Furthermore, they argue that through the establishment of the 'game rules' of power and influence, institutions also condition decisively the outcomes of such decisions.[17]

The enthusiasm shown by many European social scientists for *neo-institutionalist* theses is remarkable. Let us, however, acknowledge the fact that in Europe institutions have secularly shaped decisions and identities, and vice versa. This has been somewhat different in the case of North America, a fact that greatly explains the importance given by this new school of thought to the paramount role to be played by the institutions. Other routes for further research should be encouraged. For example, much explanatory work needs to be done to understand the mechanisms of interaction between human affinities and institutions. As one attempts to explain ethnoterritorial mobilization, one becomes aware of the interplay between reason and emotion, a relationship that does not lend itself easily to categorical and conceptual deconstruction. The reference to institutions as important sources for determining collective expectations and choices is useful but insufficient. Phenomena affecting ethnic relations are often irrational. Groups with territorial identities are actors that do not necessarily behave according to a predetermined institutional logic. Group solidarity and the self-perception of comparative grievances, for instance, can be identified as powerful instruments for mobilization without any objective reasons based on empirical evidence or any particular pattern of institutional design.

Globalization, Market Values and the Nation-State

At a time when certain universal visions of human existence seemed to indicate a fusion of both individuality and globality, group specificities have returned to the fore as protagonists of social life. Other alternative views have envisaged a process of transition to a postmodern relativism. All things considered, citizens around the world are working to revive old particularities and communal roots. In this way spatial references multiply so that their social existence can be legitimized through a reassertion of collective identities.

Ethnic myths and group affiliations continue to offer a substratum for the management of individual anxieties and aspirations. European societies in particular seem to reinforce secular ties of integration within the family or to recreate medium-sized 'intermediate' political communities, as was the case in the early Modern Age.[18]

However, divergent effects resulting from the gradual configuration of the *global village* advanced by Marshall McLuhan[19] can be observed. In the first place, the globalization and internationalization of trade encouraged by the telecommunication revolution are decisively affecting the economy worldwide, and have brought about a deep restructuring of contemporary capitalism. Other related developments have led some authors to point out that we are witnessing the emergence of a *net society* characterized by the exchange of transactions of an informational nature.[20]

Indeed, the constitution of a world market for communication schemes has been spectacular in recent times (Note that between 1984 and 1995 that market increased five-fold). At the beginning of 1996 there were 15 telephone companies with revenues over US$10 billion per year, an amount higher than the annual budgets of many small nation-states around the world. Furthermore, the use of new systems of interpersonal communication, such as electronic mail, has become almost universal in areas such as the academic sector.

The Internet and the World Wide Web have become part of everyday life. Their presence is evident not only in corporate and professional realms, but also in a wide range of leisure activities. The younger generation is increasingly adopting new lifestyles, which are greatly influenced by the use of hypertext software for personal computers and related developments.

Obviously, this informational advance reproduces the traditional dualities of 'insiders' and 'outsiders', but access to the new telecommunications is not confined to a few. In fact, the consumption costs are affordable to the majority of users. Easy accessibility and availability have greatly contributed to the dissemination of all kinds of information.

Some authors hold the view that the television will remain the primary medium in shaping peoples' behaviour and expectations.[21] They believe that the use of the Internet will reach saturation point in the not too distant future. The *homo videns* will therefore remain the central subject in the global village/s. An alternative view maintains that the major factor in overcoming the cognitive constraints produced by high TV consumption is precisely the interactive nature of the Internet. Note that in a period of three years, access to the Internet in the United States has reached 60 million households, the same market penetration that took television 15 years to achieve. By the year 2005 it is estimated that Internet traffic will be higher than the use of the traditional telephone. This trend seems to reaffirm the view that one multi-function terminal in the household will soon provide a versatile access to various means of communication, including TV and the Internet.

The other visible side of the coin concerning our discussion relates to territorial identities, the political aspirations for political autonomy of medium-sized communities and the relative obsolescence of the nation-state as the central arena for economic, political and social life. In fact, the nation-state can be regarded as just another actor –on many occasions with a supporting or secondary role – in what some authors have labelled the 'New World Order, Inc'.[22] Often, its passivity turns into inefficacy when dealing with transnational criminal rackets. These groups are well suited to operating at international level and are able to maximize the inability of individual nation-states to clamp down on organized crime.[23]

At present, national economic policies are becoming more and more dependent on external factors and constraints beyond their control. But geographical mobility does not solely affect capital flows. Other production factors are also concerned, such as industrial components and parts manufactured in cheap-labour countries and imported subsequently for assembling, marketing, and sale in core industrial countries. International freight and a legion of stateless managers are other factors, which are becoming increasingly transnational.[24]

Globalization has meant a transfer of authority and power from nation-states to the markets. The very patterns of economic competition have to comply with the new rules of global markets and the strategies of transnational corporations. Is global capitalism deprived of any sense of territoriality? In selecting locations for investment, financial analysts consider first and foremost the level of profit that they expect to achieve. Indeed, they have a much wider perspective than that determined by purely national interests.[25] But there are other crucial elements related to levels of social cohesion, the absence of political turmoil or the stability of the candidate countries' institutions which also need to be assessed. Other cultural aspects, such as educational systems or national languages, are important too. Furthermore, the processes of decision-making for investments are greatly influenced by the input made by the media and opinion leaders, neither of which can be considered territorially 'neutral'.

National governments still maintain their nominal sovereignty, empowering them to negotiate new economic frameworks (MERCOSUR, NAFTA, UEM, or WB). At the same time they also bargain with the transnational corporations. Their economic manoeuvring to offer innovative polices outside global demands is rather limited. The case of the programmes for indicative planning implemented by the first Mitterrand government in the early 1980s was symptomatic of the external constraints posed on the national sovereignty in the most statist country in Europe.

French governments after the Second World War put into action plans for economic growth. These were to be implemented in a hierarchical manner by the powerful French public sector, and were 'indicative' of the industrial priorities to be taken by private businesses. They set economic guidelines for the general development of the country. The model worked satisfactorily in the post-war period, allowing the French economy to perform at a good level. Right after the Socialist victory in the general elections of 1981, the Mauroy government attempted a different path from the policies of economic austerity followed by neighbouring European countries. The aim was to overcome the effects of the lower stages of the economic cycle by means of implementing neo-Keynesian programmes of reactivation. The experience ended in failure. In those years the majority of European countries had opted for programmes of austerity and a tight control of their national deficits. International financial markets had overwhelmingly validated these measures. Not long after their initial implementation French economic policies suffered a Copernican turn and were to align themselves with the course of action taken by the rest of Europe.

Together with the limits imposed on nation-states' sovereignty by the internationalization of the financial markets, regions and large cities have also exerted pressure on central governments for decentralization and autonomy. Both actions are having great repercussions on the power and *auctoritas* of the nation-state. Frequently, sub-state meso-governments and local authorities do not require the rationalizing intervention of central bureaucracies and élites. In fact, the rules of the 'New World Order, Inc.'

often directly concern the action and policies of these sub-state layers of governments. They can activate policies of industrial relocation or attraction of foreign capitals without the role of the intermediaries at the state's centre. By means of local incentives, urban redevelopment plans, or corporatist agreements with trade unions and industrialists, meso-governments and metropolitan authorities can have direct negotiations with the transnational corporations involved.

Meso-governments as Actors of Political Mobilization

Given this context of internationalization, the role played by medium-size polities is acquiring relevance in most aspects of contemporary life. The renewal of community life at the meso-level derives mainly from the combination of two main factors: a growing rejection of centralization in unitary states coupled with a strengthening of supranational politics, and a reinforcement of local identities and societal cultures with a territorial underpinning.

Meso-governments are no longer dependent on the state-building programs of rationalization carried out during the nineteenth and twentieth centuries. Meso-level entrepreneurs, social leaders and local intelligentsias have adopted many of the initiatives and roles once reserved for 'enlightened' élites who in the past held the reins of power at the centre of their nation-states. Positions of influence are now more evenly distributed in central, meso-level and local institutions. Besides, the cooption of regional élites to the central institutions of government is no longer the exclusive route available for 'successful' political careers.

The supranational framework provided by the European process of convergence brings with it a 'new' element of further cosmopolitanism to meso-communities and conurbations. At one point, and in the face of hard economic competition from other world regions, some analysts proposed the idea of a 'fortress Europe'. According to this view, the secession from the international world arena would preserve the maintenance of European welfare regimes. An economic 'wall' around member states of the European Union (EU) would guarantee the social rights achieved by generations of Europeans. It would also stimulate balanced growth, which, in turn, would create new employment coupled with job-sharing and the reduction of working time. Immigration would be tightly regulated. Undoubtedly this option would mean a U-turn in the cosmopolitan approach of European culture and a radical mutation in its value system. Besides, the current level of Europeanization makes the establishment of a strategy for achieving a monolithic autarky unfeasible. Thus, the very idea of a 'fortress Europe' cannot be embraced as a workable scheme.

What is acquiring major relevance in the political life of Europe is the role of meso-level communities. Two factors can be identified as having greatly contributed to enhance their significance: the re-assertion of territorial identities, and the implementation of the principle of subsidiarity. Let us briefly review both elements.

The reinforcement of local identities

This has provided civil societies with a more participative and active role. Examples in Western Europe include electoral deviations from national patterns found in regional political parties (the CiU in Catalonia, CSU in Bavaria, Lega Nord in Italy, SNP in Scotland). Social movements and local entrepreneurs have found a more flexible context for action. Central state apparatuses are often clumsy and inefficient in dealing with bottom-up initiatives. Thus, conurbations and metropolitan areas are well equipped for some innovative policies in a context more adaptable to the changing needs created by the information age. The regions of Brussels, Metropolitan Madrid, Greater London, and Paris and its urban satellites are re-creating local civic cultures alongside their cosmopolitan traditions. Despite the lack of single identities or ethnic uniformities, these conurbations are in a similar position to other meso-level communities (regions and minority nations) as regards running their own affairs, and developing their potentialities outside the *dirigiste* control of the central state institutions.[26]

Many signs seem to point towards the rise of a European type of communitarianism, which should be regarded in quite a distinct fashion from that prescribed in North America for local communities.[27] In the case of the United States, many communitarian experiences may be regarded as reactions to specific social cleavages and pressing social fractures (the criminalization of social life), as an instrumental means of socialization in response to urban constriction (suburban isolationism), or as alternative lifestyles to dominant values (possessive individualism). From this perspective, North American communitarianism can be seen mainly as socially defensive.[28]

In the EU, territorial identities are mainly proactive. They are not mere mechanisms of response for controlling the informational avalanche generated by the telecommunications revolution. The reinforcement of sub-state territorial identities is deeply associated with powerful material and symbolic referents of the past (culture, history, territories). They seem to have engaged in a process of innovation departing from a common ground, and which seeks to overcome the denaturalizing effects of global hypermodernity.[29] However, their manifestations do not take refuge in a reactive parochialism. They emerge, therefore, as 'project identities' characterized by proactive attitudes.[30]

The principle of subsidiarity

Enshrined in the Treaty of European Union of 1992, known as the Treaty of Maastricht, the principle of subsidiarity provides for decisions to be taken transnationally only if local, regional or national levels cannot perform better. In other words, the preferred locus for decision making is closer to the citizen, and as local as possible. State political élites, reluctant to further the process of European institutionalization, interpreted the subsidiarity principle as a safeguard for the preservation of traditional national sovereignty and, consequently, the powers to intervene centrally. The case of the United Kingdom is paradigmatic in this respect. According to such interpretations, the legislative supremacy of Westminster would be preserved from supranational intervention and regulation originated at the 'federal' institutions of the European Union. However, the devolution of power from the centre of the British state to the constituent nations of the United Kingdom, and to amalgamated local authorities like the former Greater London Council, could not be denied taking into account the same arguments.

The rationale implicit in the principle of subsidiarity favours the participation of sub-state layers of government in the running of public affairs, although global ones are also to be taken into account. At the same time, it encourages intergovernmental cooperation on the assumption that the role of the national states is to be less hierarchical than it has been up until now. Territorial identities are intertwined in a manner that expresses the degrees of citizens' loyalties towards the various sources of political legitimization: municipalities, regions, nations, states and the European Union. Accountability and territorial institutions should therefore reflect the political expression of people's identities and democratic participation.

Immigration from non-EU countries has certainly had an impact on growing feelings of xenophobia in Europe. Nevertheless, immigrants who are willing to take on the values of civic pluralism and tolerance find no major difficulty integrating into the economic and social life at their first 'port of entry', i.e., local and meso-level communities.

Conclusion: A New Cosmopolitan Localism

The processes of bottom-up transnationalization and top-down devolution of powers have allowed a considerable extension of a type of European *cosmopolitan localism*. This is reflected in both societal interests, which are aimed at developing a sense of local community and at participating simultaneously in the international context. There is, thus, a growing adjustment between the particular and the general.

European *cosmopolitan localism* mainly concerns medium-sized polities within or without the framework of a state. Thus, it can be detected in minority nations (Catalonia, Scotland) and small nation-states (the Czech Republic, Luxembourg, Slovenia) as well as in regions and metropolitan areas (Languedoc, Brussels, Berlin, Milan). The latter, in particular, seem to follow a pattern of re-creating those political communities that flourished in the age prior to the discovery of the New World (Italian city-states, the Hanseatic League, principalities). However, and in contrast with the Renaissance period, there is now a common institutional tie inherent in the process of Europeanization. The majority of the EU peoples have internalized European institutions, albeit rather loosely and gradually. The European Court of Justice, the Schengen Agreement, and the inception of the Euro currency can be regarded as steps advancing firmly towards the idea of European transnationalization. Even areas such as those concerning social policy and welfare development – the traditional domain of national intervention – are viewed gradually from a supranational perspective.[31]

Needless to say, all these processes in Europe are taking place in a period of relatively stable economic growth characterized by the absence of wars between once powerful colonial nation-states. Some authors hold the view that together with globalization the potential for a pessimistic scenario is just around the corner. The ever-latent possibility of rivalries between nation-states, trade conflicts between world regions or the growth of religious fundamentalism and xenophobia are potentially explosive.[32] Alternatively, a move towards a new form of civilization capable of revitalizing the old federalist congruence between unity and diversity by means of political pacts appears to be a reasonable challenge for this emerging *cosmopolitan localism*.

NOTES

1. The growing importance of households as 'part and parcel' of the world economy, and as basic units of production, should be underlined. See Immanuel Wallerstein, 'Household Structures and Labor-force Formation in the Capitalist World-Economy', in Joan Smith, Immanuel Wallerstein and Hans-Dieter Evers (eds), *Households and the World Economy* (Beverly Hills, CA: Sage, 1984) pp. 17–22.
2. Susan Strange, 'The Limits of Politics', *Government and Opposition*, Vol.30, No.3 (1995), pp.291–311.
3. On this issue, see Alberto Melucci, *Nomads of the Present* (London: Hutchinson Radius, 1989); Anthony Giddens, *Modernity and Post-Modernity: Self and Society in the Late Modern Age* (Cambridge: Polity Press, 1991), Anthony Smith, *National Identity* (London: Penguin, 1991), and Liah Greenfeld, *Nationalism: Five Roads to Modernity* (London: Harvard University Press, 1992).
4. Some authors are of the opinion that the fact that two identities can be referred to a larger entity does not preclude a possible relationship of incompatibility. See Alfonso Pérez-Agote, 'Un modelo fenomenológico-genético para el análisis comparativo de la dimensión política

de las identidades colectivas en el Estado de las Autonomías', in Justo G. Beramendi, Ramón Máiz and Xosé M. Núñez (eds), *Nationalism in Europe. Past and Present* (Santiago de Compostela: Universidad de Santiago) p.311. That would be the case, for example, of both Basque and Spanish exclusive forms of self-identification. However, the subsuming of those identities under the European confines implies a nexus – even though it is not explicitly sought – of congruence between both exclusive forms of self-identification.

5. On the concept of ethnoterritoriality, see Joseph R. Rudolph, Jr. and Robert J. Thompson (eds), *Ethnoterritorial Politics, Policy and the Western World* (Boulder, CO: Lynne Rienner, 1989); John Coakley, 'Conclusion: Nationalist Movements and Society in Contemporary Western Europe', in John Coakley (ed.), *The Social Origins of Nationalist Movements* (London: Sage/ECPR, 1992), pp.212–30; and Luis Moreno, 'Multiple Ethnoterritorial Concurrence in Spain', *Nationalism and Ethnic Politics*, Vol.1, No.1 (1995), pp.11–32.

6. Fredrik Barth (ed.), *Ethnic Groups and Boundaries: The Social Organization of Cultural Difference* (Boston, MA: Little, Brown & Co, 1969).

7. Benedict Anderson, *Imagined Communities: Reflections on the Origins and Spread of Nationalism* (London: Verso, 1983). See also Eric Hobsbawm, *Nations and Nationalism since 1780: Programme, Myth and Reality* (Cambridge: Cambridge University Press, 1990); Paul Brass, *Ethnicity and Nationalism. Theory and Comparison* (New Delhi: Sage, 1991); and Anthony Cohen, *The Symbolic Construction of Community* (London: Routledge, 1992; 1st ed, 1985).

8. The persistence of a *dual identity* or *compound nationality* in Spain is indicative of their internal ethnoterritorial relations. According to Juan Linz , 'Spain ... is a state for all Spaniards, a nation-state for a large part of the Spanish population, and only a state but not a nation for important minorities' ('Politics in a Multi-Lingual Society with a Dominant World Language: The case of Spain', in Jean-Guy Savard and Richard Vigneault (eds), *Les états multilingues: problems et solutions* (Québec: Les Presses de l'Université Laval, 1975, p.423). On the Spanish case, see Luis Moreno, *La federalización de España. Poder político and territorio* (Madrid: Siglo XXI, 1997), and Luis Moreno, *Federalism: The Spanish Experience* (Pretoria: HRSC, 1997).

9. The example of Spain is illustrative. In all 17 Spanish *Comunidades Autónomas* (regions and nationalities) there is a high proportion of citizens who claim some form of dual identity. The question addressed to them in the successive polls was as follows: 'In general, would you say that you feel ... (1) 'only Andalusian, Basque, Catalan, etc.'; (2) 'more Andalusian, Basque, Catalan, etc. than Spanish'; (3) 'as much Andalusian, Basque, Catalan as Spanish'; (4) 'more Spanish than Andalusian, Basque, Catalan, etc.'; or (5) 'only Spanish'. In the period October 1990–June 1995 a degree of duality was expressed by around 70 per cent of the total Spanish population (i.e. categories 2, 3 and 4). Approximately 30 per cent of all Spaniards expressed a single identity ('only Spanish', or 'only Andalusian, Basque, Catalan, etc.'). For an analysis of the case of Catalonia see Luis Moreno and Ana Arriba, 'Dual Identity in Autonomous Catalonia', *Scottish Affairs*, No.17 (1996), pp.78–97; and Luis Moreno, Ana Arriba, and Araceli Serrano, 'Multiple Identities in Decentralized Spain: The Case of Catalonia', *Regional and Federal Studies*, Vol. 8, No.3 (1998), pp.65–88.

10. For William Safran, one of the prominent characteristics of American social science in general, and the behaviourist-functionalist school of political science in particular, is its ahistoricist bias. History is rejected on two grounds: 'First ... as a succession of events that ... do not lend themselves to comparison and generalization. ... Second ... because it is associated with pre-modern (primitive) societies. ...' ('Ethnic Mobilization, Modernization, and Ideology: Jacobinism, Marxism, Organicism and Functionalism', *Journal of Ethnic Studies*, Vol.15, No.1(1987), p.13). 'Mainstream' Marxists have traditionally taken a functional approach to the analysis of political integration and modernization. See Walker Connor, *The National Question in Marxist-Leninist Theory and Strategy* (Princeton, NJ: Princeton University Press, 1984).

11. The cases of Catalonia and Scotland in Europe and Quebec in North America are paradigmatic in this respect. See, for example, Michael Keating, *Nations Against the State: The New Politics of Nationalism in Quebec, Catalonia and Scotland* (London: Macmillan, 1996). See also Daniele Conversi, Daniele, *The Basques, The Catalans and Spain.*

Alternative Routes to Nationalist Mobilisation (London: C. Hurst & Co, 1997) and Alain Gagnon (ed.), *Quebec: State and Society* (Scarborugh, Ont.: Nelson, 1993).).

12. See, for example, Robert Dahl, *Polyarchy, Participation and Opposition* (New Haven, CT Yale University Press, 1971), and Donald Horowitz, *Ethnic Groups in Conflict* (Berkeley, CA: University of California Press, 1985). Robert Dahl's position is in line with the views of Ernest Baker who also regarded political secessionism and authoritarianism as the two viable options in ethnocultural polyarchies.

13. Yael Tamir, *Liberal Nationalism* (Princeton, NJ: Princeton University Press, 1993).

14. On multiculturalism see Charles Taylor, *Multiculturalism and 'The Politics of Recognition': an essay* (Princeton, NJ: Princeton University Press, 1992), and Michael Walzer, *On Toleration* (New Haven, CT: Yale University Press, 1997).

15. For Will Kymlicka ethnoterritorial accommodation would not constitute a stable political solution but a previous step to secession ('Federalismo, Nacionalismo y Multiculturalismo', *Revista Internacional de Filosofía Política* No.7 (1996), p.45). However, in a subsequent writing Kymlicka shows that it would be a misrepresentation to characterize him as being pessimistic about the viability of multinational federations – see his *Finding our Way: Rethinking Ethnocultural Relations in Canada* (Oxford : Oxford University Press, 1998). Juan Linz's views are that federalism can consolidate liberal democracy in multinational states (Juan Linz, 'Democracy, Multinationalism and Federalism', paper resented at the IPSA World Congress, Seoul).

16. Marxist thinkers would use concepts such as 'class consciousness' and 'class struggle'. For both schools of thought, however, political integration and state building were the independent variables in a social analysis where culture and language were dependent categories.

17. Thomas Koelble, 'The New Institutionalism in Political Science and Sociology', *Comparative Politics*, Vol.27, No. 2 (1995), pp.231–43.

18. This is particularly relevant as regards major conurbations, regions, stateless nations, and small nation-states. Greater London, the north-east of England, Scotland, and the Republic of Ireland are instances of such communities in the context of the British Isles.

19. Marshall McLuhan, *Understanding Media: The Extensions of Man* (New York: McGraw-Hill, 1964) and Marshall McLuhan and Quentin Fiore, *The Medium is the Massage. An Inventory of Effects* (New York: Bantam Books, 1967).

20. Manuel Castells, *The Information Age: Economy, Society and Culture*, Vol.II: *The Power of Identity* (Cambridge, MA: Blackwell, 1997).

21. Giovanni Sartori, *Homo videns* (Rome: Gius, Laterza & Figli Spa, 1997).

22. Vivien Schmidt, 'The New World Order, Incorporated: The Rise of Business and the Decline of the Nation-State', in *What Future for the State?*, *Daedalus*, Vol.124, No.2 (1995), pp.75–106.

23. Besides, the informal sector of the international economy counts on the financial connivance of some transnational networks for the 'whitening' of the profits of the illegal drug trade.

24. Boeing, for instance, decided to drop its labelling as an 'American corporation'. Note that many of the components for their planes are produced in a dozen different countries outside the United States. Other companies take advantage of being a multinational consortium, as is the case of Airbus, the commercial rival of Boeing.

25. According to some authors, capital movements only take into account the potential level of profits disregarding geographical criteria; see William Greider, *One World, Ready or Not: The Manic Logic of Global Capitalism* (New York. Simon & Schuster, 1997). However, the economic crises in Japan and South East Asia in the late 1990s seem to corroborate the axiom that the international financial markets are unstable by nature.

26. A different issue is the location of central bureaucracies (or 'eurocracies', as is the case of Brussels) in their territories. Some of the officials of the central institutions cannot refrain from the perception that capital cities are the very representation of the nation-state.

27. Amitai Etzioni, *The Spirit of Community. Rights, Responsibilities, and the Communitarian Agenda* (New York: Crown, 1993).

28. Other functional identities linked to various dimensions of social life, such as cultural forms, gender, religion and individual sociobiological conditions can also be interpreted as new

forms of 'resistance'; see Richard Kilminster, 'Globalization as an Emergent Concept', in Alan Scott (ed.), *The Limits of Globalization* London: Routledge, 1997), pp.257–83.

29. De-naturalizing is used here to mean the deprivation of the rights of citizenship within an established democratic polity.

30. According to Castells, 'project identities' do not seem to originate from the old identities of the civil societies in the Industrial Age, but from the development of current 'resistance identities' against the informational avalanche. This argument is rather circular as regards its territorial dimension. In the case of the United States, sub-state spatial identities are not commensurable with the type of identities deeply rooted in the *Volkgeist* of diverse European peoples.

31. See, for instance, Bob Deacon, Michelle Husle, and Paul Stubbs, *Global Social Policy. International Organizations and the Future of Welfare* (London: Sage, 1997).

32. Noam Chomsky, *World Orders, Old and New* (London: Pluto, 1994).

II. SPANISH EXPERIENCES

Identity, Ethnicity and State in Spain: 19th and 20th Centuries

JUSTO G. BERAMENDI

The aim of this paper is two-fold: on the one hand, to present the basic patterns in the development of the national question in Spain, and on the other hand, to attempt to account for what is a quite exceptional process in Europe over the last two centuries. This explanation will focus on the origins and, where appropriate, the consolidation of regional/national identities with national referents that are different and mutually exclusive.

Given the general lack of consensus on the relevant terms of analysis, it is essential to begin by clarifying the conceptual contents of the basic terms (national identity, ethnicity), as well as other closely related words (nation, national consciousness, political culture, etc.). Unfortunately, due to spatial constraints, it is impossible to present here the full debate maintained elsewhere[1] with some of the authors[2] who have studied these questions, and especially the issue of political and ethnic identities.[3]

I will therefore begin with an analysis of the national question in Spain, in which I shall examine the different stages of development which, in my opinion, are contained in the period analysed. In each stage I shall consider how the following factors combine with one another: state actions and the reactions they provoke; the existence or absence of regional institutions of self-government; the social functions and ideological potential of ethnicity; the political identities prevalent during each stage; the particularities of socio-economic development in each area and in the state as a whole; and the convergence or divergence of interests among different élites and social classes and between them and the political institutions.

Pre-existing Conditions and the Starting Point

If we assume, as I do, that nationalisms/nations and all related phenomena develop from liberal revolutions and the reactions to them, then our starting point must lie in the first third of the nineteenth century. Nevertheless, it is clear that nothing in history arises *ex nihilo*, even during times of very

Justo G. Beramendi, University of Santiago de Compostela

radical transformations, which are always conditioned by the previous situation. Let us begin, therefore, by recalling the most significant characteristics of the *ancien régime* in Spain. These include:

1. The existence of a pre-national Spanish identity which had been generated over three centuries as a result of the domestic and foreign actions of an imperial state. At home, the state had managed to extend and consolidate a wide range of unifying elements, most of which were based on the ethnicity and institutions of Castile: the establishment of a lingua franca (Castilian) for public and intellectual uses; religious uniformity, whereby the Catholic counter-reformation as defined by the Council of Trent became a fundamental identity pillar; and the extension of Castilian public law and political institutions to most areas of the kingdom. With respect to the state's action abroad, continual confrontations with other states, cultures and religions in both Europe and America undoubtedly meant that those directly involved (soldiers, clergy, civil servants, intellectuals) saw themselves – and were seen by others – as 'Spanish'. Clearly this sense of identity would be much stronger among the inhabitants of the Crown of Castile (regardless of their ethno-cultural diversity) than among those of the Crown of Aragon, since the latter were not so closely linked to the central public administration (and the imperial venture) due to the particular conditions of unification under the Catholic monarchs. As Julio Caro Baroja noted,[4] the emergence of the first post-medieval states and their continual wars resulted in the diffusion of pre-national stereotypes throughout Europe between the sixteenth and eighteenth centuries. Naturally each stereotype had a dual nature: the positive side in its self-defined version, and the negative side in the image constructed and diffused by others. Álvarez Junco has accurately outlined the highly traditionalist nature of this pre-national Spanish identity, which he labels ethno-patriotic.[5]

2. The development of the Spanish state during the eighteenth century, combined with the population growth and economic recovery that followed the arrival of a new dynasty, also contributed to the consolidation of Spanish patriotism. At least among the reforming élites influenced by new ideas circulating in Europe, the contents of this patriotism changed, to the extent that it now became what may be described as Spanish proto-nationalism. This can be seen in the work of numerous Enlightenment writers (Feijóo, Cadalso, Forner, Masdeu) and in the tone of many official documents, in which the terms *patria* and even *nación* were increasingly used to refer to Spain. Nevertheless, the relationship between this proto-nationalism and the old pre-national Spanish identity was contradictory. On the one hand, the proto-

nationalism of the élites helped to strengthen the political and state-centred elements of identity among other sectors of the population, although it is impossible to say precisely to what extent. On the other hand, it rejected the more traditional, archaic aspects of that same pre-national identity, which began to split into two ideological-political identities: that of those who wished to keep the legacy of the past intact, and the advocates of modernization, who continued to respect political absolutism but were critical of practically everything else. These two groups would shape political developments in Spain between 1808 and 1840.

3. In spite of these trends, other identities survived. This was inevitable for two reasons: first, the great ethnic diversity of the metropolitan territory of the state, and second, because of the territorial diversity of its institutions. Besides the Catholic religion, which was undoubtedly the unifying factor *par excellence* throughout Spain, the panorama was extremely complex in terms of the other ethnic factors which would also play an important role in the future (such as language, and material and spiritual culture). Within the Crown of Castile, a number of territories coincided fundamentally in terms of ethnic and institutional characteristics (Andalusia, Old Castile, New Castile, Leon, Asturias, Murcia, Extremadura and the Canary Islands); one differed ethnically, but not institutionally (Galicia); and another two had both ethnic and institutional peculiarities (the Basque country and the Kingdom of Navarre). Within the Crown of Aragon, which consisted of four territories, the institutions of corporate self-government – the Cortes (parliament) and Generalitat (government) – had been abolished by Phillip V in 1714–15, as punishment for their support of the Habsburg pretender during the War of Succession. Of these four territories, one had no essential ethnic differences (Aragón) but the other three did (Catalonia, Valencia and the Balearic Islands).

4. Apart from other minor ethnic differences with less potential for influencing the sense of identity, we should also take into account socioeconomic diversity, particularly as far as land ownership and agrarian modes of production are concerned.

In any case, the ranking of the regional identities derived from these differences has yet to be investigated thoroughly. Therefore, we will examine certain outstanding indicators: mainly the presence or absence of significant political impact. This evidence suggests that there were a number of ethnic identities in the strict sense of the term, each with a greater or lesser social range *vis-à-vis* Castilian ethnicity, which was the foundational pre-national identity of Spain. Of all these ethnic identities, only a few seem to have served as the basis for other kinds of identities. Yet it is of particular significance that neither ethnicity, nor previous institutional peculiarities, nor a combination of the two would be sufficient conditions for the future development of anti-Spanish nationalism, although both would be necessary factors in these processes. As we know, this development only took place in Catalonia, the Basque country and Galicia. All three regions had a specific ethnicity, and the first two also had their own institutions of corporate self-government, which could be activated in fact or in memory in support of nationalist demands. But these same initial conditions were also found entirely or partially in Navarre, Valencia, the Balearic Islands and, to a lesser extent, Aragón, although strong nationalist tendencies did not develop in these areas. This would suggest that we must also take into account other factors in addition to those described above.

But first let us return to the starting point. Aside from the inclusion of Portugal in the Spanish dominions and its subsequent departure (although Portugal already had its own solid pre-national identity), two cases merit a special focus: Catalonia and the Basque country. In the case of Catalonia, the attempt to gain independence in the seventeenth century demonstrates that the combination of Catalan ethnicity and institutions of corporate self-government, along with a clear defence of regional interests by Catalan ruling groups, led to actions that revealed the existence at that time of a Catalan pre-national identity of a similar degree to those of Portugal or Spain. However, over the course of the eighteenth century and despite the abolition of its own institutions (or perhaps partly as a result of this loss), the indicators of Catalan identity weakened considerably. This was probably linked to the elimination of self-government combined with the opening up of colonial trade for Catalan products and certain state protectionist policies on behalf of the proto-industry in the region, which reshaped the interests and loyalties of the dominant or most economically advanced groups within Catalan society.

Unlike Catalonia, the Basque country maintained intact its autonomous administration and tax system. Moreover, these political and administrative institutions were the best instruments that the regional élites (clergy and *jauntxos*, or lower rural nobility) had to retain their political and socioeconomic power. Therefore, it was hardly surprising that this period saw the emergence of a discourse legitimizing Basque peculiarity.[6] This discourse was based on the historic mythicization of an ancient race, with its own language and *Volksgeist*: the Basques were a genetically pure, religious and austere people who had always maintained their independence, their simple customs and their democratic-patriarchal organization against all attempts at invasion or annexation. Their integration into the Crown of Castile had been the result of a pact with the Castilian monarchs as equals, with Basque self-government as a key aspect of this pact. This legitimizing discourse, which was propagated for centuries by the Church and governing élites, was probably also accepted by a vast majority of the population. It is, therefore, quite logical to assume the existence of a strong regional identity which, nonetheless, had never given rise to any movement in opposition to the state, except in the texts of a few isolated writers.[7] In fact, in the Spain of the *ancien régime*, the Basques (and particularly those of Vizcaya) were seen as the paradigm of honourable loyalty and exemplary service to the Crown.

Finally, it should be noted that the social status of the ethnic particularity (including language) was very different in Catalonia and the Basque country in contrast with Galicia. In this last case ethnicity was a negative social marker, due to the pronounced Castilianization of the Church and the Galician upper classes since the sixteenth century. For this reason, in Galicia, unlike the other two territories, ethnicity would have contradictory roles in the future: on the one hand it would constitute the raw material in the elaboration of Galician nationalist discourse; on the other hand, it also inhibited the social adoption of this nationalism.

Identities and the Liberal Revolution in Spain[8]

During the Frenchman's War (1808–14), later called the War of Independence, collective actions developed in such a way as to suggest that, despite the existence of numerous regional ethnic identities in Spain, the only relevant political identities at that time were the pre-national Spanish identity and reformist proto-nationalism. Due to the impact of the Napoleonic invasion and the proclamation of a foreign king (Napoleon's brother Joseph I), this proto-nationalism split into two main factions: the *afrancesados* who collaborated with the invaders, maintaining an ideological continuity that simply transferred its loyalty from one dynasty to another; and another group who transformed the proto-nationalism into a nascent liberal Spanish nationalism, which was most clearly reflected in the *Cortes de Cádiz* and the 1812 constitution which resulted. After the war, the former group disappeared, subsumed by the latter.

This liberal revolution, and the absolutist reaction to it, would dominate the political scene in Spain for almost the entire first half of the nineteenth century. This played itself out in a struggle between pre-national and national identities (both of them Spanish), and explains why other identities did not develop further. In terms of social acceptance, the pre-national identity with its historic contents (Catholicism, tradition, sense of honour, loyalty to the absolutist monarchy) was perhaps the most widespread. As the liberal revolution developed, the national identity gradually began to spread beyond the minority élites by means of a deficient diffusion (through the press, political organizations, schools and the army), mixing new and old components (ancestral yearning for freedom and independence, Catholicism, traditional values that were compatible with liberalism, patriotism and other less political elements of the resulting *Volksgeist* such as bravery, indiscipline, individualism, etc). As elsewhere, writers and historians who had been influenced by romanticism and nationalist historicism played an important role in the definition of this national identity.

Once the absolutist counter-revolution had proved itself non-viable, after 1840, the pre-national identity disappeared, bequeathing many of its components to the new national definition of 'Spanishness'. The final synthesis was therefore internally divided and conflictive, not only in an ideological-political sense (which was inevitable), but also in terms of identity. As Borja de Riquer has correctly pointed out,[9] this is even reflected – quite exceptionally – in the symbols of national identity: the national flag, coat of arms, anthem, national holidays and so on. So it would not be unreasonable to conclude that the Spanish liberal revolution, as the source of the first nationalism and of the nation itself, contained a substantive weakness right from the beginning. This 'factory flaw' prevented it from gaining sufficient social acceptance to generate a single national identity throughout the entire state. As many historians have already pointed out, the main cause of this weakness was socioeconomic underdevelopment; this gave rise to a peculiar correlation of political forces, which did not favour the most innovative sectors. This made compromise between tradition and modernity inevitable, which also explains the generally moderate nature of Spanish liberalism and its respect for certain traditional values and institutions (religion, monarchy, the central role of the Church in educating élites and so on).

All this occurred before the emergence of the other competing national identities. These initially appear and develop as regional identities in a slow, complex process that began with the consolidation of the moderate liberal state in the 1840s. Each regional identity evolved at a very different rate, with its own unique characteristics.[10]

In fact, until the first decade of the Restoration (1875–85), the only regional identity which had survived as such was the Basque identity which, as we have seen, was based more on the defence of regional institutions and the mythicization of their origin and meaning than on the politicization of ethnicity. As I have already noted, the dominant social groups in the *ancien régime* (rural lower nobility and the clergy) maintained their influence because of their control of the *Diputaciones Forales* and the specific privileges of the church. The liberal revolution threatened the former and did away with the latter. Therefore, these social groups supported the absolutist reaction carried out by Carlism in the early nineteenth century; but when they were defeated in the First Carlist War (1833–9), this Basque Carlism evolved into a regionalist movement known as *fuerismo*, which also included a minority liberal component. With its diverse ideological variants, *fuerismo* was the only movement capable of articulating a sense of identity assumed by the majority of the population.[11]

In Catalonia a series of interrelated phenomena developed over the course of a long initial period (c.1840–c.1890). First, the use and propagation of the country's language and history (a movement known as the *Renaixença*) by a large proportion of the intelligentsia gave rise to a regionalist discourse and practice which, although not assumed by the majority of the population, did lay the foundations for its later acceptance.[12] Second, agrarian transformations and industrialization fuelled the emergence of the bourgeoisie and the proletariat as proper social classes, as well as a number of intermediate social groups (the self-employed, *petit bourgeoisie* and liberal professionals). This made Catalan society qualitatively different and considerably more modern than that of other Spanish regions. Third, and as result of these developments, Catalonia enjoyed a higher degree of media networking, information and political socialization, which are all of great importance in the formation of a strong nationalism (remember Karl W. Deutsch). Moreover, the emerging Catalanism had much greater presence in this area than its real sociopolitical weight would predict. Finally, and linked to these factors, the region also enjoyed qualitatively superior sociopolitical dynamism and vitality.

All this gave rise to a major inherent contradiction (if still only latent). With rigidly centralist tendencies, the Spanish state as a whole was undergoing a slow and imbalanced process of development, to the extent that the most developed areas did not coincide either territorially or in terms of identity with the centre of political power and economic policy. Nonetheless, as long as there was still the hope of constructing a modern, progressive Spanish nation, almost all Catalan political groups – and their respective social supports – maintained their Spanish national referent, both on the right and the left of the political spectrum. The initial absolutism of the traditionalists and their rural supporters gradually gave way to reactionary Spanish nationalism or even moderate liberalism; the bourgeoisie, shopkeepers, artisans and urban workers were divided between liberal *progresistas* and democratic-republicans; and only a small minority of intellectuals and professionals took a Catalanist political stance. Nevertheless, the strength of ethnic consciousness, heightened by the actions of initial Catalanism, was reflected in the general responsiveness to ethnic identity and the vigour of the decentralizing currents, particularly present in the liberal democratic left (even though, for the time being, it remained committed to the Spanish nation).

The case of Galicia is quite different in almost all respects.[13] Despite being freed from Church mortmains, the old land-ownership system remained, along with a veritable absence of industrialization which blocked any kind of real change. The liberal revolution even respected the ancient rights of the rural *fidalguía* (lower nobility), permitting them to receive their land rents (*foros* and *subforos*), while moderate liberalism gradually provided them with a good position in the clientelist system and in the government administration. The institution which was most seriously affected by the revolution was the church. With its almost exclusively Castilian hierarchy it remained almost entirely loyal to absolutism or to striking bargains with the conservative liberals. Meanwhile, in an almost entirely agricultural and extremely underdeveloped country, the sparse bourgeoisie was mostly non-indigenous and scattered in small territorially and economically unconnected groups, who adopted the defensive strategy of staying on good terms with the central government. That left the intermediate societal groups, which were the social base of Galicianism but also of the democratizing progressive political forces whose national reference was Spain. If, in addition to this, we remember that Galician ethnicity was traditionally regarded as a negative social marker, then it is easier to understand the apparent paradox: the region with the most extensive, homogeneous ethnicity in the entire Spanish state developed the weakest nationalism, and did so considerably later than the other two. And, despite the fact that around 1840–6 a relatively large proportion of the Galician intelligentsia began to give ideological significance to the country's history and ethnicity, and the literary and historical *Rexurdimento* never fully faded, a discourse of clearly defined Galician identity remained socially marginal, and only managed to strengthen ethnic consciousness among a small proportion of the middle classes and, therefore, among a minority within the liberal left.[14]

The 'glorious revolution' of 1868, which brought down the conservative monarchy of Isabella II, then gave way to a period of unrest (1868–74) which included an attempt to democratize the state (the constitution of 1869), a change of dynasty (Amadeo I) and even a short-lived federal republic (1873). The last absolutist rebellion (centred in the Basque country and Navarre) took place during this republic. But this period finished with a failure of both the left and far right's political objectives, and the monarchy was restored, thus merely consolidating the model of a moderate, centralist liberal state (the constitution of 1876) which had already been established during the Isabelline period. For the far right this was a failure because their defeat in the last Carlist War signalled the definitive end of resorting to armed struggle in defence of tradition and the interests associated with it, and obliged all traditionalists to seek other paths. This provided the opportunity for some traditionalists to change their national referent, which happened to a very small degree in Galicia, to a certain extent in Catalonia and to a large degree in the Basque Country, where the re-channelling of a large part of Basque traditionalism would play a key role in the emergence of Basque nationalism. It was a failure for the left because the downfall of both the democratic monarchy of Amadeo I and the First Republic extinguished the hope of many that a Spanish nation could fulfil and safeguard their aspirations for political democracy and socioeconomic modernization. Nonetheless, in spite of its brevity, the republican experiment was later to play a double-sided contradictory role: for right-wing Spanish nationalism it became a 'nemesis' to fight against at all cost, and 'proof' of the terrible ills which could result from the decentralization of power; however, for the Spanish left, and for the different regionalisms and some of the alternative nationalisms, it was a model not only of maximum democratization, but also of the possible harmonization of national opponents. And this was to have major implications in both the short and medium term for the evolution of the national question in Spain.

In the short term it led to a tendency for certain sections of Spanish federalism to move into Catalan and Galician regionalism, as well as inspiring increasing respect for ethnic identity on the Catalan left (even among the working classes). This, along with the traditionalist reinforcements, led to a significant increase in the social presence of – and support for – regionalism in Catalonia during the last two decades of the nineteenth century. By the turn of the century Catalan regionalism would only require a sufficient additional stimulus in order to create a true regional identity. In Galicia, in contrast, the minor ideological and organizational advances that did take place did not significantly alter the existing situation. At this time in the Basque Country, however, there were rapid changes in the rate and nature of economic development, whose effects in the political arena, and in terms of identity, we shall consider presently.

To summarize, as elsewhere, the liberal revolution created the conditions for the emergence of Spanish national identity (although here it encountered greater limitations). There is little concrete evidence as to the level of social acceptance and strength of this identity, but ideological and political indicators reveal that throughout the first third of the nineteenth century there was only one real conflict in this field: namely, the confrontation between the old Spanish pre-national identity (of traditionalist nature) and the new Spanish national identity (with a predominantly liberal slant). We also know that the existing ethnic identities suffered no significant erosion as a result of this process; still less was there a near disappearance of these identities which characterized the falsely paradigmatic case of France. In fact, the consolidation of the liberal-moderate state during the 1840–80 period had effects which were in part contradictory. On the one hand, Spanish national identity continued to enjoy a monopoly throughout the state and (although there is no precise evidence to this effect) it seems to have become stronger and more socially diffused as a result of the nation-building mechanisms of all liberal revolutions: schools (history and values), the press, the army, the national basis of political parties and so on. On the other hand, not only did ethnic identities fail to retreat significantly, but some of them actually became stronger, and were used intensively in certain ideological-cultural revivals. Although their sociopolitical significance was still limited, they laid the foundations for the potential development of regional identities. Nevertheless, for the time being the social influence of these alternative regionalisms was still very weak; hence the possibility that they might stagnate or even weaken. An example of this is seen in the fleeting capacity of the federalist movement in 1869–74 to redirect them (except in the Basque case) towards a fully democratic and decentralized project of Spanish identity.

The resounding failure of this project, and the consequent anti-democratic centralist ebb, coincided significantly, during the first part of the monarchy restoration (1875–98) and before the so-called 'Disaster', with the growth of regionalisms that reinforced the political impact of existing ethnic identities. But the strength of the political system demonstrates that the development of alternative identities had still not reached a point of no return.

From the Disaster of 1898 to the Second Restoration

This situation changed considerably from the last decade of the nineteenth century onwards, and the effects of this change were heightened with the intensification of the protracted crisis of the Restoration political system, a crisis which began in 1898 and was only superficially settled with Primo de Rivera's coup in 1923. Indeed, the real turning point in the question of identities came with the Disaster of 1898 and its immediate consequences. The loss of the old empire's last important colonies in a humiliating war highlighted the Spanish state's impotence in the international arena, and was associated with an ineffective, essentially undemocratic political system, which had long been criticized in Spain. This provoked a violent upheaval in Spanish national consciousness, with far-reaching ideological and political consequences. Along with other factors that we shall consider later, it contributed to the transformation of the main regionalisms into non-

Spanish nationalisms (in the Basque country, in Catalonia and, subsequently, in Galicia) as well as bringing about changes in the only pre-existent nationalism: the Spanish one. Thus began the conflictive coexistence, within a single state, of four nationalisms, each referring to a different nation: Spain, Catalonia, Euskadi, Galicia. These four nations, each clearly defined and delimited in their respective nationalist discourses, did not correspond, in the realm of their social acceptance, with clearly defined territorial or ethnic areas but instead with variable portions of the population, who believed in the existence of this or that nation and acted politically in accordance with this belief. Thus, the Spanish nation comprised not only almost all the inhabitants of the linguistic-ethnic area of Castilian, but also a considerable minority of Catalans, approximately half the Basques and a majority of Galicians. Let us look briefly at the main factors that influenced the development and nature of each nationalism and, where appropriate, of each regional/national identity.

Apart from the crisis and reformulation of Spanish national identity, in which the intellectual movement known as regenerationism played a decisive role, the 1898–1936 period also saw the conversion of two regional identities into alternative national identities (in Catalonia and the Basque Country), the consolidation of one nationalism (Galicia) and the proliferation of regionalist buds (Andalusia, the Canary Islands, Aragón, Valencia, etc). Thus, the panorama in Spain changed completely and, as can be seen from the Spanish history in the rest of the twentieth century, irreversibly. The processes of alternative nation-building took place very quickly in Catalonia, more slowly in the Basque country, while in Galicia this process was still only in the very early stages in 1936. The emergence of these multiple identities stirred an already deep national conflict, with no apparent solution.

In the Basque country (renamed Euskadi by the nationalists), as we have seen, the second military defeat of Carlism in 1876 had demonstrated that it was not feasible to defend tradition through armed struggle. Consequently, this opened the doors for some of its followers to enter a new political channel asserting an alternative nationality. But the real turning point came as the result of a further stimulus in this direction: the rapid industrialization of the Basque country towards the end of the nineteenth century. The new Basque industry (iron and steel industries and shipbuilding) required a considerable concentration of capital and a numerous labour force which was generally imported from outside the region, which soon led to a radical transformation of Basque society, particularly in the province of Vizcaya. In addition to the actions of a liberal state, there was now the more frightening advance of an economic system and new social classes, which undermined the very foundations of traditional society and its values. Moreover, the new middle and working classes tended, for different reasons, to adopt the Spanish identity. The threat this posed for the leading strata of traditional Basque society, along with the recent loss – due to the 1876 defeat – of the regional institutions on which these strata had based their power, combined with the upsurge of new ideologies, values and ways of life which were wholly contradictory to those of the pre-existing Basque regional identity, all played a part in fostering the birth of a reactive nationalism which opposed modernization, and preached a national identity which, initially at least, perfectly matched the reactionary ideology and primitivism of its promoters. This reactive nationalism spread quickly and in part complemented the functions of the old traditionalism. The reaction against the ongoing transformation of Basque society are evident in the Catholic-traditionalist, racist, anti-industrial and anti-liberal ideology expressed in the work of Sabino Arana. Its radical incompatibility with modernity can also be seen in the fact that it was the only alternative nationalism in Spain, which from the outset was separatist. For all these reasons the vast majority of the new Basque bourgeoisie remained pro-Spanish and hostile towards this nationalism, as were the new working classes, which were largely drawn from other regions of Spain. Although Basque nationalism spread rapidly in rural areas and among the old middle class and artisan social groups in the urban areas, its radicalism prevented it from expanding into large portions of society; this left the country divided into two, opposing national communities. Basque nationalism thereby gained sufficient strength to generate a Basque national identity, but it did not achieve the political hegemony attained by Catalan nationalism.[15]

In Catalonia, as we have seen, the regionalist phase had paved the way for nationalism by popularizing the country's language, literature, ethnicity and history, along with drawing up a programme of self-government. The Catalan nationalist movement was ideologically diverse, comprising moderate liberals as well as those who had become disillusioned with both Carlism and Spanish federalist republicanism. However, it had little sociopolitical strength. Yet in a few years Catalan nationalism would become the hegemonic political movement in Catalonia. The factor which proved decisive in the transformation of Catalan regionalism into a nationalism was the change in the national referent among the bourgeoisie. The loss of the colonies deprived them of a considerable portion of their markets, causing them to lose faith in the Spanish nation embodied in the state and the political system. As a result, they decided to channel the defence of their interests and aspirations through a different legitimizing referent (the Catalan nation) and its political movement (the nationalism of the *Lliga*). This was done with great success due to their support, so that the first decades of twentieth century saw the formation of a Catalan party system which differed from that of the rest of Spain. The Catalanist organizations dominated this system throughout the first third of the century. The result of this was a rapid process of Catalanist nation-building, which generated a widespread, deeply-rooted national consciousness. The Catalan nation ceased to be the 'imagined community' of a handful of middle class intellectuals and minority groups, and became a viable reality as the majority of the population became convinced of its existence. But, as with every nationalism experience, this success implied the loss of ideological unity. As Catalan nationalism spread among all social classes, it could no longer reflect solely the opinions and interests of its former promoters. Despite maintaining a single national referent, its discourse and organization became more diverse. Thus, the *Lliga*, which from the outset had tried to organize Catalanism as a whole, witnessed the consolidation and growth of other nationalist political and union organizations that better represented other social sectors. In the end it was only able to represent the conservative and 'bourgeois' voice of Catalanism. The aspirations of a large part of the lower middle class, and of the peasants, artisans and white collar workers, had been channelled through small parties and cultural and union organizations which, during the Second Republic, mostly converged to form a comprehensive populist movement (*Esquerra Republicana de Catalunya*) on the left of the political spectrum, which surpassed the *Lliga* in terms of popular support. Although the majority of the working classes were not opposed to the Catalan ethnic identity, they remained unwilling to adopt Catalan nationalism, and instead tended to support 'internationalist' parties and unions, whether anarchist or Marxist. This strong Catalan nationalism, clearly more federalist than separatist in practice, predominantly democratic and in favour of modernizing both Catalonia and Spain as a whole, undoubtedly forged a Catalan national identity which would prove capable of withstanding all future attempts to erase it.[16]

The case of Galicia is also quite different. Galician nationalism, like its Catalan counterpart, was preceded by a long preparatory period in which the region's language, culture and history were recovered; as in Catalonia, it also held a pro-modernization and democratic stance for the most part. However, the conversion of Galician regionalism into nationalism took place later (at the height of the First World War), and remained until 1931 an insignificant political movement supported only by relatively small groups of intellectuals, liberal professionals and a few merchants and white collar workers. Although it began to spread abroad from this social ghetto during the Republic, and gain much more electoral support and greater acceptance among the peasants and the upper echelons of urban workers, these advancements were cut short in 1936, before Galician nationalism had acquired a sufficiently solid base to become truly consolidated. In any case, it still had no presence among employers, property owners and the clergy. This mediocre result was due to the fact that, although this period saw the weakening of nineteenth century obstacles to modernization (particularly in rural areas), neither the incipient transformations nor the serious crises of the political system brought about a major change of national loyalty among the key sociopolitical actors.[17]

Spanish nationalism also evolved during this period.[18] Like all state nationalisms, Spanish nationalism was diffuse. This means that it was an ideological component of all Spanish political options, although the relative importance of this component differed between them. Its ideological heterogeneity was therefore greater than in the alternative non-state nationalisms. As we have seen, there had been various different projects of Spanish nation-building during the nineteenth century. The crisis of 1898 and the rise of alternative nationalisms led to changes in the internal dynamics of Spanish nationalism. In the twentieth century the main manifestation of this was *regenerationism* which, among other things (and partly as a reaction against the emergence of alternative nationalisms), implied the reaffirmation of an organic *españolismo*, intended to strengthen Spain's demoralized national identity. The regenerationist ideas were not entirely original, but they differed from their nineteenth century forerunners in terms of their analytical reductionism, whereby the main cause of all Spain's ills was the political system, and the excessive emphasis on Castilian components of the Spanish spirit. On the other hand, with its political populism, regenerationism's core ideas were ideologically many-faceted. It did, in fact, inspire diverse political tendencies advocating different paths to modernization, ranging from democratizing regeneration which allowed a dialogue (albeit tense) between Spanish nationalism and the other nationalisms and the working-class left, to authoritarian regenerationism which was bitterly opposed to the working-class movement and totally uncompromising with all those who questioned the national unity of the state. The relative strength of these two fundamental tendencies of Spanish nationalism changed several times during the first three decades of the twentieth century, as conditions in the sociopolitical arena fluctuated. In 1917, the accumulated tensions erupted in the second great crisis of the Restoration; for the first time, all three dimensions (social, political and national) converged with similar intensity. And although the first great triumph of authoritarian Spanish nationalism, the dictatorship of General Primo de Rivera (1923–9), temporarily neutralized this crisis, it solved nothing in the medium-range. In fact, the underlying problems deepened in the apparent calm imposed by the military regime. When the dictator was forced to resign in 1929, the alternative nationalisms reappeared stronger and more radical than before; the working-class left attracted more widespread support and the old model of the liberal-conservative state was no longer seen as a valid option by any group.

In the face of the temporary disarray of the right and the retreat of authoritarian nationalism, the Second Republic was born as the result of an alliance of the labour movement, democratic Spanish nationalism and Catalan and Galician nationalisms. This alliance sought to establish a democratic system which would also resolve the national question (apart from socioeconomic problems) by attempting to follow a middle road between the old centralism and a federal system – which was considered too hazardous by the majority. This compromise, the so-called 'integral state' designed in the 1931 constitution (the direct precedent for the 'State of Autonomous Communities' defined in the 1978 constitution), did not satisfy the demands of any alternative nationalisms but did begin to transform the dynamics of head-on antagonism into a possible – albeit conflictive – coexistence between Spanish (democratic) nationalism and the other nationalisms.[19] Even Basque nationalism began to revise its radically anti-modern, separatist stance in order to adapt to this new situation. In time Basque nationalism finally participated in the republican institutions, although it maintained a dual language: while upholding a separatist discourse in theory, in practice it adopted an autonomist policy.

However, this semi-federal solution had rather contradictory consequences. On the one hand, it helped to deactivate the radicalism of alternative nationalisms by offering a systemic solution that attended to at least part of their demands. On the other hand, it signified the institutional recognition by Spanish nationalism of the importance and respectability of other national identities. It also involved the creation of sub-state self-government institutions and policies that were bound to accelerate the socialization of these other identities. This would inevitably help to make them irreversible, as well as having a transmission effect in other territories that, until then, had always had an exclusively Spanish identity. Sooner or later, this was bound to fuel the rise of new regional identities which would further weaken and undermine Spanish identity, or at least force it to radically redefine itself.

These phenomena, which were already visible during the Second Republic (despite its extreme brevity and highly conflictive nature), became even more marked when democracy was restored after the long era of Francoism (1939–75) with its fiercely Spanish nationalism. The 1978 constitution was based on a model of decentralization of power that has much in common with that of 1931. Moreover, the peaceful transition was possible due to an alliance of forces which was also very similar to that which had brought about the Second Republic, with the incorporation of elements favourable to reform from among the Francoists and Basque nationalists. The Catalan and Basque nationalisms emerged with equal or greater strength than before, and it soon became clear that the national identities created by them remained intact despite the dictator's endeavours to suppress them. Galician nationalism, which now was considerably more left-wing than its counterparts in Catalonia and the Basque country, managed to extend its social influence among civil servants, white collar workers, peasants and, to a lesser extent, blue collar workers. Although it has still not acquired the same strength, Galician nationalism has grown rapidly during recent years, mainly as a result of the region's socioeconomic problems, and the insufficient interest shown by the major state-level parties in tackling these problems.

Despite the fact that the Spain of 1978–98 is a much more developed and peaceful society than that of 1931–9 and, for the first time, has a truly democratic political culture, its multinational nature is also more marked than ever before. In this sense, the establishment of the current state of autonomous communities has had two major, and somewhat contradictory implications for the national question. On the one hand, by partly satisfying the demands of the alternative nationalisms, it has helped to moderate their potential radicalism (with the tragic but isolated exception of Euzkadi Ta Azka tasuna (ETA) and neutralize the pro-independence tendencies which are inherent in movements of this kind. But, on the other hand, it has also created an institutional framework which is favourable to the consolidation of these alternative national identities, thereby reducing the level of national conflict but also contributing to the stabilization of this conflict as such.

Conclusions

The long historical process outlined here reveals certain aspects of the origin and evolution of each of the national sub-state identities as well as the overall pattern of development of what we might call the Spanish national question.

With respect to the former, we have seen that the consolidation of national sub-state identities as a consequence of successful nation-building only took place when certain élites, with the support of powerful social groups, came to see nationalism as the most convenient political option. The resources and influence of these groups ensured that these pre-national traits and values were assumed to form a national identity by ever wider portions of the population. Once this process of nationalization gains a social majority, the critical threshold has been crossed: national identity becomes fully consolidated and it is very difficult, if not impossible, to reverse the process. National identity then adopts a relatively autonomous stability and internal dynamics, and its existence remains unaffected even when subsequent changes occur in the socioeconomic and institutional conditions that contributed to its rise. At the same time, this success also involves certain problems for the nationalist movement that fostered it, since the social expansion of national identity inevitably reduces ideological homogeneity. This has two consequences: the nationalist movement tends to split into different political options which more or less reflect their new social and ideological diversity; and certain components of this identity are gradually assimilated even by parties and portions of the population that do not adopt this nationalism. In other words, the development of a sub-state national identity induces two opposing phenomena: the growth of a concordant regional identity in unnationalized parts of the community, and a reaction reaffirming the national-state identity in other portions as well as among the population outside this community. In terms of identities, the region in question is divided, as it were, into three persuasions: two are built around the same specific ethnicity but in different degrees (a national sub-state versus a simple regional identity), and the third is centred on the national-state identity. The relative size of these three sectors may vary, and its changes depend on many factors, particularly on the nature and evolution of the state political system and the socioeconomic horizon.

In any case, this situation opens up a whole range of political issues and potential solutions to the dispute created by the development of the sub-state identity, since secession is not the only possible way out. Other possibilities are an autonomous or federal system that meets the minimum common denominator of the different political objectives of these three persuasions, or at least of the first two if they jointly form a majority, which is usually the case over time. The evolution of Spain since 1931 confirms this hypothesis, both in terms of the irreversibility (at least for the foreseeable future) of national identities, and of the possibility of coexistence between them, albeit with a permanent conflict which is more or less latent.

With regard to the overall national question in Spain, it remains before us to examine why the situation evolved the way it did, and not otherwise. Clearly, things could have happened very differently, as can be seen by looking at other European countries: from before the beginning of the liberal revolutions to the present day a great variety of different cases are evident, yet none of them have evolved in the same way as Spain, despite the fact that some, like France and the United Kingdom, shared very similar starting points (old multiethnic states).

Until recently there were two main explanatory models for the Spanish case. The first, of nationalist inspiration, is simple: there have always been, and still are, opposing nationalisms and national identities because objective nations have existed for so long, and were therefore bound to generate these phenomena sooner or later. The second model points to Spain's relative underdevelopment in comparison with other European countries as one of the major causes of the very specific character of the national question in Spain.[20] In my opinion, only the second explanation is worth considering, although it can be improved somewhat. So I shall now outline a comparative analysis of European states for the period in question, in which I shall consider the following relevant variables: the rate of socioeconomic development; ethnic homogeneity or heterogeneity; the age of the state; the survival of earlier institutions of sub-state power; the existence or otherwise of a modern empire with its corresponding effects of national integration; the degree of correspondence between the centre of political power and both the ethnicity's and the poles of development/underdevelopment; and the state's success or failure in the international arena. If we go on to relate *grosso modo* the precise nature of all these factors in each case with the evolution of the national question in each country and then we compare all the cases, we shall see that, as I said before, the Spanish case involves a unique combination of factors. This serves as the basis for a preliminary explanation that can at least be presented as a convincing working hypothesis.

Using the national question as a criterion for classification, we could distinguish the following groups of cases:

At the Starting Point

1. Multiethnic states: the United Kingdom, France, Spain, the Austrian Empire, the Russian Empire, the Kingdom of Sweden, the Kingdom of Denmark, the Ottoman Empire, the Netherlands, Prussia.

2. Mono-ethnic states: Portugal, the kingdoms and small states of Germany except Prussia and Austria, the kingdoms and small states of Italy.

Evolution during the Nineteenth and Twentieth Centuries

Leaving aside those groups which are of less interest to us,[21] except for the case of Italy, let us consider the following:

1. Originally multiethnic states that maintain their unity and form a single national identity: France. Characteristics: profound liberal revolution linked to industrialization and agrarian transformations, a relatively efficient state and public administration, and the construction of a modern empire.

2. Originally multiethnic states in which various national identities are generated, but which conserve their territorial integrity: Spain. Characteristics: deficient liberal revolution, relatively inefficient state and administration, very incomplete agrarian transformations, low level

of industrialization, survival of ethnic identities, no correspondence between areas of development and centres of political power, loss of traditional empire and absence of modern empire.

3. Originally multiethnic states in which a national-state identity is generated, other ethnic identities survive but are blocked and one develops as opposing national identity and achieves separation: United Kingdom (→Ireland). Characteristics: high level of socioeconomic development, previous proto-liberalism, large modern empire, integration of Wales and Scotland as secondary areas of development benefiting from the empire. Only Ireland is excluded from these benefits. It is of great significance in this case that such a strong pre-national identity as that of Scotland did not give rise to an important nationalism and a corresponding sub-state national identity until after the fall of the British Empire.

4. Originally multiethnic states in which various national identities are generated and end up splitting the state into several parts: the Austro-Hungarian Empire, the Russian Empire, the Ottoman Empire. Characteristics: weakness or absence of liberal revolution, of modern empires, of industrialization and agrarian reforms and, in some cases, no correspondence between areas of economic development and centres of political power.

5. Originally mono-ethnic states that remain intact: Portugal. Characteristics: deficient liberal revolution and socioeconomic transformations, loss of pre-modern empire but construction of a small modern empire.

As can be seen, the variations are almost infinite. However, the most relevant cases for comparison with Spain are those states that share a similar starting point: namely, France and the United Kingdom. A complete comparison of the historical development of these three cases reveals two types of differences: the first involves the question at hand (the growth/destruction of identities, characteristics of the nation-building, territorial integrity of the state); and the second concerns the other aspects of their respective historical evolutions (industrialization, agrarian transformations, urbanization, development of public administration and social services, army, educational system, empire and international role).

If we compare both groups of factors, we can see that in our case the (relative) shortcomings of the liberal state and of socioeconomic development are certainly relevant, but these factors alone can not fully explain the paradoxical Spanish case since we have only to look at Portugal and Italy to find similar deficiencies with different outcomes. On the other hand, neither should we forget that, despite the acute, persistent national and identity conflict which has prevailed in Spain over the last 150 years, the Spanish state is like a chronic patient with endless longevity; along with Portugal and Switzerland, it is one of the very few European states which has remained territorially intact throughout this period. For this reason I believe the explanation of the Spanish case should be sought in combining a greater number of factors. Some of them, and particularly the prior existence of a highly consolidated state and pre-national Spanish identity, which then became the Spanish national identity, have supported the territorial unity of the state. In contrast, the rise and development of conflict between national identities within the state has been fed by the relative weakness and particular characteristics of political and socioeconomic development, the consequent strength and capacity for reaction of anti-modern social groups, the survival of ethnic identities which are susceptible to political activation, the lack of correspondence between the centres of political power and the centres of emerging economic power, and the loss of the old empire and inability to construct a new one. The final balance today is a sort of tied game, which has always been so characteristic of the Spanish experience.

NOTES

1. See Justo G. Beramendi, 'Ethnos versus Polis? On method and nationalism', in J.G. Beramendi, R. Máiz and X. M. Núñez (eds), *Nationalism in Europe, Past and Present* (Santiago de Compostela: Universidade de Santiago, 1994), Vol.I, pp.69–110; 'La cultura política como objeto historiográfico. Algunas cuestiones de método', in *Culturas y Civilizaciones, Actas III Congreso de la Asociación de Historia Contemporánea* (Valladolid: Universidad de Valladolid, 1996), pp.73–94; and 'Identidad nacional e identidad regional en España entre la guerra del francés y la guerra civil', in *Actas Congreso Internacional Los 98 Ibéricos y el mar* (Madrid: Sociedad Estatal Expo 98, 1998), Vol.III, pp.187–215.
2. See Paul R. Brass, *Ethnicity and Nationalism: Theory and Comparison* (New Delhi: Sage, 1991); John Breuilly, *Nationalism and the State* (Manchester: Manchester University Press, 2nd edition, 1993); Walker Connor, *Ethnonationalism. The Quest for Understanding* (Princeton, NJ: Princeton University Press, 1994); Ramón Máiz, 'La construcción de las identidades políticas', *Inguruak*, No.13 (1995), pp.9–23; Antonio Melucci, *L'invenzione del presente* (Bologna: Il Mulino, 1982); Philip Schlesinger, 'On National Identity: Some Conceptions and Misconceptions Criticized', *Social Science Information*, Vol.26, No.2 (1987), pp.219–64; and Anthony D. Smith, *The Ethnic Origins of Nations* (Oxford: Basil Blackwell, 1986) and *National Identity* (London: Penguin, 1991).
3. In this note I shall briefly define some of the terms used.
   Political identity: the body of ideas, values and behavioural patterns assumed by a given sector of society, and referring to the basic characteristics of a political system (whether it actually exists or not), their national definition, the legitimate procedures to preserve or create this system, and all their desired objectives.
   National identity: the articulation of an idea of nation with the fact of the majority of the population believe to be real. In other words, national identity exists when a human group is convinced that it constitutes a specific people which differs from other groups due to a set of traits, and believes that, as a result, it is the collective subject of political rights. In short,

national identity is the self-definition of a community, which sets out its collective personality and legitimizes its real or potential sovereignty.

Regional identity: this differs from national identity in that the community in question does not imagine itself as a nation, but as a sub-national group. Hence, it is oriented towards reforming a state by achieving decentralization of power through regional institutions of self-government, without altering the unity of state sovereignty. Regional identity may or may not be based on a specific ethnicity, and may or may not evolve towards national identity.

Ethnicity: a set of objective or intersubjective characteristics which are of a non-political nature: language, specific traits of the material and spiritual culture (including religion), etc. Along with the *Volksgeist*, ethnicity can constitute the essential raw material for both the organic concept of nation, and for national identity. In any case, ethnicity is accompanied by a greater or lesser degree of collective consciousness; when this does not result in the demand for political rights based on ethnicity, then I refer to it as ethnic consciousness.

Ethnic identity: the articulation of ethnicity with a majority's social consciousness of its existence. By itself it lacks political objectives, although it is sometimes closely related to regional or national identities.

Pre-national identity: the self-image of an *ancien régime* society, which contributes to its justifying its own right to form a state. The sovereign power in these cases is based on pre-modern legitimizing principles (of a charismatic and traditionalist nature).

Proto-nationalism: ideology based more on loyalty to an absolutist state and on a pre-national identity than loyalty to the figure of the sovereign.

4. Julio Caro Baroja, *El mito del carácter nacional. Meditaciones a contrapelo* (Madrid: Seminarios y Ediciones, 1970).

5. José Álvarez Junco, 'The Nation-Building Process in Nineteenth-Century Spain', in Clara Mar-Molinero and Angel Smith (eds), *Nationalism and the Nation in the Iberian Peninsula. Competing and Conflicting Identities* (Oxford: Berg, 1996), pp.89–106.

6. See Jon Juaristi, *El linaje de Aitor. La invención de la tradición vasca* (Madrid: Ed. Taurus, 1987).

7. The best known is the Jesuit Manuel de Larramendi who proposed the independence of the Basque Country (*Corografía o Descripción General de la Muy Noble y Muy Leal Provincia de Guipúzcoa*, 1754).

8. There are few studies of the origin and evolution of identities in Spain. However, the number of works on the national question and the development of different nationalisms (of particular interest to us here) has increased so considerably in quantity and quality over the last 30 years that it is impossible to list all the relevant titles. I shall therefore mention only those which I consider to be essential, either due to my arguments or for the general overview provided of certain processes. For more detailed information about the historiography until 1993, see X.M. Núñez Seixas, *Historiographical Approaches to Nationalism in Spain* (Saarbrücken: Verlag Breitenbach, 1993).

9. Borja de Riquer, 'Nacionalidades y regiones. Problemas y líneas de investigación en torno a la débil nacionalización española del siglo XIX', in A.Morales and M. Esteban (eds), *La Historia contemporánea en España* (Salamanca: Ed. Universidad, 1996), pp.73–89.

10. On nineteenth century Spanish nationalism, see Andrés de Blas, *Sobre el nacionalismo español* (Madrid: Centro de Estudios Constitucionales, 1989), pp.13–36; José Álvarez Junco; and Luis Moreno, *La federalización de España. Poder político y territorio* (Madrid: Ed. Siglo XXI, 1997), pp.44–64, as well as the works referred to in these studies. For a general overview, see Pere Anguera (ed.), *Orígens i formació dels nacionalismes a Espanya* (Reus: Centre de Lectura, 1994) and, for ideologies, Antonio Elorza, 'Los nacionalismos en el Estado español contemporáneo: las ideologías', *Estudios de Historia Social*, Nos.28–29 (1984), pp.49–68.

11. See Javier Fernández Sebastián, *La génesis del fuerismo* (Madrid: Ed. Siglo XXI, 1991); and Coro Rubio, *Fueros y Constitución: la lucha por el control del poder. País Vasco, 1808–1868* (Bilbao: Universidad del País Vasco, 1997).

12. See Horst Hina, *Castilla y Cataluña en el debate cultural 1714–1939* (Barcelona: Ed. Península, 1986); Josep Ll. Marfany, *La cultura del catalanisme. El nacionalisme català en els seus inicis* (Barcelona: Ed. Empúries, 1995); and Pere Anguera, *El català al segle XIX. De llengua del poble a llengua nacional* (Barcelona: Ed. Empúries, 1997).

100   IDENTITY AND TERRITORIAL AUTONOMY IN PLURAL SOCIETIES

13. For the socioeconomic evolution of Galicia in the nineteenth century, see Ramón Villares, *La propiedad de la tierra en Galicia* (Madrid: Ed. Siglo XXI, 1982) and Xan Carmona, *El atraso industrial de Galicia* (Barcelona: Ed. Ariel, 1990).
14. See Justo G. Beramendi, Breogán en Numancia. 'Sobre los orígenes y pecualiaridades del galleguismo decimonónico', in Anguera, *Orígens i formació*, pp.81–120; and Ramón Maiz, *O Rexionalismo galego. Organización e ideoloxía, 1886–1907* (Sada: Ed. do Castro, 1984).
15. On Basque nationalism, see Javier Corcuera, *Orígenes, organización e ideología del nacionalismo vasco* (Madrid: Ed. Siglo XXI, 1979); and José Luis de la Granja, *El nacionalismo vasco: un siglo de historia* (Madrid: Ed. Tecnos, 1995)
16. On Catalan nationalism, see Borja de Riquer, *Lliga Regionalista:la burgesia catalana i el regionalisme* (Barcelona: Edicions 62, 1977); Enric Ucelay, *La Catalunya populista. Imatge, cultura i políca en l'etapa republicana* (Barcelona: La Magrana, 1982); and Albert Balcells, *Història del nacionalisme català* (Barcelona: Generalitat de Catalunya, 1992).
17. On Galician nationalism, see Justo G. Beramendi, *El nacionalismo gallego* (Madrid: Arco Libros, 1997).
18. On the effects of the Disaster and regenerationism on Spanish nationalism, as well as the evolution of the national question in Spain during this period, see Andrés de Blas, *Tradición republicana y nacionalismo español* (Madrid: Ed.Tecnos, 1991); S. Balfour , 'The Lion and the Pig: Nationalism and National Identity in the Fin-de-siècle Spain', in Mar-Molinero and Smith, pp.107–18; Inman Fox, *La invención de España* (Madrid: Ed. Cátedra, 1997).
19. On the national question during the Second Republic, see Justo G. Beramendi and Ramón Máiz (eds), *Los nacionalismos en la España de la Segunda República* (Madrid: Ed. Siglo XXI, 1991).
20. See, for instance, Javier Corcuera, 'Nacionalismo y clases en la España de la Restauración', *Estudios de Historia Social*, Nos.28–29 (1984), pp.249–82; and Borja de Riquer, 'Nacionalidades y regiones'.
21. These would be:
a. Multiethnic states where another national identity emerges which then separates, or states that are deprived of an ethnically different territory by a foreign power: the Netherlands (→Belgium), Denmark (→Schleswig-Holstein), Sweden (→Norway);
b. The creation of previously non-existing multiethnic states: Belgium, Yugoslavia, Rumania;
c. The creation of more or less mono-national states, constructed as result of a unifying process: Germany, Italy, Poland.

Basque Polarization:
Between Autonomy and Independence

FRANCISCO J. LLERA

Twenty years have elapsed since the Spanish constitution of 1978 established the new territorial decentralization system in Spain (the so-called 'State of the Autonomies') and 19 since the Basque country began the road that in 1983 would culminate in the formation of 17 autonomous communities. The transition from an authoritarian political system to a pluralistic regime began with the approval in December 1976 of the Law for Political Reform and ended with the ratification of the Spanish constitution in the December 1978 referendum and of the autonomy statute for the Basque country[1] in October 1979. The political transition from dictatorship to democracy between 1976 and 1978 led to a second transition, longer in time, from a centralized state to a multicultural and decentralized polity. In the periods following these referenda, the institutionalization of new governmental structures took place, leading to a third process that we can refer to as the consolidation of the democratic and decentralized system. The national and regional factor[2] has been converted into a cleavage of the first order in Spanish politics, so that the political behaviour of élites and citizens, the party system[3] and standards of governability cannot be understood if they are not attuned adequately to the splits of identity between citizen and territories in Spain.[4]

The Cultivation of Basque Ethnic Sentiment

The post-war generation of Basque nationalists comprises the children of a century and a half of civil wars and symbolic violence. This was manifested first in the Carlist Wars (1833–76) leading to a rise of the nationalist discourse and the emergence of an ethnonationalist movement headed by Sabino Arana[5] a century ago;[6] and second, in the violent resistance of the younger generations beginning in the 1960s[7] in response to the political consequences of the Spanish civil war of 1936–9 and the violent military measures imposed during the dictatorship of Francisco Franco.

Francisco J. Llera, the Basque Country University

The industrial revolution began in Euskadi[8] in the middle of the nineteenth century, changing the demographic composition and social and cultural structures of a traditional, religious, rural and conservative society. Between 1956 and 1975, industrial and social modernization produced much of the initial stress on Basque traditional culture, threatening to erase Basque traditions and the Basque language (*Euskera*) and to assimilate the Basque people into a homogeneous Spansih population. The Spanish state itself further contributed to the perception of 'us' versus 'them' by distinguishing the Basque territory from the rest of Spain through the imposition of 12 'states of exception' during the dictatorship which, by specifically discriminating against the Basque provinces, delegitimated the social reality of a unified Spanish nation and, in turn, legitimated the social construct of a distinct Basque nation.[9] Once the authoritarian state had singled out the Basque territory, it was natural that this discrimination should produce tight social cohesion. With the concomitant legal repression of everything Basque, a gulf developed between public life and private expression. This dichotomization of public and private life would become a defining feature of Basque life, particularly as the Basque symbolic space became increasingly identified with the nationalist movement and, specifically with ETA and its violent resistance to Spanish culture and state.[10]

For Basque nationalists, the essence of their identity revolved around a sacred world of values and beliefs, and developed within a 'social space' with readily identifiable members and enemies.[11] Reflecting warrior virtues and the sense of fraternity derived from extensive participation, both Basque civil wars and Catholic ritual became sanctified and gave rise to a structure of values that was broadly shared and hence morally unifying of the ethnic community. The impossibility of giving expression to the Basque symbolic universe, together with the physical repression to which Basques were subjected, contributed to the construction of a dense network of social relations in which violence, both physical and symbolic, permeated ever more deeply into Basque life.

Max Weber[12] claimed that an ethnic group is not in itself a community but merely a 'moment' that facilitates the process of 'communalization'. Later, he noted that national identity is difficult to describe objectively in any generic sense. Nonetheless, Weber indicated that since such an identity is based on particular 'differential factors'; the sharing of even subjective perceptions of such differences results in an objective differentiation between 'us' and 'them'. This symbolic universe of 'us' versus 'them' has penetrated widely through Basque society. It has served as the backdrop in which new generations of Basques have been socialized. Though politically ambiguous and lacking strategic and structural rationalization, Basque nationalism had a tremendous capacity for unilaterally mobilizing everything and everyone Basque against the state and the dictatorship.

The Basque dualism of public and private expression was reinforced by another cultural dualism whose emotional roots went even deeper, namely, the confrontation of Basque and Spanish identities,[13] which articulated competing symbolic universes (Table 1). It is not surprising, then, that objective cultural attributes, such as language, shared by members of the ethnic groups and reinforced by communal solidarity structures, became key factors in the mobilization of the Basque nationalist movement, particularly as embodied by ETA.

TABLE 1
SUBJECTIVE NATIONAL IDENTIFICATION OF BASQUE NATIVES AND
IMMIGRANTS, 1998

	Natives %	Immigrants* %	TOTAL %
Spanish Only	1.9	15.1	7.1
More Spanish than Basque	1.4	13.3	6.0
Basque and Spanish	24.8	44.7	32.9
More Basque than Spanish	27.9	14.0	22.3
Basque Only	36.0	4.5	23.4
DK/NA	8.0	8.4	8.3
N =	839	550	1,389

Source: Francisco J. Llera (EUSKOBAROMETRO).
*Including the children of immigrants.

One of the central foci of studies of ethnicity is subjective self-identification. This is based on the hypothesis that subjective elements weigh more heavily than 'primordial' factors in explaining the resurgence of ethnic demands in industrialized societies.[14] Overall, both identities, Basque and Spanish, are compatible for the majority (61 per cent) of Basque population, but more among immigrants (72 per cent) than natives (54 per cent); secondly, the extreme groups of exclusivist identities are a minority (30.5 per cent) and higher among natives (36 per cent) than immigrants (15 per cent). An examination of the evolution of the self-identification of both key groups over the past two decades shows a significant decline in the percentage of those defining themselves as Basque only (−12 per cent) or Spanish only (-6 per cent), increasing the compatibility of identities among both groups.

Change is more notable with respect to the manner in which respondents define themselves and others as 'Basque'. The most frequently selected criterion, 'the will to be Basque', was supported in the 1998 survey

(EUSKOBAROMETRO[15]) by 82 per cent of those interviewed, remaining constant from our 1989 survey. Secondly, 'to live and work in the Basque country' also remained constant, at 55 per cent. Thirdly, support for the notion that it is necessary 'to have been born in the Basque country' in order to be considered Basque increased from 41 per cent (1989) to 53 per cent. Fourthly, 'descent from a Basque family' also increased four points (to 40 per cent). 'To feel Basque nationalist' declined from 56 per cent (1989) to 36 per cent, but was selected by a majority (53 per cent) of nationalist voters. Finally, 'to speak *Euskera*' remained constant, at 31 per cent, from 20 years ago as a basis for defining one's nationality. In general, subjective criteria increased at the expense of primordial factors in defining Basque nationality, after 20 years.

Between Autonomy and Independence

It can be said that Basque political institutions (parliament, government, administration, own treasury, fiscality and police, high court of justice, public television and full control over education and health systems and in the cultural, welfare, commercial, agricultural, tourist and infrastructural fields, among others) are in very good order; they have performed efficaciously and garnered popular support from the great majority of the population, and they have been successful in significantly reducing the level of political conflict between regional and central levels of government. Nevertheless, the radical and primordial call for independence still issues forth from an important sector of Basque society. When asked about the strength of their desire for independence, respondents replied in 1995 (EUSKOBAROMETRO) in much the same way as they did in 1979:[16] the same 12 per cent said that they had a 'very great' desire for independence, while another 19 per cent (compared to 24 per cent in 1979) said that their pro-independence aspirations were 'rather great'. Not surprisingly, those who regarded themselves as Basque nationalists in 1995 responded very differently from those who did not: 69 per cent of Basque nationalists (against 12 per cent of non-nationalists) said that they had 'very great' or 'rather great' ambitions for independence. Thus, two-thirds of self-described Basque nationalists said that they had 'very great' or 'rather great' desires for independence from Spain, which reflected an increase of 19 points from 1989.

It is logical that the establishment of autonomous regional government institutions and democratic consolidation, in combination with more information about the various alternatives, have led to changes in the preferences of Basque citizens regarding the form of the state and its territorial organization. Surveys have at various intervals since the early

TABLE 2
PREFERENCES CONCERNING THE FORM OF THE STATE AMONG BASQUE (1998)
AND SPANISH (1996) RESPONDENTS

	Basques (1998) %	Spaniards (1996) %
Centralism	4	16
Regional Autonomy	37	44
Federalism	25	21
Independence	25	8
DK/NA	9	11
N =	1,600	2,500

Sources: EUSKOBAROMETRO (1998) and CIS, No.2,228 (1996).

stages of the transition to democracy asked Basques (and other Spaniards) about whether they preferred a centralized state structure, some regional autonomy, federal status or outright independence. The responses of Basque and Spanish respondents are summarized in Table 2.

Support for centralism appears to have stabilized at very low levels, although it is possible that the extent to which this alternative has been stigmatized, especially in Euskadi, may have discouraged some respondents from expressing their true feelings. The 'State of the Autonomies' model is supported by over one third of all Basque respondents (increasing ten points from 1977) and seven more points among the Spaniards, while support for federalism or 'much autonomy' is supported by about one quarter in both cases and has fluctuated in Euskadi from 1977 around a mean of about 24 per cent.[17] Support for independence, which had been declining through the transition in Euskadi (from 24 per cent in 1977 to 17 per cent in 1982), increased following the election victory of the PSOE (the Spanish Socialist Party) in 1982 and stabilized around a mean of 25 per cent (17 points higher than that for Spaniards in 1996)

Loyalty, Legitimacy, and Satisfaction

One of Juan J. Linz's central concerns about the Spanish transition was the breakdown of legitimacy in Euskadi in relation to the Spanish constitution and the Basque Autonomy Statute.[18] Our 1987 survey data revealed that two-thirds of Basques favourably evaluated the Spanish political transition, while 29 per cent held the opposite opinion. Even among the independence-seeking and violent HB or *Herri Batasuna* (Popular Unity) voters, there were as many positive as there were negative evaluations.[19]

An other empirical indicator of the lack of full legitimacy in Euskadi is the stance of the Basque population towards the Spanish constitution.[20]

Nearly ten years (1987) after its ratification by referendum, 39 per cent of Basques had internalized the message of rejection from nationalist radicalism. In the 1998, survey,[21] when respondents were asked to express their current vote towards the constitution, 46 per cent were affirmative (31.3 per cent of the census and 69 per cent of the voters in the 1978 referendum), including 57 per cent among PNV voters, and 15 per cent were negative (10.5 per cent of the census and 24 per cent of the voters in 1978). Only among HB supporters was there a majority (63 per cent) negative vote. Although some moderation of stands has taken place, as well as a pragmatic adjustment towards loyalty to the constitution, it is clear that in addition to outright rejection among radicals, the bulk of nationalists have maintained strategic reservations regarding ratification of the constitutional document.

In contrast with the constitution, the statute of autonomy was explicitly endorsed by 53 per cent of the census (91 per cent of the voters) and only 3 per cent (5 per cent of the voters) were negative. It can be said that this represents an *a posteriori* legitimation of the Spanish constitution.[22] Evaluations made in 1998 of the degree of success of the autonomy process, which began 20 years ago and is still unfinished, divide the Basque population among those who are fully satisfied (43 per cent), those partly satisfied (30 per cent) and those dissatisfied (25 per cent).The responses of Basque population over this period are summarized in Table 3.

TABLE 3
EVOLUTION OF SATISFACTION WITH THE STATUTE OF AUTONOMY AMONG
BASQUE RESPONDENTS, 1987–98

	1987 %	1993 %	1998 %
Fully satisfied	28	31	43
Partly satisfied	31	25	30
Dissatisfied	26	26	25
DK/NA	15	18	2
N =	1,800	1,400	1,400

Sources: Surveys directed by F.J.Llera.

The proportion of those fully satisfied increased significantly (+15 points), mostly during the last five years, while the proportion of those partly satisfied appears to have stabilized around a mean of about 30 per cent with slight fluctuations. Supporters of PSOE (Socialist Party, 66 per cent), PP (Popular Party 66 per cent), and PNV (50 per cent) are the most satisfied in the 1998 survey, while partly satisfied are the 'overcoat' voters of IU (United Left 50 per cent) and EA (Basque Solidarity 45 per cent). At the other extreme, those dissatisfied are stabilized in one quarter of the Basque population and account for a majority among HB supporters (83 per cent). The constitution and the autonomy statute are two sides of the same coin. Satisfactory political development within the region is dependent on their legitimacy and the political loyalties they inspire.

Political Violence

Unfortunately, violence continues to be one of the sad characteristics of the Basque polity. Of the various forms of violence that occur in Euskadi, we are most interested in those initiated by ETA's radical nationalist terrorism, the cause of most of the violent deaths that have occurred in Spain over the last 30 years.[23]

With all forms of public dissent denied to them, secrecy, activism and exile bred a *violence fondatrice* among Basques, which served as the foundation for the development of a subculture of violence in their society.[24] During the Franco regime which, by its continuous and pervasive application of coercive force, effectively limited its discourse with Basques to one of violence, the dichotomization of 'us' versus 'them' combined explosively with actual individual experiences of violence to distort both the political and social environment. Indeed, during the final years of Franco's dictatorship, violence was no longer simply a political strategy or just one more ingredient in the rethoric of Basque resistance, but rather had become the central point of reference in daily Basque life.[25] At the time of Franco's death, therefore, the dichotomization of Spain versus Euskadi was not merely cultural but political, not merely organizational but conceptual. On both sides its roots were profound, reaching to deeply-held identities and competing symbolic universes which, when confronted one with another, generated serious social conflict. The process of social development for the post-1940 generation thus coincided with an environment in which everything that symbolized Basque identity, particularly the Basque language, was endowed with enormous value and emotional appeal. To the extent that this generation of Basques has internalized the collective reality characterized by both the public and private dichotomization of 'us' versus 'them', it has come to view the confrontation between Euskadi and the Spanish state as a radically conflictive situation in which each Basque must take sides.[26]

It is not surprising that such a clash should yield violence. For the radical Basque nationalists, however, violence has not merely occurred incidentally; it has been deliberately adopted as a strategy. The passage of time appears to validate the hypothesis of Martha Crenshaw that terrorism can be a temporary occurrence within an otherwise stable society and occurs

precisely when the passivity of the mass coincides with the discontent of an
élite.[27] Although we shall not undertake an analysis of the trajectory or
sociology of Basque terrorism, it is important to note that ETA's
destabilizing and delegitimizing strategy is clearly reflected in the numbers
of persons killed at various stages in the transition.[28] By far the highest
levels of ETA violence (31 per cent of all assassinations and 41 per cent of
all kidnappings) occurred during the period 1978–80, when the Spanish
constitution and Basque autonomy statute were being negotiated and
ratified, and the first elections to the regional parliament were being held. A
second significant upsurge in terrorism also coincided with a key political
turning point, the formation of the first PNV–PSE coalition government.

    ETA clearly perceived violence as an effective way to communicate its
own position of power. Its members, therefore, sought to use violence as a
means to force the Spanish government to negotiate, a strategy that still
continues. Indeed, during its 30 years of existence, ETA has been
responsible for almost 800 assassinations, over 60 kidnappings,
innumerable bombings, countless armed assaults and robberies, more than
1,000 injuries and an extended regime of extortionist 'revolutionary
taxation',[29] as well as numerous other violent actions, counting on assistance
of its supporters of the MLNV (Basque National Movement of Liberation),
especially during the last three years (35 per cent of violent actions). ETA
bears the responsibility for more than 80 per cent of all people killed in
terrorist or police actions in Spain during the last 30 years. It is interesting
to consider the victims of ETA violence; most of the fatalities are policemen
and military officers (over 60 per cent of the total). This targeting reflects
ETA's perception of the political situation as a military occupation of the
Basque country, and as a war of the Basque people against the Spanish state
and capitalism. Additional victims who helped to make this point included
industrialists and politicians, both national and local. Between 1972 and
1983, Basque industrialists were the target of nearly 500 such attacks.
Kidnapping and personal attacks on Basque industrialists and their property
are designed both to heighten the degree of fear among the class of potential
victims as well as to inflict monetary damage on them as a result of
bombing and sabotage of their property. These attacks also serve to
reinforce ETA's position as the defender of the Basque working class.
Finally, during the last few years, politicians, especially of the PP (the
Popular Party, in the Spanish government from 1996), were the victims and
preferred target of their attacks.

    Not surprisingly, ETA is the main victim of police repression in Spain,
having had more than 90 of its members killed and more than 20,000
arrested; as of October 1998, over 600 activists and supporters were in jail
in Spain or France. ETA was also a principal target of opposition terrorist

groups (AAA, ATE, BVE, GANE, and GAL, among others), a conflict which has led to death over 90 Basque activists and which has had an important political impact, because of the implication of the state apparatus during the Socialist government.

To justify this violent activism, nationalists have relied heavily upon the collective memory of past state repression during the civil war and the dictatorship, and continuous acts of coercive force. The strategy of the action-repression-action spiral, anti-repressive mobilization, amnesty demands, the actions of prisoners and their families and organizations – all these have played important roles in maintaining the armed struggle and its social support. Further, Basque nationalism, by providing support within the ethnic group, has helped to create and protect contemporary heroes and in so doing has contributed to the overall process of reproducing the ethnic myth.

The democratic process has legitimated the use of institutional means to achieve collective aims. At the same time, however, it has raised new divisive issues for the Basques: how should Basque nationalists seek their goals in this new environment? Once the transition to democracy was initiated, tensions emerged. There was some trend towards rationalizing Basque political structures and institutions to function as effective participants in this unfamiliar milieu. Yet this option was greatly complicated by the fact that many of those involved in Basque political life had organized themselves outside of, or in opposition to, this precise institutionalizing process. Radicalized nationalists therefore rejected any participation in the new institutions as a betrayal of the Basque cause and rejected the Spanish constitution of 1978, preferring to organize as an anti-system movement.[30]

As the new political situation opened entirely different ways for change, and popular perspectives changed, the process of democratization forced the enunciation of different goals among the various nationalist factions. Most recently, despite their retention of a military strategy, many within ETA recognize that the only solution to the conflict is one of political negotiation not only between ETA and HB on the one hand and the Madrid government on the other, but also between the other Basque political parties, whether nationalist or not. The adoption of such a position by ETA reflects in part the difficulties it faces in its decision-making process at a time of enormous political and strategic importance, while most of its leaders are either in jail or deported. It also reflects, however, ETA's recognition of the *de facto* acceptance of Spanish political reforms and the concomitant enhancement and strengthening of the legitimacy of the central Spanish government within a considerable portion of the Basque electorate. In particular, the adoption of a strategy of political negotiation increases the importance of

HB as ETA's institutional voice, places an even greater responsibility on the organizations within the MLNV to mobilize popular support for the negotiation process. The Spanish reform process has, therefore, provided ETA with new opportunities for action, which have enabled it to pursue its violent campaign for independence. However, the democratization process has also confronted ETA with its most difficult task, to justify its continuing campaign of violence to those who have now accepted the alternative path of electoral politics and institutional reform.

In the light of the reaction of Basque society, ETA's terrorism campaign can be regarded as a failure. This was particularly obvious in the case of the *Pacto de Ajuria Enea* (1988–98), in which all democratic parties in Euskadi reached a consensus on the need to coordinate their policies against terrorism. One indicator of the level of legitimacy achieved by the democratic system is the response to a survey item in which respondents are asked to agree or disagree 'with those who say that in Euskadi today it is possible to defend all political aspirations and objectives without recourse to violence'. The results of 1997 survey, broken down by partisan preference, can be seen in Table 4.

TABLE 4
AGREE/DISAGREE THAT VIOLENCE IS NOT NECESSARY TO ACHIEVE
POLITICAL GOALS, BY VOTE IN 1996 LEGISLATIVE ELECTIONS IN EUSKADI
(HORIZONTAL PERCENTAGES)

	Very Much Agree	Somewhat Agree	Somewhat Disagree	Very Much Disagree	DK/NA
EA	66	21	10	–	3
HB	9	26	29	30	6
IU	68	30	2	–	–
PNV	66	31	2	–	1
PP	81	15	1	–	3
PSE	74	26	–	–	–
TOTAL	56	32	6	3	3 (1400)

Source: Francisco J. Llera (EUSKOBAROMETRO, 1997).

Nine out of every ten Basques expressed confidence in the current democratic system and rejected violence, an increase of 10 points from eight years ago. This is the majority opinion of all partisan groups except that of HB, which is strategically allied with the terrorists. Nonetheless, even its electorate is divided on this issue, which partly explains its electoral decline since 1990 and its radicalization (+19 points) from a 1989 survey.[31] Finally, let us examine the evolution of Basque attitudes towards those 'persons who are involved with terrorism', comparing our 1997 survey results with those of four earlier surveys. Respondents in all studies were asked if they regarded terrorists as 'patriots', 'idealists', 'manipulated by others' ('fanatical' in 1996), 'crazy' ('terrorists' from 1996), or 'criminals'('killers' in 1996). The results are presented in Table 5.

TABLE 5
EVOLUTION IN ATTITUDES TOWARDS ETA ACTIVISTS, 1978–96

ETA activists are...	1978 %	1979 %	1989 %	1993 %	1996 %
Patriots	13	17	5	9	8
Idealists	35	33	18	13	16
Manipulated/Fanatic*	33	29	11	25	12
Crazy/terrorists*	11	8	16	14	32
Criminals/killers*	7	5	16	21	21
DK/NA	1	8	34	18	11
N =	1,140	1,011	2,386	600	1,800

Sources: For 1978–9, J.Linz (1986); for 1989–96, F. Llera (CIS, No.1,795; CICYT, 1993, and EUSKOBAROMETRO, 1996.
* Categories have changed from 1996 survey.

The generally favourable attitudes of Basques towards terrorists in the first years of the transition had turned to radical rejection and disgust ten years later. During this period, the percentage of respondents who considered activists to be 'patriots' or 'idealists' declined from 50 to 24 per cent, very similar to the evolution of the percentage of respondents for 'manipulated/fanatical' (from 33 to 12), while those who regarded activists as 'crazy/terrorists' or 'common criminals/killers' rose from 13 per cent to 53 per cent. Equally noteworthy is the increase in those without an opinion, who amounted to over one third of all respondents in the 1989 study, showing the great change of Basque public opinion against ETA at the end of the 1980s. On closer examination, these respondents tended to be those without political identification or supporters of nationalist parties.

Studying these perceptions of terrorists by vote in Spanish legislative elections of 1993 (EUSKOBAROMETRO, 1996) and comparing these data with those of Juan Linz for 1979,[32] one notices a striking change within each partisan group. Without doubt, the most significant changes are those among supporters of the PSE, although shifts among Basque nationalist voters in general are quite substantial. Positive opinions among Socialist voters declined from 46 per cent to 9 per cent ('idealists'), while negative assessments increased from 47 to 87 per cent. The smaller change was among Spanish centre-right voters: the overwhelmingly negative attitudes of PP (91 per cent) were almost identical to those of former UCD voters in 1979 (76 per cent), while positive opinions show the greatest stability from 17 to 4 per cent ('idealists'). Among PNV supporters, the percentage of negative assessments also increased from 54 to 74 per cent of respondents in both surveys, and positive evaluations declined from 40 to 21 per cent. In this respect, the relatively positive stance of EA (the radical nationalist split in the PNV in 1986) voters (among whom 41 per cent held favourable opinions) stands in contrast. Among HB supporters, meanwhile, negative attitudes remained stable between 7 and 4 per cent, and positive evaluations declined from 85 to 75 per cent, while those without an opinion increased from 10 to 20 per cent.

The Basque Party System: Polarization and Fragmentation

The fragility and difficult crystallization of the Basque party system become clear as soon as we take a backward glance to what has happened since the beginning of the Spanish political transition.[33] In order to better understand the evolution of the Basque party system, we can differentiate five periods: the first, from the inaugural election of 1977 to the autonomy referendum at the end of 1979, is the Basque political transition; the second, from 1980 to 1984, is the first Basque regional legislature and is one of internal institutionalization; the third, from 1984 to 1986, is one marked by the crisis of hegemonic nationalism and the schism within the PNV; the fourth, from 1986 to 1998, is one of democratic consolidation in the Basque country; and the fifth is beginning and could be one of pacification (see Tables 6 and 7).

TABLE 6
POPULAR VOTES IN BASQUE REGIONAL ELECTIONS, 1980–98

Parties	1980 %	1984 %	1986 %	1990 %	1994 %	1998 %
PNV	38.0	42.0	23.7	28.5	29.8	27.6
EA	–	–	15.8	11.4	10.3	8.6
PSE/EE	14.2	23.0	22.0	19.9	17.1	17.4
EE	9.8	8.0	10.9	7.8	–	–
PCE/IU	4.0	–	–	1.4	9.1	5.6
HB/EH	16.6	14.6	17.5	18.4	16.3	17.7
UCD/CDS	8.5	–	3.5	–	–	–
AP/CP/PP	4.8	9.3	4.8	8.2	14.4	19.9
UA	–	–	–	1.4	2.7	1.2
Nationalists	64.4	64.6	67.9	66.1	56.4	53.9
Turnout	59.8	68.5	69.6	61.0	59.7	70.0

Calculations by the author.

TABLE 7
SEATS IN BASQUE PARLIAMENT, 1980–98

Parties	1980	1984	1986	1990	1994	1998
PNV	25	32	17	22	22	21
EA	–	–	13	9	8	6
PSE/EE	9	19	19	16	12	14
EE	6	6	9	6	–	–
PCE/IU	1	–	–	–	6	2
HB/EH	11	11	13	13	11	14
UCD/CDS	6	–	2	–	–	–
AP/CP/PP	2	7	2	6	11	16
UA	–	–	–	3	5	2
TOTAL	60	75	75	75	75	75

All regional elections from 1980 produced a nationalist majority in a very pluralistic arena, in which the PNV's predominant status was confirmed. This last period is just beginning, and is characterized by the political manifesto of the nationalist front (*Declaración de Estella*) and the truce announcement by ETA in September. The increase of terrorism against the Popular politicians, and the extension of street violence by the radicalized nationalists during the last two years produced social mobilization[34] and more tension between nationalist and autonomist political parties. The government's anti-terrorist policy of firmness and the agreement of Socialists and Populars to isolate HB provoked a reaction from PNV for a radicalized strategy change. From the beginning of 1998 PNV had secret talks with HB and ETA in order to find a peaceful way together; the first result was the so-called 'Ardanza's peace plan', rejected by the PP and PSE, and the second consequence was the rupture of the *Pacto de Ajuria Enea* after its ten years of existence. This new polarized political scene also produced a coalition split and the regional government Socialists' exit at the end of the last legislature.

After a stressful and polarized electoral campaign, but without terrorist violence for the first time, the high voting turnout (70 per cent) in these sixth regional elections of October 1998[35] reproduced the same political pluralism, and the radicalized PNV repeated its electoral success. Small but significant changes are the polarization of electoral support for extreme options (PP and HB/EH), the thin Socialist recovery, and decline of all others, especially the smaller parties. The great change could be a new coalition government of all nationalist parties (PNV, EA and HB/EH), which could lead to the end of ETA's terrorism, the pacification process and the integration of HB/EH into the democratic game, but showing respect to the Basque political pluralism.[36]

Rarely is there such unanimity among scholars[37] as there is in classifying the Basque party system as one of 'polarized pluralism'.[38] There are numerous indicators that justify such a designation: an average of seven significant parliamentary parties, the two largest of which only received 47.5 per cent of valid votes cast in the last regional election; an index of parliamentary fragmentation of .79;[39] important ideological tensions; and an anti-system party openly supporting violence during the last 20 years and receiving 17.7 per cent of the vote. Fragmentation would not be so significant if it were not linked with an ideological polarization between parties, which affects the dynamics of competition, acceptance or rejection of political institutions, and the basic conceptions of the social system. This polarized pluralism has exacerbated confrontations over identities, symbols, territoriality, and integration/seccesion.

In the aftermath of these last regional elections, the party system could be regarded as consisting of seven partisan groups: three are Basque nationalist (PNV, HB/EH and EA), three others are statewide parties (PP, PSE-EE and IU), and one is provincialist (UA). Examined from a different perspective, partisan politics within the region is dominated by four parties on the right (PNV, PP and UA), one on the centre (EA), and the other three on the left (HB/EH, PSE-EE and IU). Finally, it is important to note that one of them, HB (with a new denomination after these elections, *Euskal Herritarrok* or 'we the citizens of *Euskal Herria*'), is an anti-system party.

Fragmentation

One of the first indicators of fragmentation is the number of relevant parties, defined either through their coalition formation ability or their blackmail potential. Given the roles played by various parties and the level of electoral support they have had since the first regional parliament, we can conclude that there are seven relevant parties. This is one of the preconditions for classification as a case of extreme pluralism. Table 8 shows the party system format and its evolution.

As can be seen, in spite of changes in the internal structure of the Basque party system, its high degree of fragmentation remained almost constant throughout this period. The dispersion of parliamentary forces has increased slightly, virtually precluding the re-emergence of an absolute majority in support of any one party, let alone the establishment of a hegemony by any party. The PNV, having recovered from its crisis of 1986, has returned as a central political force, not as an hegemonic actor, but as a dominant one. The succesful experience of the centripetal and basic PNV-PSE alliance has moderated Basque political life for 14 years. Given the great complexity of Basque territorial institutions and this distribution of parliamentary seats, coalition governments have been the way to governability in Euskadi.[40]

Most parties shared coalition experiences at different institutional levels (PNV-PSE, PNV-EE-PSE, PNV-EA-PSE in the regional, provincial and local governments; PNV-EE-EA in the regional government; EA-EE in Guipúzcoa; PNV-EA-(PP) in Alava; PNV-PP in Bilbao; PNV-UA in Vitoria; and PNV-PSE-IU also in Bilbao). Given its anti-system stance, HB has been left out of all these coalition scenarios so far, but this situation could change with the new nationalist policy, and next regional coalition government could be formed by a minority alliance PNV-EA and parliamentary supported by EH(HB).

TABLE 8
FORMAT OF THE BASQUE PARTY SYSTEM, 1980–98

Indicators	1980	1984	1986	1990*	1994	1998
Parliamentary Fragmentation Index	.81	.72	.81	.81	.82	.79
Corrected Parliamentary Dispersion	.87	.90	.94	.94	.96	.92
Electoral Volatility Index	–	13	25	11	15	8
Number of parliamentary parties	7	5	7	7	7	7
Percentage of seats for largest party	41.7	42.7	25.3	29.3	29.3	28.0
Percentage of seats for second party	18.3	25.3	22.7	21.3	16.0	21.3
Difference between the two	23.3	17.4	2.7	8.0	13.3	6.7
Largest Party	PNV	PNV	PSE	PNV	PNV	PNV
Second party	PSE	PSE	PNV	PSE	PSE-EE	PP
Percentage of seats for two largest	60.0	68.0	48.0	50.6	45.3	49.3
Min. no. of parties for party majority	2	2	3	3	3	3
Parties in Government	PNV	PNV	PNV/ PSE	PNV/ EE/EA	PNV/ EA/PSE	PNV/EA (EH)

Calculations by the author.
*1991–94: PNV-EE-PSE

Polarization

Two main dimensions of polarization have characterized Basque electoral behaviour in the course of 20 years of elections: left-right identification and nationalist sentiment. Both ideological dimensions have been operationalized as self-placement scales of ten-point continua: the classical left(1)/right(10) and the new independence(1)/centralism(10) one. Although we lack survey data concerning perceived ideological positions of party supporters in every election, both regional (1980, 1984, 1986, 1990, 1994 and 1998) and general (1982, 1986, 1989, 1993 and 1996), since 1980 it is possible to get an idea of their ideological evolution from some post-electoral surveys. We have chosen the first regional election (1980), a more recent regional election (1994), and the most recent (1996) general election (see Table 9). Although it should be pointed out that we are mixing data from two different kinds of elections, we believe that it is safe to infer that

TABLE 9

MEAN SELF-PLACEMENTS OF PARTY SUPPORTERS ON THE TEN-POINT LEFT-
RIGHT AND INDEPENDENCE-CENTRALISM CONTINUA IN 1980, 1994 AND 1996
ELECTIONS IN EUSKADI

Party Supported	Left-Right			Independence-Centralism		
	1980	1994	1996	1980	1994	1996
Partido Popular (AP,1980)	6.4	6.8	6.0	7.6	6.9	6.7
Unidad Alavesa	–	6.5	–	–	7.0	–
Partido Nacionalista Vasco	4.6	4.8	4.9	3.2	3.1	3.3
Eusko Alkartasuna	–	4.0	4.5	–	2.4	2.5
Partido Socialista de Euskadi	3.8	4.1	3.7	5.5	5.7	5.9
Euskadiko Ezkerra	3.1	–	–	3.1	–	–
Izquierda Unida (PCE,1980)	3.1	3.2	2.8	–	4.9	4.5
Euskal Herritarrok (HB,80/94)	2.3	2.4	2.2	1.6	1.7	1.7

Sources: Surveys directed by F.J. Llera.

significant real change did take place along these fundamental dimensions of Basque political behaviour.

As can be seen, a centripetal shift has occurred among many voters and this, coupled with significant changes in relations and discourse among parliamentary parties, has facilitated the pacts and coalitions of the most recent period and reduced the overall level of polarization. It is also possible that this increased moderation has reduced the level of voter turnout.

Indices of polarization (see Table 10), as measured by the distance between the mean self-placements of supporters of the parties at either extreme,[41] reveal that high levels of political division have been slowly reduced. The disappearance of the UCD and the restructuring of the right produced an increased polarization on the left-right dimension in 1986; conversely, the electoral realignments among the state-wide parties reduced it since 1993. At the same time, the extent of polarization on the independence-centralism continuum remained virtually unchanged until 1990, while it declined from 1993, both by the centripetal political dynamics of PNV-PSE coalitions and by the more moderated PP.

TABLE 10

EVOLUTION OF THE INDICES OF POLARIZATION ON THE LEFT-RIGHT AND
INDEPENDENCE-CENTRALISM DIMENSIONS IN EUSKADI, 1980–96

Dimension	1980	1982	1986	1989	1990	1993	1994	1996
Left/Right	.46	.55	.63	.61	.62	.50	.49	.42
Independ'ce/centr'ism	.66	.67	.65	.57	.63	.53	.59	.55

Sources: surveys directed by F.J.Llera.

Electoral competition is a function of these cleavage dimensions – the manner in which they interact with each other, and the way they are dealt with in partisan electoral strategies. The data indicate that, in the aggregate, there was no significant reduction of polarization on the independence-centralization dimension, nor in left-right polarization.

However, it is also apparent from these data that there has been a certain convergence towards the middle of the two continua, especially with movement towards the political centre on the part of the PNV, PSE and PP, in addition to the fusion between PSE and EE (PSE-EE) and the solid alliance of reconciliated PNV-EA. This has had the effect of further isolating the extremes (HB and UA), as well as facilitating relations among the moderate parties. As they converge, however, one unanticipated consequence may be an increase in competitive tensions and volatility, as distances between parties are narrowed.

Conclusions

During the last 12 years Basque politics and society have undergone a solid process of consolidation for the autonomy institutions and their plurality. The political climate was increasingly characterized by the consociational patterns of consensus, pact, and coalition. In the midst of a growing and widely accepted pluralism, the Weberian ethic of reality is emerging victorious over that of principles, and the nationalist utopia has been pragmatically adapting to accepted political responsibilities.

Political pluralism, volatility, and the heterogeneity of the political geography have increased in Euskadi, giving rise to a greater party-system fragmentation. Nevertheless, ideological tensions have moderated, putting an end to 'adversarial politics'. The stage of institutional consolidation, led by the moderate governing PNV-PSE alliance, as well as by the *Pacto de Ajuria Enea*, has reinforced centripetal tendencies within the system.

In spite of ETA's truce, however, the fear of expressing oneself politically has still not disappeared from Basque society, and the conflict of identities remains alive. Basque public opinion remains immured between longings for peace and freedom and the fear of the political consequences of a collective failure. The nationalist hegemony, however, has shifted to a more 'voluntaristic' model, implying the predominance of assimilationist attitudes towards immigrants and those natives who do not regard themselves as nationalists. The linguistic question, which has found a solution in the education system and the national policy of 'positive discrimination (affirmative action)' a way for its solution, has moderated tensions in political terms, but it remains alive.

Autonomy has been consolidated, and independence demands have not only lost much of their political power, but with current nationalist radicalization have became an object of conflict and political tension between national and state-wide parties. The nationalist front and its coalition government are conditioned by the ETA's truce and its goal is to achieve peace. The peace process needs political normalization and consensus, but one runs the risk of going back to 'adversary politics', which could be a serious difficulty for that process.

Rather than the East-European syndrome of micronationalist disintegration, it has been the political integration of Western Europe (and the Irish peace process) that, for the moment, has exerted influence on the political climate in Euskadi, moderating centre-periphery tensions and encouraging the policy of pacts and coalitions. It has also led to a reduction of political conflict with Madrid, except in the area of antiterrorist policies.

The greatest change, however, concerns attitudes towards violence, now overwhelmingly rejected by Basque society. Indeed, following the inter-party consensus on this issue established in 1988, the citizenry has been mobilized in its opposition to violence. This consensus and the overall legitimacy of the democratic system have taken root among Basques, leading them not only to abandon violence as a political method, but also to abandon the political goals of the terrorists. However, nationalist parties are changing their moderate strategy and are trying to convert their electoral decline and the political defeat of terrorists into a more nationalist institutional status for the Basque country.

Levels of consensus and legitimacy are still inadequate among Basques, but a significant reduction in the intesity of conflict, in combination with consolidation of the autonomy process, have made it much more possible for Euskadi to conform to consociational patterns of political behaviour.

ACKNOWLEDGEMENTS

This contribution was made partly with the financial support of the Comité Interministerial de Galicia y Tecnologia (CICYT) [SEC. 94-0247].

NOTES

1. The Basque Autonomous Community consists of the provinces of Alava, Guipúzcoa and Vizcaya, while Navarra is a separate *Comunidad Foral*, both with 'historical rights' recognized by the Spanish constitution.
2. Juan J. Linz, 'Early State-Building and Late Peripheral Nationalisms Against the State', in S.N. Eisenstadt and S. Rokkan (eds), *Building States and Nations: Models, Analyses and Data Across Three Worlds*, Vol.2 (Beverly Hills, CA: Sage, 1973), pp.32–112.
3. Richard Gunther, Giacomo Sani and Goldie Shabad, *Spain After Franco: The Making of a Competitive Party System* (Berkeley, CA, and London: University of California Press, 1986).
4. See, among others, Juan J. Linz *et al.*, *Informe sociológico sobre el cambio político en*

España (Madrid: Euramérica, 1981); also Françesc Pallarés, José R. Montero and Francisco J. Llera, 'Non State-wide Parties in Spain: An Attitudinal Study of Nationalism and Regionalism', *Publius: The Journal of Federalism*, Vol.27, No.4 (1997), pp.135–69.

5. The founder of the PNV (Basque Nationalist Party).
6. Javier Corcuera, *Orígenes, ideología y organización del nacionalismo vasco, 1876–1904* (Madrid: S.XXI, 1979).
7. Goldie Shabad and Francisco J. Llera, 'Political Violence in a Democratic State: Basque Terrorism in Spain', in Martha Crenshaw (ed.), *Terrorism in Context* (Philadelphia, PA: University of Pennsylvania Press, 1995), pp.410–69.
8. This is the name given to 'the fatherland of all Basques' by Sabino Arana Goiri, the founder of Basque nationalism in the late nineteenth century. For Basque nationalists, the Basque country or *Euskalherria* is an ethno-lingüistic unit made up of the Spanish provinces of Alava, Guipúzcoa, Vizcaya and Navarra, and by the French Districts of Labourd, Soule and the Lower Navarre in the département of Pyrénées Atlantiques.
9. Alfonso Pérez-Agote, *La reproducón del nacionalismo vasco* (Madrid: CIS, 1984).
10. Robert P. Clark, *The Basque Insurgents: ETA, 1952–1980* (Madison, WI: University of Wisconsin Press, 1984).
11. See Jon Juaristi, *El linaje de Aitor. La invención de la tradición vasca* (Madrid: Taurus, 1987) and *El bucle melancólico. Historias de nacionalistas vascos* (Madrid: Espasa, 1997); also Mikel Azurmendi, *La herida patriótica* (Madrid: Taurus, 1998).
12. Max Weber, *Economía y sociedad* (México: Fondo de Cultura Económica, 1979), p.318.
13. See the evolution in Juan J. Linz *et al.*, *Conflicto en Euskadi* (Madrid: Espasa-Calpe, 1986) and in Francisco J. Llera, *Los vascos y la política* (Bilbao: Univ. del País Vasco, 1994).
14. Juan J. Linz, 'From Primordialism to Nationalism' in E.A. Tiryakian and R. Rogowski (eds), *New Nationalisms of the Developed West* (Boston, MA: Allen & Unwin, 1985), pp.203–53.
15. It is the name for pèriodical surveys conducted by Francisco J. Llera at the Basque Country University.
16. Linz *et al.*, *Conflicto en Euskadi*, p.89.
17. Ibid., p.98.
18. Ibid., pp.669ff.
19. Francisco J. Llera, 'Continuidad y cambio en la política vasca: notas sobre identidades sociales y cultura política', *Revista Española de Investigaciones Sociológicas*, Vol.47 (1989), p.118.
20. See Linz *et al.*, *Conflicto en Euskadi*, pp.226ff.
21. Francisco J. Llera, 'Conflicto en Euskadi Revisited', in R. Gunther (ed.), *Politics, Society, and Democracy. The Case of Spain* (Boulder, CO: Westview Press, 1993), p.189.
22. Linz *et al.*, *Conflicto en Euskadi*, pp.258ff.
23. See its evolution in Gurutz Jauregui, *Ideología y estrategia política de ETA. Análisis y evolución entre 1959 y 1968* (Madrid: S.XXI, 1981); Luciano Rincón, *ETA (1974–1984)* (Barcelona: Plaza & Janés, 1985); Joseba Zulaika, *Basque Violence: Metaphor and Sacrament* (Reno, NV: University of Nevada Press, 1988); Robert P. Clark, *Negotiating with ETA. Obstacles to Peace in the Basque Country, 1975–1988* (Reno, NV: Univ. of Nevada Press, 1990); Florencio Dominguez, *De la negociación a la tregua. ¿ El final de ETA ?* (Madrid: Taurus, 1998).
24. Michel Maffesoli, *La violence fondatrice* (Paris: Champ Urbain, 1978).
25. Ander Gurrutxaga, *El código nacionalista vasco durante el Franquismo* (Barcelona: Anthropos, 1985).
26. Alfonso Pérez-Agote, *El nacionalismo vasco a la salida del Franquismo* (Madrid: CIS, 1987).
27. Martha Crenshaw, 'The Causes of Terrorism', *Comparative Politics*, Vol.13 (1981), pp.379–400.
28. Llera, *Los vascos y la política*, p.99.
29. The name used by ETA when collecting money from employers to finance organizational activities.
30. José M. Mata, *El nacionalismo vasco radical. Discurso, organización y expresiones* (Bilbao: Univ. del País Vasco, 1993).

31. Centro de Investigaciones Sociológicas (CIS), Study No. 1795.
32. Ibid., p.639.
33. Francisco J. Llera, *Postfranquismo y fuerzas políticas en Euskadi* (Bilbao: Universidade del País Vasco, 1985) and *Los vascos y la política*.
34. Maria Jesus Funes, *La salida del silencio. Movilizaciones por la paz en Euskadi, 1986–1998* (Madrid: Akal, 1998).
35. Francisco J. Llera, 'Las elecciones autonómicas vascas de 1998', *Cuadernos de Alzate*, Vol.19 (1998), pp.177–98.
36. Dominguez, pp.105ff.
37. See Francisco J. Llera, *Postfranquismo y fuerzas políticas*, pp.112ff; Linz et al., *Conflicto en Euskadi*, p.317; and Gunther, Sani and Shabad, p.312.
38. Giovanni Sartori, *Partidos y sistemas de partidos* (Madrid: Alianza, 1980), pp.166ff.
39. Douglas Rae, *The Political Consequences of Electoral Laws* (New Haven, CT: Yale University Press, 1971), pp.47ff.
40. Francisco J. Llera, 'Pluralismo y gobernabilidad en Euskadi (1980–1994)' in M. Alcántara and Maria A. Martínez (eds), *Las elecciones autonómicas en España, 1980–1997* (Madrid: CIS, 1998), pp.413–43.
41. S.C. Flanagan, 'Models and Methods of Analysis' in G.A. Almond, S.C. Flanagan and R.J. Mundt (eds), *Crisis, Choice and Change* (Boston, MA: Little Brown, 1973), pp.682–96.

Autonomist Regionalism within the Spanish State of the Autonomous Communities: An Interpretation

XOSÉ-MANOEL NÚÑEZ

The role played by *regionalisms* and *regionalist movements* in Spanish history is ambiguous. The development of regional identities contributed to the formation of the nineteenth-century Spanish nation-state, in a similar fashion to other nation-building processes. But the strong survival of the so-called 'historical regions', and therefore of territorial identities forged in the course of the Middle Ages and the early modern period, also resulted in a necessary precondition for the emergence of several peripheral nationalisms during the last third of the nineteenth century (Catalan, Basque and Galician nationalisms). These nationalist movements denied the existence of a Spanish nation occupying the entire territory ruled by the state, and sought to achieve self-determination for their respective territories. In fact, peripheral nationalisms usually have regionalist forerunners, and have also been accompanied by the emergence or development of regionalism in various forms.

This makes Spain a good case for examining the ambiguities of the processes of region-building and nation-building. A scientific definition of a region seems as elusive as providing a definitive answer to the question: what is a nation? Geographers, economists and social scientists coincide in pointing out that no single definition of region is sufficient: regions are economic entities, historical territories, frontier areas and geographical units delimited by natural elements. But they are also a form of collective identity, with uncertain limits that vary according to the spatial representation imagined by the inhabitants of a given territory.[1] Similar problems arise when defining the term regionalism. According to M. Hroch, in the Central European context, regionalism meant a form of supra-ethnic territorial loyalty similar to *Landespatriotismus*, which was not infused with ethnic content and hence could be shared by linguistically or ethnically diverse segments of the population, to the point of becoming an alternative concept to ethnonationalism.[2] Nevertheless, this definition cannot be

Xosé-Manoel Núñez, University of Santiago de Compostela

applied to all Western European areas, since in many cases the construction of regions has also implied the 'rediscovery' of history, traditions, languages and disappearing local cultures. Some authors hold that regionalism has three characteristics in common with minority nationalisms: the shaping of a territory-bound collective identity; the existence of a centre/periphery conflict of a cultural, economic or political nature within the state; and the existence of social mobilization and/or political organizations of a territorial character. In this manner, regionalism and minority nationalism could be considered as two parallel manifestations of a conflict or social mobilization on an ethnoterritorial basis, with a rather unclear line of demarcation.[3] Two common elements to regionalism and minority nationalism would be ethnic mobilization and an appeal to the territory defined as a political unit.

Under the influence of modernization theory, classical definitions of nationalism presupposed that an increase in social communication and a weakening of local and regional meso-territorial identities were necessary preconditions for nation-building. Therefore, regional identities were implicitly seen as pre-modern remains of the past, as opposed to modern national identities.[4] The modern form of collective identity, which was also linked to the legitimacy of power, was asserted to be the nation, while the regions remained as spaces for traditional culture, folklore, social mores and so on. In fact, the French-Jacobin version of nation-building attempted to erode any form of pre-national territorial identities by assimilating the whole state territory under one unified and codified culture. From this perspective, which has also permeated historical and sociological research on the matter, the survival and especially the robust maintenance of regional identities and of any form of regional claims during the modern period should be considered as a symptom of weak nation-building and a possible forerunner of minority nationalisms. This assumption has decisively influenced Spanish academic research on the national question. For instance, historical studies on Basque, Catalan or Galician nationalism, have led social scientists in other regions to emphasize any form of regional affirmation and/or local claim for autonomy, by merely applying the same explanation to all cases. Regionalism was held to precede minority nationalism, and within regionalism every possible and ideologically diverse forerunner (federal republicans, monarchists, cultural folklorists) was included in a sort of catch-all movement, which would result in the emergence of a new peripheral nationalism, or some elusive form of 'particularism'.[5]

This article will examine the relationship between region- and nation-building by focusing on the political dynamics of regionalism in Spain during the last quarter of the twentieth century, as well reviewing the theoretical and doctrinal aspects of regionalist discourses. Recent historical research in other European states tends to tone down the classical assertion that region-building is opposed to nation-building, and even stresses the contrary thesis: nation-building may also imply region-building, to the extent that the former may be highly dependent on the latter, and/or vice-versa.[6] Collective identities and feelings of belonging may be regarded as overlapping concentric spheres, which complement each other; and, as with all forms of collective identity, they are the result of dynamic historical processes.[7] Nationalist movements and states which carried out nation-building policies also contributed, in many cases, to the reaffirmation of local and regional identities in order to help *national* identity take stronger roots among the population. Moreover, this phenomenon manifested itself as common to diverse currents and versions of nationalism, as can be seen in nineteenth-century Germany and also, to some extent, in France. To promote regional symbols and identities meant, first of all, promoting *national* identities at the very bottom level.[8]

However, not all forms of collective identity have the same weight and political significance, and not all expressions of local and regional identity are infused with present-day political implications (that is, claims for self-determination), as are nationalisms and national identities. Consequently, not all forms of regional identity necessarily lead to conflict with national identities, and not all regional (meso-territorial) affirmation discourses may evolve towards nationalist discourses. But some of them do, if a certain set of social/ political factors and historical circumstances interact appropriately. Regional identities may have a historical tradition, common cultural elements, and a memory of previous collective political institutions. The relationship between nation- and region-building is not a fixed one, but rather is subject to constant change over time. Moreover, the basic discussion underpinning current research on nationalism – are nations given and pre-existing entities, or are they a construct of nationalist doctrines and movements? – may also be applied to regions, regional identities and regionalisms. What came first: the region or regional identity? Why are some regional identities successfully constructed (or, if one wishes, invented) while others are not? Are regional identities complementary to, or opposed to, national identities? Can regional identities be constructed from above, according to the interests of political élites?

This paper builds upon the premise that, although regional identities as collective identities have many precedents in the Middle Ages and the early modern period, they have also been constructed during the modern period by diverse actors (the state, local élites, institutions and political movements). These actors generally established the criteria for defining a region as a collectivity, in some cases even demanding a certain degree of regional political rights, but never proclaiming the right to self-determination and full sovereignty. In the course of this construction process, regionalists find themselves forced to appeal to arguments which are very similar to those used by nationalists. But, in contrast with the latter, the regionalists maintain their belief in the existence of a nation, which enhances their region as well as *other* regions, and may see regional identity and regionalism as a first step in consolidating the *nation*, defined as a superior collectivity.

The Spanish case shows how some region-building processes may become specifically nation-building, while others may not; how both identities are shifting and sometimes contradictory over time; and also how different social actors have constructed differing concepts of the region. In fact, until the outbreak of the Spanish Civil War (1936), regionalist discourses in Spain were to a greater or lesser extent shared by both the political Left and Right. These discourses came mainly from three ideological sources:

- nineteenth-century progressive liberalism, subsequently reinforced by the appearance of federalism; this current was opposed to the centralizing policy of the moderate liberals who carried out the task of building the new liberal Spanish state from 1833 on;
- the survival of a pre-liberal idea of the Spanish political community, based on the dynastic principle and loyalty to the Catholic faith, relying on the preservation of 'unity in diversity' among the variegated kingdoms, territories, legal codes and privileges existing in the various territorial units which had merged into the Spanish monarchy since the end of the fifteenth century; and
- the ideological influence of Peter Kraus's organicist doctrine on Spanish liberalism from the mid-nineteenth century, as well as the regenerationist (*regeneracionista*) thought of the beginning of the twentieth century. For some thinkers and regional politicians, a regeneration of the 'decadent' Spanish nation could only be achieved by revitalizing the 'purest' and healthiest parts of the 'national body', that is, the regions and the municipalities, by eradicating centralism and political clientelism.[9]

The post-1975 situation has certainly been characterized by a new set of circumstances. The re-emergence of peripheral nationalisms (Basque, Catalan and Galician) during the first years of the democratic transition, along with the accompanying demonstration effects in other Spanish regions, led to a complex mixture of reactions and imitations from Andalusia to Cantabria. But two conditioning factors were now present, which deeply influenced and reinforced the new forms of regionalism: the deficit of legitimacy of Spanish nationalist discourse, due to its appropriation of and identification with the Francoist legacy, which pushed almost all political parties of the democratic spectrum towards decentralizing proposals; and the implementation of a decentralized territorial structure extended to the whole of Spain, creating 17 administrative and political units under the 1978 constitution. The generalization of all-round home rule made it possible for formerly marginal or irrelevant regionalist discourses to become politically functional and useful for new political élites in search of new legitimacy for the new meso-territorial governments and administrations. This process has given rise to a Janus-faced phenomenon. On the one hand, regionalist discourses emerged as a new presentation of Spanish nationalist tenets that were considered illegitimate when expressed openly. But regionalism has also contributed to the reinforcing of territorial loyalties and interests, and hence may be considered a potential prerequisite for the emergence of new nationalist discourses where there formerly had been virtually no historical tradition of peripheral nationalism. At the same time, the presence of 'regionalist' discourses stressing 'equal treatment' and 'symmetry' among all territories of Spain makes the balance of power between Spanish nationalism, peripheral nationalism and the state even more intricate.

Region-building in Post-Franco Spain

Spanish nationalist discourses, and especially their left-wing and liberal tendencies, underwent a deep identity crisis during Francoism, which forced Spanish left-wing parties to defend regionalist claims and even uphold self-determination rights for Catalonia, the Basque country and Galicia. This gave rise to a more or less rhetorical 'regionalism', or even peripheral nationalism, among almost all left-wing political options during the transition period.[10] Free from legitimacy problems, after 1975 peripheral nationalisms re-emerged in Spain as strong as in 1936, demonstrating their strength at the first two general elections, in 1977 and 1979. Basque and Catalan nationalism soon became socially hegemonic in their respective territories, while Galician nationalism remained in a weaker position. Andalusian regionalism went through a period of relative strength (1977–89) as a leftist tendency, and the Canary Islands' radical left nationalism, with its origins going as far back as the 1960s, gained some electoral support.

The pressure of peripheral nationalisms on the young Spanish democratic state, seeking satisfactory self-government status within it, led to a new territorial structure, instituted by the 1978 constitution. Spain became a 'state of autonomous communities' and was divided into 17 territorial entities which encompassed the previously existing 50 provinces. These new entities were granted a generous level of administrative and legislative autonomy. A political and institutional compromise resolved the dispute between the post-Francoist reformist right, which preached the unitary character of the Spanish nation and was only willing to recognize a certain degree of administrative decentralization; the Spanish left, which theoretically defended a federal state; and Basque and Catalan peripheral nationalists, who argued that Spain should explicitly be a multinational federalized state. According to part VIII of the constitution, Spain is defined as the sole political nation, which delegates sovereignty from above to the new regional entities, baptized as 'autonomous communities'. But it also established that those regions which had passed a home-rule statute before 1936 deserved the special status of 'historical nationalities' and were granted a different and 'faster' procedure for achieving full autonomy (article 151 of the constitution), as well as a higher lever of power. They were soon joined by Andalusia, while the other 13 had the right to achieve autonomy through a 'slow' procedure (article 143).[11]

The new autonomous communities are neither uniform nor comparable as far as their geographical size, economic structure, income levels and population are concerned, and some of them do not correspond with traditional 'historical regions'. This was the case with Madrid (which became a single-province community), Murcia (which lost the Albacete province to Castile-La Mancha), La Rioja (the ancient Logroño province, which had traditionally been a part of Old Castile) and Cantabria (the ancient Castilian province of Santander). In other cases, such as the demarcation of the limits and provinces included within the new autonomous community of Castile-León, problems arose due to the reluctance of some provincial institutions, such as the *Diputaciones*, to transfer powers to the meso-territorial governments created from nothing.[12] All new regions achieved their home-rule statutes between 1978 and 1982, and started implementing new decentralized administrations. Hence began the consolidation process of the so-called 'state of the autonomous communities'.

Spain's new regional structure seemed to be the definitive solution for the 'national problem', which has been at the centre of Spanish twentieth-century history. Nevertheless, two factors contribute, and still contribute, to the failure of the system of autonomous communities to stabilize definitively:

- the difficult fit of Basque and Catalan nationalism, especially the former, within the new state. Peripheral nationalisms do not explicitly accept the present regional structure and keep aiming at deeper autonomy within a

multinational state (not to mention the existing pro-independence tendencies within them);
• the improvised and ambiguous distribution of powers between the town-councils, the autonomous communities and the central government, that has been – and still is – negotiated through permanent political bargaining.

Some of the present problems have to do with setting up a mechanism for financial transfers from richer to poorer regions, creating a forum for political cooperation and participation between the autonomous communities and the central state, and clarifying the role that the regions will play in the decision-making process within the European Union.[13] Aside from this, the rapid creation of regional administrations has frequently led to a duplication of bureaucracies. Finally, since the beginning of the 1990s town councils' representatives have protested against financial and political 'discrimination' by both the central state and the 'centralism' of the autonomous communities. In good measure resurrecting the old 'municipalism' from the nineteenth century, they have insisted upon the principle of the autonomy of municipalities as the basic entities of administrative organization, underpinning the significance of meso-territorial governments.[14]

The Rise of 'Autonomist Regionalisms'

A third – fundamental – problem is the fact that the system of autonomous communities has unexpectedly contributed to the rise of 'regional claims' and regionalisms all over Spain. To a certain extent these autonomist regionalisms are a new incarnation of pre-war regional movements, and, in fact, they reproduce some of the characteristics of historical regionalism present during the first third of the twentieth century. Today regionalisms have emerged in the course of a sort of chain reaction, caused by the imitation effect produced by peripheral nationalisms, that 'show the political path' to be followed by other regions in the process of gaining power. At the same time, most of them insist upon their Spanishness and protest against 'unfair' discrimination by the state in favour of Catalonia or the Basque country, which are perceived as seeking unique privileges and therefore accused of lack of solidarity. But there is now a further factor encouraging the emergence of 'autonomous regionalisms': the fact that the consolidation of a decentralized political system created an additional arena of political power and competition (regional parliaments, meso-territorial administrations and elections, and so on). Regional élites now encounter greater opportunities for achieving power and controlling resources. In other words, regional administrations imposed from above, which very often did not correspond to any regional consciousness by a majority of the respective populations,[15] caused *regionalism* to be promoted by both traditional – some of them deriving from late Francoism – and new regional political élites.

Some regionalist parties certainly emerged before the 1978 constitution had been approved. The Aragonese Party (*Partido Aragonés*, or PAR) was founded in 1977 by a handful of Zaragoza's conservative-oriented bourgeois, some of them former members of Francoist local institutions. Their political aim was to proclaim a regional identity while, at the same time, roughly expressing opposition to the neighbouring Catalan nationalism. The party therefore sought home-rule for Aragón on a principle of equality with Catalonia, so that it would not be 'discriminated' against by another region. Its representatives in the first Spanish parliament (1977–9) argued against the distinction between regions and nationalities contained in article 2 of the Spanish constitution, since the sole *nation* had to be Spain, while all regions should receive similar treatment and an equal degree of self-government delegated from the central state.[16] This position was maintained in the following years, once the 'state of the autonomous communities' had begun to be implemented. For the regionalist president of Aragón's regional government in 1987, the development of the decentralized system established by the 1978 constitution should lead to an equality of powers among all regions, and therefore avoid having some autonomous communities receive larger power transfers than others; at the same time, the idea of the Spanish nation was considered as non-negotiable, since 'it is above any form of political organization that may be adopted'. Nevertheless, the PAR was opposed to federalism, relinquishing any claim to full sovereignty for Aragón and preferring instead to focus on economic claims and demands for competencies and powers from the Madrid government.[17]

A strong degree of anti-Catalanism was also a characteristic of the Valencian right-wing and regionalist party Valencian Union (*Unión Valenciana*, or UV), founded in 1981, whose main concern was the defence of Valencia's particular regional personality against so-called 'Catalan cultural imperialism', to the point that the party supported the academic standardization of the Catalan-Valencian dialect as a distinct language from Catalan. The social network which supported Valencian regionalism derived mainly from the clubs and traditional associations involved in organizing the local celebrations of the *fallas* in the city of Valencia. It included a blend of populist appeal, regional traditions and Spanish affirmation.[18] The Regionalist Party of Cantabria (*Partido Regionalista Cántabro*, or PRC) was also founded in 1978, with the purpose of achieving for Cantabria – the former coastal Castilian province of Santander – a separate autonomy from that of Castile. It expressed its political goals and ideas in a confused manner, blending arguments from Christian personalist thought and from pre-war regenerationism in order to defend the need for regional decentralization.[19] But these parties and other regionalist options such as La Rioja's Progressive Party (*Partido Riojano Progresista*, or PRP, afterwards renamed as La Rioja's Party, *Partido Riojano*), hardly presented any well-defined regionalist creed, at least from a theoretical point of view. They mainly consisted of pluralistic but tendentially conservative platforms with very diffuse and improvised ideological principles, relying on the mobilizing appeal of the complaints against the privileges afforded by the central state to the historical nationalities, along with a demand for funds from the Madrid government in order to further improve their regions. This inter-class appeal was common to all regionalist parties, and a good example may be seen in the purely 'functionalist' approach to regional policy adopted by La Rioja's Party, whose main aim so far seems to be to counteract the competition of the neighbouring Basque autonomous community in the area of industrial policy and financial powers.[20]

Only in the case of the main party in Navarre, the strongly conservative Navarrese People's Union (*Unión del Pueblo Navarro*, or UPN), can a specific regionalist tradition be traced back to the nineteenth century. It was maintained through Francoism thanks to the survival of the Navarrese *foral* institutions, in combination with enduring Traditionalist postulates – since Navarre has been a historical stronghold of Carlism. At present these have been transformed into a conception of the Spanish nation based on traditional 'regional liberties', which supposedly date back to the late Middle Ages and have been preserved under the Spanish monarchy. This creed was also reinforced by its opposition to Basque nationalism, which would seek to assimilate the region into the Basque country or *Euskal Herria*.[21] Alava's Union (*Unidad Alavesa*, or UA), the regionalist party of the Basque province of Alava, has a somewhat similar character. It was founded towards the end of the 1980s after a split from the provincial branch of Spanish right-wing People's Party (*Partido Popular*, or PP), and during the first half of the 1990s has maintained third place in Alava's politics. Like UPN, UA's historical roots date back to the pre-war traditional reticence of the overwhelmingly Spanish-speaking Alava to become fully integrated into the autonomous (or eventually independent) Basque country. This was manifest in its peculiar interpretation of the *fuerista* legacy, understood as a provincial claim opposed to the other Basque province of Vizcaya's 'hegemony', and also as a vindication of the provincial autonomy maintained by the *Fueros* as more important than Basque regional home-rule. Alavese regionalism may also be interpreted as a way of legitimizing a local variant of Spanish nationalism which has not yet fully overcome its post-1936 identity and legitimacy crisis – which is particularly enduring in the Basque country. Hence, for instance, UA has taken up the defence of the 'discriminated' Spanish language against the linguistic policy of the Basque government, but does so by campaigning for protection for the so-called 'Alavese language', as a part of the territory of Alava's historical tradition. The defence of the unity of the Spanish nation, consecrated by the 1978 constitution, is taken to be compatible with the respectful preservation of regional liberties as legitimized by history and identified with a progressive understanding of individual rights. As the Popular Party has progressively increased its vote in the Basque country since 1994, thanks to its more convincing approach to regional home-rule, the only way for UA to differentiate its position from that of the Spanish conservatives has been to demand the transformation of the province of Alava in a new autonomous community. Hence its slogan for the last Basque regional elections (October 1998): 'Alava [should be] like Navarre'.[22]

In spite of their confusing ideological principles and variegated political character, the new autonomic regionalisms have proved to be very able pragmatic improvisers, and in this sense they have benefited from a favourable political context. Moreover, they flourished and expanded between 1982 and 1989 thanks, among other factors, to the spectacular fall after the 1982 parliamentary elections of the main Spanish centre party which had led the transition process since 1977, the Democratic-Centrist Union (*Unión de Centro Democrático*, or UCD). UCD had agglomerated a good number of local élites from the late Francoist period, for whom a conversion to regionalism became the best way to reorient their political activity and to retain their influence after 1982.[23] Thus, regional parties either emerged or received the reinforcement of these new members. Many local UCD representatives from Aragón, a number of whom had already occupied posts in Franco's administrations, subsequently joined the PAR. Another good example of this process was the formation in 1984 of the Galician moderate 'nationalist' party *Coalición Galega*, shaped by some local bosses from the rural provinces of Lugo and Ourense, who had inherited the clientelistic networks of UCD, and another minority nationalist party.[24] Something similar happened in 1990–2 after the final defeat of the remaining centre party (the Social and Democratic Centre (*Centro Democrático y Social*, CDS) led by the charismatic ex-president of the government, Adolfo Suárez. A large part of today's 'nationalists' in the Canary Islands came from the regional branch of the CDS and from insular post-Franco élites, as well as former UCD members. They merged with other political groups (such as the left-wing nationalists) to form a new regionalist party, Canary Coalition (*Coalición Canaria*, CC), which today receives around 22 per cent of regional votes.[25]

Moreover, the regionalist option has become a typical catch-all label which may be adopted by any local politician in a pinch. A very significant and almost ridiculous example was provided by Nicolás Piñeiro, regional parliamentarian from the autonomous community of Madrid, who, after leaving the PP in 1988 due to internal problems, founded along with some family members a regionalist party for Madrid, which claimed that Spain's capital should become a historical region and vindicate its 'personality' against the challenges posed by peripheral autonomous communities.[26] Similar examples can be seen in several regions during the second half of the 1990s. In Galicia, the recently-shaped (1997) 'nationalist' party Galician Democracy [*Democracia Galega*] was founded by two former leading figures in the Spanish right-wing parties UCD and PP. And a very recent example has been offered at the end of 1998, with the emergence of a new regionalist organization in Asturias out of a split in the regional branch of the PP, led by the president of the autonomous community, Sergio Marqués. The dissidents set up a new regionalist party, Union for the Renewal of Asturias (*Unión Renovadora Asturiana*, URAS), and its founding conference in February of 1999 included some moderate Asturian ethnonationalists, drawn there by the strong regionalist appeal of the organization. In fact, URAS declares itself an inter-class party, which seeks to defend Asturias' regional interests, above any other political or social cleavages.[27]

During the 1980s and part of the 1990s, and especially after the 1987 regional elections, some of the regionalist parties (the PAR, for instance) came into power in their respective autonomous communities (always in coalition with other Spanish national parties – either the socialist PSOE or the right-wing PP), and then succeeded in giving political content to their recently-achieved home-rule status. In this sense, there is a clear imitation dynamic, or 'institutional mimicry', following the nationalist-ruled autonomous governments of Catalonia and the Basque country.[28] Neither the PSOE nor the PP were able to avoid this, since they are constantly under pressure from their regional branches to favour regional interests. The 'slow track' autonomous communities promoted regional consciousness among their citizens, as some were forced to 'invent' new regions and therefore new identities, as in the case of La Rioja, Cantabria or even Castile-León and Castile-La Mancha, in order to provide arguments that justified and legitimized the existence of the present political institutions and territorial frameworks. As a Castilian PP politician expressed it, 'It is particularly urgent to emphasize the political dimension of the autonomous community of Castile-León, given its low level of collective identity in this respect.' Although secessionism was entirely rejected as a political issue, regional home-rule should not be justified merely on an economic basis: according

TABLE 1
ELECTION RESULTS OF REGIONALIST PARTIES IN FIVE AUTONOMOUS
COMMUNITIES, 1983-1995 (REGIONAL ELECTIONS ONLY)
(% of valid votes)

	1983	1987	1991	1995
Aragón	20.64	28.48	24.68	20.46
Valencia	–	9.24	10.41	5.72
Navarre	23.51	31.18	34.95	49.90
La Rioja	7.52	6.49	5.38	6.66
Cantabria	6.77	12.29	6.36	14.63

Source: Historia 16, No.200 (1992), and *El País*, 29 May 1995.
The following parties are included: for Aragón, Partido Aragonés (PAR); for Valencia, Unión Valenciana (UV); for Navarre, Unión del Pueblo Navarro (UPN), Convergencia de Demócratas Navarros (CDN) since 1995 – in 1995 UPN presented itself in coalition with the Popular Party (PP). For La Rioja, Partido Riojano (PRP); for Cantabria, Partido Regionalista de Cantabria (PRC). The mostly populist-oriented Unión del Pueblo de Cantabria (Cantabria's People Union), founded by the former president of the autonomous community of Cantabria, Juan Hormaechea, after being expelled from the PP, has not been included because of its purely 'charismatic' and populist character, since its regionalist positions are virtually undefined.

to him, 'the autonomous communities must know how to create their own political space, in spite of present difficulties'.[29] Propaganda campaigns, cultural and schooling policies, an appeal to historical forerunners (more or less real, more or less imagined) and invented traditions,[30] as well as the permanent – and always useful – argument of enduring discrimination in comparison with other 'favoured' regions, have also contributed to spread regional consciousness among the population and to legitimize the existence of all the autonomous communities. At the same time, autonomous regional governments and institutions have benefited from a period of expanding public expenditure (1982–92), which has served to implement a sort of micro-welfare state at the regional level. This took place at little cost to the regional governments, since they had the power to spend, but did not have the responsibility of directly collecting taxes (with the exception of the *foral* systems of the Basque country and Navarre). Two examples of this would be the fact that the public expenditures of the autonomous communities tripled between 1986 and 1992, and that the number of civil servants employed by regional governments increased from 44,475 in 1981 to 565,460 in 1991; during the same period, the number of civil servants dependent on the central government decreased from 1,181,820 to 900,576.[31]

This provided a demonstration for citizens of the positive effects and services that regional institutions could provide, and gave a more concrete meaning to the previously rather diffuse sentiment of 'loyalty to the region', which subsequently was expressed in the high rates of satisfaction exhibited by citizens with regard to the system of autonomous communities two decades after its implementation.[32]

Self-affirmation Dynamics: From 'Region' to 'Nation'?

The dynamics of new region-building undertaken by the ruling élites of the autonomous communities have also had another effect: increasing pressure on the central government to solve almost every serious problem that directly affects the regions, such as labour conflicts or economic adjustments, by making 'Madrid' responsible for them. The need to justify their own regional power leads new regionalists, as well as regional élites from the Spanish political parties, to demand further powers for their autonomous communities, greater decentralization and equal treatment with the 'historical nationalities', in order to avoid comparative 'injustices'. Some of the UCD ministers who took part in the articulation of the new decentralized state structure at the beginning of the 80s, such as the Andalusian M. Clavero Arévalo, saw it as a necessity in order to preserve Spain's territorial cohesion.[33] Nevertheless, the present dynamics of regional affirmation make this prediction seem far too optimistic. A clear example of 'competition for resources' occurred during the so-called 'water conflict', which broke out in 1994 between three autonomous communities (Castile-La Mancha, Murcia and Valencia), all of them ruled at that time by the same party, due to the disputes over usage of the water from the Guadiana and Tajo rivers. The Madrid government was unable to provide a solution.

Moreover, as has already been mentioned, regional governments of the 'slow track' autonomous communities constantly press for achieving the status reserved for the historical nationalities. This self-affirmation dynamic has even led some regionalist parties, such as the Aragonese PAR, rhetorically to uphold new peripheral *nationalist* tenets with the purpose of transforming Aragón into a 'nationality' within the limits established by the 1978 constitution. These claims have sometimes received a certain degree of popular support from the regional population, as expressed in several mass demonstrations between 1992 and 1994. Nevertheless, doctrinal coherence was, in this case, less important than the publicity effect: according to Hipólito Gómez-de las Roces, there was no difference between *regionalist* and *nationalist* parties as long as they were not in favour of secession. At the same time, the youth section of PAR declared itself to be *nationalist*, although explicitly relinquishing the claim to self-determination, while other leaders and members of the same party insisted instead upon prioritizing socio-economic questions. Every possible forerunner was included within the invented historical heritage of the party, from the so-called 'Aragonese lobby' of the enlightened absolutism of the

134   IDENTITY AND TERRITORIAL AUTONOMY IN PLURAL SOCIETIES

eighteenth century (a group of aristocrats of Aragonese origin in the Bourbon kings' court) to the isolated and sparse Aragonese nationalist ideologues of the 1920s and 1930s, such as Gaspar Torrente. The ideological blend resulting from this mixture caused increasing confusion among PAR's membership, to the point that, during its January 1996 conference, the party was forced to abandon the label 'nationalist' in order to avoid further misunderstandings among its rank-and-file members and supporters. However, the main aim of the party continued to be the achievement of official recognition of Aragón as a 'historical nationality', obtained in 1998.[34] An Aragonese intellectual close to autonomist positions has expressed that permanent ambiguity in the use of the concepts of 'nation' and 'nationality' by local regionalists in the following fashion: 'Aragón does not need to be labelled in any way. But if, to be heard and respected we have to call ourselves a nation, let's call ourselves a nation.'[35]

Following the same tendency, the Valencian party, UV, has attempted to adopt an entirely 'nationalist' terminology and to advocate the transformation of Spain into a vaguely defined federal state, carrying the flag of linguistic distinctiveness while suffering from several splits headed by the most conservative sectors of the party.[36] Canary Coalition has also established as its political objective the 'definition of the Canary Islands as a nationality, with all its implications, within the framework of article 2 of the constitution, which considers Spain to be composed of nationalities and regions'. The rest of its programme principally emphasizes economic objectives and the defence of regional interests within the European Union.[37] Finally, it is worth mentioning that the Navarrese party UPN, which entered into a permanent coalition with the PP in 1990, underwent a split in April of 1995 due to leadership disputes and ideological friction over its own identity as a party, and the extent of self-government to be sought for Navarre. The dissident faction was headed by its former president, Juan-Cruz Alli, who founded a new party, Convergence of Navarrese Democrats (*Convergencia de Demócratas Navarros*, CDN), which is supposed to be more regionalist than UPN and has even advocated the existence of a *Navarrese nationality*, which distinguishes itself from both the Basque and the Spanish identities. From a theoretical standpoint, Alli intended to elaborate a new and more sophisticated ideological synthesis of Spanish and Basque nationalism, a sort of vindication of a deeper regional consciousness for Navarre that would enable the region to play a prominent role in the process of European unification.[38] In contrast, a platform of Spanish regionalist parties constituted at an assembly held in Cáceres in December of 1998, with the objective of achieving a 'symmetrical Spain [built on] solidarity' and a national idea of Spain that would be 'entirely respectful of the Constitution', was able to include only 12 organizations from throughout Spain, such as the Alavese UA and La Rioja's PRP, while older parties like the PAR, UV or the Navarrese CDN refused to join it.[39]

The new regionalist creed advocated by Alli's supporters is partially based on Christian-personalist thinking following the influence of the Bavarian right-wing party Christlich-Soziale Union (CSU). This approach is also shared to a certain extent by former Francoist minister and presently president of Galicia, Manuel Fraga. Fraga's new regionalist theory – which is full of theoretical vagueness regarding the distribution of powers between the central state and the regional administrations – does not deny Spain the condition of one single nation, but advocates a more prominent role for the subnational units within the future borderless European union, as well as reinforcing regional identity, following the 'subsidiarity principle' which enshrines decentralization as fundamental basis for individual freedom.[40] This 'regionalization' of the political creed of the Spanish conservatives, and especially of their fellow Galicians, has increased since PP's rise to state power in 1996 and its subsequent strategy of moderating its image, to the point of declaring itself as a party located at an ideological mid-point between the 'extremes' of peripheral nationalism and Spanish nationalism. According to one of the 'emerging stars' of the Galician PP, the present secretary of state for local administration X. Rodríguez-Arana, the entire intellectual and political tradition of Galician nationalism prior to 1936 may be assimilated into a new form of 'Galicianism'. His vague proposals emphasize the need to combine regional self-government and a reinforcement of subnational cultures, defined in an essentialist fashion (but respectful of individual rights), with Spanish patriotism, based upon common loyalty to a historical fatherland (Spain) legitimized by the existence of a common Hispanic political community since the 15th century.[41]

As a result of the complex mosaic of political interactions and diverse processes of identity-building taking place in the present Spanish state of the autonomous communities, one may conclude that region-building in Spain at the end of the twentieth century is still an open and evolving matter. The decentralized system established by the 1978 constitution has proved itself to be a useful formula for peacefully integrating the majority of the peripheral nationalisms within the new Spanish democratic system. In spite of its terminological vagueness and lack of congruity, it has also proved to be a surprisingly functional, flexible and robust provisory solution.[42] But it has not yet fully incorporated the peripheral nationalisms in a definitive manner, since they tend to consider their present autonomy statutes as a minimal solution, hence the persistent claims for self-determination in the long term. This lack of satisfaction periodically rises to the fore of political debate, expressing itself in an increasingly bold-faced fashion since 1998.

Thus we may conclude that the state of the autonomous communities is still in progress, and not yet totally consolidated. The proliferation of autonomist regionalisms in several autonomous communities determines contradictory relationships with the peripheral nationalisms and with the state. On the one hand, regionalisms depend on the pressure that Catalan or Basque nationalism exert on the central state in order to gain additional transfers of power; on the other hand, they demand 'equal treatment' with the historical nationalities, without allowing for the fact that the nationalists seek to preserve their uniqueness, either by asymmetric federalism, or by pursuing a confederation integrated by the 'historical nations' (the Basque country, Catalonia, Galicia and the 'Castilian lands', more or less imprecisely defined). The regionalization proposals of the main Spanish parties, such as the 'single administration' advocated by Manuel Fraga (which consists of full devolution to regional administrations and the virtual elimination of the provinces) are another attempt at 'renationalizing' Spain from the bottom up and to counteract the increasing demands of peripheral nationalism.

Finally, one must keep in mind that the process of European integration may affect the roles of the regions, provinces and states within the new European Union. Without being 'europessimistic', it is reasonable to say that it does not seem that state-wide national loyalties in Spain will be entirely replaced by regional and European allegiances in the near future. Even in the Basque country, and particularly in Catalonia, both Spanish and Basque/Catalan loyalties clearly dominate in a complementary form which has been labelled 'dual patriotism'. Neither the regionalist nor the peripheral nationalist parties have been fully successful so far in taking the place of Spanish national loyalties and some form of Spanish patriotism. In any case, regionalist autonomism has also contributed to make loyalty to the system of autonomous communities gain broad acceptance among a majority of the Spanish population, without necessarily implying a decrease in the feelings of Spanish national identification among the citizens of most regions.[43] But it has also contributed to make far more complex the territorial balance of power and of identities between the state and minority nationalisms.

Some General Conclusions

What lessons can be drawn from this overview of the dynamics of region-building in the Spanish state of the autonomous communities? In my view, the following six may be highlighted:

1. Region-building follows historical dynamics which, to a certain extent, are similar to those of nation-building. As a basis for its arguments, the former tends to use similar elements (history, tradition, culture) that may

be assumed or defended by élites when certain sufficient interests are present. The theoretical difference between the *region* and the *nation* lies in the notion of *present collective sovereignty*, which is held to be an attribute exclusive to the nation. Hence the differences that arise between nationalist and regionalist discourses.

2. The Spanish case illustrates how these dynamics converge and diverge over time, and in any case they are deeply interrelated since both have similar historical origins.[44] The relatively unfulfilled character of state-promoted Spanish nation-building in the nineteenth century and therefore the strong persistence of regional identities, as well as the existence of local élites in need of preserving given social or economic interests, may lead regionalisms to become minority nationalisms if confidence in the previous nation-state fails or if the interests of one or more social groups require a complete change of national loyalties. In fact, almost all European minority nationalisms have developed from a previously existing form of collective identity. Throughout Spanish history groups of regional intellectuals have often elaborated a 'nationalist' discourse from a regionalist forerunner, but then proceeded to experience no social support. This would be the case with the tiny Asturian or Castilian 'historical' and present-day nationalist movements, for instance, as well as Lombardy's or Tuscany's ethnonationalist groups in Italy (not to be confused with the Northern League).

3. Peripheral nationalisms create a clear demonstration/imitation effect for regionalist movements to follow. This may have a decisive influence on the level of theoretical discourse and ideology, but hardly contributes at all to the social extension of new nationalisms.

4. Regional identity is also, in Anderson's words, an imagined community.[45] Its construction is first carried out by élites and intellectuals, but regional consciousness is also spread thanks to the presence of institutional mechanisms, as Breuilly and other authors emphasize with regard to nation-building.[46] Hence, the more power regional institutions have, the more they will consciously promote the territorial loyalty of the citizens in order to reinforce their own legitimacy. Potential legitimizing arguments are built on more or less 'objective' factors, such as history, the existence of a distinct codified language, cultural traditions, economic conditions, etc. But these may also act as preconditions that shape strong pre-political meso-territorial identities.

5. In the study of the historical evolution of nationalist movements, more attention must be paid to the underlying ideological and political dynamics which may transform regionalisms into nationalisms.

6. Regionalism and regional affirmation do not imply *per se* a

contradiction or opposition to nation-building. Nevertheless, in some cases they may insert some elements of ideological friction in the regional political arena, which under certain circumstances may result in the development of an alternative nationalist discourse. Of course, whether this new output receives the support of the targeted population is another matter. Even peripheral nationalist parties in the Basque country, Catalonia and Galicia receive votes from people who do not fully identify with any exclusive sentiment of national identity, but who tend to reconcile regional loyalties and interests with some sort of loyalty to the national state as a whole. Conversely, it is not amazing that those regionalist parties which have conveniently seized the opportunity to play the *ethnonationalist card* have not lost votes or social support because of it.

NOTES

1. See P. Anderson, *The Invention of the Region 1945–1990* (Florence: European University Institute, 1994), Working Paper EUF 94/2.
2. M. Hroch, 'De l'ethnicité à la nation. Un chemin oublié vers la modernité, *Anthropologie et Société*, Vol.19, No.3 (1995), pp.71–86.
3. See e.g. K. Symmons-Symonolewicz, *Nationalist Movements. A Comparative View* (Meadville: Maplewood Press, 1970); L. Moreno, *La Federalización de España* (Madrid: Siglo XXI, 1997), pp.11–23; D. Petrosino, *Stati, nazioni, etnie. Il pluralismo etnico-nazionale nella teoria sociologica contemporanea* (Milan: Franco Angeli, 1991), pp.93–4.
4. See for instance K.W. Deutsch, *Nationalism and Social Communication* (Cambridge, MA: MIT Press, 1953).
5. See X.M. Núñez, *Historiographical Approaches to Nationalism in Spain* (Saarbrücken/Fort Lauderdale, FL: Breitenbach, 1993).
6. See a good sample of case-studies in H.-G. Haupt, M.G. Müller and S. Woolf (eds), *Regional and National Identities in Europe in the XIXth and XXth Centuries* (The Hague/London/Boston, MA: Kluwer Law International, 1998).
7. A. D. Smith, *National Identity* (London: Penguin, 1991).
8. For the German case, see C. Applegate, *A Nation of Provincials. The German Idea of Heimat* (Berkeley, CA: University of California Press, 1990); for the French case, see among others H.G. Haupt, 'Die Konstruktion der Regionen und die Vielfalt der Loyalitäten im Frankreich des 19. und 20. Jahrhunderts', in G. Lottes (ed.), *Region, Nation, Europa. Historische Determinanten der Neugliederung eines Kontinents* (Heidelberg: Europa-Verlag, 1992), pp.121–6, or G. Rossi-Landi, 'La région', in J.F. Sirinelli (ed.), *Histoire des Droites en France. 3: Sensibilités* (Paris: Fayard, 1992), pp.71–100.
9. For a historical overview covering nineteenth and twentieth century developments, see X.M. Núñez, 'Region-building in Spain during the 19th and 20th centuries', in G. Brunn (ed.), *Region und Regionsbildung in Europa. Konzeptionen der Forschung und empirische Befunde* (Baden-Baden: Nomos, 1996), pp.175–210.
10. See, among others, B. de Riquer, 'Aproximación al nacionalismo español contemporáneo', *Studia Historica – Historia Contemporánea*, Vol.12 (1994), pp.11–29, and A. de Blas-Guerrero, 'El problema nacional-regional español en los programas del PSOE y del PCE', *Revista de Estudios Políticos*, Vol.3 (1978), pp.155–70.
11. For a general overview of the process, see J. Solé-Tura, *Nacionalidades y nacionalismos en España* (Madrid: Alianza, 1985); J. Botella, 'The Spanish "New" Regions: Territorial and Political Pluralism', *International Political Science Review*, Vol.10, No.3 (1989), pp.263–71;

P.A. Kraus, *Nationalismus und Demokratie. Politik im spanischen Staat der Autonomen Gemeinschaften* (Wiesbaden: Universitäts-Verlag, 1996); F. Fernández-Rodríguez *et al.*, *La España de las autonomías* (Madrid: Espasa-Calpe, 1985); D. Nohlen and J. González Encinar (eds), *Der Staat der autonomen Gemeinschaften in Spanien* (Opladen: Leske and Budrich, 1992).

12. See P. Altares, M. González-Herrero and A. Carretero, *La autonomía de Segovia y la reivindicación regional de Castilla* (Segovia: Consejo de Comunidad Castellana, 1981).

13. See, for example, Kraus, *Nationalismus*; A. Hildenbrand and D. Nohlen, 'Regionalismus und politische Dezentralisierung in Spanien nach Franco', in W.L. Bernecker and. J. Oehrlein (eds), *Spanien heute. Politik-Wirtschaft-Kultur* (Frankfurt am Main: Vervuert, 1993), pp.41–75; and A. Hildenbrand, 'Das Regionalismusproblem', in W.L. Bernecker and C. Collado-Seidel (eds), *Spanien nach Franco. Der Übergang von der Diktatur zur Demokratie 1975–1982* (München: Oehrlein, 1993), pp.104–26.

14. See the tenets advocated by A Coruña's socialist mayor Francisco Vázquez in J.A. Silva, *V de Vázquez* (Barcelona: Ronsel, 1994), pp.89–92; also Federación Española de Municipios y Provincias (FEMP), *Informe de la Asamblea General Extraordinaria. La Coruña, 5 y 6 de noviembre de 1993. Resoluciones* (Madrid: FEMP, 1994).

15. See a first sociological survey in M. García-Ferrando, *Regionalismo y autonomía en España, 1976–1979* (Madrid: CIS, 1982). On the rather confusing views held by the local press regarding the issue of decentralization during the late Francoist period, see M. Parés-Maicas, *La ideologia regional de la premsa espanyola (1966–1973)* (Barcelona: Ed. 62, 1984).

16. See PAR, *Diez años luchando por Aragón (1977–1987)* (Zaragoza: PAR, 1987). On the views of the PAR parliamentarian H. Gómez-de las Roces on the constitutional draft, and especially on the concept of the Spanish nation to be included in the Constitution, see X. Bastida, *La nación española y el nacionalismo constitucional* (Barcelona: Ariel, 1998), pp.142–3, where one finds that Navarrese and Aragonese regionalists were among the first to denounce the introduction of the term 'nationalities' in the constitution, not only because of its terminological ambiguity (the sole nation should be Spain), but also because of the distinction, which was considered discriminatory by regionalists, between 'regions' and 'nationalities'.

17. See H. Gómez-de las Roces, *El Estado del Estado de las Autonomías* (Zaragoza: Diputación General de Aragón, 1988).

18. On Valencian regionalism and its relationship with anti-Catalanism, see the article of A. Cucó, 'Notes sobre la Transició política i la qüestió nacional al País Valencià´, *L'Avenç*, Vol.201 (1996), pp.8–19. For some authors, Valencia's conservative regionalism has occasionally adopted the role of a far-right organization, by competing with the regional branch of PP. See X. Casals, *El fascismo. Entre el legado de Franco y la modernidad de Le Pen (1975–1997)* (Barcelona: Destino, 1998), p.84.

19. See the brochure *Partido Regionalista de Cantabria (PRC)* (Santander: PRC, 1978).

20. See contribution of M.A. Ropero (president of La Rioja's Party) to C. Navajas-Zubeldía (ed.), *Actas del Primer Simposio de Historia Actual de La Rioja* (Logroño: Gobierno de La Rioja/Instituto de Estudios Riojanos, 1996), pp.215–9. Another example would be the confusing inter-class appeal of the ideological tenets of the Partido Regionalista del País Leonés (PREPAL). Its second point establishes as its main purpose, 'the defence of Spain', while 'the defence of the interests of the Ancient Kingdom of León' appears in seventh place. See PREPAL, *Estatutos y Reglamento* (Salamanca: n. ed., 1984).

21. See an exhaustive exposition of UPN's founding tenets in the writings of one of its early leaders, L.F. Medrano y Blasco, *El partido foral necesario* (Madrid: n. ed., 1984), where Spanish nationalism, interpreted in a 'foral' way, goes hand in hand with extremely conservative tenets regarding the social role of the family and women, along with fiercely anti-Basque statements. For the historical background see also M.C. Mina, 'Navarrismo', in A. de Blas-Guerrero (ed.), *Enciclopedia del nacionalismo* (Madrid: Tecnos, 1997), pp.353–6.

22. For the historical background see S. de Pablo, *Los problemas de la autonomía vasca en el siglo XX. La actitud alavesa (1917–1979)* (Leioa: UPV, 1991); and for an extensive eyewitness account, as well as an exhaustive compilation of documents by a former founding

member of Unidad Alavesa, see J.G. Laburu, *El orgullo alavés* (San Sebastián: Sendoa, 1992). At the founding congress of UA there were delegates from UV, PRP and other regionalist parties, including two – much weaker – twin organizations from the Basque provinces of Guipúzcoa and Vizcaya.

23. See C.R. Aguilera-de Prat, 'Balance y transformaciones del sistema de partidos en España (1977–1987)', *Revista Española de Investigaciones Sociológicas*, Vol.42 (1988), pp.137–53, and M. Alcántara and M. A. Martínez (eds), *Las elecciones autonómicas en España, 1980–1997* (Madrid: CIS, 1999).

24. See J. de Juana, J. Prada and R. Soutelo, 'Transición y élites políticas: el nacimiento de Coalición Galega en Ourense', in J. Tusell *et al.* (eds), *Historia de la Transición y Consolidación Democrática en España (1975–1986)* (Madrid: UNED, 1995), Vol.I, pp.475–95.

25. See D. Garí-Hayek, 'Los nacionalismos periféricos ante la construcción política europea: el caso del archipiélago canario', in J.G. Beramendi, R. Máiz and X.M. Núñez (eds), *Nationalism in Europe: Past and Present* (Santiago de Compostela: USC, 1994), Vol.II, pp.447–67; J. Hernández-Bravo de Laguna and A. Millares-Cantero, 'Los partidos de centro-derecha en la Transición canaria: subestatalidad e insularismo', in Tusell *et al.* (eds), *Historia de la Transición*, pp.87–99; J. Hernández-Bravo de Laguna, *Historia popular de Canarias. Franquismo y Transición política* (Santa Cruz de Tenerife: Centro de la Cultura Popular Canaria, 1992).

26. See an extensive exposition of the enthusiastically proclaimed 'Madrid regionalism', by N. Piñeiro, *Madrid. Capital y región* (Madrid: n. ed., 1991).

27. 'El nuevo partido de Sergio Marqués le proclama presidente y candidato electoral', *El País*, 28 Feb. 1999, p.25; P. San Martín-Antuña, 'La configuración del sistema asturiano de PANE', unpublished paper, 1999.

28. The term 'institutional mimicry' was coined by W. Genieys for the study of the Andalusian case since the implementation of the state of the autonomous communities: see W. Genieys, *Les élites espagnoles face à l'État. Changements de régimes politiques et dynamiques centre-périphéries* (Paris/Montréal: L'Harmattan, 1997), pp.244–6 *et seq.*

29. J.L. Cascajo-Castro, 'El marco institucional', in J. Jiménez-Lozano *et al.*, *La identidad regional castellano-leonesa ante la Europa comunitaria* (Madrid: Centro de Estudios Ramón Areces, 1991), pp.31–58.

30. See a good example of 'invention of regional tradition' in the monumental work of I. Granado-Hijelmo, *La Rioja como sistema* (Logroño: Gobierno de La Rioja, 1993), 3 vols., particularly Vol.3, *La identidad riojana*. The author admitted, some years later, that the main motivation for undertaking this task had been to seek historical, ethnological, literary and all other arguments to buttress its main conclusion: 'La Rioja does exist, and consists of a diachronic, complex system of systems that are perfectly comprehensible, not only in their natural and social dimensions, but also ... from the perspective of the identity which serves as basis for the whole' (I. Granado-Hijelmo, 'La Comunidad Autónoma de La Rioja en el proceso autonómico español (1975–1996)', in Navajas-Zubeldía, pp.169–88). Similar endeavours to 'invent' a regional history for a new autonomous community have been undertaken in Cantabria: see the analysis of these attempts in the last chapter of M. Suárez-Cortina, *Casas, hidalgos y linajes. La invención de la tradición cántabra* (Santander: Límite/Univ. de Cantabria, 1994), as well as several examples in B. Madariaga-de la Campa (ed.), *Antología del regionalismo en Cantabria* (Santander: Diputación Provincial, 1989).

31. Data from Kraus, *Nationalismus*, pp.190–1.

32. F. Mota-Consejero, *Cultura Política y opinión pública en las Comunidades Autónomas: un examen del sistema político autonómico en España 1984–1996* (Barcelona: ICPS, 1998), Working Paper No.153.

33. M. Clavero-Arévalo, *España, desde el centralismo a las autonomías* (Barcelona: Planeta, 1983).

34. Gómez-de las Roces, p.38; PAR, *Por el progreso y la identidad de Aragón* (Zaragoza: PAR, 1991), pp.23–7, 54–7 and 73–5; PAR-Secretaría de Prensa, *Hablando desde Aragón* (Zaragoza: Guara Ed., 1992); J. González-Antón, *España y las Españas* (Madrid: Alianza, 1997), p.678.

35. E. Fernández-Clemente, 'Una reflexión sobre el nacionalismo desde Aragón', *Riff-Raff. Revista de Pensamiento y Cultura*, Vol.5 (1995), pp.29–33.
36. In the case of UV, two new parties emerged between 1995 and 1998: *Iniciativa de Progrés de la Comunitat Valenciana* and *Alternativa Valenciana*. Moreover, the youth branches of UV (Joventut Valencianista) also split from the party because of its lack of 'nationalism'. See S. Giménez, 'La fugida endavant d'Unió Valenciana', *El Temps*, Vol.22, No.11 (1998), pp.34–35.
37. Coalición Canaria, *La Primera Fuerza Política de Canarias. Un programa para Canarias* (n.p.: n. ed., 1996). A similar level of ambiguity and lack of congruity in its ideological definition was also noticeable in the Galician party *Coalición Galega*, whose 1985 political programme simultaneously declared Galician nationalism and full identification of Galicia with the 'Spanish nation'. See *Así faremos que Galicia sexa respetada. Programa de Coalición Galega* (Pontevedra: n.ed., 1985), pp.6–7.
38. In December of 1992 Alli stated at the UPN Party Conference that 'Navarre is a nation' (*El País*, 27 Dec. 1992, p.25), and he has subsequently attempted to develop his own doctrinal approach to the question of the 'Navarrese nationality'. See the briliant analysis of Navarrese regionalist tenets by B. Loyer, 'Nations, États et citoyens en Espagne', *Hérodote*, No.73–74 (1994), pp.76–91, as well as J. Cruz Alli's contribution to the book *El regionalismo en Europa* (Soria: Fundación Alfonso X, 1994).
39. 'Los partidos regionalistas acuerdan crear una plataforma', *El País*, 14 Dec.1998. p.16.
40. See M. Fraga, *Da acción ó pensamento* (Vigo: Ir Indo, 1992); id., *Impulso autonómico* (Barcelona: Planeta, 1994).
41. Among these theoretical elaborations of a 'cultural vindication' of Galician self-government without questioning the definition of Spain as a political nation, see X. Rodríguez-Arana and A. Sampedro-Millares, *O galeguismo* (Santiago de Compostela: FOESGA, 1998) and F. González, 'Nacionalismo', *La Región*, 19 Feb. 1999, p.29.
42. As P.A. Kraus has labelled it ('Der Autonomiestaat: Ein funktionsfähiges Dauerprovisorium?', *Tranvia. Revue der iberischen Halbinsel*, Vol.49 (1998), pp.24–6).
43. See, among others, F. Llera, *Los vascos y la política* (Bilbao: UPV, 1994); D. Petrosino, 'Autonomia e indipendentismo in Sardegna, in Catalogna e nel Québec: un tentativo di comparazione', in *Le autonomie etniche e speciali in Italia e nell'Europa mediterranea* (Cagliari: Consiglio Regionale della Sardegna, 1988), pp.214–31; M. García-Ferrando, E. López-Aranguren and M. Beltrán, *La conciencia nacional y regional en la España de las autonomía* (Madrid: CIS, 1994); Moreno, pp.129–35.
44. This point has been emphasized by B. de Riquer and E. Ucelay-Da Cal, 'An Analysis of Nationalisms in Spain. A Proposal for an Integrated Historical Model', in Beramendi *et al.*, Vol.II, pp.275–301. See also J.G. Beramendi's paper in this volume.
45. B. Anderson, *Imagined Communities. Reflections on the Origin and Spread of Nationalism* (London/New York: Verso, 1983).
46. J. Breuilly, *Nationalism and the State* (Manchester: Manchester University Press, 1993, 2nd ed.).

National Identity and Self-government in Spain: The Galician Case

ANTÓN LOSADA

The Autonomous Community of Galicia: An Institutional Description

The ratifiction of Galicia's statute of autonomy in 1981 ended the so-called 'provisional pre-autonomous regime'. The present model, called 'autonomía', implies very important levels of self-government and decentralization. The principal powers of the autonomic institutions (CCAA) and the Spanish central state are distributed into three different levels:

- Powers exclusive to the autonomous communities (AC): institutional organization, territorial organization, urban policies, health, fishing within domestic waters, education, culture, etc.
- Shared powers: the state determines the bases for these powers and the autonomous communities then legislatively assume and execute them. They are such matters as development and planning of economic activity, industry, agriculture, corporate credit institutions and savings and loans (*cajas de ahorros*).
- Powers expressly reserved for the national government: international relations, defence, foreign commerce, the monetary system, etc.

The institutional model of this autonomous community[1] (AC) falls within the most extended type in Spain. It is composed of a legislative assembly that includes 75 representatives; a governing council (*Xunta*) that directs the administration, and a high court of justice integrated within the general organization of the state justice administration. The parliament selects from among its members the president of the community, who in turn names and presides over the governing council.

The political history of the Galician *Xunta* has been characterized by instability due to the successive coalitions of the various political parties on the scene. This has marked the uncertain development of its institutions and

Antón Losada, University of Santiago de Compostela

has meant that administrative organizational problems regularly occupy a secondary position on Galician political leaders' agendas.

The pre-autonomic stage (1979–81) saw the centrist UCD as principal political force, mainly dedicated to the constitution of a legal and institutional framework for the Galician autonomous community. The first legislative period (1981–5), under Fernández Albor, with the *Alianza Popular* (AP) party governing in a minority, resulted in an administration that experienced grave difficulties in coordinating and directing its growth in an orderly fashion.

The second legislative period (1985–9) was marked by the intense political shock wave that occurred due to the mid-term crisis caused by the vice president, until then a veritable strong man of the Galician government, Xose Luis Barreiro. The departure of Barreiro, and a small group of representatives, from Alianza Popular left Fernández Albor and the AP in a situation of 'transition', a parliamentary stalemate and the loss of all political initiative and leadership capacity, which did not change until 1987. A convulsive motion of censure forced the end of the AP government. A three-party coalition took over in government: Partido Socialista Obrero Español (PSOE), and for the first time in Galician history, two moderate nationalist parties – the *Coalición Galega* and the *Partido Nacionalista Galego*. The rise to power of this tripartite coalition put the presidency in the hands of socialist González Laxe. This government would experience a critical point when Barreiro, once again vice president, faced the charge of abuse of power and was forced to resign.

The political weakness evident in the birth of the Galician autonomous community,[2] and a political arena dominated by the Spanish parties, along with the very limited presence of strictly nationalist forces, would generate throughout the 1990s a negotiation process for transferring resources that was subject to the priorities and necessities of the Spanish central administration, in contrast with what was taking place in the two other historic communities, Catalonia and Euskadi.

This process has been somewhat dysfunctional due to the high number of policy areas to be covered by the new-born Galician administration, in contrast with the limited material and human resources available. The temporary nature of a good number of the solutions adopted during the transfer process have severely hampered its development. In this sense, for example, although the bulk of the services and human resources necessary for executing the autonomic responsibilities had already been transferred, Galicia did not have its own legal framework for administration until the public administration law of 28 March 1988. This was subsequently modified in part by the law of 8 March 1991, during the Fraga government's first term, initiating an administrative reform project for Galicia.

The reform and modernization of the administrative structure of the Galician *Xunta* has gained a relevance under the Fraga government that had not formerly been experienced. It has progressively become one of the 'star' policies of this government and its position on the political leader's agenda has been clearly reinforced. This development occurs in conjunction with a clientelist use of administration resources, thus consolidating the Popular Party (PP) of Galicia as the manager of the resources flowing from the autonomic budget and European funds.

A radical change in the Galician political scene took place due to the overwhelming electoral victory of Manuel Fraga and the Popular Party (PP) in 1989, subsequently confirmed in 1993 and 1997, along with the strong rise of the previously almost non-existent Bloque Nacionalista Galego (BNG), which abandoned its more radical strategies. The BNG grew to proportions that threatened the PSOE's position as second Galician force, and in fact surpassed it in the autonomic elections of 1997. The parliamentary configuration for the first and second legislative terms (1981–5 and 1985–9) presented no political force with an absolute majority of the regional parliament's seats. During this time the governing parties in relative majority experienced processes of internal fragmentation and progressive loss of parliamentary support, with a concomitant political crisis and governmental instability. In contrast, after the autonomic elections of 1989 the party led by Manuel Fraga held an absolute majority in parliament, which should have sustained a solid government exhibiting clear leadership.

For the first time a solid leader was at the helm of the Galician government, based on stable and overwhelming parliamentary and social support, with an indisputable position as leader – both within the autonomous government and his own party – which citizens also clearly saw.[3] The hegemony of the PP was translated into a broad legislative programme and a normal functioning of the Galician *Xunta*, which gave rise to a notably stable political period, especially in comparison with the recent past in autonomic politics.

From this institutional perspective, and after these first stages of development and popular satisfaction over recovering self-government, Galicia and its *autonomía* face an increasing problem due to public perception of poor levels of regional performance. This problem is a part of a major question: how to ensure its institutional consolidation?

There are few sources of information available on levels of public satisfaction with institutional performance. There is a multiplicity of electoral surveys by the media, along with many public debates, but in the end there is insufficient information about the autonomous state. From the perspective of public policy analysis, we may note the work of a group of researchers from several Spanish universities (the ERA Project[4]). The first ERA report was published in 1997. Within Galicia public perceptions about *autonomía* present the following main characteristics:

- Growing acceptance of the levels of self-government: from 19 per cent in 1984 to 31 per cent in 1992.
- 40 per cent of Galicians demand more autonomy (Report 2.211, CIS 1996).
- 62 per cent of Galicians believe that decisions by the regional government have a direct impact upon their lives. This percentage is similar to percentages in other historical regions, like Catalonia or Euskadi.
- Galicians express a moderate degree of satisfaction with the performance of the regional government. The percentages are similar to those on the performance of the central government.

The legal development of the AC has been very intense: 146 regional laws have been approved between 1981 and 1995 (annual average: 9.7).[5] This level of activity means that Galicia is the fifth region in terms of legal production, following Navarra, Catalonia, Madrid and Euskadi. Of these, 74 laws can be defined as innovative in terms of contents and range, and some of these laws (four) regulate issues for the very first time.[6] ERA defines these regional regulations as more interventionist (50 laws) than regulative, a common characteristic among these regions with low degree of social and economic development. Most regional laws include a strong emphasis upon aspects of 'institutional design', including the creation of semi-private organizations as tools for public management and provision of public services; and, secondly, a very important degree of institutional socialization, including the creation of stable ways of participation for concrete social or professional groups.

This kind of situation highlights one of the main problems of Galicia as a nation: defining the real terms of the relationship between public power and society. The powers and resources of the *Xunta* have grown very quickly. The PP's long tenure in public office has stimulated the creation and consolidation of networks of exchange akin to forms of clientelism. The presence and involvement of the regional government is very high, creating a societal dependence on it. A key question for the future will be to re-define these relationships in the context of scarce public resources.

The Impact of Regional Institutions

Galicia's contemporary history presents two main elements: a low level of social and economic development, and the long process of consolidation that Galician nationalists forces have had to follow to achieve significant levels of political organization and electoral results – from the beginning of the twentieth century to the 1990s. The development and consolidation of regional institutions has had a very significant role in the radical transformation of both traditional characteristics.

The Social and Economic Impact of the AC

Galicia has traditionally been an agrarian region. Until the 1970s, the percentage of the working population in the primary sector was always above 50 per cent. This is especially relevant if we consider several sociological components of the primary sector in Galicia. These are:

1. A subsistence economy and a very high degree of property fragmentation.
2. A scattered population. In order to reduce costs, the population tended to settle down in small villages where familiar relations and traditions are very important. There were also very significant deficits in terms of communications, education and cultural formation.
3. The strong impact of very intense migration abroad.

After 1960 a process of increasing and sustained social and economic development began. During Franco's regime, the national plan of economic stabilization meant the creation of commercialization networks within agriculture, along with a slow process of modernization and industrial development. After a first great migration towards South America during the first part of the century, a second great migration took place, heading for Madrid, Catalonia and other parts of Europe.

TABLE 1
EVOLUTION OF THE WORKING POPULATION (%)

	1960	1981	1989	1991
Primary Sector	67.74	48.6	36.7	30.2
Industrial Sector	16.1	27.44	23.74	25.9
Tertiary Sector	16.16	23.96	39.56	43.9

Source: Instituto Galego de Estadística.

Table 1 shows the evolution of the working population from 1960 till now: the sustained growth of the industrial and service sectors has always been below Spanish average. It is important to point out that, despite all its weaknesses, this trend had significant consequences: an increasing concentration of population, greater urban development – in the leading as well as medium-sized cities – improvement in communications and, in the long term, the creation of new opportunities to break local isolation.

This process of urban development, nevertheless, has one relevant characteristic with very important consequences: urban and industrial development did not mean that people gave up agricultural activity. The introduction of capitalism was made in line with the land property fragmentation, in part because of slow industrial development.[7] This dynamic had several effects: it delayed the formation of a modern urban reality; it produced a particular synthesis between rural and urban realities – blue-collar workers maintaining agricultural activity; and it delayed the consolidation of an urban culture, favouring a slow modernization of rural social traditions.

The decade of the 1980s was a very important period for this modernization process in the Galician economy. The increasing importance of tertiary sector is the most relevant fact. The tertiary sector became the main force in this process of urban concentration and job creation, and also was the main protection against crisis in the other economic sectors.

TABLE 2
DISTRIBUTION OF THE WORKING POPULATION (%)

Sectors	Galicia 1995	Rest of Spain, 1995
Agriculture and fishery	28	8
Industrial	15	21
Construction	10	9
Services	47	62

Source: Instituto Galego de Estadística, INE

TABLE 3
EVOLUTION OF THE ECONOMIC STRUCTURE OF GALICIA
(% Gross Added Value)

	1955	1975	1981	1985	1991	1995
Agriculture	36.2	17.8	12.8	11.4	9.1	7.8
Industry	19.1	25.8	22.7	23.8	21.9	20.3
Building	7.2	8.5	9.0	7.4	11.4	11.7
Services	37.5	47.9	55.5	57.4	57.6	60.2

Source: Papeles de Economía Española[1]

TABLE 4
SECTORAL DISTRIBUTION OF GNP, 1993 (%)

	Galicia	Rest of Spain
Agriculture and Fishery	8.5	4.5
Industry	30.0	29.2
Services	61.5	66.3

Source: Fundación FIES[2]

Tables 2, 3 and 4 exemplify the economic evolution of Galicia, and also give us an idea of its impact on regional social conditions. The Galician economy has experienced a process of adaptation and structural change. This change has also taken place in the rest of Spain, and so the relative position of the Galician economy has not improved. This fact has put in doubt the global effectiveness of the entire process and set of policies implemented by all public administrations.

Despite all these problems, we can still identify very important opportunities for economic development: a high capacity for energy production, the creation and consolidation of an important industrial focus, the renovation of economic entrepreneurship, a strategic geographic position – near Portugal and within the Atlantic focus of development– and a very high level of institutional development for the region's financial system, especially the very important role that the AC is playing within the regional economy.

In fact, the real levels of self-government that the AC implies have been one of the most important determinants in the evolution of the Galician economy's growth. These are derived, first, from the importance of regional decisions for the allocation of public resources which traditionally were managed by the Spanish central government, along with their impact on the productive and social infrastructures; and secondly, from the political capacity of the regional government to articulate and organize regional economic and social interests in the Spanish and European arenas. The *Xunta* has a very broad range of powers: Galicia is one of the ACs with highest level of autonomy, close to that of Catalonia or Euskadi. Table 5 clearly illustrates the increasing impact of autonomic actions and decisions on the whole Galician economy.

The regional governments have implemented a very wide range of policies: both innovative policies with a high net value – such as fishery policies– which mean the implementation for the very first time of a global regulation and a global strategy, and also more conventional but equally necessary policies such as

- infrastructure policies, especially, road communications, services for industry and so on;
- education policy – increasing the number of educational services and universities (from one to three) and also encouraging a broad review of all curricula;
- communication policies: the development of regional public media and support for the development of modern communications networks (digital facilities);
- health policy: the creation of a regional public service (SERGAS), with

TABLE 5
PUBLIC EXPENDITURE EVOLUTION IN GALICIA
(in millions of pesetas)

	State	AC	Local	Total	% GNP
1985	53,874	113,822	73,619	541,15	33.0
1986	398,771	137,646	82,189	618,06	33.8
1987	428,332	155,120	82,577	666,29	31.1
1988	457,894	181,076	105.961	744,31	31.1
1989	562,972	240,179	135,66	938,17	35.0
1990	645,157	288,917	142,85	1,076,659	36.1
1991	10,509	468,396	164,66	1,243,071	39.6
1992	679,700	607,727	177,44	1,464,471	44.1
1993	760,066	645,590	190,06	1,595,762	45.0
1994	804,342	653,810	196,29	1,654,281	44.0

Source: Alvarez Corbacho 1996[3]

an important network of centres for primary care, and also the designing of new global regulations for health services (*Ley General de Sanidad*) and implementation of new models for financing and providing health services.

All these policies are having a very significant impact on the entire region, despite the absence of a global model for economic development for Galicia, a model to deal with the increasing problems arising in the traditionally principal economic sectors:

• Agricultural policy: problems of productivity and problems with European policy and its limits on production;
• Fishery policy: exclusion from a great number of foreign fishing waters like Argentina or Namibia;
• The global crisis in areas such as naval construction, timber management, and so on;
• Unemployment;
• An absence of real policies for the development of science and technology;
• Permanent infrastructure deficits: Galicia is still the only Spanish region with no highway communication with the rest of the country.

There are other factors that also constitute very important parts of the whole problem: an increasingly elderly population, the presence of a high percentage of workers with low skills, a more and more competitive general context, the weakness of civil society and its dependence on public resources, and inter-territorial competition with other Spanish regions for resources and political influence over the central government.

The decade of the 1980s has been a very significant period of modernization and urbanization in Galicia. During these years there has been a process of urban consolidation and also a very important process of improving communications and transport facilities. This process, along with the return of a very significant number of emigrants, has meant a breaking down of traditional isolation and localism.

This process of modernization has been very important in itself. But the limits and problems of the process have also been very important. The restructuring of the naval construction sector – a decision taken by the central government – the economic crises in agriculture and fishery – a consequence of the process of integration into the European Community – and the dramatic problem of unemployment have brought conflict both to the cities and to rural areas, which are traditionally conservative and highly conflict-averse. These dynamics have had two relevant consequences. First, important and broad social sectors have become aware of the existence of a common economic space with specific interests that can be articulated through regional institutions, and also the possibility of real conflict with other regional interests, the central government or European policies. As a result, an arena for conflict has been created, where nationalist forces can play a very important role and can obtain significant improvements in terms of consolidation, electoral results and political influence. If economic modernization is a basic cause for the weakening of localism, the crises of traditional economic sectors are a basic factor in the creation and representation of a new common identity

Policies and strategies implemented by regional institutions have also played a very important role throughout this process – by functioning as economic, legal or technical support for regional sectors in conflict, and by acting as a voice and a real leader for those regional interests in conflict within the Spanish political arena or even at the European political level. This role has also helped to consolidate a common perception among Galicians of a common space of economic and political interaction. This perception has reinforced pre-existing historical and social preconditions: language, culture, economic particularities and so on.

Finally, concerning the financial structure of the AC we can say that Galicia belongs to what is called a 'common regime for autonomous communities' developed on the basis of a general law passed by the Spanish parliament, plus a particular budget for financing health policy. European founds and general transfers from the central government are the largest part of regional budgets. There is also an increasing use of regional public debt as a source for financing regional institutions (in 1996 it was 8.7 per cent of GRP, the highest regional public debt in Spain).

TABLE 6
BUDGETS OF GALICIAN XUNTA
(In millions of pesetas)

Concept	1995	1996	Concept	1995	1996
Ordinary Revenues	642,431	684,219	Ordinary Expenditures	606,345	639,675
Capital Revenues	74,644	80,804	Capital Expenditures	150,048	156,536
Financial Revenues	62,797	54,602	Financial Expenditures	23,230	23,414
Total	779,872	819,625	Total	779,623	819,625

Source: Xunta de Galicia, official data

TABLE 7
EVOLUTION OF REAL INVESTMENT IN GALICIA
(In millions of pesetas)

Concept	1991	1992	1993	1994	1995
Real investments	98,533	101,679	105,091	93,074	94,431
GNP	3,135,097	3,313,812	3,544,307	3,753,861	4,035,944
ri/GNP	3.14	3.06	2.96	2.48	2.29

Source: Xunta de Galicia, official data

Because of all this, the financial future of Galicia presents several dilemmas:

• The increasing fiscal autonomy that it is being implemented by the central government (autonomous communities are responsible for 30 per cent of general taxation) can became a great opportunity for development of the regions and regional governments, but can also become a severe risk for it.
• This new situation is leading to increasing inter-territorial competition for public resources. The political influence of each regional government is a key factor in this kind of competition.
• Galicia does not have a real model of fiscal organization, nor a fiscal policy. This is still an open matter, and so questions arise concerning the relationships between public power and society. Tables 6 and 7, showing the increasing importance of regional budgets and the increasing importance of ordinary costs and the decreasing impact of real investment are good illustrations of this lack of real policy.

Social and Political Impact of Autonomous Community Status

Galicia presents a strong differential linguistic ethnicity, which is reinforced by a multiple cultural particularities such as customs, traditions, family relations and common strategies of production, due to the stunted social and economic development of the region. Nevertheless, this very strong differential base has traditionally presented a peculiar political and institutional deficit.

This historical failure of Galician nationalism to build a concept of nation accepted by a majority may be explained by very adverse social preconditions: a rural economy, a rural society, localism, strong domination relations through ownership of the land, the Catholic Church linked to the local élites, massive emigration, communications deficits, low urban development, lack of a bourgeoisie.[8] As a consequence, all through the last 200 years, Galician nationalism has faced a very adverse political opportunity structure. If we examine the recent history of nationalism in Galicia, we observe three main dynamics:

- Permanent tension between a conservative and traditionalist nationalism (Brañas, Grupo Nós, Vicente Risco) and a liberal one (Grupo de A Coruña, Villar Ponte, Pereira, Bóveda, Castelao).
- A strong imbalance between the very important cultural development of nationalism and its very low levels of political and organizational development.
- Constant 'communication problems' between nationalist groups and élites – urban professionals and other people with little interest in rural problems – and the majority composed of rural people. This implied an absence of 'master symbols' that could be perceived as identification labels for the entire country.

The Spanish Civil War and Franco´s regime broke the slow political progress of nationalism that had evolved from the beginning of the twentieth century until the Second Republic, within which nationalist parties had obtained their best electoral results and the autonomy statute was approved and passed. Nationalist forces had to begin anew under Francoism. This stage resulted in a radical discontinuity. Official repression was highly selective and especially hard for left-wing nationalist parties. The leaders had to choose between abandoning political action and exchanging it for some kind of 'cultural action' or exile abroad. As a consequence, new generations faced a process of 're-founding' political nationalism. This process meant breaking with the political tradition of republican nationalism and the evolution of several groups towards some kind of 'radical anti-colonialism'.

During these years there were three main forces within the nationalist groups: socialists, Christian democrats and extreme left. The most organized nationalist political party was the *Unión do Pobo Galego* (UPG), on the extreme left. UPG was inspired by principles such as Marxist-Leninism, a third world vision, anti-colonialism and proletarian nationalism. The absence of a moderate nationalist party in Galicia similar to those present in Catalonia or Euskadi is especially relevant. This can be explained by considering the difficulties in incorporating the Galician middle class, a group that had its interests well represented by Spanish parties.

The Spanish transition to democracy and the constitution of 1978, the first democratic elections and creation and development of the *estado de las autonomías* model, in addition to the improvement in social and economic preconditions in Galicia, have meant a radical transformation of reality and the creation of new political opportunities for nationalism.

The political and electoral dynamics between the approval of the Spanish Constitution in 1978 and the great Socialist victory in 1982 in the Spanish general election have been characterized by three main variables:

• Weakness in political participation (see Figure 1). Two provinces of Galicia (Lugo, Ourense) are among those with the lowest electoral participation in Spain.
• The existence of a certain degree of moderate pluralism and relatively short ideological distance between the main parties, and especially, a predominance of conservative voters and its logical consequence – conservative parties (UCD, AP, PP) always win in Galicia (see Figure 2).
• Weak presence of nationalist parties within an electoral space clearly dominated by Spanish parties.

The severe electoral defeat of nationalist parties in 1982 (80 per cent of votes went to Spanish parties) meant a massive rejection of their proposals. This defeat opened a process of redefinition of political space: a reduction in the number of parties and the formation of a system composed of three main political parties, with the following dynamics:

• An internal crisis within the UPG and left-wing nationalism, followed by the creation of two political forces: *Esquerda Galega* and the *Bloque Nacionalista Galego* (BNG). *Esquerda Galega* was to vanish, after relative electoral success in 1985; BNG developed after 1985 a strategy of moderation. This strategy, plus great organizational capacity and high levels of activism, allowed the BNG to increase its presence within the electoral space of Galicia. The BNG subsequently concentrated both nationalist votes and organizations. The strategy of moderation implied giving up traditional ideological positions, accepting the Spanish

FIGURE 1
ELECTORAL NON-PARTICIPATION IN GALICIA

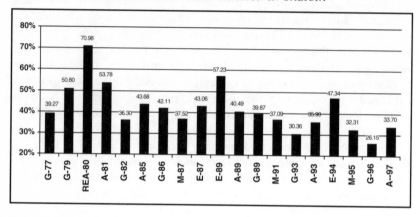

G: General elections
REA: Referéndum Estatuto de Autonomía
A: Autonómic
M: Local
E: European Parliament

Source: Official data

FIGURE 2
DISTRIBUTION OF SEATS IN REGIONAL PARLIAMENT

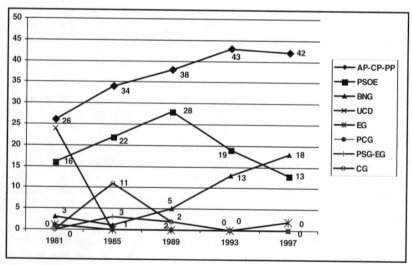

Source: Official data

constitutional framework and developing an integrative discourse (the 'common project') characterized by calculated measures of populism and ambiguity ('the defence of the interests of Galicia').

- A temporary presence – in the elections of 1985 – of one moderate nationalist party (*Coalición Galega*, or CG). This party achieved notable levels of organization, institutional presence and electoral results (24 per cent of the votes in 1985 elections). The fragmentation of CG meant a temporary loss of power by the PP due to the creation of a coalition between three parties: PSOE, CG and PNG (a group that came from CG).

- The appearance of Manuel Fraga, a traditional leader of the Spanish right, during the 1989 regional elections. Manuel Fraga clearly won the election and this gave rise to a period of relative political stability (he went on to be re-elected in 1993 and 1997). Manuel Fraga also opened a new stage of internal evolution inside the PP. This stage has been characterized by an evolution towards regionalism along with the reinforcing of the party's political organization and institutional presence. Other elements include the intensive use of cultural and folk elements and a strategy of conflict with the Spanish Socialist government based on a regionalist dialectic.

- The disappearance of moderate nationalist parties – this electoral space was taken over by the PP – and also of moderate left-wing nationalism.

- Great problems and internal crises suffered by the socialist party (PSOE), locked into a very complicated situation. The policies implemented by the socialist central government (many of them with a very high cost for the economy of Galicia), a very conservative organization and also the defeat of the party in the Spanish elections of 1997, can explain why the BNG obtained more votes than PSOE in the last regional elections.

- Decreasing levels of non-voting. During the 1990s levels of participation in regional elections and Spanish elections tended to become similar.

The modernization of political life in Galicia has been promoted both by the moderation process within left-wing nationalism and the evolution process within the main right-wing party towards regionalism.[9] These processes have also meant increasing levels of electoral participation in Galicia, nearing those of the rest of Spain, and an increasing *galleguización* (Galicianization) of political life: all political forces – nationalists or not – now assume the discourse of regional difference and the need to use the regional language. This has helped create a common base or master frame, which is used by all the parties: defence of the culture and language of Galicia, defence of 'Galicia's national interests'. This process of construction has been encouraged by the development of regional public media, which constitute a very visible space for debate and political interaction.

In Figure 3, we clearly see which are the main paths of political evolution in Galicia: the clear dominance of one right-wing regionalist party (PP), the failure of the main Spanish left wing party (PSOE), and the growth of a left wing nationalist party (BNG). The reasons for this growth can be traced to the social and economic changes that accompanied the process of modernization and urbanization of Galicia during the twentieth century; to the severe crises in the industrial, agricultural and fishery sectors which are very important elements in forming a kind of 'common interests matrix' in opposition to those interests represented by the European Community and the rest of Spain, and especially central government policies; to the institutional impact of autonomic institutions and autonomic policies; and to a successful mobilization of organizational and interpretative resources.

FIGURE 3
EVOLUTION OF VOTING IN ALL ELECTIONS

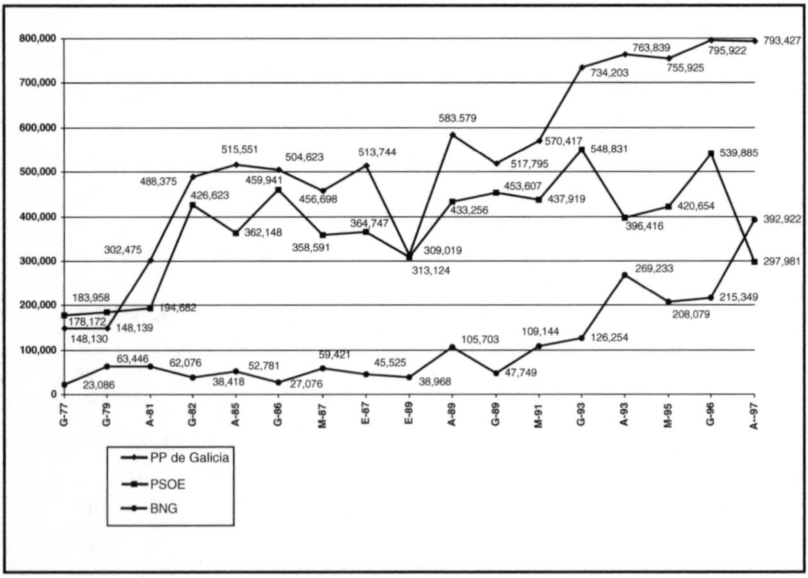

G: GENERAI
A: Autonomics
M: Local
E: European

Source: Official data

Institutions Matter: The Impact of Autonomy on National Identity and Some Ideas for Further Study

The hypothesis underlying this work can be summarized as that the creation and rapid development of the autonomous community and its institutions function as one of the key variables that have altered, and continue altering, the social preconditions for nationalism in Galicia. This variable is also helping to create a political opportunity structure that favours the development of nationalism. This progression is clearly visible if we take a look at recent electoral results and the evolution of the main parties. Autonomy is also favouring the process of building a 'Galician nation', the process of political, organizational, discursive 'production' of a nation – following the assumption that a nation as such is not something 'natural' or 'given', but rather the result of a process of social and political construction. Autonomic institutions are doing this in several ways:

- The consolidation and institutionalization of an ethnic base (language, culture, history, and institutions) that it is being built upon a pre-existing raw materials. This base is now being elaborated, manipulated and re-defined, in part through institutional action by the regional administration: through language normalization, through the creation and development of regional services and media and so on.
- The mobilization of resources and its impact on the social and economic preconditions for mobilization: greater social mobility and supra-local communication, more important economic, legal and technical resources, the formation of a common matrix of interests.
- The re-creation of a new political structure of opportunity: better access to institutions – the creation of new institutional settings, greater political participation and so on.
- The creation of nationalist 'interpretative frames' and their institutionalization through particular policies (education, health, culture, communications.)

It seems relatively simple to identify particular regional public policies, their outputs and outcomes (see Table 8) that are operating in this sense. These policies are a direct result of regional action, and they have a direct impact upon the building process of a national identity accepted by the majority.

A deeper analysis of this initial information allows us to formulate, and even confirm, our hypothesis: policies implemented by the regional government and their relative success have contributed to institutional consolidation of the autonomous community and have contributed to the consolidation of a national identity. Certain policies, their results and outcomes (see Table 8), directly and exclusively result from autonomic activity and have significant impact upon the construction process of a broadly accepted national identity. This helps to develop a certain political self-image as a broadly accepted collective identity which becomes extended enough to reach the mass level.

The policies carried out by the Galician *Xunta* and their relative success are contributing to the institutional consolidation of the autonomous community and this in turn brings about certain relevant effects on what we might label the 'political, institutional and identity production' of the Galician nation. This process of construction may be understood as the combination of the following elements:

Political. The idea of nation and of national identity as the determinant factors in the legitimacy and representativeness of the political actors and parties; the expansion of the political competition sphere centered around the national space; an increase in the stability of electoral alignments, open doors and access for nationalist forces to the institutions; the incorporation of these élites into the process of institution building.

Institutional. The growth of the nationalist or regionalist groups' organizational and material resources, the expansion of the institutional spaces that nationalist forces have access to, the capacity of these institutions to compete for the allocation of resources in the national and supranational arenas.

Identity. The discursive and mythic/symbolic processes that identify a collective national identity with its own interests and objectives based on 'national' solidarity *vis-à-vis* other forms of collective solidarity (class, etc.); the legitimation of national public policies and cultural homogenization, the development of a centre/periphery discourse and competition with other nationalities for resources during a process of state construction.

These effects are caused by policies implemented by the AC. These effects are a direct, and almost exclusive, product of this regional action. No other administration has worked in this direction at any prior time. These effects are producing new situations:

- There are concrete changes in substantial aspects: the articulation of a solid common identity; better levels of organization in defending common interests; and support for processes of political, organizational and discursive construction of the nation, such as an increasing use of and institutionalization of the regional language (*Gallego*), better communications, the weakening of localism, educational and cultural changes, the institutionalization of nationalist values and the nationalist interpretative frame (history, culture, traditions, mobilization of resources in defence of 'Galician interests').

- Regional policies have become the most important institutional arrangement in many areas of public action: health, education, and fisheries. Regional laws and regulations have become real game rules for most actors; they act, handle conflicts and demands, and achieve solutions within a regional regulatory context. They also organize themselves using regional support.

- The political, economic and social actors of Galicia now use the regional arena as the main space for developing their strategies and relationships. They also employ the regional arena and regional institutions as a sort of 'spokesman' for their common interests. Regional government has became a key element in competition for resources and policies with other Spanish or European regions. Developing this function, the regional government has also supported different processes oriented towards a better articulation and organization of several economic sectors of Galicia in order to defend their common interests within the Spanish or European arenas.

- The regional government – and administration – has consolidated its position and has improved the perceptions other regional actors have about its relevance and performance. They use it to gain support, as an element of reference and also as an opponent, and so the legitimization of regional institutions is no longer in doubt.

Some empirical data seem to indicate this by showing the clear impact of policies implemented by the regional government on people's perceptions about the autonomous community and regional institutions, especially if we compare them with what was available at the beginning of the 1990s.

Various electoral surveys published by the media before regional elections in 1997 showed that about 50 per cent of Galicians have a positive evaluation of regional government activity, while 36 per cent do not. About 48 per cent of Galicians believe that Galicia is better off with the AC. Another survey, this one done by the regional government, shows that a majority – 64.4 per cent – of the people who have interacted with the regional administration have a positive evaluation of this administration, and this percentage clearly increases for people living in rural areas. The most extended criticism refers to slowness in administrative procedures. More recent and reliable data – the first public opinion barometer done by the University of Compostela political science department, in March 1998,

TABLE 8

THE IMPACT OF AUTONOMIC INSTITUTIONS ON NATIONAL IDENTITY

Arena	Output	Outcome	'Nation production'
Health policy	• SERGAS • Health regulation • Assistance network	• Regional health network • Increasing financial resources	*Institutional* 1. Administrative and geographic identification of a common service *Political* 2. Visible inter-regional competition for resources and services 3. Integration of professional élite
Education policy	• Academic programmes • Language regulation	• Increasing use of Galician language • Nationalist revisionof history, culture, etc. • New universities and investigation units	*Institutional* 1. Administrative and geographic identification of a common service *Political* 2. Integration of professional élite *Identity* 3. Increasing use of a common language 4. Increasing culture identification 5. Institutionalization of political and cultural national ist myths
Public administration	• Regional, visible administration • SGPA • Information system	• Regional bureaucracy • Financial, legal and technical resources	*Identity* 1. Institutionalization of Galician language *Political* 2. Integration of professional élite 3. Creation of a professional élite *Institutional* 4. Common administrative identification 5. Materialization of a common identity 6. Creation of procedures

Communication	• TVG • RAG	• Creation of regional media space	*Identity* 1. Increasing use of Galician language 2. Mass diffusion *Institutional* 3. Creation of an audiovisual network based on language *Political* 4. New arena for political competition 5. Integration of professional and business élite
Fisheries policy	• General regulation	• Economic organization of a key sector	*Political* 1. Common identity: regional interest competing with foreign interests *Identity* 2. Supranational conflicts for resources *Institutional* 3. Administrative and geographic identification of a common service
Transport policy	• Official Plan for highways and roads	• Better communications	*Political* 4. Breaking local isolation 5. Optimizing common space *Institutional* 6. Administrative and geographic identification of a common service

Source: Author.

also shows a clear evolution in the perceptions of Galicians concerning regional institutional significance: a third of the population evaluated positively recent regional government action. This evaluation is especially positive in areas of public action such as road construction and transport policies (82.8 per cent), housing policy (51.4), health policy (44 per cent) and education policy (43 per cent). This evaluation is, in turn, especially negative about areas of public action such as employment policy (52.2), agricultural policy (49.5 per cent) and fishery policy (41.8 per cent).

Other significant results of this survey are that Galicians have a positive attitude towards the performance of regional institutions (45.5 per cent); that a majority demands increased levels of self-government (56.9 per cent); that Manuel Fraga and the leader of the BNG, X.M. Beiras, are the political leaders who receive the highest approval rates (6.26 and 5.32) and greatest confidence (55.8 per cent and 41.2 per cent); and that the PP and BNG are perceived as those political forces that have the best capacity to defend the interests of Galicia (37.8 per cent and 35 per cent), but that the PP is the party that really has enough public confidence to be able to govern (53.6 per cent compared to 19.4 per cent for the BNG).

These data are, of course, just indicative. Deeper and more specialized research will be needed in order to confirm that regional institutions matter – and how– in the building process of Galician national identity, and if so, why, when and how they do.

NOTES

1. For a more detailed explanation of the institutional model of Galicia and its functioning, see F. Caamaño, R. Máiz, X.M. Rivera and X. Vilas, *O Sistema Político galego: as Institucións* (Vigo: Editorial Xerais, 1994).
2. The statute of autonomy was approved in a referendum in which fewer than 40 per cent of electors voted, and the subsequent autonomic elections barely exceeded 50 per cent participation.
3. In recent electoral surveys (Voz de Galicia, Decembre 1996, July 1997 and October 1997) Manuel Fraga appeared as the most valued leader and the most recognized Galician politician. The rest of the Galician government occupied much lower positions in the ranking and only one of them, José Cuiña, was recognized by more than 50 per cent. For a more detailed insight see R.L. Blanco Valdés, *Galicia. Informe Comunidades Autónomas 1996* (Barcelona: Instituto de Derecho Público, 1997), Vol.1, pp.291–313; N. Lagares, *Genesis y Desarrollo de Partido Popular* (Madrid: Tecnos, 1999).
4. Informe ERA, *Informe España 1996, Una Interpretación de su Realidad Social* (Madrid: Fundación Encuentro, 1997.)
5. ERA information, 1997.
6. Ibid.
7. For a more detailed examination of the introduction of capitalism in Galicia see: E. Pérez Touriño, *Agricultura y capitalismo. Análisis de la pequeña producción campesina* (Madrid: Ministerio de Agricultura, 1983), and also J. Cabrera Varela, 'Las Precondiciones Sociales

de la Identidad Colectiva de Galicia', *Historia y Crítica,* No.4 (1994), pp.209–39; J.
Carmona Badía, *El Atraso Industrial de Galicia; 1750–1900* (Barcelona, 1990); R. Villares,
La Propiedad de la Tierra en Galicia 1500–1936 (Madrid, 1982); R. Villares, *A Historia*
(Vigo: Galaxia, 1984).
8. For a deeper analysis of the historical evolution of nationalism in Galicia see X. Beramendi,
O Nacionalismo Galego (Vigo: A Nosa Terra, 1995); X. Beramendi, *De provincia a Nación.*
O galeguismo político 1840–1936 (Vigo, 1998); Ramón Máiz Suárez, *O Rexionalismo*
Galego: Organización e Ideoloxía (Publicacións do Seminario de Estudios Galegos,
Edicións do Castro, 1984); id., 'Nación de Breogán: Oportunidades Políticas y estrategias
Enmarcadoras en el Movimiento Nacionalista Gallego (1886–1996)', *Revista de Estudios*
Políticos, No.92 (Abril-junio 1996), pp.33–78; id., *A Idea de Nación* (Vigo: Xerais, 1997).
9. For a deeper analysis of recent trends of political life and the evolution of the main political
parties see X.M. Rivera Otero, *Os Partidos políticos en Galicia* (Vigo: Xerais, 1998).

III. VARIATIONS ON THE THEME OF
IDENTITY, AUTONOMY, AND NATIONALISM

Autonomy of the Sacred: The Endgame in Kosovo

STEVEN MAJSTOROVIC

The ongoing conflict and tragedy in Serbia's southern province of Kosovo[1] (see Figure 1) brings into sharp focus the issues of state sovereignty, territorial autonomy, separatism, irredentism, independence, human rights, war crimes, and international recognition in the post-1989 international system. In the Balkans, ethnic conflagrations are rarely contained within a compact territory and often spread beyond their original flashpoints. Consequently, there is a sense of urgency in the international community, to limit the strife before this latest round of Balkan warfare metastasizes beyond Kosovo.

Kosovo's relatively small 6,200 square miles of territory presents a history of shifting demographic balances and migration and expulsion patterns over the centuries. Perhaps only the struggle between Israelis and Palestinians over the tiny West Bank is as emotionally charged and is similarly characterized by competing and generally incommensurable interpretations of history. The conflicting interpretations of history between the Serbs and Albanians over Kosovo cannot be resolved, but any reasoned analysis of Albanian-Serbian relations, particularly during the twentieth century, reveals a tit-for-tat pattern in which each side has taken turns oppressing the other, and an exclusive focus on either side of the argument is extremely ahistorical.[2]

During the Balkan wars in the early twentieth century Kosovo changed hands from Ottoman Empire dominance to Serbian control, and then after World War Two shifted from a demographic balance between Albanians and Serbs to a population that was 90 per cent Albanian at the beginning of 1999. Moreover, since 1968 the status of Kosovo gradually changed from an autonomous region within the former Yugoslav Federation's Serbian republic to quasi-republican status by 1974, and since the late 1980s, back to Serbian control and the loss of autonomous status for the province. Until the NATO bombing campaign in the spring of 1999, Kosovo's Albanians and Serbs both made maximal demands. The Albanians pursued both violent and non-violent strategies toward secession and an independent

Steven Majstorovic, University of Wisconsin at Eau Claire

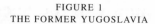

FIGURE 1
THE FORMER YUGOSLAVIA

Albanian Kosovo, which would become part of a greater Albania. The Serbs used the levers of state repression to enforce a *status quo* that bordered on apartheid in order to protect what they consider the cradle of Serbian civilization and cultural identity.

The conflict essentially remained non-violent from 1989 to 1996. The leadership of Ibrahim Rugova and his strategy of Albanian passive resistance to Belgrade garnered a lot of international support, but the situation remained static. Since 1996, however, a new force, the Kosovo Liberation Army (KLA) began a violent anti-Serb insurrection. By the spring and summer of 1998, intense fighting between the KLA and both Yugoslav army and special police forces resulted in the expulsion of 60,000 to 80,000 Albanians from Kosovo's western border in order to establish a 'cordon sanitaire',[3] but this did not solve Belgrade's problems. By August 1998, another 150,00 Albanian civilians were driven from their villages in the central part of the province as Serbian forces pursued the overmatched KLA secessionists. At the same time the KLA terrorized and kidnapped Serb civilians and in some cases, Serb populations also were driven from their villages.[4]

The situation changed dramatically in early October 1998 as the US decided to bypass a strategy of getting UN Security Council agreement to bomb the Serb military positions and instead garnered NATO support for a credible military ultimatum to force the Serb leader, Slobodan Milosevic, to back down and withdraw the bulk of his troops from Kosovo.[5] The NATO effort was led by special US Ambassador Richard Holbrooke, who made it clear that if Milosevic had not made some important concessions, the Serbs would certainly have been bombed toward the end of October.[6] What galvanized the international community was a particularly gruesome slaughter of a dozen Albanian women, children, and elderly. A man who survived the incident claimed that Serb paramilitary forces wearing masks descended on his village and massacred the helpless civilians.[7] Yet despite the ominous military threats throughout most of October 1998, the Serbian forces only reluctantly withdrew.[8] The situation, however, quickly destabilized as thousands of Albanian villagers returned to their destroyed and looted homes and the KLA moved into the areas vacated by the Serbs. Since the KLA was not a party to the agreement signed between Holbrooke and Milosevic, the KLA leadership vowed to continue its campaign to establish an independent Kosovo.[9]

By February 1999, the violent repression of Kosovo's Albanian population by the Yugoslav military, along with the KLA's campaign of assassination and terror, precipitated the direct involvement of the United States in a series of meetings in Rambouillet, France. The US decided to bypass the UN Security Council, and Russian or Chinese resistance, and declare Kosovo a European issue that would fall under NATO's sphere of interests. Although the meetings were called 'negotiations', the Serbs and Albanians never engaged in any direct face-to-face talks. The 'peace agreement' that the US drafted required the pull-out of all Yugoslav troops from Kosovo and the introduction of NATO peacekeepers. However, the language of the proposal did not technically relinquish Yugoslav state sovereignty over the province and both the Albanian side (dominated by the KLA) and the Yugoslav side refused to sign. But within a few days the KLA was persuaded to sign on to the proposal when the language of the new draft included a proposal for a referendum on independence after a three-year interim period and the Serbs were left with an ultimatum: sign or be bombed. Typically, the Serbs refused and in March NATO commenced to bomb Yugoslavia and Kosovo for almost 80 days.

The results of this action are now well known. Over 700,000 Kosovo Albanians were ethnically cleansed from their homes and escaped into neighboring Albania, Macedonia, Montenegro, and even Serbia. Hundreds and perhaps even thousands of Albanian men were executed by Serbian paramilitary units and the civilian population terrorized and humiliated.

Despite the efficacy and precision of NATO's weapons, up to 5,000 Serb civilians were killed in what was referred to a 'collateral' damage and many Albanians were killed in Kosovo itself as civilian targets were also included along with military ones. NATO warplanes defied international norms and even used cluster bombs to root out Yugoslav troops. Unfortunately, their anti-personnel weapons also took a heavy toll of civilians' lives.[10]

Eventually the Serbs capitulated to NATO's demands only after the Russians became an intermediary in the negotiations and because the new agreement did not call for a three-year interim period to be followed by a referendum on independence. This detail was extolled as a victory by Milosevic as he surveyed his environmentally damaged[11] and destroyed country and contemplated his indictment for war crimes by the Hague tribunal. In the wake of NATO's victory, the Albanians began to flood back into Kosovo. Spearheaded by the KLA, Albanian Kosovars now began to attack Serb civilians and make them victims of terror and ethnic cleansing. Thousands of Serbs fled Kosovo despite the guarantees of slowly arriving NATO forces, who could not fill the vacuum that the KLA quickly exploited in the immediate aftermath of the bombing halt. Within a few days after the end of the NATO campaign, grisly scenes of mass graves of Albanians were discovered. How many civilians were killed by the Serbs and how many were killed by NATO bombs is still debatable, but most observers would agree that the majority of the Albanian victims died at the hands of the Serbs. For their part, the Albanians and the KLA continued the Balkan tradition of revenge as they killed Serb civilians, looted and burned homes, destroyed Orthodox churches, and were even caught using a torture chamber in the town of Prizren where dozens of Serbian and Roma victims were found by NATO troops.[12]

Instead of exclusively military solutions, however, this essay will explore a possible conflict resolution arrangement than can be best described as mixed autonomy. In this arrangement, the issues of Albanian territorial aspirations would be balanced with the powerful ethnic identity markers that Kosovo and certain areas within Kosovo symbolize for Serbs. This paper suggests that such a mixed autonomy solution can satisfy the bulk of Albanian territorial and demographic demands and can also reassure the cultural identity needs of the Serbs. Before this recommendation can be explored, however, it is necessary to plunge into the murky waters of Balkan history to support the contention that in Kosovo, as in the rest of the Balkans, agnosticism is the reasoned approach and is the best way to avoid the pitfalls of ethnophilism in support for any particular group. One of the directors of the United States Institute of Peace, Chester Crocker, contends that many factors are involved in considering the varieties of pre-emptive conflict intervention and in assessing the conditions necessary for success.

Crocker makes it clear that 'it helps to know something about the place in which intervention is to occur. When a great nation decides to engages in the affairs of distant regions, it should first make sure that the necessary homework has been done.'[13]

History in the Making and Unmaking

Almost every ethnonational group in Eastern Europe can remember or 'imagine' a medieval golden age when it reached a pinnacle of cultural achievement and territorial expansion, and it is this territorial expanse that many of these groups still believe should be their true borders today. But despite the heights reached in antiquity, much of the second millennium found these groups under the domination of one great empire or another, be it Ottoman, Austro-Hungarian or Russian.[14] But the glories of the past still exercise a powerful psychological hold on contemporary nations like the Serbians and Albanians.

For the constructionists and instrumentalists in the field of ethnic studies it has become chic to assume that ethnic or ethnonational identity is malleable and populations, especially uneducated peasants, can easily be manipulated and led into war. A strict primordialist orientation toward the genesis of ethnonational identity, which sees identity as an ontological given and evokes terms like 'ancient hatreds', is generally limited to sociobiological perspectives.[15] The mainstream anthropological approaches to primordial identities do not assume an unchanging given in examining a particular ethnic identity but do leave some room for change over time.[16] These intellectual differences can be resolved to some extent when we realize that although the state is modern, the modern nation has its past firmly rooted in a history that predates the modern nation-state. This past has been invented, imagined, constructed, remembered, and reconstructed by ethnic élites and nationalists in an ongoing process that combines history and contemporary events for the preservation of national identity. In short, this past is a sort of geological project in which historical layers and sediments are chosen for particular exploitation by ethnic entrepreneurs. But the past also limits and constrains the choices that ethnonational leaders make and – as will be discussed later in this paper – Slobodan Milosevic, without foresight, came to power by using Kosovo as a call to arms to the Serbs, and it may be that Kosovo will also be his undoing.[17]

Consequently, at any given historical juncture such as the recent ethnonational confrontation in Kosovo, the past and the present are collapsed in an ongoing narrative that is an endless iterative process of identity reinforcement and adjustment. This process, which can be labelled 'primordialization',[18] seeks justification for today's behaviour through the remembrance of the past. For the Albanians and the Serbs this can be a heady brew that is hard to put down. The subjective nature of this narrative makes the presentation of 'objective' history an almost fruitless endeavour. In simple terms, in order to understand the motivations of Serbs and Albanians it must be stressed that what has behavioural consequences is not what *is* but what people *believe to be*. Thus it is tragic and unfortunate that when it comes to the history of events in Kosovo, what the Serbs believe and what the Albanians believe are rarely in agreement and the competition between competing narratives is more than just a bloodless academic exercise. The limits and constraints imposed by historical memory, for both masses and élites, has outcomes that often result in death and destruction.[19] If one could induce a state of historical Alzheimer's disease throughout the Balkans, then everyone could start over with a blank slate. But ethnonational groups do possess shared memories; this historical clay of memories is reshaped by each generation, and what has been shaped in a previous epoch constitutes a constraint on the political élites in a subsequent historical period. In the case of Kosovo, the shape of the historical clay also limits the choices for peace and compromise.

The great ethnonational enterprise of the Albanians since World War Two has been to establish the link between the modern Albanian nation and the ancient Illyrians in order to prove that the former has been in constant existence in both Albania proper and in Kosovo. The archaeological effort has been somewhat successful in Albania, especially along the Adriatic coastline. However, an extensive effort in the mid 1980s to unearth evidence of Albanian settlements in Kosovo that predate the Slavic migration in the sixth century has only produced evidence of Roman and pre-Roman artefacts but no proof of extensive Albanian settlement before that century. But west of Kosovo, the name 'Albanii' had came into common usage by that time, and their language was called Albanian.[20] It should be noted that some Albanians consider the link between the ancient Illyrians and the ancient Greeks a strong one and they surmise that the contemporary Albanians are the true descendants of Aristotle and Plato.[21]

The Serbian connection to Kosovo is a product of the Slavic migrations into Eastern Europe during the fifth to seventh centuries. The Serb move into the Kosovo region during the sixth century was simply the migration of undifferentiated Slavic tribes. The Greeks Christianized the Serbs by the ninth century and through a series of royal dynasties, especially the Nemanja dynasty of the thirteenth century, the Serbs established their own autocephalous Serbian Orthodox church under the leadership of St Sava, a royal prince turned monk. This was the beginning of Serbian ascendancy in the Balkans and during the fourteenth century under Tsar Dusan, the Serbian empire was the dominant force in the Balkans. Dusan's empire covered an area from the Adriatic at Dubrovnik to the Danube, into western Bulgaria and into most of Albania and some areas in northern Greece. Dusan also continued and accelerated the practice[22] of monastery building. These beautiful structures with ornate frescos and icons in the interior were built everywhere in what today is modern Serbia, Montenegro, and Macedonia. Most of the monasteries and churches, however, were built in Kosovo. It is the presence of this historical reminder of past glories that brings the past into the present for most Serbs. Dusan's empire was in a sense an early example some of the trappings of a modern state. He established a uniform legal code throughout the empire, and the rights of nobles and peasant were clearly spelled out.[23]

After the death of Dusan in 1355, the centralized system that he established began to unravel as the Serbian nobility competed for power. This unravelling was temporarily halted when Prince Lazar came to power in 1371. But this last period of what the Serbs consider their golden age soon came to an end on 28 June 1389 (15 June in the Julian calendar that is still followed by much of the Orthodox faith) at Kosovo Polje (the field of blackbirds), which is just a few miles out side modern Kosovo's provincial capital of Pristina. 28 June is a critical day in Serbian mythology. This day, called *Vidovdan* (St Vitus' day), commemorates the Battle of Kosovo, the assassination of Austrian Archduke Ferdinand by a Bosnian Serb (Gavrilo Princip) in 1914, and the date of the first Yugoslav constitution in 1921. Along with Christmas, Easter, and the saint's day (Slava) of the Serbian family, it is considered the holiest of days.

The confrontation between the Serbs and the Ottoman Turks was in the immediate aftermath of the battle perceived by the Ottoman Empire as either a pyrrhic victory or indecisive. In fact, the Serbian state survived for another 70 years of infighting while the Ottoman Turks left to lick their wounds, marshal their superior resources, and finally return to conquer the Balkans. The cataclysmic nature of the battle, however, was the prime stuff of which legends and myths are made. In this battle, which lasted eight to ten-hours, the losses were incredible on both sides and most scholars estimate that approximately 120,000 fighters were killed. Moreover, the events toward the end of the battle seemed to be out of a Hollywood movie. Prince Lazar was captured and was beheaded along with his son in front of the Turkish Sultan Murad. A Serb noble asked permission to catch Lazar's head in his robe so that it would not have to touch the ground, and the Sultan was so impressed by this request that he granted it. A short period before Lazar's execution, another Serb knight, Milos Obilic, knelt in front of Murad to feign surrender and submit to vassal status. When he had the chance, Obilic stabbed Murad, disembowelled him, and it was thus a dying Murad who shortly thereafter witnessed the beheading of Lazar. The plot thickened even further when Murad's two sons came into the drama and one son murdered the other and became the leader of the Ottoman Turks. The final part of the plot was the alleged treason by the Serbian noble Vuk Brankovic. The Serb version of history claims that Brankovic turned from the battle at the very moment when the tide was in the favour of the Serbs. Whatever the particular details of the Brankovic issue, the battle created a myth-making apparatus that has consumed and shaped Serbian ethnonational consciousness over the intervening 600 years.[24] Even Albanian folklore valorizes the battle as an epic event and although the interpretation of events differs slightly from the Serbian version, the cast of characters and dramatic sacrifice remain integral.[25]

Clearly, the battle at Kosovo Polje ended Serbian hegemony in the Balkans and the Ottomans paid a price that took 70 years to overcome. But almost immediately after the battle Serbian Orthodox priests, poets, and peasants began to spread the notion of a Christian martyrdom by the Serbian people, Prince Lazar, and Milos Obilic, and of course the Judas-like betrayal of Vuk Brankovic. Legend has it that Lazar was visited by a falcon that flew from Jerusalem to Kosovo on the eve of the battle and presented Lazar with a choice between an 'earthly kingdom' via vassalage under the Turks or a 'heavenly kingdom' through sacrifice on the battlefield. According to Serbian legend, Lazar choose the latter and it is this mythicized refusal to accept ultimatums that has shaped Serbian political behaviour since Kosovo.[26] This refusal to bow down pragmatically like a 'good soldier Schweik' was evident in Serbia's rejection of Austria's ultimatum in 1914, in the Serbian *coup d'état* and the rejection of Hitler's ultimatum in 1941, in the hard-line position of the Bosnian Serbs when confronted by NATO throughout much of the war in Bosnia, and in Milosevic's cynical attempt to be a modern day Lazar by refusing NATO's ultimatum in March 1999.

The Kosovo battle's memory became a Serbian passion play acted out in daily life and the primordialization of the events is a powerful example of how ethnic groups aggrandize real historical events to reinforce identity. This event was a combination of primordial reality, myth construction, and instrumental manipulation by élites. It is this combination (primordialization) that has been used by Serbs over the centuries and eventually spawned Slobodan Milosevic. The difficulty in transcending this myth for the Serbs is that the event actually occurred. Even the perspective of the Ottoman Turks mirrors many of the traditional Serbian accounts of thematic martyrdom and cataclysmic struggle.[27] In fact, the Turkish accounts extol the bravery and virtues of the Serbs while Serb accounts do not address the courage and the skills of the Ottoman forces.

At the time, the battle was the largest ever fought on European soil and military historical surveys routinely include the Kosovo battle not only as one of the top ten military defeats but also one of the most important battles in history.[28] The result of all this historical celebration not only by the Serbs, but also by the Turks, military historians, and even the Persians is that the Serbians are shackled by an identity marker whose ubiquity is almost impossible to escape. Even if all the myth and legend surrounding the battle were erased, there is unfortunately enough historical evidence left, so that it is unlikely that anyone can separate fact from belief. Sometimes myths are somewhat real and the Kosovo albatross cannot be wished away.[29]

The Serbs were not alone at Kosovo. An ally of Lazar, King Tvrtko I of Bosnia, sent a contingent of troops. More important, there was also a combined Albanian-Serbian force that arrived to fight the Ottomans. This force was led by John Kastrioti, who was of mixed Albanian-Serbian origin and whose son, Skenderbeg, was venerated by Albanians as the founder of their nation. The Albanians at the time were Christian and their solidarity with the Serbs was not difficult to comprehend. A Hungarian force also showed up, and although Kosovo was mainly a Serbian effort, it is also fair to suggest that the battle was a combined Balkan-Christian enterprise to repulse the Ottoman Turks.[30]

By the early fifteenth century, the Ottoman incursion affected the Albanians as well, and Kastrioti's son, Gjergi, was taken hostage and held by the Turks. The younger Kastrioti eventually renounced his Christianity and adopted the Muslim name of Skender. He quickly reached the rank of general and was given the title of *beg* (thus Skenderbeg); soon afterwards he deserted the Ottoman army. From 1444 until his death in 1468, Skenderbeg renounced Islam and managed partially to unify the clannish Albanian tribes in their resistance to the Turks and despite rarely exceeding a force of 10,000 men, the Albanians admirably fought the Turks in numerous skirmishes and battles. As in the case of Lazar, however, his effort was futile and the Albanians, as the Serbs before them, could not resist the might of the Ottoman Empire.[31] But unlike the Serbs, the Albanians were pragmatists and in the sixteenth and seventeenth centuries converted to Islam in large numbers. By the end of the seventeenth century, two-thirds of Albanians followed Islam. In Kosovo the Turks encouraged their new Muslim allies to come in from Albania and bestowed upon them the privileges of nobility and landowning and accorded them socioeconomic privileges that put them in the top tier of the Ottoman two-tier *millet* system. Unlike Albania itself, which always maintained a sizeable Christian minority, the Albanians of Kosovo were almost exclusively Muslims.[32]

The solidarity of 1389 between Serbians and Albanians was in the distant past in Kosovo when the Austro-Hungarian empire pushed the Turks as far south as Kosovo in 1689. The Serbs enthusiastically joined the fight against the Ottoman Empire, but the anti-Turk campaign was soon crushed and the Serbs were left to face the Turks and the Albanians. Unlike pogroms after sporadic Serbian uprisings over the previous century, the Turks exacted a horrible revenge. In 1594, after a previous rebellion, the Turks disinterred the body of St Sava from Kosovo and burned it at a public funeral pyre outside Belgrade in order to convince the Serbs that Kosovo was a memory to be forgotten. In 1689, after a failed rebellion, the Serbs decided not to wait for Turk and Albanian reprisals and migrated north. On New Years' Day in 1690, Patriarch Arsenius III left the Pec monastery in Kosovo and led an exodus of 39,000 Serb families north to what is now the present day Serbian province of Vojvodina. This very real exodus contributed to the further embellishment of the Kosovo myth and its biblical connotations. One of Serbia's most famous paintings is a great canvas, painted in 1896 by Paja Jovanovich and displayed in Belgrade, which depicts a Moses-like figure leading the Serbs away from, instead of to, the promised land.[33]

Another Austrian advance during 1714 was a repetition of 1689 and this time another 30,000 *families*, led by Arsenius IV, migrated north.[34] There is much speculation over how many people this involved. Although much of Kosovo was depopulated of Serbs, there were apparently enough Serbs left in the province that by the end of the nineteenth century they still made up a third of the population. Nevertheless, Serb nationalists claim that families in those days were large in comparison with today; using Serbian Orthodox Church records, they contend that these migrations totaled 500,000 people. Other researchers dispute the Serb claim and, using Albanian sources, suggest that only a few thousand individuals left Kosovo during the migrations.[35] Although there is no resolution of this typical Balkan impasse over historical interpretation, one can assume that nearly 70,000 families with an average of just three or four individuals per family would still comprise a sizeable number.

Almost a century passed from the time of the last Serbian migration to the first of the anti-Ottoman nationalist uprisings in the Balkans during the nineteenth century. The Ottoman Empire was in early decline and the Serb uprising in 1804, led by Karadjordjevic, a pig farmer, surprised not only the Ottomans but also the Albanians and the Europeans with its effectiveness. Like previous rebellions, the 1804 uprising was short-lived, but this time it took on a different character, as other Balkan peoples realized that the Ottoman Empire was beginning to weaken. By 1850, the Greeks and the Bulgarians were involved in resistance. Through one uprising after another the Serbs were able to extract more and more autonomy from the Turks during the middle of the nineteenth century. The Russians also went to war against the Turks and the Ottoman Empire, the 'sick man of Europe', could not resist an assault on all fronts.

The Treaty of San Stefano in 1878 recognized Serbia as an independent state after almost 500 years of Ottoman control. Greece and Bulgaria also became recognized states, but to the Albanians the treaty of San Stefano was not as welcome. Because so many Albanians had converted to Islam, unlike the Serbs, Greeks, and Bulgarians, the great powers identified the Albanians with the Ottoman Turks instead of considering Albanian aims and ideals. The rise of Albanian national consciousness was delayed because of the nature of Ottoman rule, and it was not until 1912 that Albania achieved independence.[36]

In the social system built by the Ottomans the Muslim converts were landowners and freeholders while the overwhelming majority of peasants who were taxed heavily and lived as second-class citizens in Kosovo were Serbs. Of particular interest for an understanding of present-day ethnic frictions in Kosovo is that as the Ottoman empire eroded and was forced to make concessions to subject populations it was in Kosovo and Bosnia where the local Muslim landlords were the most reactionary and hostile to any changes that threatened their paramountcy.[37] After the Treaty of San Stefano, along with Skenderbeg, Kosovo also became part of Albanian myth and national consciousness. A conservative group of Albanian élites, mostly from Kosovo and Macedonia, met in Prizren, Kosovo in 1878 to protest against the San Stefano treaty and to begin the organization of an Albanian national movement.

Unfortunately for the Albanians, the Ottoman system of privileges made them unable to conceive of a Balkan alliance with the Serbs and the Greeks, and it was not until the twentieth century that Albanians began to consider whether dismembering the Ottoman Empire was in their interest. Still, the Prizren League is an ideological and ethnic identity marker for Albanians, especially those in Kosovo. Moreover, the crushing of the Prizren League in 1881 by Ottoman forces at the urging of the great powers further imbued the league with the mantle of martyrdom and legend in the minds of the Kosovo Albanians.[38] While the Albanians considered their weakened position in the new Balkan calculus, the Serbs in Kosovo found it harder to survive in an environment where the Albanians became more insecure and violence against Serbs forced 150,00 to 200,00 to flee from Kosovo to the north during the years from 1890 to 1910.[39] The stage was now set for the Albanian-Serbian tit-for-tat violence that has characterized relations during the twentieth century.

The Century of Revenge: 1912–98

In 1912, Serbia, Greece, Montenegro, and Bulgaria declared war on the Ottoman Empire and within a short time drove the Turks out of the Balkans to the edges of Turkey. The sudden success of the campaign stunned Europe and an autonomous Albanian state was quickly recognized before the Greeks and the Serbs carved up all of Albania. The Serbs had already reached the Adriatic in northern Albania: the Austrians were incensed and concerned that the upstart Serbs might set an example for other restive Slavic populations in the Austro-Hungarian Empire. The area of Macedonia itself was divided among the Bulgarians, Greeks, and Serbians. But it was Serbia's move into Kosovo that resonated in a manner beyond words for the Serbs and concerned the Albanians in Kosovo. What the Serbians saw as the 'liberation' of Kosovo and a reversal of 500 years of history, the Albanians saw as a horrible situation. When Serbian soldiers returned to the Field of Blackbirds in the winter of 1912, they crept over the snowy field barefoot so as not to disturb the fallen warriors from the 1389 battle. This certainly was an instance where historical memory seemed to reach mythic dimensions. Accounts at the time describe impromptu speeches and uncontrollable weeping.

The war in the Balkans in 1912 also continued the Balkan tradition of vengeance and reprisal as Muslim populations suffered horribly at the hands of advancing Christian armies. Many Turks and Albanians escaped to Turkey but many others stayed and suffered. The horror of the Balkan Wars was recorded by the Carnegie Endowment for International Peace in a book, *The Other Balkan Wars*, published in 1913 (and recently republished).[40] During this period it was the Albanians and other Muslim populations who bore the brunt of the suffering, although the Albanians still made the Serbs pay a heavy price in areas where the Serbian armies were not in control.[41]

By 1914 the Austrians were fed up with Serbia's new status and issued a series of ultimatums which the Serbs typically could not completely comply with. In June of that year, Archduke Francis Ferdinand came to Sarajevo in 1914 to make it clear to Serbia that with the Turks gone it was the Austrians who now controlled Bosnia and Hercegovina. Unfortunately, the Archduke had picked *Vidovdan*, the day of the battle of Kosovo Polje, for the visit and he was assassinated by a Bosnian Serb. It should be mentioned that two of the five-member team of assassins were Bosnian Muslims. Austria immediately declared war on Serbia and the Serbs initially repulsed the Austrians until the Germans came into the picture. The Serbian army, along with members of the government, the Serbian monarch, and the mummified remains of Lazar, began a historic retreat through southern Serbia and into Kosovo and Albania, where it was now the Albanian turn to exact revenge. Of the 500,000 men during the retreat over the Albanian mountains in the winter of 1914–15, over a third succumbed to the elements or to Albanian snipers. This 'army of skeletons' eventually reached the island of Corfu and returned to the Salonika front in 1916 and by 1917 had driven the Austrians and the Germans out of Serbia, although by the war's end the Serbs had lost 52 per cent of their adult male population.[42]

The end of Word War One saw the entrance of a host of new states created from the remnants of collapsed empires. Serbia ceased to exist as an independent state and a Yugoslavia was formed in which the Serbs made up almost 40 per cent of the total population while the Albanians only made up 3.6 per cent.[43] But in Kosovo the ethnic balance still favoured the Albanians over the Serbs. In the inter-war period the Serbs started a programme of Serbianization and colonization in Kosovo. There was no problem in finding settlers willing to 'return' to Kosovo. During this period the demographic balance shifted from a two-to-one Albanian majority to an approximate balance between Albanians and Serbs. From the Serb perspective the period is chauvinistically remembered as a time when the Serbs were out to 'civilize' the Albanians and 'help' them to modernize and transcend their peculiar clannish culture that practised blood vengeance and tribal retribution. The Albanians, of course, understood the inter-war period as a time of domination and the imposition of foreign colonial rule, during which any Albanian uprisings had been put down with a maximum of force.[44]

When World War Two arrived, the Serbs again found themselves, along with the Greeks, as the only Balkan actors on the side of the Allies, while the Albanians received immediate support from Mussolini. Although the slaughter of Serbs in Kosovo was not nearly on a par with the activities of the *Ustashe* puppet state in Croatia, the Albanians managed to keep the Balkan tradition of vengeance alive from 1941 to 1945. About 100,000 to 150,000 Serbs were immediately driven out and (according to Serb accounts) about 10,000 Serbs were massacred. Towards the end of the war the Serbian resistance under General Drazha Mihailovic first took control of parts of Kosovo back from the Albanians but it was the Partisans under Tito's leadership who eventually consolidated Yugoslav state control in Kosovo. From 1945 until early 1950s there were continual anti-Yugoslav insurrections in Kosovo, which were gradually eradicated by the communist government in Belgrade. However, Tito, who was both a Marxist and a Croat, thought it would be useful for proletarian solidarity if the 'false consciousness' of ethnonational identity could be eroded in the Serbian mind. Consequently, both the Serb settlers of the inter-war period and Serbs native to Kosovo who had fled in 1941 were not allowed to return. In order to placate Enver Hoxha, the communist leader in Albania, who wanted a greater Albania, Tito let 200,00 to 240,000 Albanians into Kosovo in the period after the war[45] and by 1961 the Albanian population in Kosovo had more than doubled to almost one million from a pre-World War Two population of less than 500,000.[46]

During the post-war period until 1966, Yugoslavia's communist party ran Kosovo with an iron hand under Aleksander Rankovic, the minister of the interior. Although loyal to Tito, Rankovic was hostile to the Albanians in Kosovo because of the guerrilla uprisings in the late 1940s and early 1950s. When his excesses came to light in 1966, he was sacked.[47] Much to the consternation of the Serbs, the autonomous status of Kosovo was increased incrementally from 1947 until 1969, when it became, after Rankovic's fall, the autonomous province of Kosovo. In 1968 the Albanians were allowed to celebrate the 500th anniversary of the death of Skenderbeg[48] and by 1974 the new Yugoslav constitution elevated both Kosovo and Vojvodina to near-republican status in Yugoslavia's federal system. The Albanians also received the right to fly the Albanian national flag next to that of Yugoslavia. Moreover, in Yugoslavia's system of six republics and two autonomous provinces (both within Serbia), the Serbs, who made up almost 40 per cent of the population of Yugoslavia, were often left with one vote out of eight because both Vojvodina and Kosovo had the constitutional authority to veto any legislative action that originated in the Serbian republic.

Despite anti-Serb riots in 1968 and continual calls for secession and a greater Albania, there was one decision that proved to be the undoing of any hope for ethnic harmony in Kosovo. The university in Pristina underwent a process of Albanization, not only in the student body but also in the faculty, which was augmented by professors from the University of Tirana in Albania, who espoused an irredentist anti-Serb ideology.[49] Ethnic relations in Kosovo deteriorated as the Albanians started to erect an apartheid system that excluded the Serbs. Often, the hostilities were directed by the Albanian faculty at the university in Pristina. Serbs were assaulted in the streets, crops and farms were demolished, and many Serbian Orthodox churches, monasteries, and shrines were destroyed by the predominantly Muslim Albanians. Thousands of Serbs and Montenegrins started to leave Kosovo. Albanians even desecrated Serbian graves by destroying headstones and digging up the dead.[50]

The 1970s in Kosovo were marked by the Albanization of security forces so that Serbs had little protection against terrorism.[51] The increasingly Albanian-dominated communist party in Kosovo kept federal authorities from becoming involved in much of Kosovo's security operations because these were concerned about the return of Serbian control. The Albanians kept federal authorities in the dark about the growing separatist organizations in Kosovo. Furthermore, internal intelligence in Kosovo was usually published in Albanian so that the Serbians in Kosovo would remain unaware of the volatile situation.[52]

Kosovo exploded in March and April of 1981. The turmoil started when 2,000 Albanian students at the university in Pristina rioted, and the number of rioters quickly grew to 30,000. Anything Serbian-owned or remotely related to the federal government was attacked. Eventually the violence escalated to street battles against the police. Many of the rioters were able to use young girls as protection against police bullets,[53] since male-dominated Albanian society refrained from sending girls to school and thus the children were available as shields.[54] The violence soon spread throughout Kosovo and by early April over 2,500 people were dead.[55]

The imposition of military control did not calm the Albanians down. Sabotage was rampant and eventually schools were closed.[56] Kosovo continued to experience violent outbursts through most of 1982. The hostilities finally started to abate by the end of 1982 and the Albanian professors at the university were removed along with the books that the communist authorities considered counter-revolutionary. The communist party in Kosovo was also purged of over a thousand members and many Albanians were sentenced to long prison terms.[57]

The events in Kosovo were the prelude for the arousal of the (politically dormant) Serbs. In April 1987, 10,000 Serbs and Montenegrins gathered around the Hall of Culture in Kosovo Polje to lodge grievances about their treatment at the hands of the Albanians. While the Albanian police used clubs on the crowd outside the hall, the head of the Serbian communist party, Slobodan Milosevic, listened to the complaints of 300 Serbian and Montenegrin delegates in the hall. When Milosevic heard that Serbs were being assaulted in the middle of Kosovo Polje, Serbia's most holy place, he stepped outside. He shouted at the police to stop clubbing the people and told the crowd, 'Nobody, either now or in the future, has the right to beat you.'[58] When Ibrahim Rugova, moderate leader of the non-violent Albanian movement in Kosovo, was asked by former US Ambassador to Yugoslavia, Warren Zimmermann, about how the Serbs were treated by the Kosovo Albanians before the rise of Milosevic, Rugova replied that 'unfortunately, many crimes were committed against the Serbs'.[59] Unlike most ethic élites in the Balkans, Rugova was willing to admit that interethic violence in Kosovo was not a one-way street.

For Milosevic, April 1987 was a surprising moment for a bloodless bureaucrat who had few inclinations toward nationalism but whose thirst for power was relentless and who was willing to exploit the heavily primordialized historical clay that is Serb memory. This moment also signaled the death of Yugoslavia and in 1989, for the 600-year anniversary of the Kosovo battle, over a million Serbs gathered at the site to commemorate the event. Along with the living there were the dead, in particular Prince Lazar's body, which had toured almost every major Serbian area in Yugoslavia during the previous two years. Lazar and history had finally come full cycle.

A 'Least Worst' Solution for an Intractable Problem

Clearly, the recent conflict in Kosovo is not something new or sudden. Many have suggested that the best solution for Kosovo is for the Serbs simply to realize that the demographic imbalance is an undeniable fact. Giving Kosovo up completely, however, is an unlikely option for the majority of Serbs. The 1981 census revealed that there were 1.2 million Albanians and 250,000 Serbs in Kosovo. By 1991, there were almost 1.8 million Albanians and only 200,000 Serbs.[60] The Serbs claim that the Albanians have inflated their numbers while the Albanians claim that they are undercounted. The Albanians present a similar contention in Macedonia where they comprise from 25 per cent (the Macedonian Slav claim) to 40 per cent (the Albanian claim) of a population concentrated on the borders of Kosovo and Albania. To complicate the demographic debate even further, the Roma population of Kosovo claims that it has been ignored in the numbers game and that there are 400,000 Roma in Kosovo who have suffered at the hands of the Albanians and have been under great pressure to 'pass themselves off as Albanians and not as Roma'.[61]

One of the problems with any current conflict resolution formula is that the international community is still undecided whether the Kosovo Liberation Army (KLA) has undermined Ibrahim Rugova as the leader of the Kosovo Albanians. A rebel spokesman for the KLA, Jakup Krasniqi, insisted in an interview with *Der Spiegel* that the KLA goal was a greater Albania that would unify Albania with Kosovo and much of Macedonia. For those reasons, Krasniqi suggested that Rugova had lost legitimacy in the eyes of the Kosovo Albanians and had failed in his policies of non-violence.[62] Thus, the strategy of the KLA was to escalate the fighting, intimidate and kidnap Serb civilians, and then fight valiantly as Milosevic's special police descended on an Albanian village, reduced it to rubble and drove out innocent peasants.[63] Here it should be noted that the KLA is not a recently formed organization. The KLA had been active in assassinating Serb policemen and Albanian 'collaborationists' for over three years before the NATO bombings[64] and Krasniqi remarked in the *Spiegel* interview that he looked to the PLO as his organizational model.

Even the name of Kosovo is part of the struggle. The Albanians have used the term Kosov*a* for much of the post-World War Two period. Although the term Kosov*o* is strictly Slavic in origin and Kosov*a* has no original meaning in Albanian, this does not reduce the importance of this difference. In early May 1998 the daily Radio Free Europe/Radio Free Liberty report changed its editorial policy from using Kosov*o* to an exclusive use of Kosov*a*. When questioned about the change, one of the editors simply stated that 'some weeks ago we decided that, in cases where official names for places differ from those preferred by the majority of the population, we follow the usage of the majority.'[65]

Whether in Kosovo, Timor, or Tibet, the issue is nation-state sovereignty versus autonomy for compact minorities. Some have even suggested that the walls of sovereignty may be broached when human rights violations in places like Kosovo become a concern.[66] Autonomy will certainly become a buzzword in the coming decades. Autonomy, however, comes in many flavours; the degree of autonomy that can be pursued can cover a wide spectrum from simple recognition of cultural, religious, and linguistic rights to the creation of autonomous units that resemble sovereign mini-states. The next step could be an internationally recognized independent Kosovo that would immediately destabilize Macedonia and soon after that two NATO members, Greece and Turkey, would confront each other if the recent tensions in Cyprus do not abate. Moreover, China does not want a precedent set for Tibet and Russia is still sensitive over Chechnya and other Muslim areas within its southern borders.

Democratic alternatives in deeply divided societies have been explored thoroughly by political scientists over the past 30 years. The consociational approach envisioned by Lijphart as a possible solution is perhaps the most discussed one.[67] This approach demands that 'élites cooperate after election to form multiethnic coalitions and manage conflict; groups are autonomous; [and] minorities are protected'.[68] This solution was attempted in Yugoslavia after Tito's death but any interethnic cooperation was quickly outflanked by ethnic élite outbidding through playing the ethnonationalist card. To imagine that this level of cooperation would be possible in Kosovo with its irreconcilable interpretations of history, language differences and some very divergent cultural norms is to imagine the impossible. Timothy Sisk has modified the consociational approach to include an 'integrative' strategy in which 'parties [are] encouraged to create coalitions before elections, creating broadly inclusive but majoritarian governments'.[69] The integrative approach, however, would also be doomed. Noel Malcolm suggests that the conflict could be resolved if the Serbians simply let go of Kosovo and decide *en masse* that their national myths are inaccurate and should be either disbelieved or at least dramatically changed. He insists that it is more important for the Serbs than for the Albanians to do this because Serbs pose a greater threat to stability in the region.[70] Malcolm's suggestion is not unlike the comment above about inducing historical Alzheimers' disease in the Balkans. The chance that the Serbs would completely reinterpret or forget most of their national myths is quite unlikely; such a psychological change would necessitate a denial of identity.[71]

The least worst approach to resolving the Kosovo impasse is to give both parties most of what they really want and for the international community to realize that not all states are completely sovereign,[72] Many states are 'soft' states and are amenable to some social engineering. What the Albanians in Kosovo want is independence, connection to Albania, and control of territory. According to Ibrahim Rugova, the Kosovo Albanians do not want partition.[73] What the Serbs want is preservation of, and access to, their holy places. Most of all, they do not want to give up the symbols of the unifying the myth that shapes the core of what comprises Serbian national identity. Many Serbs may never visit Kosovo Polje, but they need to believe that they can do so if they wish. What the Kosovo Albanians have to give up is complete control over about 25 per cent of Kosovo's territory and what the Serbs have to give up is 75 per cent of their monasteries but not all of the most important ones.

The demographic balance of 80 to 90 per cent Albanians and 10 per cent Serbs in Kosovo (assuming that it is restored) actually works towards a solution. The Serbs have to a great degree been 'pre-cleansed.' Imagine how democratic the Czechs or Poles would be today if there were still three million Sudeten Germans in the Czech Republic or if Poland was still home to more than three million Jews and hundreds of thousands of Germans. Of course, this observation cannot sit well with those who believe in the individual rights that evolved out of the Protestant Reformation and the Lockean formula for government. But in Eastern Europe as in much of the rest of the world, democracies are 'illiberal', and the existence of parties and free elections does not guarantee the type of outcomes that are a Western norm.[74] After all, the Czech Republic seems quite Western until one discovers that the most dangerous place in Europe for a Roma to walk the streets is in Prague.[75]

Despite their small population of only 200,000, most of the Serbs in Kosovo are concentrated in the northern part of the province. Although some have called for complete partition in Kosovo,[76] this arrangement would not be fair to the large number of Albanians who also live in the northern section of Kosovo. Consequently, a framework of mixed autonomy, territorial autonomy and personal autonomy is perhaps the only way out of the quandary short of further warfare and the ethnic cleansing of the Serbs. The map in Figure 2 depicts a Kosovo that contains a collection of over 1300 Serbian holy places. The map also depicts a proposed division that falls a little short of partition and the errors of the Dayton Accords, a little short of formal independence for Kosovo, and a little short of preserving all of Kosovo as a Serbian ethnocultural museum. To the south of the dotted line drawn on the map, the Albanians would have complete and broad autonomy and could pursue contacts with Albania and even apply for dual citizenship. For the Albanians, the quasi-holy city of Prizren would be totally under Albanian control and the connection to the Albanians in

FIGURE 2
KOSOVO

Macedonia would be free and unencumbered by the Serbian military; Macedonia itself might consider a similar model and become part of a regional conflict-resolution process. The process would also result in the creation of a softer and smaller version of a Greater Albania but that would be part of the compromise that Serbia, Macedonia, and the international community would have to accept.

As for the Serbian monasteries under Albanian control, the Albanians could do whatever they wanted with them. They could expel the monks and nuns (which has already begun to occur), convert the monasteries to barns or hotels, or even preserve the shrines and invite Serbian tourists to visit. The Serbs in this section of Kosovo would be on their own and could not depend upon NATO or any international monitors to help them; again, this is a situation that has already occurred. The Albanian-controlled section of Kosovo would be functionally independent and only autonomous in a formal sense in order to placate the international community and to conform to the UN Charter on state sovereignty and the inviolability of international borders.

The area north of the line on the map would be quite different. In that area, a system of 'personal autonomy'[77] would prevail in which the individual rights of both Serbs and Albanians would be protected by NATO and a team of international monitors. The Serbs would retain control of the original seat of Serb orthodoxy at Pec, the Decani monastery, and of course the area around Kosovo Polje and the Gracanica monastery. The cities of Pristina and Mitrovica might look like Montreal with a large French (Albanian) section and a smaller English speaking (Serbian) section. Pristina would be the headquarters of the international community's monitoring effort. Pristina could in the future even evolve as a site of Serbian-Albanian *rapprochement* if enough individuals could transcend their conception of rights within a collective context and reconceive rights in an individual context. By eventually concentrating the bulk of NATO troops and of international monitors on the fraction of Kosovo still inhabited by Serbs, peacekeeping efforts would have a much more reasonable chance of success.

It is evident that the government in Belgrade would still be technically sovereign over the northern fraction of Kosovo – but it would be a 'soft' sovereignty compared to the exclusive monopoly of power by the state in Serbia proper. Except for national extremists in Serbia, most of the Serbian population would be more than satisfied with an arrangement that could preserve their identity markers, especially if the presence of the Russian troops in Kosovo could help in this effort.[78] The names of the two sections of Kosovo could even be tinkered with so that the northern section would be called Kosov*o* while the southern section would be Kosov*a*.

Perhaps the most difficult Rubicon to cross in the scenario suggested above is not the one in the minds of the Albanians or Serbs but the one in the minds of those in the international community, and particularly the United States. This Rubicon can be labelled 'presentism', an ahistorical, postmodern affliction in which policymakers can only understand a historically rooted conflict in the immediate context. From this perspective one could only conclude that the Albanians are the overwhelming victims while the Serbs should pack their bags and move to Belgrade. And perhaps this might be the result if people only see the Serbs as manifestations of Slobodan Milosevic's consciousness and Albanians as KLA terrorists or, conversely, as innocent victims. The urge to help the Albanians and the Serbians to come to terms with the limits of their aspirations must be stronger that the urge to simply punish the Serbs and assume that 'the Serbian people will suffer, but so they must.'[79] Being addicted to history with one's feet stuck in the mud of memories is certainly a Serbian, and to some degree, an Albanian problem. Conversely, the assumption that ethnonational groups, particularly the masses, can be influenced and manipulated by their élites in an unlimited manner, despite historical memory, is also a counterproductive assumption that hinders the vision needed for political solutions to complex problems. Slobodan Milosevic came to power over the issue of Kosovo and a real solution that ends the conflict is not in his long-term interest. But Milosevic might yet come through as the supposed guarantor of another agreement in the Balkans. It cannot be stressed enough how much Milosevic's claim to power stems from his 1987 remarks at Kosovo Polje. It is still very possible that if some type of resolution is reached that can satisfy most of the demands listed above for both Albanians and Serbians, then Milosevic's reason for being will evaporate and his hold on the levers of power in Belgrade will quickly weaken. The most ironic observation that one can make about the recent Balkan war is that if democracy does come to Serbia, then multiethnic authoritarian Serbia will become the only multiethnic polity to emerge from the carnage of Yugoslavia's wars of secession. Finally, if the conflict in Kosovo is some day brought to heel by a solution that meets most of the needs of the antagonists, then not only will this particular Balkan tinderbox have been doused but the beginning of the end for a Balkan dictator will not be far behind.

ACKNOWLEDGEMENTS

The research for this project was funded by a US Institute of Peace grant to attend an extensive colloquium on conflict and peacemaking during the summer of 1995. This work was completed with the support of a 1999 research stipend from the University of Wisconsin, Eau Claire.

NOTES

1. Kosovo was officially called Kosovo-Metohija for most of the twentieth century, with 4,200 square miles within Kosovo and 2,000 within Metohija. Since its autonomy in 1968, Metohija has fallen out of usage and Kosovo is now used generally for the entire region. See Alex N. Dragnich and Slavko Todorovich, *The Saga of Kosovo: Focus on Serbian-Albanian Relations* (New York: Columbia University Press, 1984), pp.4–5.
2. See Miranda Vickers, *Between Serb and Albanian: A History of Kosovo* (New York: Columbia University Press, 1998) for an analysis that clearly implicates both Serbians and Albanians at different times in an alternating pattern of oppression, particularly in the twentieth century.
3. See Chris Hedges in an interview with Terry Gross, US National Public Radio, 23 June 1998.
4. Chris Hedges, 'Albanian Rebels Are Reportedly Targeting Serbian Civilians', *New York*

188 IDENTITY AND TERRITORIAL AUTONOMY IN PLURAL SOCIETIES

Times, 24 June 1998; Mike O'Connor, 'Rebel Terror Forcing Minority Serbs Out of Kosovo', *New York Times*, 31 Aug. 1998; 'Captured KLA Men Say Serb Civilians Were Executed', Reuters, 28 Aug. 1998.

5. Jane Perlez, 'Milosevic Accepts Kosovo Monitors, Averting Attack', *New York Times*, 14 Oct. 1998.
6. 'NATO Almost Decided to Bomb Yugoslav Forces, Holbrooke Says', *New York Times*, 29 Oct. 1998.
7. Jane Perlez, 'Survivor of Kosovo Massacre Describes the Killing Garden', *New York Times*, 2 Oct. 1998.
8. Steven Lee Meyers, 'Serbian Pullouts Lead NATO to Postpone Attack Indefinitely', *New York Times*, 28 Oct. 1998.
9. R. Jeffrey Smith, 'Kosovo Rebels Plan for Renewal of War', *Washington Post*, 22 Oct. 1998; R. Jeffrey Smith, 'Kosovo's Warriors Not Ready For Peace', *Washington Post*, 30 Oct. 1998.
10. Paul Watson and John-Thor Dahlberg, 'Dozens of Kosovo Albanian Civilians Killed in Nighttime Raid', *Los Angeles Times*, 15 May 1999.
11. See Christopher Walker, 'The Environmental Impact of the NATO Campaign', Radio Free Europe/Radio Free Liberty (RFE/RFL), 3 June 1999.
12. See Paul Watson and Marjorie Miller, 'Defying NATO, Rebels Try to Grab Government Control', *Los Angeles Times*, 19 June 1999; Christopher Lane, 'US and NATO Have Put the Fox in the Chicken Coop; Installing the KLA as the Dominant Power Broker Ultimately Will Prove to be Bad', *Los Angeles Times*, 23 June 1999; John Ward Anderson, 'KLA Accused of Beating Gypsies', *Washington Post*, 19 June 1999; David Brodie, 'Kosovar Attack on Gypsies Reveal Desire for Revenge', *New York Times*, 7 June 1999; and Philip Smucker, 'Accusations Fly as KLA Tightens Grip on Kosovo', *Pittsburgh Post-Gazette*, 24 June 1999.
13. Chester A. Crocker, 'The Varieties of Intervention: Conditions for Success', in Chester A. Crocker, Fen Osler Hampson, and Pamela Aall (eds), *Managing Global Chaos: Sources of and Responses to International Conflict* (Washington, DC: United States Institute of Peace Press), p.192.
14. See Michael G. Roskin, *The Rebirth of East Europe*, 3rd ed. (Englewood Cliffs, NJ: Prentice Hall, 1997), pp.12–23.
15. See Pierre L. Va de Berghe, 'Race and Ethnicity: A Sociobiological Perspective', *Ethnic and Racial Studies*, Vol.1, pp.401–27.
16. See Clifford Geertz, *The Interpretation of Cultures* (New York: Basic Books, 1973) and Edward Shils, 'Primordial, Personal, Sacred and Civil Ties', *British Journal of Sociology*, Vol.7 (1957), pp.113–45. For a critique of the primordialist position see Jack David Eller and Reed M. Coughlin, 'The Poverty of Primordialism: The Demystification of Ethnic Attachments', *Ethnic and Racial Studies*, Vol.16 (1993), pp.183–201. And for a spirited response to Eller and Coughlin see Steven Grosby, 'The Verdict of History: The Inexpungeable Tie of Primordiality – A Response to Eller and Coughlin', *Ethnic and Racial Studies*, Vol.7 (1994), pp.164–70.
17. See Anthony Smith, *The Ethnic Origins of Nations* (Oxford: Basil Blackwell, 1986) and 'The Nation: Invented, Imagined, Reconstructed?' *Millennium: Journal of International Studies*, Vol.20 (1991), pp.353–68.
18. See Steven Majstorovic, 'Ancient Hatreds or Elite Manipulation?', *World Affairs*, Vol.159, No.1 (Spring 1997), pp.171–72.
19. For the best insight into this subjective perspective see Walker Connor's work in a volume of his collected essays, *Ethnonationalism: The Quest for Understanding* (Princeton, NJ: Princeton University Press, 1994).
20. Miranda Vickers, *The Albanians: A Modern History* (London: I.B. Tauris, 1995), p.2.
21. While attending a conference organized by the United States Institute of Peace in Washington, DC, on 25 Feb. 1998 entitled 'A Dialogue on Bosnia in the Balkans: Exploring Regional Approaches to Peace', the author had an extensive discussion with two members of the Albanian embassy in the United States. These very articulate and kindly gentlemen took great pains to express their thanks for my interest in the subtleties of Albanian identity and history and it was here that I first was exposed to the argument that the modern Albanians have a direct connection to the ancient Greeks.

22. See Tim Judah, *The Serbs: History, Myth and the Destruction of Yugoslavia* (New Haven, CT: Yale University Press, 1997), pp.20–23. Although Judah's work is a critical, negative and quite detailed deconstruction of Serbian history, the combination of this work along with Dragnich and Todorovich's *The Saga of Kosovo* provides a useful way for the scholar to split the difference in the search for historical trajectories that are neither overtly pro-Serb or Serbophobic.
23. See Dragnich and Todorovich, p.12, and Judah, p.24.
24. See Nicholas C.J. Pappas and Lee Brigance Pappas, 'The Ottoman View of the Battle Kosovo', in Wayne S. Vucinich and Thomas A. Emmert (eds), *Kosovo: Legacy of a Medieval Battle* (Minneapolis, MN: University of Minnesota Press, 1991, pp.41–60.
25. See Albert B. Lord, 'The Battle of Kosovo in Albanian and Serbocroatian Oral Epic Songs', in Arisha Pipa and Sami Repishti (eds), *Studies on Kosova*, (New York: Columbia University Press, 1984), pp.65–83.
26. See Rev. Bishop Atanasije Jevtic, 'The Heavenly Kingdom in Serbia's Historic Destiny', in Bill Dorich and Basil W.R. Jenkins (eds), *Kosovo* (Allahambra, CA: Kosovo Charity Fund, 1992): pp.63–9.
27. Pappas and Pappas, p.53.
28. See Robert Cowley and Geoffrey Parker (eds), *The Reader's Companion to Military History* (New York: Houghton Mifflin Company, 1996), p.497.
29. For an example of a work that seeks to de-mythicize the Serbian perspective on Kosovo and uses many Albanian Muslim sources see Noel Malcolm, *Kosovo: A Short History* (New York: New York University Press, 1998).
30. Dragnich and Todorovich, p.21.
31. Vickers, *The Albanians*, pp.7–9.
32. Dragnich and Todorovich, pp.45–57.
33. See Judah, pp.1–2, 38–39; and Dragnich and Todorovich, pp.66–67.
34. Dragnich and Todorovich, p.66.
35. Malcolm, *Kosovo: A Short History*.
36. Vickers, *The Albanians*, pp.30–1.
37. Donia and Fine, *Bosnia and Hercegovina*, pp.78–119; and see Francine Friedman, *The Muslims of Bosnia* (Boulder, CO: Westview Press, 1996), pp.61–80.
38. Vickers, *The Albanians*, pp.30–44.
39. Dragnich and Todorovich, p.94.
40. See Carnegie Endowment for International Peace, *The Other Balkan Wars* (Washington, DC, 1913, 1993).
41. Dragnich and Todorovich, pp.100–110; and Judah, pp.84–9.
42. Dragnich and Todorovich, p.11; and Judah, pp.98–101.
43. Ivo Banac, *The National Question in Yugoslavia: Origins, History, Politics* (Ithaca, NY: Cornell University Press, 1984), p.58.
44. Dragnich and Todorovich, pp.119–27; and Judah, p.107.
45. See Stevan K. Pavlowitch, 'Kosovo: An Analysis of Yugoslavia's Albanian Problem', *Conflict Studies*, Nos.137/8 (1982), pp.7–21.
46. See Prvoslav Ralic, *Minority Rights in Serbia* (Belgrade, 1992), p.21.
47. See Pedro Ramet, *Nationalism and Federalism in Yugoslavia: 1963–1983* (Bloomington, IN: Indiana University Press, 1984), pp.156–7.
48. Ibid., p.159.
49. *The Economist*, 2 May 1970, p.37.
50. F. Singleton., 'The Roots of Discord in Yugoslavia', *The World Today*, Vol.28 (1972), pp.172–73.
51. Mile Veljovich, 'Yugoslav-Albanian Relations', *Review of international Affairs*, Vol.37 (1985), p.16.
52. Mark Baskin, 'Crisis in Kosovo', *Problems of Communism*, Vol.24 (1983), p.26; and *NIN*, 7 June 1981, pp.11–12 and 21 June 1981, p.13.
53. Ramet, p.164.
54. I spoke with Rade Smiljenic in Vojvodina who was serving with the federal police in Kosovo at the time and he confirms that the Albanians used young females as shields. He said that it

190   IDENTITY AND TERRITORIAL AUTONOMY IN PLURAL SOCIETIES

was hard to believe that while the rioters were shooting at him they fully expected him to fire back. Interview, July 1990.
55. *New York Times*, 7 Apr. 1981, p.A3.
56. Ramet, pp.370–82.
57. *Christian Science Monitor*, 2 Sept. 1981, p.7; *Dragnich and Todorovich*, p.172.
58. *The Chicago Tribune*, 17 Oct. 1988; Associated Press, 25 Apr. 1987.
59. Warren Zimmermann, *Origins of a Catastrophe* (New York: Times Books, 1996), p.80.
60. Judah, pp.314–7.
61. Romnews (The Roma National Congress), 18 June 1998.
62. See William Drozdiak, 'Rise of Kosovo Guerrillas Puts NATO Powers in a Bind', *Washington Post*, 8 July 1998, p.A19.
63. See Alan J. Kuperman, 'False Hope Abroad', *Washington Post*, 14 June 1998, p.CO1.
64. Patrick Moore, 'More Attacks on Serbian Police', RFE/RFL, 5 Aug. 1997.
65. This was a 20 May 20, 1998 e-mail message to the author from RFE/RFL editor Patrick Moore.
66. See Judith Miller, 'When Sovereignty Isn't Sacrosanct', *New York Times*, 18 Apr. 1999; and Neil A. Lewis, 'The Rationale: A Word Bolsters Case For Allied Intervention', *New York Times*, 4 Apr. 1999.
67. Arend Lijphart, *Democracy in Plural Societies: A Comparative Exploration* (New Haven, CT: Yale University Press, 1977).
68. See Timothy D. Sisk, *Power Sharing and International Mediation in Ethnic Conflicts* (Washington, DC: United States Institute of Peace Press, 1996), p.35.
69. Ibid, p.35.
70. Malcolm, *Kosovo: A Short History*.
71. Noel Malcolm, 'Independence for Kosovo', *New York Times*, 9 June 1999.
72. See Ruth Lapidoth, *Autonomy: Flexible Solutions to Ethnic Conflict* (Washington, DC: United States Institute of Peace Press, 1997), pp.41–7.
73. Rilindja (Tirana), Rugova news conference, 30 Mar. 1996.
74. See Fareed Zakaria, 'Illiberal Democracies', *Foreign Affairs*, Nov./Dec. 1997.
75. 'Women Drowned in Skinhead Attack', *Associated Press*, 17 Feb. 1998. This report is representative of many reports of attacks on the Roma population in the Czech Republic.
76. See Marco Dogo, 'Kosovo: Pleading in Defense of a Division', *ISIG*, Aug. 1998, pp.14–15; John L. Mearsheimer, 'A Peace Agreement That's Bound to Fail', *Washington Post*, 19 Oct. 1998; and John Mearsheimer and Stephen Van Evera, 'Redraw the Map, Stop the Killing', *New York Times*, 19 Apr. 1999.
77. Lapidoth, p.39.
78. See Anatol Lieven, 'What Role for Russia?', *New York Times*, 14 June 1999.
79. Anthony Lewis, 'Proof of the Pudding', *New York Times*, 5 June 1999

Internal Unit Demarcation and National Identity: India, Pakistan and Sri Lanka

SWARNA RAJAGOPALAN

As the physical embodiment of the vision of the state,[1] territory is sacrosanct. When the state is described in the constitution, there is usually some indication of what regions it comprises. It is not just the list of included territories that is inviolate, but also their definition, their relation to one another and to the collective. In other words, territorial sanctity pertains to both the collective and the individual unit(s) of territory. Alterations in either alter the nature of the collective, and that threatens the survival of the state. Equally, however, the sense of identity of any group of people seems to be related to some portion of land, larger or smaller.

Territorial demarcation is a feature of modern nation-states. The dynastically-identified polities that preceded them had a core area, beyond which their decreasing control yielded at some point to another polity. People were known by many things – family, village, language, religion, or occupation, and of these only the village was spatially bound. Therefore, even a people with a distinct cultural identity and a long history, such as the three communities in this study, had no need to say 'This is where we end and someone else begins.'

One of the circumstances in which visions seek territorial manifestation is in response to the territorialization of an alternative vision. So those who were a people, unbounded by geographical limits, would claim a geographical space for themselves when they were confronted by another definition of their space. For instance, the literature and folklore of Tamils in India described their space vividly – from Tirupati to Kanyakumari. However, the modern territorial sense of a Tamil homeland came with the recognition of an Andhra province in the north-eastern part of Madras – a large colonial administrative unit. As linguistic minorities within Madras acquired their own areas, the need to have the remainder recognized as Tamil country was overwhelming. Likewise, in the case of Karachi, by searching for a territorial space for the *muhajireen* (those who migrated to

Swarna Rajagopalan, James Madison College, Michigan State University

Pakistan during the 1947 Partition), the Pakistan government forced the Sindi to claim primacy and primary 'ownership' of Karachi. The creation of administrative units in the colonial period and then the conversion of those units into state and sub-state units provided the impetus for other collectivities in the polity to articulate their spaces. Sometimes, where the unit coincided broadly with the areas occupied by an ethnic group, the members of that group came to cast their past within the confines of that unit, claiming for the form of the unit a standing and legitimacy that antiquity alone lends. In Gaston Bachelard's words, 'An entire past comes to dwell in a new house.'[2]

The demarcation of units within a polity is often tantamount, if not to the throwing down of a gauntlet, then to the assertion of a particular dispensation or vision. As it pleases some, so must it displease others. Those displeased find it easiest to articulate their dissent or formulate their demands in territorial terms. Territorial demands also are a 'front' for other grievances. The territory claimed as homeland or nation represents a sanctuary from repression or a haven where, by definition, the group will thrive. Often, it is not the demand voiced most vociferously that is the concession or privilege sought. The land that is claimed in such cases is the 'motherland', the land that will nourish, as opposed to the territory of others who deprive and repress the group. The claim is sometimes extended to people who have never lived there and who would be hard-pressed to do so. Colombo Tamil claims to belong to Jaffna fall in this category. The claims are no less valid for being rhetorical since they are an instrument to draw attention to something that is not right.

If we accept this, then there is no question that the demarcation of units is a tangible, physical statement of the state or nation-state's self-image as well as its image of the 'place' of its units. For instance, the Indian Constituent Assembly's argument for calling India a 'union' (see below), or the view of India as people coming together to reorganize themselves as states (units within the whole), denies the units' history by saying that they did not exist before the constitution. At the same time, even though the constitution (i.e., the entity of India) did not exist before the people came together, it precedes the units in history. Thus, the whole appropriates to itself a history that it denies the units. When, as in the case of the Indian union, the union can create and alter the shape and form of the units more or less unilaterally, then the unit is totally dependent on the state for its present and future (having already been denied a past).

The question of unit demarcation within the state is thus a question prior to that of power distribution within the state. There are two parts to this question. First, states (framers of constitutions) must decide how many tiers the governmental structure shall have, and what the distribution of power and 'lines of command' shall be. Second, and this is the crux of this paper, states must choose what the basis shall be whereby the primary unit of administration is demarcated. Is it to be language, geography, electoral considerations, or something else? Given that in most states, and in all of the three states that are studied in this project – India, Pakistan and Sri Lanka – the life and existence of the units is constitutionally derived from what Taussig calls the 'state of the whole',[3] it is contended that the vision of the units is derivative of the vision of the state as a whole. Where the vision of the state is contested, the vision of the unit is apt to be contested. To achieve reconciliation in the polity, agents of the state and of civil society must, first, find a way to reconcile the competing and seemingly incompatible visions of what should constitute the unit.

There is more than one vision of the state and more than one vision of its parts. The state is not a unitary actor, and its agents, functionaries and interpreters speak in a multiplicity of voices and act on a myriad versions of the constitutional vision – which is in effect, if not in law, merely one among equals. The 'groups' or 'regions' are also not unitary actors. First of all, unlike the state whose territorial limits are hermetic enough that they simulate perfect definition, the borders/membership of other human collectives are/is still murky around the edges, and it is hard to say who belongs and who does not. Indeed, this definition forms the substance of politics within the collective.

Therefore, there are many visions of the 'state-of-the-whole' and many visions of the parts thereof. It is not a simple good-versus-evil, dark-versus-light contest. These visions may be at odds with each other, and so may the visions of the parts. Any task of reconciliation involves some consensus-building across all these visions.

Each vision of the 'state-of-the-whole' gives rise to a predictable, consistent vision of the parts of that whole. Each vision of a part has a corollary vision of the 'state-of-the-whole.' For instance, to envision the Malaysian state as primarily a Malay state, is to predetermine what the place and role of other parts shall be. To envision the United States as an English-speaking state was until recently to create a rationale for learning English and assimilating non-English speaking immigrants. To envision Bangladesh as Bengali is to raise questions about the identity of the non-Bengalis and their *bona fides* as Bangladeshis. Conversely, for Québécois to define themselves as separate and distinct undermines the idea of Canada as a bilingual, bicultural state. For increasing numbers of Asian immigrants in the United Kingdom and North African immigrants in France to make their presence felt in the political process in the last two decades is to undermine respectively the primordial 'British' and 'French' nature of those states. For China's new region, Hong Kong, to assert its distinctive political and economic, but also cultural characteristics, *vis-à-vis* the state-of-the-whole is to call into question the 'state-of-the-whole' itself.

This relationship is even stronger territorially. Kashmir is only the most contentious example in South Asia, symbolizing the founding argument for Pakistan and its Indian counter, and holding ransom in its valleys the legitimacy of both those state ideologies. In all the three states in this study, the vision of the state has led to certain internal dispensations which have been negotiated over the years. Pakistan was founded as the South Asian 'homeland' for Muslims, but when it became an 'Islamic Republic' one of the first experiments was 'One Unit' – which erased the more conventional demarcation of regions, particularly in west Pakistan and which therefore de-ethnicized the nature of the units. In Sri Lanka, the demand of the Tamils for a separate unit – whether we speak of those that are fighting for a sovereign state or those who are campaigning for federalism – challenges the unitary vision of the state identified with the Sinhala-Buddhists. In India, the dialogue between visions of the 'state-of-the-whole' and parts of the state has been constant, resulting in revisions on all sides.

All kinds of visions seem to have one thing in common: a propensity under certain circumstances to be grounded in a territorial space. This is not irreversible and the territorialized vision is not immutable. We have discussed this earlier as the embodiment of a hitherto abstract vision. The contest in the political arena between a variety of visions would be hard enough to resolve without the visions being concretely manifested in land, in physical and human resources and in geopolitical configurations. As long as a collective vision rests in the realm of ideas, negotiation is facilitated by a reinterpretation of ideas. The moment the idea is 'grounded', it acquires a binary cast – either Tamil country includes Tirupati or it does not. Negotiation on that position is more difficult; it is hard to reinterpret the loss of arable land or to justify the transfer of a village full of Tamil-speakers out of what they have been told is Tamil country. There is much writing on devotion to language and to religion, but both of these are intensified if and when they come to be associated with specific pieces of land.

In order to survive, and in order to minimize conflict, the state has to find ways in which such a dialogue is sustained. This dialogue is carried on in different arenas and through different media. The arenas may be politics, economics, culture and custom. The media include schooling, communications, and formal legislation and rules. In this paper we trace the history of unit demarcation in post-colonial India, Pakistan and Sri Lanka largely through the sequence of changes in units initiated by the 'state-of-the-whole', usually in response to complaints or demands from regionally-based groups within the state.

India

Since 1935, India has experimented with three kinds of units. The variations have been introduced in response to specific group-state exchanges, and they have not been sweeping system-wide transformations. The fundamental position of the constitution has not changed. Differently demarcated units exist side by side, and the reorganization is extra-constitutional in that the constitution does not specify that any particular basis is to be adopted.

British India was ruled largely as a unitary state until the passage of the Government of India Act (1935) which provided the core of what became the constitution of free India. This legislation introduced for the first time the idea of a 'federation' whose units were of two types: provinces that were under direct British rule (governor's provinces and chief commissioner's provinces) and princely states. The princely states never gave their consent to this arrangement; therefore, it prevailed only with regard to the British-ruled provinces. The act of 1935 created two new provinces – Sind out of Bombay and Orissa out of Bengal and other provinces. Sind had been annexed in 1843 and in 1847, it was merged with the Bombay presidency. From then until 1935, Sind was a non-regulation province administered by a commissioner, and it was treated as distinct within the Bombay presidency in that special regulations and administrative arrangements were often made for Sind. Historians of Sind read this period, nevertheless, as one of neglect. Hamida Khuhro for instance, says that not only was Sind a very low priority for the Bombay presidency, but even projects of importance to the empire like the development of Karachi harbour were also delayed.[4] Therefore, the demand for the re-creation of the province of Sind was raised by the business community, first in 1913, at a Congress meeting, then in 1925 at the Congress, Muslim League and Khilafat conferences. In 1927, the Congress backed the principle of linguistic demarcation of provinces and backed the separation of Sind from Bombay as a place to begin.[5]

What is interesting here is the deployment of different rationales for the same demand. The demand for separation was first raised by Hindu merchants in Sind who did not want to compete with the merchants in Bombay. It was raised on the grounds of regional neglect. When the Congress took it up, it was transformed into a demand for a linguistic province. When the Muslim League took it up, it took on the dimension of protecting the (native) Muslim population of Sind. What happened was that the 1935 act separated Sind from Bombay, but the event took on three different hues, and each of these had something to say about the nature of the whole of which Sind was a part. Sind was an autonomous region in a larger polity whose concern with local welfare was minimal; Sind was a linguistically self-determined province in a larger imperial holding, whose separation was the first step towards a larger self-determination; Sind was sealed off in such a manner as to reduce the immigration of non-Muslim outsiders, sowing the seeds of a separate homeland for Muslims in South Asia. When the imperial holding became two states, these visions of Sind had implications for the new 'state-of-the-whole' to which it was appended – Pakistan.

The question of what is the appropriate basis for the demarcation of units is one of the most controversial ones in independent India. The 1950 constitution of India begins by describing India as a 'Union of States.'[6] According to D.D. Basu, Dr B.R. Ambedkar, the chairman of the constitution-drafting committee, had justified the committee's preference for this term 'to indicate two things, viz., (a) that the Indian federation is not the result of an agreement by the units, and (b) that the component units have no freedom to secede from it.'[7] In other words, the Indian federation is constitutionally a product of devolution by a unitary state. The very next two articles qualify this, giving the central legislature the power to admit or establish new states,[8] and also to form new states from old ones, to alter the area and composition of any state or rename a state.[9] These changes require little more than a simple majority in Parliament. There is some mention of consulting the legislature of the state in question, but it is not a prerequisite:[10] 'the affected State or States may express their views but cannot resist the will of Parliament'.[11] Therefore, it is a 'union' where the very existence of the units depends to some extent on the union. The union comprises states and union territories, where union territories are centrally administered and under the direct control of Parliament. States enjoy greater autonomy than union territories, and also have greater access to resources, a fact which explains the demand for statehood in many former union territories such as the North-East Frontier Agency (now Arunachal Pradesh), Goa and Delhi.

The first set of units in independent India followed largely *administrative* lines. As they acceded, units were placed in three categories within which they ranged in size, composition and the terms of their relationship with the centre. Independent India was a union, and as the argument in the Constituent Assembly went, the units had no existence prior to the formation of the union. They came into existence as a feature of the union. Therefore, as India commenced, apparently without history, on the basis of the social contract of its peoples, so did the units into which it was divided. When you do not recognize the historicity of units, the question of other historically rooted or shared characteristics becomes irrelevant. Therefore, in the India of modernizing leaders like Nehru, the past and its legacies are not relevant. They must be disregarded as obstructions and it is

India's 'unity in diversity' that must be celebrated. In such a vision of India, administrative efficiency can be the only basis for unit demarcation.

The idea of the administratively defined unit did have historical roots, though.[12] As the British expanded their control over Indian states, they simply appended them to whichever presidency was adjacent. Particularly on the frontier, security and development were the driving forces of any administrative arrangement they devised. The ultimate goal was political stability at the edges of the empire. Administrative (and security) considerations were paramount in the case of frontier provinces, because the administrators needed to be neutral *vis-à-vis* local politics and also the lines of communication needed to be clear and quick to the centre, in the interests of defending the empire. This has always been the justification in large empires for integrative action that tends towards centralization and towards coercion.[13] This is borne out, too, by the fact that Arunachal Pradesh (post-colonial India's North-East Frontier Agency) was only granted statehood as late as 1987. Until then, it was a centrally administered territory. So it seems that the degree of formal central control increases as one moves away from the centre, in order to maintain the natural advantage of the centre.

What might constitute 'administrative efficiency'? When Lord Curzon partitioned Bengal in 1905, the rationale proffered was administrative convenience. Leaving aside for the moment the political motivation (divide and rule) commonly ascribed to the act, what made it convenient to partition Bengal? The partition of Bengal was meant to facilitate the independent development of Assam and to streamline the administration of Bengal. That it did not serve these purposes well is irrelevant for this discussion. It was part of a larger scheme of reorganization of provinces which took into account area, resources, land tenure and other usages and even culture.[14] This represents a corrective to the earlier British practice of simply creating large units by adding new acquisitions to adjacent units, suggesting that perhaps there is to administrative organization a pattern of large, centralized units until the centre is sure of its paramountcy, followed by a confident downsizing and decentralization. Is administrative organization itself the choice of new systems where the control of the centre has not been established over the periphery and where the ruling class is not yet familiar with its new outer acquisitions? Is there a historical moment for each of these bases of demarcation?

The protest movement that followed the partition presents the first instance of linguistic politics in the subcontinent, almost suggesting that such a transition – from one form of administrative unit to another – triggers the demand for a shift to another basis for unit demarcation. The fact that linguistic identity had so much to do with the reversal of the partition underlined the diversity within Bengal, with its Oriya, Bihari, and Assamese minorities who did not have their own province. The emphasis shifted away from administrative to identity concerns, from the wider to local interests.

In a period of mass mobilization, linguistic politics was a handy way to organize and it was all the more useful for the fact that the British view on this subject differed so starkly from the Indian. The British did not favour unit demarcation on the basis of language at all. The Montagu-Chelmsford Report (1918) rejected linguistic provinces as impracticable as well as inadequate without equal consideration of other factors like resources, geography and defence. At the Nagpur session of the Indian National Congress, language was accepted as the basis for demarcating units within India. In 1917, the linguistic areas of Andhra (Telugu-speaking) and Sind (Sindi-speaking) had been designated 'Congress Priorities.' In 1920, the Congress was itself reorganized into 21 *pradeshiya* or provincial committees, each of which was linguistic. In the period of the freedom movement, the Congress regarded linguistic provinces as the local expression of the self-determination impulse. Partition changed this view somewhat.

The Dar Commission, which was appointed in 1948, rejected the notion of linguistic provinces on the grounds that they would result in a loss of administrative efficiency, that each such province would also be home to other linguistic communities – minorities within that province – and that they would threaten national unity. 'Administrative convenience' was the principle it favoured, especially in the case of Madras, Bombay and the central provinces. In December 1948, the Congress Party appointed a linguistic provinces committee, comprising Jawaharlal Nehru, Vallabhbhai Patel and Pattabhi Sitaramayya. Their mandate was to look at the question politically rather than administratively. Although this committee also concluded that the idea of linguistic provinces was not a good one, they acknowledged that the demand for them might escalate to a point that not to concede them would harm national unity more. They cited the instance of Andhra as one where the claim to a linguistic state might be legitimate. This opened the floodgates. In 1953, Potti Sriramulu's fast-unto-death forced the hand of the central government. The state of Andhra Pradesh was created in October 1953 and was the first linguistic state.

Although the terms of reference of the states reorganization committee were to keep in mind national unity and the viability of units, the principle of reorganization was implicit in their mandate. The commission did its work over two years in the midst of much debate and discussion on the issue. It recommended that Madras be further reorganized to take into account the sentiments of the Kannadigas and Malayalis, but in the case of Bombay, merely recommended that Vidarbha be carved out of Bombay and Madhya Pradesh. This led to riots as the Marathi-speaking people left in

Bombay had no wish to be marginalized by others in the state. The problem was finally resolved in 1960 with the splitting of Bombay into Maharashtra and Gujarat, keeping Vidarbha in the former.[15] Further, even in the case of Madras, while Andhra Pradesh, Karnataka and Kerala were carved out on the basis of language, Parliament continued to resist designating the remainder of Madras state as Tamil Nadu, a principle that the Pradesh Congress and the Dravida Munnetra Kazhagam both endorsed. It seems that in this case, the view that linguistic reorganization was undertaken to checkmate the growing support in the south for Dravidastan was unfounded. The terms of reorganization left the secessionist party dissatisfied and the rhetoric of separation gathered force until 1962–3. In 1963, with the formation of Nagaland as part of the settlement of that long-running insurgency, there were 16 linguistic states, several of which had minorities that spoke other languages. Forty years later, on 15 August 1996, the prime minister of India, H.D. Deve Gowda, announced in his Independence Day address that the government was going to grant statehood to a region within India's largest state: Uttarakhand out of Uttar Pradesh. This is the region of the northern Himalayan foothills. The announcement set in motion a renewal of demands from other regions within large states, like Vidarbha in Maharashtra, Gorkhaland in West Bengal, Telengana in Andhra Pradesh, and Jharkhand in Bihar.[16]

The Uttar Pradesh had resolved a couple of times earlier to recommend to the centre that a separate state should be created out of the eight hill districts of the state. This was a proposal favoured by successive state governments. The centre had not been known to favour the proposal before this, although the arguments were old and had been presented to the states reorganization commission: the hill districts were culturally and geographically distinct and now, in the intervening years, had been neglected. It was thought that setting up special hill development councils or schemes would redress the neglect, but over the years, all political parties in the area seemed to have come around to the view that statehood or some measure of the sort was inevitable. At the time of Deve Gowda's announcement, however, there was no consensus about the form it should take. The procedure for drafting the requisite legislation began on 16 August 1996 as per article 3. Not much has changed since then.

Thus we see that in the Indian case, the bases of unit demarcation were reviewed repeatedly as a response to the struggles of identity groups for autonomy. The first shift to a rationale of administrative convenience was prompted by the complaints of Sind and Andhra that they were being neglected – although both were also identified as 'linguistic provinces' by some political groups like the Congress. The second shift, in 1956, also followed the Andhra agitation. The occasional promotions to statehood of former union territories also amount to recognition that the people of the state have 'come of age' as an identity group and that they will now take their place in the polity at large. Finally, with the Uttarakhand province, we see echoes of the arguments heard in Sind in the 1920s and 1930s. In sum, each change in demarcation has been prompted by a challenge to the identity of the 'state-of-the-whole'.

Pakistan

Pakistan has always been a federation, and so it behoves us to ask why its internal structure has so consistently been a source of political discontent. To answer this, let us pick up the narrative of Pakistan's constitutional development at the moment of partition and independence. India received independence as the successor-state of the British Empire, having to deal with the integration only of those parts that had *de jure* been outside the empire. In contrast, Pakistan, which seceded from the empire, was formed as a result of provincial legislatures and leaders choosing to form a separate state.

In 1947, under Mountbatten's plan for partition, the legislatures of Bengal and Punjab would each meet in two sections, comprising in each case the Hindu and Muslim majority districts. The decision against partition would have to be unanimous. If either section chose to separate, then the process of partition would be under way. The section would also determine which constituent assembly would draft its constitution. The Sind legislative assembly would also choose which of the two constituent assemblies would frame its constitution. A referendum would be held in the Northwest Frontier Province (NWFP), and some mechanism would be worked out for Baluchistan. A referendum would be held in Sylhet to determine whether it would remain in Assam or be transferred to East Bengal. Thus, all the provinces that came together to form Pakistan had to choose to do so. Contrast this with the provinces of India that lay outside the heartland – even using multiple definitions of heartland.[17] These provinces were deemed, by virtue of their Hindu majority, to be part of India. Where anybody had a choice – for example, the princely states of Junagadh and Hyderabad – *realpolitik* limited that choice. Theoretically, the formation of Pakistan is an act that is closer to the creation of a social contract than was the formation of India or Sri Lanka. For the most part, within the limits imposed by representative rather than direct democracy, this was an act reinforced by overt consent. Why was Pakistan the first country in the post-colonial era to experience secession?

Many answers are offered for this – the role that India played; the dominance of one ethnic group (the Punjabis); the nationalism of the

Bengalis – and all of them are correct. It is argued here, however, that one needs to look at the nature of Pakistani federalism to see what made all of these things possible. Yes, Pakistan was a federation, but it was a federation whose federating units were demarcated in a manner that was deeply ambiguous and that lent itself to a variety of interpretations.

The ambiguity of Pakistan's unit demarcation stems from four facts. First, the provinces and regions of Pakistan predate Pakistan itself. K.K. Aziz, who has undertaken to trace the genesis of the idea of Pakistan through every speech and article on the subject, identifies several views on how to resolve the Hindu-Muslim equation in the subcontinent.[18] These fall into three groups: those who sought electoral representation (separate electorates), those who sought a federalist solution, and those who favoured a separate sovereign state. In the 80 years or so (1858–1940) that Aziz's survey covers, influence shifted from the first to the last solution.

Unlike most other cases of separatism, Indian Muslim separatism had no 'natural territory', no obvious home, no 'traditional homeland'. There were areas in which Muslims had ruled, and areas in which Muslims had long been a majority, but until this historical moment, there was no area that in common political talk would have been necessarily and naturally a Muslim homeland. Muslims lived all over the subcontinent. So the task of those who spoke of either federal or separatist solutions was to identify territorial units for federating or for a separate state. It was easy to identify the Muslim *qaum* (people, nation), and therefore, separate electorates were easy to conceive. In order, however, to organize a dispersed population with some pockets of concentration into a state, some scheme of territorial allocation is called for. There were several ideas that attempted to meet this need.

The argument of this section is that it is significant that most of these were lists of ethnoterritorial entities or units – Sindhis/Sind, Punjabis/ Punjab, for instance.[19] To envision Pakistan thus and then to expect the different identities to be effaced is unrealistic. The territorial bases suggested for the Muslim state ranged from the simple division of the subcontinent into two parts, north and south of the Vindhyas, to the elaborate rearrangement of populations and jurisdictions.[20]

The earliest proposals for a separate Muslim state divided the subcontinent into a Muslim north and a Hindu south (Akbar Allahabadi, 1905; Rahmat Ali, 1915; Wahabuddin Kamboh, 1923; Sardar Gul Khan, 1923; Abdus Samad Rajisthani, 1938). They gave way to those proposals that were a little more specific about what constituted the north. Initially, it is interesting that the proposals (at least those discussed by Aziz) focus on the north-western part of the subcontinent; Bengal and Hyderabad enter into the discussion later. In 1879, Jamaluddin Afghani is said to have proposed a Muslim republic comprising Muslim central Asia, Afghanistan, and

Muslim-majority areas in the north-west. In 1918, the Aga Khan visualized a north-western Indus province in a south Asian federation comprising Sind, NWFP, and Baluchistan. Ten years later, he talked about joining Muslim provinces of north and west India into a separate state. In 1920, M.A.Q. Bilgrami suggested the partition of Punjab and Bengal, and the creation of a separate province of Sind. In 1928, M.A.K. Maikash is quoted as suggesting a Muslim national homeland comprising Punjab, Sind, Baluchistan and NWFP. In 1930, Iqbal suggested a state comprising Punjab, NWFP, Sind and Baluchistan.[21] In 1933, Rahmat Ali made his famous suggestion that a separate state – Pakistan – be formed comprising Punjab, NWFP, Kashmir, Sind, and Baluchistan. In 1937, M.H.Gazdar proposed a separate federation of Punjab, Sind, NWFP and Baluchistan. In the same year, Rahmat Ali advocated the creation of a separate Muslim state of Bang-i-Islam constituted by Bengal and Assam, and two years later, he added Osmanistan (Hyderabad) to the list of states he advocated.

As the clamor for partition mounted among the Muslim leadership and as it seemed more and more inevitable to the Muslims, schemes for partition became very detailed and involved massive transfers of population. Some of their features include corridors to link the north-west with Bengal, the creation of a Muslim block in the Gangetic heartland with the migration of populations from other areas and, most dramatically, the suggestion that the Maharajah of Kashmir and the Nawab of Hyderabad exchange their states! It is important to note that almost every way of visualizing what would constitute the new Muslim state involved the listing of regions that are identified by the ethnic community residing there (or the other way around, but the point is that there is a dominant ethnic group in each of these areas). This clearly indicates that in the creation of Pakistan, the building blocks were regions with forms and histories that preceded Pakistan. The 'state of the whole' is created by the coming together of the parts here, and therefore, is *either equal to or more than* the sum of its parts, but it cannot be *other than* what its parts are, taken together.

When Pakistan finally came into existence, it came into existence with two wings – an eastern wing comprising East Bengal and the Sylhet district of Assam, and a western wing, comprising West Punjab, NWFP, Sind and Baluchistan. (Parts of Kashmir subsequently came under Pakistani control.) The two wings were divided by Indian territory, and formed two 'natural' units of the Pakistani state. This would seem to simplify the question of unit demarcation, except that the ethnic composition of the two wings was not anywhere similar. The eastern wing was preponderantly Bengali-speaking, although there were Biharis who had migrated there during partition, as well as Assamese and Chakmas. The other groups were very small minorities, and the Bengali impress upon the eastern wing gave it a homogeneous cast.

The western wing was quite different. Not only was it composed of provinces/regions that had been the building-blocks of the idea of Pakistan – Punjab, Sind, NWFP and Baluchistan, to say nothing of Kashmir – but it also had tremendous cultural diversity within it. Several of the communities had occupied their region for centuries and the land bore the mark of their histories ineffably. To treat the two wings as similar units, as the 'one unit' system did, was to ignore this fact. It was also to raise the question of what, other than the accident of geography, was the basis of unit demarcation. In the east, it would seem to have been ethnicity as well as geography, and in the west, it was merely geography.

When you work your way back from the resulting 'vision' of the unit to the 'vision' of the whole, you have two different takes on what post-colonial Pakistan actually was, as opposed to what the vision had been prior to independence. If you were from East Pakistan, then as your unit might well have been defined by ethnicity, the state would seem to have to be a culmination of many singular ethnic units. Therefore, the actions of such a state *vis-à-vis* cultural policy must seem like the actions of either a state that is a composite of many ethnic groups or one that is not ethnically neutral. The reaction of the East Pakistanis to Urdu as the national language bears this out. If the state was a composite of their dominant ethnic group and others, then that was the action of a state that had chosen one of its components over others. From the perspective of the West Pakistanis, this was not as much of an issue largely because it was their language that had been selected, but there is also the fact that since they now formed a unit in which their individual identities had been effaced, the state from their perspective was a legal composite of two geographical wings. It does not follow, from a unit that has no ethnic basis, that the state would have one. Their anxieties surrounded the population differential between the two wings, and the fear of always being outvoted by the East.

Two different, if not contrasting, visions follow from the ambiguity of the basis of unit demarcation. To be sure, it was a function of geography, but were there ways of undermining that geography? The creation of smaller units in either wing, for instance, might have undermined the ethnic basis in the east – but would the natural next step in the west have been the retention of the old ethnoterritorial regions, thus reversing the situation? Any single system of unit demarcation would have proven problematic sooner or later, given the awkward geography of the post-colonial Pakistani state. In 50 years, the state has, however, experimented with three systems. In 1947, as noted, the Pakistani state was created out of the constitutive choices of its units. These, it left initially as they were, except for carving Karachi out of Sind as the federal capital – a choice which would have grave consequences for Karachi in the 1980s and 1990s.

In 1955, the 'one unit' system was introduced. By this system, a false parity was introduced between East and West Pakistan, by consolidating them into the two federating units in the state. The four constitutive provinces of West Pakistan were merged to create that unit. The idea was that this would help the west balance the numerical dominance of the east. That is, the population of East Bengal was so much larger than that of the provinces in the west that the east would have dominated any federal legislature. By creating two units of equal importance, the potential dominance of the east was diminished. From the perspective of the east, it would now be underrepresented in the federal legislature. On the other hand, regional parties and leaders were unhappy over their displacement as their spheres of influence disappeared overnight. More importantly, 'one unit' meant greater centralization and the result pleased no one save the centre.

After the secession of Bangladesh, the old provinces were restored in another federal arrangement. Today, their relation to the federal government is no more equal than before, but they do have their identities.

Finally, the identity of the 'state of the whole' suggested that there could be no differences within, contradicting the first three facts. Pakistan has been an Islamic state in all its three constitutions. The state is exhorted in each of these to create such a climate that the differences between Muslims are erased, that Muslims are no longer divided among themselves. Where does this leave a state which was first formed as a union of regions which had Muslim majorities, but was nonetheless as a union of regions? The normative emphasis on erasing differences, and the need for groups and regions to retain their identity and relative autonomy, are framed in classic opposition here.

Karachi exemplifies this. In the early years after independence, when the federal capital was located at Karachi, the city attracted a large number of migrants from India (*Muhajirs*). These people came from those provinces in India that had lent the greatest support to the Pakistan movement. They settled in Karachi and they dominated the administrative class. Over decades, the combined immigration into Karachi of labour from nearby provinces and the growing dominance of the *Muhajir* community led to the marginalization of the 'indigenous' Sindi population. On the one hand, undeniably, Karachi made its appearance in history as a Sindi city, but on the other, like all port cities, it has always attracted outsiders, particularly after Sind was merged with the Bombay Presidency. The *Muhajir* settlement of Karachi was not even the latest of the waves of immigrants in the city's history. In the battle for Karachi, three claims are at stake and all three are fundamental to the identity of the collective that makes them. The Sindis claim Karachi because their dominance in their eponymous province is restricted to the rural areas. The *Muhajirs* claim Karachi because they have nowhere else in Pakistan. The state has an interest in neutralizing either claim because like Bombay in India and Colombo in Sri Lanka, Karachi is the economic magnet for labour from its hinterland and thus it is critical to the state that no parochial claim is entirely recognized. Cities like the three mentioned above epitomize the secularizing, modernizing, identity-effacing drive of the modern nation-state. The identity of the state-of-the-whole of Pakistan is written also in the identity of Karachi, as it is in all other units.

The demarcation of units may not be the most pressing issue in the politics of Pakistan, but it appears in the post-colonial political history of the state as one of the consistent threads in the warp and weft of its fabric. Units appear in the early visions of the state, and they come together to create the state. The state's experiments with their demarcation render its own definition ambiguous and finally, when the units reappear, they do so in strange contrast to the monochrome assumed by the state-of-the-whole. In fact, Pakistan is the most telling example of the relationship between identity and internal unit demarcation that is outlined here.

Sri Lanka

How do you manage a unitary state composed of two peoples with territorial bases who view themselves as distinct nations? This is the question that Sri Lanka has grappled with for five decades.

The unitary state that the Colebrooke-Cameron reforms initiated in 1829 continues in independent Sri Lanka. The British were the first to extend their sovereignty over the entire island and their creation of the unitary state is attributed to a wish to increase and institutionalize their control over the island. The first would be achieved because the unitary, centralized state would diminish the importance and therefore, power of the Kandyan chieftains. The second would be accomplished as a centralized administration would be better able to plan and develop a communications system for the island. This is similar to their early policy in India.

In the early years, representation in the political arrangements in Colombo served as the bone of contention between rivals in the Colombo élite, who happened also to be ethnically different. However, this rivalry enlisted the rhetoric of two distinct nations,[22] who must be represented in one state. Battles over representation involved definition of the group to be represented and part of that definition was territorial. In the 1940s, S.W.R.D. Bandaranaike, who was minister for local government affairs, began to espouse the creation of provincial councils. This idea was stillborn, however, although it was closely identified with Bandaranaike's support base and with the Federal Party.

In its founding resolution in 1949, the Federal Party asserted that Tamils needed to have 'their own autonomous state guaranteeing self-government and self-determination for the Tamil nation in the country.'[23] K.M. de Silva says that in the original Tamil version of the Federal Party's resolution, it is hard to tell whether the Tamils wanted autonomy or separatism. Therefore, that agenda of the Federal Party lent itself to every incarnation of the Tamil nationalist impulse. In 1951, the Federal Party claimed that 'the Tamil-speaking people in [Sri Lanka] constituted a nation distinct from that of the Sinhalese in every fundamental test of nationhood'.[24] The Federal Party also raised the allegation of 'colonization' – or the relocation of Sinhalese in the newly irrigated areas of the north-east. They alleged that the government was trying to alter the demographic balance between ethnic groups in the area. The 'traditional homelands' of the Tamils made their first appearance at this time as the Federal Party resolved that the 'Tamil-speaking people have an inalienable right to the territories which they have been traditionally occupying.'[25] In 1956, at its national convention, the Federal Party referred to the 'traditional homelands of the Tamil-speaking people', who were being overwhelmed 'in their own national areas.'[26] These areas were soon after identified as the Northern and Eastern provinces. Thus, the 'traditional homelands' idea was first mooted and used in the context of the government's resettlement policy and was an element of the solution proposed by the Bandaranaike-Chelvanayagam Pact to this problem. If a local authority was going to make decisions about the allocation of reclaimed arable land and employment, what was to constitute 'local'?

The Bandaranaike-Chelvanayagam Pact was signed in January 1956. At this point, the 'communal' element was still seen as being in the minority within each community.[27] In the quest to isolate it, the pact agreed that regional councils would constitute the unit of devolution, where the Northern Province would constitute one province and the Eastern Province would constitute two or more regions. This was in recognition of the diversity of the Eastern Province. Regions might merge, with the merger subject to ratification by Parliament, and they might collaborate. The right of Tamils to use their language for administrative and court business was also recognized. The regional councils were granted power to make decisions about local development issues and about the re-settlement of population in newly irrigated areas. While the regional councils were welcomed, the pact did not recognize the north-east as a Tamil area in the way that linguistic states in India did. The Bandaranaike-Chelvanayagam Pact's proposal to create regional councils was abrogated within a year, faced with opposition from the Eksath Bhikkhu Peramuna, the United National Party and the Tamil Congress. Thereafter, the demand for regional autonomy abated.[28]

The 1965 agreement between Dudley Senanayake and S. J. V. Chelvanayagam settled on the district as the unit of devolution, setting up district councils whose powers would be agreed upon in the national interest. Tamils should get priority for resettlement in the newly irrigated areas of the north. Early legislation providing for the use of Tamil in administrative transactions all over the island was to be implemented. Stopping far short of the Bandaranaike-Chelvanayagam Pact, this was however, accepted by the Federal Party, a member of which assumed the local government portfolio in the Cabinet. The Federal Party described this pact as a stage in the ongoing negotiation of a settlement between the two communities. Critics accused the Tamil leadership of placing class interests before the interests of the Tamil masses, a charge that still resonates in Tamil circles today. Fissures also developed between the Tamil parties and the left.[29] With the formation of the Tamil United Front (TUF) in 1972, an attempt was made to bring together the now-splintered Tamil leadership of the Federal Party and the All-Ceylon Tamil Congress.

Parallel to the brewing ethnic crisis, there was some debate and progress on decentralization in the context of development administration in Sri Lanka, with the discussion focusing on district development councils. The 1972 and 1978 constitutions established Sri Lanka as an ethnically identified and explicitly unitary state. The 1978 constitution specified that the unit of devolution was the district and listed their names. In rejection of the 1972 constitution, S.J.V. Chelvanayagam resigned from Parliament. By the time that he campaigned for his seat again, the complexion of Tamil politics had changed enough that the idea of *Tamil Eelam* [homeland] had crept into the campaign rhetoric.[30] The traditional homelands idea gained ground even as the grievances of Tamils grew in number. In 1976, in the Vaddukodai Resolution, the Tamil United Liberation Front (TULF) espoused the idea of a *Tamil Eelam* for the first time. To do so, they drew on a history of Tamil statehood that had been narrated authoritatively and persuasively by scholars like C. Suntheralingam.[31] *Tamil Eelam* was to consist of the Northern and Eastern provinces of Sri Lanka. In the period of Indian mediation in the crisis, Tamil 'traditional homelands' were part of the Tamil representation to the Indian government, and the success of that representation was evident in the selection of the province as the unit of devolution and the merger, albeit temporary, of the Northern and Eastern provinces.

After the 1983 riots, the TULF withdrew from Parliament and an all-party conference was convened to discuss the political crisis. The conference set up one committee to look expressly into the question of the unit of devolution. The conference faced a deadlock between two non-negotiable positions: one that would concede nothing more than district councils and the other unwilling to settle for anything less than regional councils. President Jayawardene's solution was to promote inter-district cooperation. Later in 1984, the conference managed a consensus on many questions short of supporting provincial councils as the main subnational unit. The hierarchy of government went, top-to-bottom, thus: the national government in Colombo – inter-district coordination – district councils – urban and municipal councils – *pradeshiya mandalaya*. This was rejected by the TULF. As India became more and more involved with the process of negotiation in Sri Lanka, Indian government officials came up with their own suggestions, but the thrust of all of them was to favour the region or the province as the unit of devolution. Although this was originally anathema, the turn of events saw the passage of the Pradeshiya Sabhas Act in 1987 and the establishment of the provincial legislatures. Ten years after the Indo-Sri Lanka Accord of 1987, while the province seems to have replaced the district as the first unit of devolution, there is still no consensus about the basis of its demarcation (as opposed to level).

In the case of Sri Lanka, the unit of devolution was contentious for three reasons. The first point of contention had to do with whether the district or another level of government (such as the province) should be the unit. This is what the discussions in the 1980s revolved around. The second point of contention was whether the creation of a new unit or level of government meant the changing of the basic nature of the unitary state. This is what fuels the strongest opposition to devolution. But the third point remains the most contentious to date, even as the idea that some kind of devolution is unavoidable is accepted, no matter how reluctantly. This is the question of what shall demarcate the unit. The Tamil demand for devolution assumes that the unit of devolution will be coterminous with the traditional homeland they claim. The problem with that is twofold. One, the historical bases of that claim itself are specious. Two, the category 'Tamil' in this claim is also contested. Tamils have tended to include the Muslims of Sri Lanka in their number because they are largely Tamil-speaking. So the category 'Tamil' is actually 'Tamil-speaking.' The Muslims, however, have never regarded themselves as part of this community. The more conservative among the Sinhalese, in their dispute with the Tamils, use this as an additional reason not to concede the extent of devolution desired by the Tamils.

Thus, in Sri Lanka, we see that as the idea of the 'state-of-the-whole' became more and more contentious, ideas of alternative ways of demarcating spaces within that whole – in this case, an island – crystallized into expressions of that contestation. Again, the relationship between the idea of the 'state-of-the-whole' and the way in which that whole is structured is shown to be close, even symbiotic.

The Identity-Unit Demarcation Relationship: Closing Thoughts

The three cases examined here suggest that the idea that national identity is expressed through internal unit demarcation bears further investigation. In India, changes in the bases of unit demarcation follow demands from identity groups for greater autonomy. In Pakistan, national identity is the sum of consenting units with distinct identities. In Sri Lanka, the rejection of the national identity is expressed as the demand for a separate unit. The larger work from which this paper is drawn also studies the histories of regional groups in these countries. Those histories reinforce this view of the relationship between identity and internal unit demarcation. A sense of self and the concomitant demands that a group makes acquire a territorial dimension soon enough, and it is really at this point that the contest between them and the state intensifies.

If this holds, then reorganization of units is in fact the conflict resolution measure as India has used it. More often than not, states do not have a choice, and creating a new unit may buy the state some time before a group goes from identifying to actualizing as a new state the embodiment of its vision. The rule of thumb, experience suggests, is flexibility. What distinguishes the Indian experience, all its failures notwithstanding, seems to be the willingness of the state-of-the-whole, by and large, to enter into *ad hoc*, case-by-case arrangements of its territory and polity. This has resulted in a plethora of special provisions and awkward exceptions to the neat hierarchy of administrative units, but it has kept conflict to a minimum. It is in those instances and periods that the state has been unwilling to do this, that conflict has become unmanageable. The idea that internal unit demarcation is an expression of national identity explains this reluctance – in India, in Pakistan and in Sri Lanka. Equally, unilateral decisions about unit demarcation undermine group identity or the terms on which the group has acceded to the national identity, and therefore they too are bitterly contested, as we see with Pakistan and the 'one unit' arrangement.

If the territorialization of collective vision is detrimental to the goal of a lasting and sustainable integration in society, then how is it to be prevented? What cannot be done is to change overnight the nature of an inter-state system that begins with territorial units. Short of that, there are a few things that can be attempted, by state and non-state agents.

- Pre-emptive alleviation of the proto-territorial collectivity's fears and insecurities.
- The suggestion of alternative histories to those laying claim to the territorial space of an administrative unit.
- The facilitation of communication and interaction that diminish the salience of internal boundaries.

IDENTITY AND TERRITORIAL AUTONOMY IN PLURAL SOCIETIES

- The devolution of power to those regions that might become 'traditional homelands', but without their recognition as such, prior to the association of the area with such a claim.
- Demarcation of administrative units within the state, not as a fiat, but as a consultative process, so that the bases of demarcation shall be commonly agreed.
- Recognition that for a state, external boundaries are much more important than internal, and that therefore flexibility and responsiveness on questions of internal demarcation are possible.

This paper is part of a larger effort to establish inductively the terms and conditions whereby a 'national community' may be forged by a state within its populace. The argument that territory and identity are closely related is given operational form here as the establishment of a relationship between the identity of a collective and the way in which space is organized within, reflecting the relationships in which the collective holds its components. The argument may be now further tested in a larger number of historical cases to determine its veracity and validity.

NOTES

Barry Buzan, *People, States and Fear* (Boulder, CO: Lynne Rienner, 1992), p.65.
2. Gaston Bachelard, *The Poetics of Space* (New York: The Orion Press, 1964), p.5.
3. Michael Taussig, *The Magic of the State* (New York: Routledge, 1997).
4. Hamida Khuhro, *The Making of Modern Sind: British Policy and Social Change in the Nineteenth Century* (Karachi: Indus Publications, 1978), pp.14–15.
5. Suhail Zaheer Lari, *A History of Sind* (Karachi: Oxford, 1994), pp.179.
6. *The Constitution of India*, Part I, Article 1(1).
7. Durga Das Basu, *Introduction to the Constitution of India* (New Delhi: Prentice-Hall of India, 1982), p.49. He points out that constitutions as varied as the US, South Africa (1909) and the USSR (1936) all have used the word 'union.' In the pages that follow, Basu provides a discussion of what constitutes a federal constitution and the points of consonance and dissonance between the Indian constitution and such a constitution.
8. *Indian Constitution*, Article 2.
9. Ibid., Article 3.
10. 'Provided that no Bill for the purpose shall be introduced in either House of Parliament except on the recommendation of the President and unless, where the proposal contained in the Bill affects the area, boundaries or name of any of the States, the Bill has been referred by the President to the Legislature of that State for expressing its views thereon within such period as may be specified in the reference or within such further period as the President may allow and the period so specified or allowed has expired.' *Indian Constitution*, Article 3, proviso.
11. Basu, p.67.
12. The main source for the historical information in the paragraphs that follow is B.B. Misra, *The Unification and Division of India* (Oxford: Oxford University Press, 1990). Misra has provided a detailed and authoritative account of the process of integrating the territories of princely India and British India into post-colonial India.
13. Swarna Rajagopalan, 'Regime Maintenance in Two Pre-Modern Indian Polities', unpublished, 1993.

14. Misra, pp.158–67.
15. In 1995–6, the United Front government at the centre has accepted in principle the idea of smaller states, throwing open the issue of Vidarbha and other regions once again.
16. 'Uttarakhand, not the last', *The Indian Express*, pp.8–17, 96.
17. In the context of British India, the heartland could be construed as the Hindi heartland, or the three presidency areas, whose claim to be 'centre' was stronger in the political economy sense in this period.
18. K.K.Aziz, *A History of the Idea of Pakistan*, Vols.1–4 (Lahore: Vanguard, 1987). The first three volumes survey and discuss the context, content and historiography of each contribution to the development of the idea. At the end of the third volume, Aziz sorts the ideas and their authors in a variety of ways – by idea, by period, by education, by origin. The last volume is a bibliography of works cited. Two companion volumes of *Prelude to Pakistan 1930–40: Documents and readings illustrating the growth of the idea of Pakistan*, edited by K.K.Aziz, were published by Vanguard, Lahore, 1992. Together, the two sets form an invaluable resource for students of Pakistani history, given the paucity of historical writing in that country in the post-colonial period. This section draws on Aziz's comprehensive account.
19. Aziz's Table 13 in Vol.3, *A History of the Idea of Pakistan*, encapsulates the territorial demands made by 15 proponents of partition.
20. While the following section talks only about schemes originated by Indian Muslims, there were several Europeans and Indian Hindus who also proposed territorial divisions. It should be noted that Aziz discusses the problems of attribution and sources for each of these at length. In this section, I have decided to ignore that discussion because it is not germane to our discussion whether Afghani, for instance, did in fact propose what he did, when it is widely believed that he did so. We are concerned with the ideas with which people are believed to have come up, and to the visions of the state that these have built.
21. This is usually interpreted as a suggestion for a separate state, but Aziz contests this interpretation. Again, while Aziz is convincing, since it is the commonly held ideas about the territorial bases of the Pakistani state we are researching, this will be included here.
22. It is interesting that this is something that happened in Sri Lankan politics and in the politics of the Dravidian movement at this time, and that it parallels the Pakistan Movement. The latter appears to have inspired at least the Dravidian movement by their own admission and allusion. It would be an interesting study that asked to what extent the Dravidian movement influenced changes in Sri Lankan politics.
23. Quoted in K.M. de Silva, *The 'traditional homelands' of the Tamils* (Kandy: International Centre for Ethnic Studies, 1995), p.6. This monograph is the main source for the information in the next few paragraphs. It provides an excellent account of the development of this idea, and then critiques its historical validity.
24. Ibid., p.7.
25. Ibid., p.7. The centrality of colonial arguments to much that happens today is illustrated by the fact that one of the sources most often cited as proof of this claim is Cleghorn's Minute (1799) – the work of a British administrator, Hugh Cleghorn. The minute states that from the earliest times, the island has been occupied by two distinct nations, concentrated and 'possessing' very different parts of the island.
26. De Silva, p.8.
27. Ketheshwaran Loganathan, *Sri Lanka: Lost Opportunities* (Colombo: Centre for Policy Research and Analysis, University of Colombo, 1996), p.20.
28. The next two paragraphs are based on the account in Victor Gunawardena, 'Provincial Councils System: A Critical Perspective', in Chanaka Amaratunga (ed.), *Ideas for Constitutional Reform: Proceedings of a series of seven seminars on the Constitution of Sri Lanka conducted by the Council for Liberal Democracy, November 1987–June 1989* (Colombo: Council for Liberal Democracy, 1989).
29. Loganathan, pp.36–7.
30. Ibid., pp.57–9.
31. De Silva, p.12.

The Political Demands of Isolated Indian Bands in British Columbia

DENNIS L THOMSON

The identity and autonomy of the native peoples of Canada are not straightforward issues. Canada is a country which has invested considerable political effort into discussions of multiculturalism, language and the identity of its citizens. Yet the Canadian Indians[1] have not always benefited from that discussion or from the legislation which has followed. There are several layers in the Canadian consideration of ethnicity. First is the problem of Canada trying to distinguish itself from Britain, with whom it was closely tied for over two centuries as a colony and still remains tied as a member of the Commonwealth. There is not much evidence that other peoples were much concerned or confused about the bonds between Canada and Britain. Politically they were seen as allies, but externally they were viewed as separate nations with the same language. Secondly, the Canadians have been concerned with distinguishing themselves from the Americans to the south. There was initially an antagonism which remained after the American War of Independence when non-separationist Americans fled north into then colonial Canada and promoted their biases. This antagonism resulted in the War of 1812. Since then, as the United States grew in size, population and power there has remained a concern about a sense of identity. Canadians remain quick to point out what distinguishes them from Americans, although it is often a tortured explanation. But it was important for the Canadians to have a distinct national identity to justify their existence, particularly with regard to the United States and Great Britain.

Finally, and constantly on the agenda, is the role and recognition of French foundations and language, not only in Quebec, but by law throughout the country. There has existed a myth that French Canadians were one of the two 'founding races', the other being the British, but not the aborigines. Thus, the French Canadians were given a privileged position in Canadian history, while the Indians were not. When the Royal Commission on Bilingualism and Biculturalism was created in 1969, its mandate was not to consider the culture and language of the Indians, but of the French-

Dennis L Thomson, Brigham Young University

speaking Canadians. And in 1971, in response to the commission's report, there was a governmental policy that recognized biculturalism and bilingualism. Eventually the term biculturalism was replaced by multiculturalism, but the emphasis did not change perceptibly.[2] Interestingly, multiculturalism has become one of the things 'Canadian' that distinguishes the country from the United States and Great Britain. Canada acknowledges and celebrates this distinction, whereas the United States does not.

The Canadian Indians are not a unitary group. Historically there are tribal divisions, which have been accepted both internally and externally. Thus we know of the Cree, the Mohawks, the Blackfeet, and others. They are known as tribes, an anthropological term, but in effect they are communities of people who live in some organized status. In some instances they are indeed nations which have interacted with other nations on the international scene, most often in the past. Interestingly, as Europeans became acquainted with the various communities, each was dealt with as an independent entity. Later, the European governments and their successors dealt with the Indian communities collectively as if their interests and needs were the same. While many, probably most, of the Canadian Indians have a strong desire to maintain some of their traditional ways, they have nonetheless become a part of the larger nation. Many are urbanized; most wish to participate fully in the national economy; most have adopted the basic living patterns of the European cultures; their language is that of the dominant society; and they aspire to education and recognition by the majority. Our focus here is a subset of Canadian Indians who have not found a reason to abandon their traditional life patterns for a European lifestyle and who have not seen in the alternative culture any benefits that would cause them to abandon that traditional culture they have inherited.

It is difficult to define a traditional culture. Culture is not static as it changes over time; so that it is difficult to determine at what point it is no longer traditional. Nearly all Canadian Indians would claim that they adhere to tradition. But there are significant levels of acculturation differences. As Légaré reports,

> Aboriginal leaders are placed in a defensive position, continually forced to ... 'prove' the purity and continuity of their own culture. The land claim of the *Gitskan-Wet'suwet'en* Tribal Council is a recent example. In that case, one of the government lawyers argued that, because they watched television and ate pizza, the *Gitskan* had no basis for their land claims. ... In ruling against the *Gitskan-Wet'suwet'en*, Chief Justice McEachern noted he had to reject many of the defendants' claims that their culture has 'always been more or less as it is now'.[3]

These kinds of attitudes induce the Indians to suppress the many sides of their identities to avoid criticism.

To allow themselves to continue in a traditional lifestyle, the Indians have had to maintain a degree of isolation from the dominant society. In doing so they follow somewhat the pattern of other peoples in the world whom I have called cultural isolationists.[4] These are groups who have preferred to isolate themselves and not participate in the processes of government because they do not wish to be influenced or coopted, who do not want to share in the rewards and resources distributed to others,[5] and who want to maintain their distinctive group identities in isolation.

The cultural isolationists often pursue values not consistent with the actual policy practices of government. In general, 'they are groups that wish to remain pastoral, agrarian, isolated, or non-mechanized, who reject the supposed benefits of modern technological society or who at most accept some of these benefits as secondary to higher goals or values. They adhere to traditions, customs, language or dress out of preference.'[6]

I argue that in a country like Canada, where the idea of cultural pluralism plays an important role in national policy, it can best be judged if the country respects the cultural isolationists. If cultural pluralism is an important aspect of democratic governance in a country, then it is strengthened and made more secure by its manifestation on the edges of majoritarian society. The issues engendered by cultural isolationists are not so fundamental to the foundations of the Canadian or, for that matter, the US political systems that resolution to accommodate the isolated minorities would harm society, but instead it would strengthen the concept of pluralistic governance embodied in the Trudeau policy of multiculturalism. The cultural isolationists do not seek to confront society, but live on its edges. The Amish and the Hutterites in Canada and the United States and the Sami in Norway are examples of cultural isolationists in their respective countries. The sources of cultural differentiation found among those who attempt to maintain distinctive group identity may be religious, ethnic or linguistic, or a combination of those.[7] The Indians in Canada, or the United States, for that matter, who seek cultural isolation have as their sources potentially a combination of all three. To be a cultural isolationist one does not have to live in isolation, though that helps. At the core, it is an attitude.

The Anglo-Saxons in Canada, with their culture and religion, continue to dominate society; thus rights, privileges, and recognition of others come from the Anglo-Saxon hands. For practical reasons of national unity and recognition of their economic and political strength, the French of Quebec have been included; thus, they and their Northern European cousins were exempted from the melting-pot. Everyone else was supposed to become subservient to the political and economic élites of Ontario and Quebec.[8]

Many of the attributes of nationhood which had been built on unitary values with an identifiable ideal as a reference point affect current policies.[9]

Canada accepts political pluralism, but it is a pluralism that is primarily based upon the French and English language and upon voluntary participation in competing political parties and (socioeconomic or professional) interest groups. Government, however, has never automatically accepted cultural, racial, linguistic or even religious diversity as being legitimate, and there are numerous instances of conflict between groups of this sort and the government. In Canada, eventually biculturalism and bilingualism have become accepted institutionalized policy, but it was not always so. Those pluralistic groups that are politically accredited may or may not be seen as participants in the public policy process. They have had to be justified, and sometimes rejustified, each time they attempt to become involved in the political process. Furthermore, to the extent to which the Canadian Indians have been seen as participants in the public arena they have been regarded as an entity, a unitary whole rather than as many peoples with distinctive interests and attitudes towards the larger society.

Canadian Indians as a class have been subjected to a system of values different from those they have traditionally held. In addition to an external economic standard, Indians have been subjected to a foreign concept of territoriality, including residence, place, and property. As such many Indian communities have been restricted in their movement. Some of them have been nomadic, while the majority has insisted that they should settle in one spot. For some, like the Mohawks, national boundaries have divided tribes and restricted north/south movement.

In a significant way the religious side of the tribes' ethnicity is a very important aspect of their identity, one that has been eradicated by majoritarian society. European and North American religious organizations, churches, and missionary societies have been engaged to assist in the governmental acculturation programs. There are many instances where missionaries have been given access to tribal and band territories, while at the same time traditional religious practices have been restricted. There are no cases where indigenous religion has been protected.

In the Constitution Act of 1982, the aboriginal peoples of Canada were defined as Indian, Inuit and Metis. Traditionally they have been considered as two categories – status and non-status Indians. A status Indian is one who qualifies as an Indian, and is registered, or is entitled to register, as an Indian under Canadian law. In fact, the Indian Act of 1876 defined an Indian as 'a person who pursuant to this Act is registered as an Indian, or is entitled to be registered as an Indian.' One did not have to belong to an Indian community that had signed a treaty in order to qualify. Today, about two-thirds are status Indians. 'Non-status' Indians are those who have not registered. They do not have official definition, yet it is recognized that there are Indians who have no legal status but are still identifiable as Indians. For example, children of an Indian woman married to a non-Indian lost their right to status. Numerous variations cropped up over time. Furthermore, the Canadian government uses the term 'band' rather than 'tribe' to describe Indian communities. A band is what the government has declared it to be.

It has been difficult to identify Indian communities that remain a group in cultural isolation. There are many Indians who long for a return to traditional ways and beliefs, but not many seriously pursue that goal. The Mohawks of eastern Canada are certainly militant in defence of their culture; but they participate in a major way in the Canadian economy and engage in militant behaviour towards governments. In Canada the Indians who come closest to being cultural isolationists are in British Columbia. They inhabit areas that, for the most part, have not been in the path of development. Thus, they can remain physically isolated from the paths of acculturation, though there are none who are fully isolated either physically or culturally.

There are a considerable number of Indians in British Columbia who remain physically isolated. For example, the Kincolith Band of the Nishga Indians live in comparative physical isolation from society on the lower reaches of the Nass River on the coast of upper British Columbia. There are no roads into their area; yet they have ready contact with the outside world by radio-telephone, daily floatplane service, and satellite television. In my interviews with band officials they never expressed any concern about maintaining their culture, but they were single-mindedly interested in getting more benefits from the Canadian government.

There are still others, like the Fort Ware Band of the Sekani Indians, who became isolated by the construction of the Bennett Dam on the Finlay Reach of the Peace River in upper British Columbia. The valley floor became flooded and they were shut off from the outside world. They still survive, but do not have a viable society. Government officials report that there is extensive drug abuse, alcoholism, and child abuse. Vandalism is common in the community. Most of the people have guns and use them. The Ingenika Band was also flooded out by the Bennett Dam. Its members were forced to move and squatted on provincial crown lands at the north end of the Finlay Reach. They have been left there, although no reserve boundaries have been determined. The village of Portage of the Tlazten Band is near Stewart Lake near Fort St James. It first got road access about ten years ago, yet it still remains isolated. The community is a troubled one with many social problems. Its members would like to break away from the band, but they have no leadership to make it happen. Another group is the El Gacho Band of the Carrier Indians who live on the shores of Anaheim Lake about 80 miles from the coast. They are still nomads. They gather berries, fish and hunt moose, and derive their income from trapping. They have little interaction with the government. Some of them will drop into an Indian office and pick up a welfare cheque because it is there. Then they disappear again with no routine for regular contact.

Let us consider two bands who attempt to stay culturally isolated; they are organized and live in peripheral contact with the larger society. For the most part they govern themselves, but with the financial backing of the Canadian government. They are the Nemiah Valley Chilcotin and the Kluskus band of the Carrier who live on the West Road River west of the village of Nazko. Both live in central British Columbia. They are not necessarily more traditional than some other Indian bands, but they are more independent. They make demands, but they do not organize politically to get their demands met nor do they persist in a lobbying effort to achieve their wants.

The Nemiah Valley Band of the Chilcotin number about 360 people. There are six other bands in the Chilcotin tribe. They live in a fairly arid area just north of the Fraser Valley. They live traditionally and still use the ancient Chilcotin place names. The Indian personal names have disappeared, but they are returning to the practice of giving their children traditional Chilcotin names. All of the population speak Chilcotin, and no English is spoken on the reserves. However, most of them are also able to speak English because they learn it in school. Band meetings are held in Chilcotin.

There is a school in Nemiah Valley, which was built in 1978. At first it offered grades one through seven; in the early 1980s it was expanded from kindergarten through grade nine. Children from grades ten through 12 still go to the town of Williams Lake, a hundred miles away, where the band office is. There they board with a few band members who are permanent residents in the town. Significantly, they teach the Chilcotin language up to grade three. Part of their education is tied to the traditional religion, which teaches respect for the land, wildlife, water and people through tradition and legends. These teachings are contained in stories of the seasons. When children live at home they hear the full range of stories; when they go away to boarding schools they miss out on the stories of some of the seasons. In their tradition they also had a well-defined role for women, which was lost, but is now coming back.

Their economy is mostly ranching, though they do not function in a commercial sense. They raise cattle, but do not necessarily sell them in the fall market; rather, they sell them piecemeal as they need cash. They raise a lot of horses, but these are not for sale; rather, they are used as a measure of wealth. Many of the people still hunt, pick berries and trap for furs, but trapping has declined because of the decline in fur prices. They fish and dry the fish for later use. Their area has not yet been touched by logging, although they have been threatened by the timber industry as it has moved close by. They find it increasingly difficult to live off the land, because there is constant pressure of encroachment into their territory. Trap lines are interrupted and roads bring in outsiders with different interests.

The Nemiah Valley Chilcotin are governed by a traditional chief and council. They have their own elections and notify the Department of Indian and Northern Affairs (DINA) when they are over. Although the DINA has required elections every five years, the Chilcotin elected their chiefs every two years until this year, when they adopted a five-year term –for their own reasons, they insist, and not because of government demand. The current chief is Roger William, a member of the band council since 1988, who was elected chief in 1991 and reelected in 1993, for a five year term. The previous chief was a woman, who is now the band's manager.

The Nemiah Valley Chilcotin have accepted DINA funds, but on a selective basis. A number of their people accept welfare payments, but not all. They make use of the Canadian health programmes and have accepted money for economic development and for water and housing. In addition to a government-funded school, they recently applied for money for an apprenticeship training programme and now have four persons enrolled. Yet they have rejected a government sponsored electrification project. In 1989 the Canadian government offered to bring power into the valley, but it was turned down. They believed that the availability of power would induce non-natives to move in the valley.

The Chilcotin Indians do not mind using Canadian institutions to get what they want, and they are not averse to using direct action if they are unsuccessful through 'normal' processes. In 1991 they got a court injunction against logging inside their traplines – which delineates a fairly large area. And on 7 May 1992, they used a roadblock to keep loggers out of an area called the Brittany Triangle, which is outside the traplines but is the winter range for moose and deer. They then sought and got a three-month injunction against logging the area until a management plan was made. The plan, which was completed in 1992, provides for a potential agreement for the lumber companies to take 'beetle kill' trees only, but no green wood. At the time of writing, the British Columbia Ministry of Forests, the lumber companies, and the band were still in negotiation.

Nemiah Valley ranchers are charged range fees, as required by the Canadian government, but they pay the fees to the band. They have done this without government assent. There are a few non-native ranchers in the valley who abide by band practices. There is one German-owned tourist lodge in the area. It has an agreement with the band that whenever groups go out Indians will be the guides and there will be no hunting. The band, in effect, serves as the coordinator for the area. The band itself anticipates the possibility of tourism into the area, but under its control. In 1989, the Nemiah Valley Chilcotin unilaterally declared their valley area an aboriginal preserve. Essentially, the declaration provided that a park surrounding Nemiah Valley would be set up within which the band would be able to function and control outsiders, including those who came to recreation areas that the band intended to build. The band has been told that the province has not looked at their declaration.

The Kluskus live due north of the Chilcotin and are one of the Carrier Indian bands. They only number about 150 people; 90 of them live on the reserve and 60 outside, primarily in Quesnel, Vancouver and Edmonton. About 75 per cent of their population are over 40 years old. Two hundred years ago, according to some estimates, there were 2,500 to 3,000 Kluskus. After the smallpox epidemic, there were 55 in 1920 and by 1930 only 50 remained. They live in an ancestral area which still has no road into it. Access is by horse, foot, or air. They continue to speak the Carrier language. They converted to Catholicism in the 1920s,.but they have retained an overlay of traditional tribal values. They tend to marry very young, often from age 15 on, and by the age of 30 they will have most of their family. The Kluskus still rely on hunting for much of their food supply. They do not hunt in the fall, when allowed by the Canadian government, but in February or March when the moose are the fattest. They undertake a moose count in July and February to assure their supply. Everybody has horses which are preferred to all-terrain vehicles (ATVs) or snowmobiles. They are considering an offer to have buffalo brought in. Only two families have small herds of cattle.

As early as 1924 the government tried to put in a school, but it was refused. Up to the 1960s some of the Kluskus' children went to a missionary school in Williams Lake, and there were complaints that some of the children were abused by priests. In 1970 the Department of Indian and Northern Affairs ran a school at Road River which some attended. Finally, in 1991, a school was opened at the Kluskus reserve, which now has about 40 to 50 students. The band hires the teachers, preferably those who have strength in the Carrier language and culture as well as in mathematics and English. After grade eight the children had gone to Quesnel for more schooling under a boarding arrangement funded by the Canadian government. There are now two or three children enrolled in high school. The Kluskus would like to develop a vocational training centre as 95 per cent of the youth have quit school after grade eight. There are a few who go back to school after they are 20 to 25 years old. Of the few who have gone on to finish grade 12, most have returned to the band. There is one who is a college graduate and one who is now in college. Their school curriculum is now aimed at local experiences and local conditions.

The band has about 95 per cent unemployment. Its economy is made up primarily of welfare payments and trapping, which traditionally was the main source of income. But trapping is now unstable: lynx are nearly extinct and beaver pelts do not bring a high enough price. The Kluskus set up a forestry programme in 1974. The tribal leaders argue that clear-cutting ruins the trap lines; that the lumber companies do not put enough back into the soil; and that they leave the earth too clean, making it easier for the moose and the dear to eat the seedlings that are planted. The Kluskus log with horses and do not want heavy machinery to intrude into the area.

Welfare grants run from $3000 to $4000 a year. According to the tribal chief, that welfare problem was deliberately set up to fail; indeed, the Kluskus are always in deficit. What few are employed work for the band on projects paid by Canadian government funds. In the 1980s, the Kluskus became so frustrated with government policies and funding programmes that they gave back all funds except welfare payments for the elderly. They survived from 1980 to 1986 without government funding before they rejoined the programmes. The Canadian government has been willing to bring electric power to the reserve at an estimated cost of $2 million, but the Kluskus have rejected that offer, in part because they would not have had adequate local control. Until 1986 there was only one house on the reserve; then the Canadian government provided $10,000,000 for housing, a water system and the school. The band organized a council-owned construction company which has built about a dozen log homes on the reserve. With the skills and experience they gained the company has been doing some work outside the band area.

The Kluskus have a traditional government – a chief and four clan heads, now called councillors. The current chief had occupied this position for 20 years. At the time of writing, all four of the clan councillors are women. The chief has veto powers over council decisions, but has used that authority rarely. He and the councillors split the responsibility for the major services, such as education, welfare, and housing. The band administers an annual budget provided by the DINA, part of it in direct grants. The money is programme-driven, based on formulas. For example the government provides $4500 for each student, including adults who may enroll in school. This is also provided for post secondary education with an additional supplement for rent.

Government funding has carried certain risks; in the words of the chief, 'the more money we got, the more it appeared that we were burying our people'. Prior to when they withdrew from federal funding in 1980 they used to bury from six to eight people a year. During the non-funded years the deaths were only one or two a year, mostly from natural causes. Since the early 1980s most of the elders have quit drinking. More money brings on alcoholism and 'fancy trucks', and suicide becomes an issue. There was even an AIDS scare in 1991. Ten people were tested, but the band argues that the results were withheld from the people by the provincial and federal authorities.

The Kluskus are not particularly confrontational, but they are not wallflowers. In June, 1993, they blocked the trail from the Fraser River to the Pacific Coast to a group which was reenacting the trek of Andrew Mackenzie and the *voyageurs* across Canada.

The Nemiah Valley Chilcotin unanimously, and the Kluskus Carriers nearly unanimously, voted against the Meech Lake Agreement in the October 1992, referendum. As one said, 'Our system is over one thousand years old; why should we adopt something that was worked out in two or three weeks?' Neither group is supportive of the ongoing treaty process in British Columbia. According to the Kluskus chief, 'nearly one thousand treaties [have been] signed; everyone [has been] broken.' Both bands are affiliated with the Union of British Columbia Indian Chiefs, which opposes the treaty commission and is isolated from the government, although it, too, is funded by the government. The union, which operates out of Vancouver, argues that negotiations should be from the top down rather than from the bottom up. The union officials see the Canadian government as reneging on its responsibility, both in negotiation with the tribes and in devolving programmes to the provinces. They believe that the negotiating partner of the tribes, as independent nations, should be not the province but the sovereign entity, namely the Canadian government.

Government policy towards Indians in Canada has had a long, tortured history. Upon first contact with Europeans, the Indians were autonomous self-governing nations. The attitude of Europeans who came to North America was that they were entering an uninhabited land. They knew, of course, that there were people who were living here, but these were 'savages'. They were considered to be more like animals who roamed over the land and as such never possessed it. In what was to become Canada the French functioned as though it was empty territory. The British found it preferable to assume that the various Indians they encountered had some sort of centralized authority with whom they could make treaties. Though treaties were the instruments of engaging in agreements between sovereign nations, there is no evidence that the treaties which were made with Indians in North America were considered as such. Although treaties were negotiated and signed as if the Indian signatories were representatives of sovereign entities, these treaties were not presented to the British Parliament through normal procedures. There is ample evidence that the Europeans in fact never considered the Indians with whom they dealt to be sovereign.[10] For that reason, the treaties appear to be merely agreements of convenience. Rather than invent new ways to treat with an entity that is not considered to be a state, the Europeans used old methods to create one-sided results. On the other hand, the Indians appear to have had some concept of what treaties were for and how they could be used between nations; but they only had experience of making agreements with other Indians. As those agreements had been entered into in good faith, it was understood that agreements with the British would be carried out in the same fashion. For the British, a treaty was a ruse; for the Indians it was an agreement. As treaties were made over time it is evident that the Indians were not always back-pedalling and acceding to the British or French for whatever they requested. In 1765, for example, Pontiac signed an agreement with the British providing that while they could assume control of the French forts that had been surrendered to the them, it did not mean that they could assume control of the Indians' land. The British would be there under the same condition as the French, who had been tenants.[11] At the same time, the French and the British had seen fit to sign treaties of alliance with various Indians in their battles with each other and later with the American colonists. These agreements were not the contracts offered to mercenaries, but were treaties made with allies. After the American Revolution and its subsequent aftermath, the War of 1812, the position of the British in North America and the boundaries within which they were to operate were settled. The Indians were no longer valuable as allies, but were looked upon as troublesome subjects. First, they stood in the road of settlement; and second, they were an embarrassment to the British as their numbers were rapidly declining and they lived in deplorable social conditions – poor health, little education, and squalid housing. Of course, these were the Indians that had been touched by European civilization. Initially, the British response was either to isolate or assimilate them.

In 1763, the British posted a royal proclamation that extended British sovereignty and protection over the Indians west of Upper Canada. It recognized that Indians had a continuing right to their lands except where they had ceded them voluntarily. The proclamation further prohibited the Indians from selling their lands to any entity other than the state.

In the late 1830s, as the result of a parliamentary inquiry into the conditions of aboriginal peoples throughout the British Empire, Parliament passed the Crown Lands Protection Act, which declared Indian lands to be Crown lands. This act took away any political rights of Indians based on individual property qualifications.[12] To some degree it recognized communal property rights, but it also effectively alienated Indian title to their land in favour of the state.

The act was contrary to any efforts that were made to assimilate the Indians. Further provisions to promote assimilation were more demanding on Indians than on white resident immigrants. The 1857 Act for the Gradual Civilization of the Indian Tribes of the Canadas provided for the enfranchisement of male Indians over 21 who were literate in French or in English, had minimal education, were of good moral character and free from debt, and who had passed a three-year probation. In return, the enfranchised Indian would lose his tribal status. A decade later, only one person had availed himself of that law. As Dickason has observed, 'not only did the dominant society demand assimilation, it reserved to itself the right to dictate the terms by which it could proceed'.[13]

The other policy option to isolate the Indians was achieved by placing them on reserves. The British had established this policy in 1763; they proceeded to clear the western lands of Indian title by treaty, in return for gifts and annuities and the establishment of reserves. By the time of the creation of the dominion, the government had established reserves and retained the right to sell any reserved lands not being used by the Indians without consultation.

The British North America Act of 1867 made one reference to the Indians, namely, to declare them a federal responsibility. At the same time, each of the provinces, as they entered the federation, brought with them a different set of experiences and different attitudes towards the Indians within their boundaries.[14] Nowhere was this more true than in British Columbia, which once had the greatest concentration of Indians in Canada; now its Indian population is second to that of Ontario. It is estimated that at least over 300,000 Indians were in British Columbia prior to European contact.[15] Tennant lists 31 tribal groups with 199 bands and about 68,000 status Indians in 1987 with an approximately equal number of non-status Indians in that province.[16] Of the nearly 2,300 reserves in all of Canada, 1,629 are in British Columbia, whose government asserted that the royal proclamation of 1763 never did apply to its territory. Yet nothing happened in British Columbia prior to 1849 to challenge ownership of the territory. James Douglas was made governor of Vancouver Island in 1851 and began to make treaties with the local Indians, in which he recognized the title of the land as belonging to the Indians. In 1860 he asked the colonial legislature 'to provide means for extinguishing, by purchase, the native Title to the Lands'.[17] Within two years Douglas was governor of mainland British Columbia as well as Vancouver Island. In a change of heart, he proceeded to ignore Indian land rights, and the idea of Indian ownership of land dropped from the public debate over the next decade.

East of the Rocky Mountains, the Canadian government proceeded to negotiate treaties to extinguish Indian title to the land. This was done through a series of ten treaties before 1906, which covered large sections of territory. Only Treaty 8 reached into northern British Columbia, but it provided evidence that Indian title to the land had been recognized within the province of British Columbia in 1899 – which meant that the principles and procedures set forth in the Proclamation of 1763 were applicable to Indians and Indian lands in that province. The treaty negotiations were accomplished in large part before the settlers arrived in the prairies. West of the Rockies, neither the Canadian nor the British Columbia governments made the same arrangements. In fact, where reserves had been created in the east under federal control, minimal lands were allowed to Indians in the far west, and these were under provincial control.[18] On the prairies the white settlers were being allowed to pre-empt 160 acres and purchase an additional 480 acres; Indians in the same area were allowed to pre-empt 160 acres only. Earlier in British Columbia, Indians had been allowed 200 acres per householder, but later they were allowed only 10 acres. Then in 1873 a negotiated compromise allowed 20 acres per family. In 1870 the Indians lost the right to preemption through the Preemption Act of 1870.[19] Where east of the Rockies Crown lands belonged to the federal government, in British Columbia Crown lands were left under the control of the province. Thus, a situation arose where the federal government was responsible for the Indians, but the provincial government controlled the land.

Traditionally, the Indian communities had separate chiefs for different segments of activity and who were, for the most part, installed for life. The 1857 act, however, had provided for a system of electing band chiefs and members of band councils for three-year terms (who could, however, be deposed by the governor). This policy was not effective, in part because traditional chiefs continued to function alongside or instead of the elected chiefs. Therefore, in 1876, the federal Indian Act was amended to include a provision prohibiting traditional chiefs to exercise any power unless they had been elected. To ensure that an end would be put to the system of traditional (and unelected) chiefdoms in British Columbia, the provincial Indian Act of 1880 provided for the federal cabinet to have power to depose 'life chiefs' and affirmed that they should not exercise the powers of chiefs unless they were elected. At the same time, the provincial Indian superintendent did not trust any of the bands to have an elected council.[20]

The purpose of the federal Indian Act of 1876 was to further regulate the Indian peoples and to assimilate the Indians into the Canadian population. This act is still the basis for Indian administration in Canada. In 1920, the deputy minister of Indian Affairs said, 'Our object is to continue until there is not a single Indian in Canada that has not been absorbed into the body politic, and there is no Indian question, and no Indian department.'[21] While Canadian legislation was intended to turn Indians into Canadians, it also reached into every facet of the Indians' lives, sometimes making it difficult for them to achieve whatever transition was hoped for and certainly regulating them more than the people to whom they were to assimilate. Until 1923, for example, the Indians on the north coast who engaged in commercial fishing were not allowed to operate boats with engines. There was an attitude that the whites could best define what a traditional life ought to look like – and then deny the Indians the traditional life. 'Whites apparently took it for granted that Indians would prefer not to be Indians.'[22] Indian agents inspected households for cleanliness. Children were removed from their homes and put into boarding schools usually run by churches.

The system of Indian schooling had profoundly important consequences for pan-Indianism and Indian political organization in British Columbia. By bringing together children from different tribal groups and widely separated communities and by keeping them together for long periods [and] away from traditional influences, while at the same time isolating them from white society, the schools promoted a new and wider Indian awareness and identity.[23]

Furthermore, Indian schooling for decades was tied to Christian missionary programmes. In the 1960s, the government had finally removed religious organizations from Indian educational programmes. The Indian agents tried to suppress potlatches as well as other traditional practices, such as matrilineal inheritance, customary marriage ceremonies, the use of Indian names rather than 'Christian' ones, and use of the native languages.[24] Indians were even prohibited from wearing traditional clothing or performing traditional dances at white rodeos. So extensive was the control by the government agents over the Indian bands that they would negotiate the sale of reserve lands. An amendment to the Indian Act in 1911 allowed portions of reserves to be expropriated by companies, railways, or municipalities.

> As the power of the agents grew, it became steadily more arbitrary. Their duties accrued until they were expected to direct farming operations; administer relief in times of necessity; inspect schools and health conditions on reserves; ensure that department rules and provisions were complied with; and preside over band council meetings and, in effect, direct the political life of the band.[25]

Along the way, Indian administration had been passed around from agency to agency. It started out in the Department of the Secretary of State, then was moved to the Department of the Interior in 1873, then to the Department of Mines and Resources in 1936, on to the Department of

Citizenship and Immigration from 1950–54, and now to the Department of Indian and Northern Affairs.

There was a time just a few years ago when DINA personnel were seen as the enemy of the people they were to serve. Now the emphasis is on the provision of services if the Indians want them. DINA has gone from a service provider to a funding agency. Most of the federal funds are dispensed by programme to the bands who administer the funds. Even Indian Affairs personnel will admit that the degree to which such Indians as the Kluskus and Nemiah Valley bands depend on the government is because the government has made them that way.

Public policy has affected the value structure, life patterns, and internal governance of Indians. On the one hand they are isolated and neglected, and on the other they are the objects of integration and involvement. In the late 1930s, native groups in Canada gained access to the Canadian judicial system, a development that resulted in the constitutional recognition of Indian rights and allowed them to make claims upon governments. The clarification of self-government, rights, and land title continued from the late 1980s into the 1990s. First came the Meech Lake Accord and in 1992, the Charlottetown Accord, both of which failed, and more recently, in 1996, the report of the Royal Commission on Aboriginal Peoples. The assimilationist paradigm was challenged from 1945 to 1965 by aboriginal leaders, social scientists, and government officials who pointed out the policy failure of the Canadian government in 'civilizing' and assimilating the native peoples.

The Canadian government has kept the Indians on small reserves so that no large group was created. The 780,000 or so Indians in Canada are divided into 604 bands on 2,200 reserves. Canadian reserves are much smaller than American reservations. Therefore, there is no Canadian Indian band as large as the Navajos of the United States. However, in the 1960s there was a cross-band effort created by the secretary of state. In British Columbia, where nearly all of the Indians have failed to sign treaties establishing territorial reserves, these are generally only village size with no attendant supporting territory. Only in the past decade has the provincial government recognized aboriginal land rights in British Columbia.

For most Indians, the choice to stay on a reserve is a choice for cultural maintenance. They recognize that when they move into the city they become acculturated. Conversely, living on the reserve is more demanding economically, spiritually and intellectually. There is no reliance on the external culture to provide an answer for the problems that occur. The Indian culture must bear both the blame and the praise for the results of communal existence. In any case, to stay on the reserve is a choice which protects the individual. The Indian has not been as able to adapt to outside or dominant cultures. In the Indian Act of 1951, the government dropped the legal ban on certain Indian customs and began to promote traditional arts and crafts with financial assistance.[26]

Indians cannot survive simply by preserving the culture they pretend to maintain. The issue of survival is also a matter of economics and fundamental belief. For example, in most instances Indians speak English rather than the native language, a language without which they will only preserve a race, not a culture. The government, however, cannot give special status to a race. In their 'management' of the Indians, the Canadian government has imposed western structures upon them. Rather than react defensively or attempt to develop protective mechanisms, a large proportion of Canadian Indians has moved wholly into the western system introduced by the government and its societal allies. Thus we find that the band councils are responsive to Ottawa rather than to some internal cultural demands. The band councils act as administrators rather than as representatives of the band. The leaders form a sub-culture both on and off the reserve – they form a community of their own, and they do not see themselves as representing the community. This is the fault of the system, with its reward structures established by the government, which forces the leaders to respond in the fashion described here. In their relationship with the government, however, the Indians have developed expectations far beyond what the government is willing to provide. To some degree band government is similar in form, to nineteenth-century territorial government in the United States. Although the Indian leaders are not carpetbaggers, they are responsive to external forces.[27]

The Indian concept of territoriality was never the same as the western one. Indians were not concerned with sovereignty over territory, or of territory as concomitant of statehood. Their idea of territory was to support the community, which was their basis of nationhood. Thus, when they seek land claims against the governments today, it is in the context of the fact that they have already made a concession to European legal strictures, which understand land as owned. What they seek is functional autonomy, but in order to be understood by the outside entities they have to seek territorial autonomy:

> The cultural isolationists never mount a competition. By not competing in the political system the absent groups tend to be ignored by legislatures and bureaucracies. Thus legislation and administration are aimed [at sustaining] interest demands which often run counter to specific avowed group concerns.[28]

However, the isolationist bands feel that they have asserted a degree of independence. And by being selective in adopting governmental programmes and maintaining their distance from the larger society, they sense a preservation of their traditional community. Though some of their culture has disappeared, they believe it can be retrieved. Rather than seeking exemption from governmental policies when they rub up against the traditional ways, the Indians ignore these policies. Rather than seeking specific benefits to meet their needs, they go without.

The native policy community has moved towards self-government, peaceful coexistence, and mutual understanding of the role and status of government and of traditional Indian societies, but these aims have not yet been fully achieved.[29]

ACKNOWLEDGEMENTS

The research for this article was conducted under a Canadian Studies program grant from the Canadian Embassy in the United States.

NOTES

1. I use the term 'Indian'advisedly to describe a people who were original inhabitants of the American continents. In their own languages the most common description of themselves by these peoples is translated as 'The People'. There are numerous other terms used. The preferred term in Canadian government now is 'aboriginal peoples' and this is accepted by most of the Indians, although many refer to themselves collectively as 'First Nations'. Although 'politically incorrect', I will use the term Indian because that designation has the most meaning across cultures.
2. Evelyn I. Légaré, 'Canadian Multiculturalism and Aboriginal People: Negotiating a Place in the Nation', *Identities*, Vol.1, No.4 (1995), pp.347–66.
3. Ibid.
4. Dennis L Thomson, 'Comparative Policy Towards Cultural Isolationists in Canada and Norway', *International Political Science Review*, Vol.13, No.4 (1992), pp.433–49.
5. Antonia Pantoja and Barbara Blourock, 'Cultural Pluralism Redefined', in Antonia Pantoja *et al.* (eds), *Badge and Indicia of Slavery: Cultural Pluralism Redefined* (Lincoln, NE: Cultural Pluralism Committee, University of Nebraska, 1975), p.6.
6. Thomson, p.434.
7. Crawford Young, *The Politics of Cultural Pluralism* (Madison, WI: University of Wisconsin Press, 1977), pp.47–65.
8. Karl Peter, 'The Myth of Multiculturalism and Other Cultural Fables', in Jorgen Dahlie and Tissa Fernando (eds), *Ethnicity, Power and Politics in Canada* (Toronto: Methuen, 1981), p.65.
9. Thomson, p.437.
10. Olive P. Dickason, *Canada's First Nations* (Norman, OK: University of Oklahoma Press, 1992), pp.176–7. Tennant disagrees; he argues that the Royal Proclamation of 1763 'does not take its assertion of British sovereignty as incompatible with continuing Indian land ownership. Precisely the opposite is the case.' See Paul Tennant, *Aboriginal Peoples and Politics: The Indian Land Question in British Columbia, 1849–1889* (Vancouver, BC: University of British Columbia Press, 1990), p.11.
11. Dickason, p.184.
12. Ibid., p.247.
13. Ibid., p.252.
14. Ibid., pp.257–8.

15. Tennant, p.3.
16. Ibid., pp.5 and 10.
17. Ibid., p.21.
18. Ibid., pp.36, 67.
19. Dickason, pp.261–3.
20. Tennant, p.51.
21. Peter Sherrill, 'Government Treatment of Native People in Canada, Mexico, and the United States.' Unpublished paper, University of Arkansas at Little Rock, 1993.
22. Tennant, p.71.
23. Ibid., p.81.
24. Ibid., p.75.
25. Dickason, p.319.
26. Sherrill.
27. This paragraph was developed in a discussion with Menno Boldt on 17 June 1988.
28. Thomson, p.446.
29. Michael Howlett, 'Policy Paradigms and Policy Change', *Policy Studies Journal*, Vol.22, No.4 (1994), pp.631–49.

Why Territorial Autonomy is Not a Viable Option for Managing Ethnic Conflict in African Plural Societies

SHAHEEN MOZAFFAR and
JAMES R. SCARRITT

The central argument of this contribution is that territorial autonomy is not a viable option for managing ethnic conflict in sub-Saharan Africa. The structural, historical and political conditions that are generally considered to favour territorial autonomy elsewhere are essentially absent in the 48 countries that make up sub-Saharan Africa. Some of these countries may approximate one or more of these conditions, but a number of other important factors distinct to the continent seriously diminish their influence in fostering territorial autonomy as an effective political option. As a result autonomy has almost always been pursued only as a last resort by ethnopolitical groups in countries with the most authoritarian regimes who have felt unable to protect their vital interests in any other way. Since these regimes have been the ones least willing to grant autonomy, demands for it have usually been associated with lengthy rebellions involving high levels of violence.

Territorial autonomy may apply only to the area inhabited by a single ethnic group, or it may be part of a more general mechanism of ethnic conflict management in which territory is attached political significance, such as *regional devolution, federalism,* or *confederalism.*[1] The use of territorial autonomy to manage ethnic conflict depends on a number of favourable structural, historical and political conditions. This contribution briefly discusses these conditions in the next section. It then describes and explains their absence or infrequent occurrence in contemporary Africa, identifying a number of important factors – including group morphology, territoriality, changing bases of ethnic identity, and the nature of state responses to ethnopolitical mobilization – that are distinct to African countries. Given the importance of these factors, this article next shows that communal contention within multiethnic coalitions is a more effective alternative than the quest for autonomy for resolving ethnopolitical conflicts, at least under more pluralistic regimes. Finally, the recent and

Shaheen Mozaffar, Bridgewater State College; James R. Scarritt, University of Colorado, Boulder unique Ethiopian case of a state policy of ethnic-based territorial autonomy is shown to have problems that illustrate the lack of viability of this option.

Favourable Conditions for Territorial Autonomy

A combination of structural, historical and political conditions facilitates the use of territorial autonomy as a political device for managing ethnic conflicts in ethnically plural or deeply divided societies. These conditions, however, are not static but vary across space and time, generally according to broader pattern of social and economic modernization.

Structural Conditions

Two structural preconditions for the use of territorial solutions to ethnic conflicts are the presence of a substantial population sharing one or more traits that define ethnicity (an ethnic group) and its concentration in a particular region. These preconditions underpin the historical treatment of ethnicity and territory as essential sources of national identity. In public international law, ethnicity and territory correspond, respectively, to two distinct criteria of national identification, citizenship by descent (*jus sanguinis*) and citizenship by birth (*jus soli*).[2] Several factors, however, complicate the relationship between the two criteria and their straightforward application in devising territorial solutions to ethnic conflict. The first factor concerns the essential territorial basis of the modern state. Members of an ethnic group may occupy an imprecisely defined territory or may predominate in a well-defined one. In either case, the territory may not coincide with the boundary of the sovereign state. The problem, of course, is compounded if members of the same ethnic groups are concentrated in adjoining territories under the jurisdiction of two sovereign states.

Second, regardless of their actual territorial distribution, members of an ethnic group may harbour an attachment to a real or imagined 'national homeland' that may be occupied or dominated by another ethnic group. Pressing claims on this homeland is not only likely to provoke counter-historical claims to the territory by the alien ethnic group, but will also probably challenge the sovereignty of the state controlling that territory. The problem, of course, is compounded if the state and the alien ethnic group are closely identified with each other.

Finally, variability in an ethnic group's territorial distribution (its concentration/dispersion) and in its demographic majority or minority status in 'its territory' also complicates the use of ethnicity and territory as criteria for devising territorial solutions to ethnic conflicts. For instance, when an ethnic group is concentrated in a territory in which it also constitutes a very substantial majority, an unambiguous basis obtains for the use of territorial autonomy in managing ethnic conflicts. But the two criteria do not always coincide. An ethnic group may be concentrated in a territory in which non-members of the group constitute a majority or large minority. An ethnic group may be dispersed across a territory in which it constitutes a majority. Finally, an ethnic group may be dispersed across a territory in which non-group members constitute a majority.

These complications suggest that the historically acknowledged 'structural givens' of ethnicity and territory neither reflexively nor uniformly facilitate the use of territorial solutions to ethnic conflicts. They suggest, more importantly, that ethnicity and territory are not so much structural *givens* as structural *variables* that become salient bases of ethnopolitical demands for territorial autonomy as a result of a number of long-term historical developments and shorter-term political contingencies.

Historical Developments

By definition, ethnopolitical demand for territorial autonomy presupposes the presence of ethnicity as a sense of group identity and the activation of ethnic identity as a basis for organizing collective political action. Ethnicity and ethnic identity, however, are not primordially fixed. Their social relevance and political salience stem from the strategic use of varied ascriptive markers by a group of people to foster internal group cohesion and differentiate itself from other groups, as well as from similar behaviour by outsiders. This social construction of ethnicity within the limits imposed by ascriptive markers may or may not lead to political mobilization of ethnic identity in support of demands for territorial autonomy.

Ethnicity and Ethnic Identity. The activation of ethnicity as a subjective sense of group identity involves the self-conscious use and definition of objective cultural markers as criteria of group inclusion and exclusion. Ethnic identity formation, however, is not a singular event, but a secular iterative process of 'intensifying the subjective meanings of a multiplicity of symbols (objective cultural markers) and striving to achieve multi-symbol congruence among a group of people defined initially by one or more central symbols'.[3] In the context of demands for territorial autonomy, one of these central symbols is territory. Historical patterns of migration and settlement produce territorial concentrations of people who over time become reciprocally linked by such potential sources of ethnic identity as language or religion.[4] The mere existence of territorially concentrated people linked by language, religion, and/or other markers, however, is insufficient to foster a sense of ethnic identity. Fostering a sense of ethnic identity also involves some degree of strategic construction, an endogenous process involving the self-conscious transformation of one or more of the ascriptive markers that define ethnicity into a composite social criterion for simultaneously assimilating and differentiating ethnic groups and investing these markers with normative and symbolic significance.[5] Three exogenous processes – two long-term and one short-term – structure its political dynamics. The two long-term processes are the rise of the modern state and a history of autonomous rule. The short-term process is the uneven impact of modernization.

The Rise of the Modern State. The political salience of ethnicity is a primarily modern phenomenon closely linked to the rise and the globalization of the modern state. The rise of the modern state expanded the ecological scale of human activities, correspondingly altering the bases of social, economic and political relations. This broad-based transformation, even as it created national polities and markets, imposed growing diseconomies on localized small-scale social organizations based on myriad of particularistic criteria (e.g., family, kinship, lineage, clans) by under-mining, and in most cases destroying, their 'institutional completeness'.[6] The new opportunities in the national arena created incentives for social actors to merge their heterogeneous local identities upwards into more encompassing identities to conform to the larger political and economic arenas and institutions. The encompassing identity, 'to which the label of ethnic group is commonly attached',[7] became internally consolidated and externally differentiated from other similarly constructed identities in the course of political and economic competition. Political actors adjusted their social identities by combining and recombining the ascriptive criteria that defined those identities to forge solidarity groups for collective political action.[8]

More importantly, territorial sovereignty, the quintessential legitimating principle of the modern state, establishes and legitimizes the geographic basis of ethnopolitical demands for territorial autonomy. The existence of the territorially sovereign state, in other words, precedes and is an essential reference point for demands for territorial autonomy. The state defines citizenship as the over-arching national identity, which prompts the reactive articulation and mobilization of ethnicity as a basis of collective identity for territorially concentrated peoples. The state is established and sustained as a political organization by the singular process of internal unification and external differentiation of citizens living within its territorial jurisdiction. Demands for territorial autonomy also aspire to create a similar basis of collective identity and political organization for the people living in the territory. These demands receive added legitimating impetus if the territory and the people living in it had enjoyed some degree of political autonomy prior to their incorporation into the state.

History of Autonomous Rule. A prior history of autonomous rule for the territory in question, the nature of its incorporation into the state and the resulting pattern of its relationship with the centre establish the facilitating condition for the mobilization of ethnic identity in support of demands for territorial autonomy. In Western Europe, for instance, varied patterns of modern state formation led to varied patterns of annexation and control of the periphery by the core. In one pattern, exemplified by Ireland, Wales and Brittany, the weakness of pre-existing institutions and the resulting absence of extended autonomous rule in the peripheral regions permitted their outright annexation and direct control by the core. However, their weak factor endowments and geographical remoteness contributed to their economic underdevelopment, although the latter enabled them to maintain cultural autonomy. In a second pattern, exemplified by Scotland, Catalonia and the Basque country, an extended history of autonomous rule reflected in strong pre-existing political and social institutions enabled the peripheral regions to retain substantial autonomy after incorporation into the core. The second pattern is more likely than the first to experience coherent and successful demands for territorial autonomy.[9]

Modernization. The uneven impact of social and economic modernization associated with colonial rule in the Third World and with the post-1945 development strategy of combined economic growth and social welfare in Western Europe has encouraged the strategic construction of ethnic identity behind demands for territorial autonomy. Different levels and rates of economic growth and the spread of education and other benefits of modernization produce regional differences that engender perceptions of relative deprivation in the disadvantaged region. To the extent that ensuing inter-regional comparisons produce expectations of continued deprivation, they are likely to precipitate demands for amelioration through some form of territorial solution.[10] If not satisfactorily accommodated, these demands can, and often do, escalate into demands for territorial autonomy and eventually secession.[11] Modernization thus creates the conditions for ethnic conflict, but more significantly, also helps to 'sculpt the institutional structure and ideological character'[12] of ethnic politics. It fosters, in other words, the political contingencies that jointly determine the form, content and success of ethnopolitical territorial demands: patterns of élite conflict; opportunities for the political organization and expression of ethnic identity; and the substantive policy content embodied in territorial autonomy.

Political Contingencies

Political conflicts associated with demands for territorial autonomy are conflicts between central and regional élites and among regional élites.

Conflicts between central and regional élites usually involve differences over the appropriate allocation of power and resources to the regions. These differences are usually resolved within mutually agreed rules by which regional élites join the central government as representatives of the region so long as they possess a demonstrably legitimate constituency in it. To sustain this constituency, they need to secure a steady stream of central resources for the region. Conflicts among regional élite groups usually involve these incumbent élites dependent on the centre and upwardly mobile groups excluded from power. They are engendered by a combination of visible regional disparities and reduced resource flows from the centre, which the emergent élites have an incentive to exploit to challenge the centre-dependent incumbents. Conflicts among regional élites are more likely to precipitate and exacerbate demands for territorial autonomy.

The extent to which they are likely to do so, however, depends on the institutional opportunities available for the political organization and expression of ethnic identity. In Western countries since the 1960s, for instance, democratic elections have permitted the emergence of regional political parties as the primary instruments for mobilizing ethnic identity in support of territorial autonomy demands precipitated by growing regional disparities. In the former Soviet Union, *de facto* 'ethno-federalism' enabled entrenched ethnic cadres in the economically advanced Baltic and Caucasian republics to launch successful demands for territorial autonomy in the unstable political environment precipitated by *perestroika* and *glasnost* to counter regional political opponents allied to the central government and the all-union affirmative-action policies favoured by the economically disadvantaged Central Asian republics. In the absence of supportive institutional opportunities, territorial autonomy demands in multiethnic societies are less instrumentally motivated to secure political autonomy for the group and more expressively inspired to guarantee group survival against real or perceived threats to it by other groups.[13]

The Absence of Favourable Conditions in Africa

The preceding paragraphs have identified a number of structural, historical and political variables that combine in different ways across space and time to establish the supportive conditions for the rise and successful realization of territorial autonomy demands. This section examines the distinctive ways in which these variables combine in contemporary Africa to establish conditions that militate against successful territorial autonomy demands.

Structural Conditions: The Morphology of African Ethnic Groups

One important obstacle to territorial autonomy demands in contemporary

Africa is the morphology of African ethnic or (as defined below) ethnopolitical groups. Compared to countries in other regions of the world, African countries contain large numbers of small groups, none with sufficient numerical strength to constitute a majority in a country. In some cases, and depending on how ethnicity is defined, an ethnic group might constitute a plurality of the population, as, for example, the broadly defined Hausa-Fulani, who constitute roughly 30 per cent of the population of Nigeria. In the rare case where an ethnic group does constitute a majority, it sometimes does so barely. For example, the Mossi constitute 50 per cent of the population of Burkina Faso, with 29 other groups making up the rest. Moreover, even when a group is numerically dominant, differences among sub-groups – present in virtually all groups – weaken group loyalty and unity. In Zimbabwe, for example, the Shona constitute 77 per cent of the population. However, the term 'Shona' is a broad political designation that subsumes six distinct groups, four of which have political significance and continually shift political alliances, but have frequently united as Shona in political competition with the Ndebele (who constitute 20 per cent of the population) and the Whites (three per cent). A recent encyclopedia, moreover, identifies over 1,200 African ethnic groups, but including sub-groups and dividing those that cross country boundaries would increase this number to several thousand.[14] To how many of these should territorial autonomy be granted to resolve which conflicts?

African ethnopolitical groups also exhibit the highest degree of territorial concentration of any region in the world.[15] Their small size, however, militates against territorial autonomy as a viable option. Territorial concentrations of ethnopolitical groups occur within administrative boundaries and sometimes spill over them. Since these boundaries often date back to the colonial period, they encompass not only politically salient ethnic subdivisions but also people who are not members of the ethnopolitical group. This means that the administrative unit, the ethnopolitical 'homeland', and subdivisions of the latter are all potential candidates for autonomy, and conflict is likely to occur over which is selected.

Even when ethnic groups are territorially concentrated in areas large enough to support political autonomy, the territory they occupy often falls under the sovereign jurisdiction of more than one state. For example, the Hausa are concentrated in a large area that covers northern Nigeria and southern Niger. The Yoruba are concentrated in an area that covers western Nigeria and eastern Benin. The Ewe occupy an area that covers eastern Ghana and western Togo.[16] Moreover, due to historic trade patterns and colonial rule, members of the same ethnic group are occasionally widely spread across several countries. For example, Hausa are found in virtually every country across the Sahel between Lake Chad and Senegal, while Fulani are found in Benin, Cameroon, Mali, Mauritania, Senegal, and Sierra Leone. Any attempt at territorial unification of dispersed ethnic groups in this context would immediately threaten the territorial sovereignty of virtually every state on the continent.

Structural Conditions: Territoriality and Autonomous Rule in Africa

African ethnic groups also cannot lay claim to a history of autonomous rule based on control over a well-defined territory. The concept of territoriality as a basis of rule is a colonial innovation introduced in Africa with the concept of the modern state. This is not to suggest that territory was not an important basis of political organization before the onset of colonial rule. However, the significance of territory for organizing people and circumscribing the physical boundaries of political authority varied according to the power capabilities of different types of polities in pre-colonial Africa. But nowhere did territory take on the juridical meaning commonly attached to it in the modern state. Precolonial African polities reflected a *mélange* of political organizations and governance structures, which can be placed between two polar types for analytical convenience. The first polar type involved large numbers of small acephalous polities with politically fragmented non-centralized governance structures. Their political authority extended over a small number of people and limited territory. The second polar type involved a limited number of kingdoms with centralized governance structures (army, bureaucracy, taxation) that were more approximations of 'proto-states' than actual modern states. Their political authority over people and territory was established and maintained through a combination of cooperation, warfare, tribute, extraction and outright conquest. Territorial control, however, weakened with increasing distance from the capital.

Colonial rule was imposed on these polities by a combination of military conquest and treaties by which African chiefs, in return for financial compensation, ceded territories they did not control or whose people were not culturally similar to their own. It was formalized by geographical boundaries determined at the 1884–85 Berlin Conference primarily to avoid a European war over Africa. Drawn through a combination of a strategically rational response to the limited information available about the social demography and the ethnographic structure of contemporary Africa and the realities of physical occupation before and after the Berlin Conference, these boundaries often divided potentially homogenous groups into separate territorial jurisdictions or otherwise brought diverse indigenous polities within a single territorial jurisdiction.[17] Very rarely (e.g., in Lesotho) did they encompass an ethnically homogenous population. Colonial rule established the political, social and economic conditions for the emergence of ethnicity as strategic political resource in contemporary Africa. As a pragmatic cost-effective response to the contradictory imperatives of accumulation and control, colonial policies relied on African intermediaries to administer and legitimize alien rule, increasing their political authority and improving their groups' access to economic resources. These policies favoured centralized pre-colonial kingdoms with some degree of cultural unity. Elsewhere, especially in varied acephalous societies, the administrative divisions of the colonial state entrenched or created local 'traditional rulers', created a wide range of localized heterogeneous sources of potential ethnic identity, and reduced incentives for African intermediaries to control larger territories and aggregations of people. Most significantly, colonial boundaries established the conditions for juridical statehood and became the national boundaries of successor postcolonial states.

For the majority of African rulers who came to power at independence an explicit proscription of territorial autonomy was in their mutual self-interest, since virtually all of them inherited multiethnic societies with secessionist potential. Their fears were not entirely unjustified, as the (albeit unsuccessful) secessionist attempts of Katanga (1960) and Biafra (1967–70) clearly exposed the territorial vulnerability of their new states. As a result, they had these boundaries, already sanctified by international norms, legitimized by the newly created charter of the Organization of African Unity (OAU). Specifically, Article 4 of the charter declared the inherited territorial boundaries inviolable, erecting a strong institutional barrier against potential territorial autonomy demands and fostering a mindset that defined any such demand as an initial step towards secession.

However, the juridical legitimation of the sovereign territorial state in Africa, even as it has suppressed prospects for territorial autonomy demands, has nevertheless established the institutional framework for the political construction and mobilization of ethnic identity. The political salience of ethnicity in contemporary Africa, in other words, is not an atavistic remnant of 'traditional' societies. As elsewhere, it is pre-eminently a modern phenomenon inextricably tied to the central role of the state in allocating resources and structuring the accompanying political interactions and outcomes. *Politics, in other words, moulds and sometimes creates ethnopolitical identity and animates its mobilization as a strategic resource to organize collective action.* What is distinctive about contemporary Africa is the fluidity of politicized ethnicity stemming from the multiplicity of criteria that define ethnic identity on the continent.

Historical Processes: Changing and Varied Bases of Ethnic Identity in Africa

The ascriptive markers that define ethnicity and distinguish ethnic groups in Africa are markedly flexible and varied among groups and over time. This variety and change is due primarily to interaction among the historical processes discussed in the preceding section of this chapter: ethnic identity formation, the imposition of the modern state in the form of colonial rule, and modernization.

First, to the extent that physiognomy is a politically salient distinguishing marker, its relevance is limited largely to interactions between indigenous Africans and peoples introduced under colonialism. The European-privileging apartheid systems in pre-1990 South Africa and pre-1989 Namibia and their replication in less severe form in the former Southern Rhodesia (now Zimbabwe) are the most prominent examples of the legal recognition of race as a basis of group identity. Physiognomy is also politically relevant in countries with a significant 'mestizo' population, as for example, in Angola and Mozambique. It is also invoked in countries where groups from the Levant (in a number of west African countries) or from the Indian subcontinent (in east and southern Africa) occupy key economic sectors. Finally, indigenous Nilotic, Nilo-Hametic, Hametic, and Pygmoid peoples are also differentiated partially on the basis of physiognomy. In general, however, physiognomy is not a politically salient distinguishing marker in much of Africa.

Language, which elsewhere is central to the definition of group identity, is only one politically salient distinguishing marker in Africa, and not necessarily the most important one. In virtually every African country, the European language inherited from colonial rule remains the pre-eminent, if not the only, national language. Language policies also recognize the *de facto* dominant language (or languages) as the national language in a country. Thus, Hausa, Yoruba and Ibo, the languages spoken by each of the three major ethnic groups in Nigeria, are also official languages of the country. In Senegal, Wolof, the language of the dominant ethnic group of the same name, is an official language widely-used as a lingua franca along with French. And in Zimbabwe English, Shona and Ndebele are all national languages. Regional linguae francae (notably Hausa in west Africa and Swahili in east Africa) facilitate interactions between groups distinguished by other criteria. Most ordinary people in Africa, moreover, tend to be multilingual. Depending on the context (home, market, school, business, political interactions), their varied language repertoires include the simultaneous use of distinct local languages and dialects with pidgin, creoles and European languages.[18] Language alone thus provides a weak basis for crafting and sustaining ethnopolitical identity across Africa.

Religion is one important component of ethnopolitical identity in some countries that are divided between Christians and Moslems, although narrower ethnopolitical identities are also important in these countries. The Christian-Moslem religious divide, created by colonialism and associated with modernization, is the primary but not exclusive basis of ethnopolitical cleavages only in Sudan and Comoros, although it is also significant in at least ten additional countries. In recent years, the spread of Islamic fundamentalism has witnessed increased radicalism and sectarian violence. However, these have remained localized incidences limited to regions of the continent where there is a sizeable receptive population, such as in northern Nigeria with its conservative brand of Islam. Neither these incidences nor debates about the adoption of Shari'a law in several countries or about joining the Organization of Islamic Conferences (OIC) in Nigeria and Tanzania have led to the consolidation of ethnic identities along religious lines.[19]

The principal religious cleavage between Christianity and Islam interacts with other sources of social cleavages that modify its systematic role in defining a politically salient ethnic identity and sustaining collective political action among the followers of these religions. In the first place, the two major religions exist alongside a wide range of traditional religious practices that dilute the doctrinaire purity of each and effectively foster syncretistic beliefs and practices. Second, intra-religious divisions by sect and denomination further vitiate the prospects of ethnic unity based on broad religious affiliations. Third, in many instances, religious affiliations are often subordinated to other social connections, such as ancestral birthplaces and family and kinship groups. Such micro-level affiliations usually cut across religious lines; it is not uncommon to find, for instance, different members of the same family with different religious affiliations. Widely prevalent and socially significant at subnational levels, these multiple cleavages serve to moderate the otherwise divisive religious conflicts at the national level.[20]

Finally, processes of change have created multiple levels of ethnopolitical identity for all Africans. Particularistic subnational identities remain spatially anchored in ancestral villages, towns and regions where they remain intimately tied to patterns of property rights, land use, economic consumption and capital accumulation. Social and economic modernization permits spatial mobility by which these heterogeneous subnational identities are carried into urban settings, where the potential exists for aggregating them into an over-arching composite basis of broadly-defined ethnopolitical identity based on 'invented tradition'.[21] For individual carriers of particularistic identities, the incentive to merge into the larger identity derives from the fact that it provides important social capital in the competitive urban environment.[22] The construction of the larger ethnopolitical identity, however, does not mean the rejection of the particularistic identities. The 'syncretistic inclusivity'[23] of the former allows for the persistence of the latter; the two identities represent mutually beneficial social capital. The larger urban-based ethnic identity provides access to valued economic and political resources (jobs, public contracts, government positions) in a competitive environment, resources that become valuable investment capital for sustaining a diversified portfolio of particularistic localized identities. The latter serve as important sources of political support for both incumbents and potential élites in the struggle for power and resources at the national level.[24]

The availability of diverse ascriptive markers enables ethnic identity construction and ethnopolitical mobilization as joint processes of syncretistic aggregation of multiple identities into a single composite identity. But the heterogeneity of ascriptive markers involves quantitative variety, not socially relevant qualitative differences, in the sources of emergent ethnic identity. As a result, the emergent ethnopolitical groups in Africa are not distinguished by sharp cultural differences. Nor are these low cultural differences highly correlated with political and economic differences. While the accrued benefits of the uneven spread of colonial rule and modernization often corresponded to ethnopolitical identities that were newly-created by educated Africans serving as cultural entrepreneurs, most groups have limited economic resources and most countries cannot be effectively ruled without some degree of support from multiple groups. As a result, African ethnopolitical groups are characterized by relatively low economic and political differences. When severe and reinforcing differences do exist, they are the direct result of politically motivated discriminatory policies (e.g., in apartheid South Africa).[25]

Because of the combination of modal characteristics of ethnopolitical groups in Africa – many small and relatively similar groups that do not differ greatly from one another by global standards, the heterogeneity of these differences, multiple levels of ethnopolitical identity, the absence of long histories of autonomous rule, and significant changes in the ethnopolitical landscape – most African countries are *not* deeply divided societies. They are more accurately characterized as *multiethnic* societies comprised of large numbers of relatively evenly balanced, or dispersed, communal groups. Only Burundi, Rwanda, Sudan, South Africa, and pre-independence Namibia and Zimbabwe can be accurately characterized as *deeply divided* societies in which communal groups are sharply polarized by overlapping social, economic and political cleavages. South Africa, moreover, has rejected the enforced territorial autonomy of *apartheid* in favour of federalism that has only overtones of ethnicity, while territorial autonomy in Burundi and Rwanda would require more extensive ethnic cleansing than witnessed in Bosnia and Kosovo.

Political Contingencies: Regime Differences and Strategic Choice

In the absence of supportive historical and structural conditions for territorial autonomy, the political struggle for power and resources centred on the state has been the principal determinant of ethnopolitical identity construction and resulting ethnopolitical conflicts in contemporary Africa. Ethnicity is a cost-effective strategic resource for political organization because alternative bases of political organization, such as class, are weak or non-existent in most African countries. In this organizational vacuum, ethnicity becomes a means of incipient class formation mediated by the central role of the state in macroeconomic management. Ethnic identity, moreover, is an indispensable social capital that efficiently solves collective action problems and serves as a strategically rational link between political élites and followers. For ethnic followers, ethnic political leaders serve as a means to access state resources. For risk-averse ethnic élites involved in uncertain political competition in the context of economic decline and diminishing state resources, ethnicity serves as a valuable social capital for demonstrating political power *vis-à-vis* the state and other groups and in maintaining access to land, labour and food during economic hard times.[26]

Given this intrinsic comparative advantage of ethnicity in organizing and sustaining group behaviour, post-independence political regimes distinguished by their governance institutions and associated orientations and policy responses have been critical in structuring the political expression of ethnicity and the articulation of ethnopolitical demands.[27] For instance, hegemonic-control regimes, displaying an *essentialist* orientation to ethnopolitical demands, have typically pursued zero-sum hegemonic strategies aimed at controlling these demands through subjection, isolation, cultural assimilation, avoidance, and displacement. Essentialist hegemonic strategies have relied heavily on coercion to suppress ethnopolitical demands, occasionally imposing forced self-determination on subordinate ethnic groups without any major concessions, as, for example, in the creation of 'homelands' for Africans in apartheid South Africa. By attempting to suppress ethnopolitical demands without any accommodation, hegemonic-control regimes have provoked violent rebellions in Africa.[28]

Hegemonic-exchange regimes, by contrast, have displayed a *pragmatic* orientation to ethnopolitical demands, typically pursuing affirmative action policies in the allocation of economic resources and state positions as well as power-sharing strategies in which key ethnopolitical élites secure political representation in inclusive coalitions.[29] These pragmatic accommodations are buttressed with informal agreements negotiated between contending ethnopolitical élites over reciprocal exchanges of state-controlled resources for political support. Because hegemonic-exchange regimes contain ethnopolitical conflicts within informal quid-pro-quo routines, creating incentives for élites to moderate their demands, they have experienced more non-violent protests than hegemonic-control regimes when such routines have broken down.[30]

Finally, polyarchies, displaying a *reciprocative* orientation toward ethnopolitical demands, have successfully accommodated ethnopolitical conflicts through competitive elections and public accountability in governance. Until the recent democratic transitions, notable African examples of polyarchies included Botswana, Gambia (until 1994) and Mauritius. One of the most multiethnic societies in the world, Mauritius has sustained a successful parliamentary democracy continuously since independence in 1968. A combination of institutional factors and policies reflecting the reciprocative orientation of multiethnic polyarchies account for Mauritius's enigmatic success.[31]

The Politics of Ethnopolitical Conflict in Africa: Communal Contention v. Ethnonationalism

Ethnopolitical conflicts in contemporary Africa thus reflect the interplay of historically configured social structures and the strategic choices of political actors involved in traditional struggles for power and resources. For the most part, these conflicts have involved the activation of ethnicity to define group *interests* and articulate political demands concerning equity and proportionality in the allocation of cabinet positions, administrative appointments, public sector jobs, and development funds. These instrumental demands are generally negotiable and readily accommodated within the existing institutional framework of the state through the use of 'ethnic arithmetic' in forming multiethnic government coalitions and formulating affirmative action policies. More problematic are ethnopolitical conflicts that involve the activation of ethnicity to define group *identity* and articulate expressive demands dealing with the very survival of the group against real or perceived threats to it. These demands are difficult to deal with because they usually require a fundamental restructuring of the state, for example, the transformation of a unitary to a federal system, the creation of additional units in an existing federal system, or outright secession.[32]

As indicated above, political regimes are the primary determinants of ethnopolitical demands and associated types of ethnopolitical action. Ethnopolitical groups in polyarchies with competitive party systems and to a lesser extent in hegemonic-exchange regimes with single-party systems have participated in multiethnic coalitions to realize instrumental demands or engaged in political protests when such demands are unmet. *Ethnopolitical groups, however, have articulated expressive demands and pursued territorial autonomy almost always as a last resort in countries with the most authoritarian hegemonic-control regimes where they have felt unable to protect their vital interests in any other way. Since these regimes have also been the ones least willing to grant autonomy, demands for it have usually been associated with lengthy rebellions involving high levels of violence.*

These statements are supported by systematic data on political interactions in the 1980s between states and (a) 74 minorities at risk classified in terms of their political orientations and demands in phase I of the Minorities at Risk Project and (b) 68 such minorities from phase III of that project (including 51 from phase I).[33] In the former universe, 30 groups are classified as 'communal contenders', culturally distinct groups who accept the existing national boundaries and compete over political power and economic distribution in the context of stable multiethnic coalitions. Twenty-one groups are classified as 'ethnonationalists', sizeable populations of regionally concentrated peoples with a history of organized political autonomy who have pursued separatist objectives at some time in the past 50 years.

The groups classified as ethnonationalists have justified their pursuit of autonomy demands by historical claims to autonomous rule. These claims, however, date back at most to the colonial period when the exigencies of colonial rule created administrative divisions that became the basis of political autonomy for these groups within the larger territorial jurisdiction of the colonial government. More commonly, the erosion of this autonomy by the successor postcolonial states' attempt to establish sovereign control over their territories, combined with subsequent political discrimination against the previously autonomous groups, precipitated their autonomy demands. Thus, the pursuit of political autonomy for even ethnonationalists in contemporary Africa is a direct response to political factors. These demands, moreover, remained unfulfilled largely because of state repression and lack of international and regional support. Finally, compared to ethnonationalists globally, territorial autonomy demands by African ethnonationalists that combine putative cultural differences and past political autonomy are extremely rare. Autonomy demands in Africa are not those of natural primordial communities, but are last resort actions against perceived political repression.

More significantly, in the universe of 74 minorities at risk, 30 are cross-classified in two categories, although this is not done in the universe of 68. Of these, 24, including 12 ethnonationalist groups, have secondary classifications as communal contenders. Thus, 54 of the 74 groups (73 per cent) have always or often acted as communal contenders who accept the existing sovereign territorial jurisdiction of the state but employ ethnic identity as a critical organizing resource to compete for access to the power and resources controlled by it. The prevalence of communal contenders in contemporary Africa and especially the political origins of their ethnic identity and resulting conflicts among them are reinforced by the fact that, among all the politicized communal groups, they exhibit the least amount of cultural and economic differences. Politics, in other words, remains the principal cause of intergroup differences and conflicts among communal contenders in contemporary Africa.

The autonomous impact of politics on ethnopolitical differences and conflicts in contemporary Africa is reinforced by analysis showing that objective group differences and group grievances are less important than previous patterns of group political actions and state characteristics in predicting ethnopolitical mobilization (nonviolent protest and rebellion) in the 1980s.[34] Ethnopolitical groups that engaged in non-violent protest and rebellion in support of their political demands in the 1960s and 1970s tended to repeat these forms of political actions in the 1980s because most grievances remained wholly or partially unsatisfied; the conditions that gave rise to them did not change significantly, and no group was able to attain all or even most of its goals in a situation of competitive mobilization, varying degrees of repression, and increasing economic decline. As we have seen, state accommodation of these demands varied according to regime types. Hegemonic-exchange regimes and polyarchies were sufficiently accommodative of varying degrees of continuous ethnopolitical protest to prevent conflict from taking other forms. Hegemonic-control regimes repressed continuous ethnopolitical rebellions sufficiently to prevent them from attaining territorial autonomy, but not sufficiently to end them.

It is possible to strengthen this analysis by extending it to all ethnopolitical groups in sub-Saharan Africa through the use of a newly created data-set that identifies 375 such groups, divided into up to three levels of inclusiveness in some countries.[35] This data-set includes all groups found in both phases of the Minorities at Risk project, as well as a number of others that are actually or potentially relevant for multiparty political competition in the 1990s even though they have not engaged in rebellion or even in substantial amounts of protest. Although this data-set does not include explicit coding of rebellion or demands for territorial autonomy, Minorities at Risk data supply the former while the procedures used to identify groups in the new data-set supply the latter, although a few groups are difficult to code on both variables. Approximately 45 ethnopolitical groups (not counting their sub-groups) have engaged in violent rebellion in the post-independence period, and only four of these groups – the Hutu and

Tutsi of Rwanda and Burundi – were clearly not seeking autonomy. Chaotic situations such as those recently found in Liberia and Sierra Leone do not allow for reliable coding of rebel demands. Approximately the same number of groups have sought autonomy, and, apart from the ambiguous cases of the Afrikaners and Zulu in South Africa, only islands – Mahore, formerly but not presently (with decisive French support) part of the Comoros, Bioko in Equatorial Guinea, and Zanzibar and Pemba in Tanzania – have done so without participating in rebellion. This expanded data-set shows that over 80 per cent of African ethnopolitical groups have neither rebelled nor sought autonomy.

Ethiopian Ethnic Federalism

In the Minorities at Risk project, Ethiopia had the highest score of any African country on ethnopolitical rebellion between 1960 and 1990. Strictly speaking, this score was inflated by the inclusion of the Eritrean rebellion, which was not really ethnopolitical, since Eritrea is ethnically extremely heterogeneous, but rather was delayed anti-colonial nationalism, negating the decision of the World War Two British victors to allow Ethiopia to absorb this former Italian colony.[36] On the other hand, since the Eritrean rebellion was a model for actual ethnopolitical rebellions in other parts of the country, it might be considered part of the pattern of such rebellions. The current government of Ethiopia, which came to power in 1991, was an amalgam of ethnopolitical rebellious movements, led by the Tigrayan People's Liberation Front (TPLF). Emerging out of this inheritance, and contrary to the policies of virtually every other African country, it has established a system of ethnic federalism with 11 regions. Nine – Tigray, Afar, Amhara, Oromiya, Somali, Benishangul-Gumuz, Gambella, Harari, and Southern Nations and Peoples – are designated as the ethnic homelands of single ethnic groups or combinations thereof, while two are multiethnic cities. None of the former regions are ethnically homogeneous and none contain all members of the ethnic group for which they are named. In the short term, the major problem has been the inability of the government – now uniting various ethnopolitical parties into the Ethiopian People's Revolutionary Democratic Front (EPRDF) – and the opposition, itself composed mostly of ethnopolitical parties competing with those in the EPRDF for the support of the same groups, to agree on the rules of democratic contestation.

In the longer term, however, a number of analysts suggest that ethnic federalism itself is likely to exacerbate rather than mitigate conflict.[37] The various arguments advanced by these analysts add up to a position very similar to that taken in this chapter:

- no boundaries can be drawn for autonomous federal units that are ethnically homogeneous because of the mixing of peoples and the variety of markers that can be used to differentiate them;
- heterogeneous regions have experienced substantial conflict;
- conflicts about the appropriate boundaries between ethnically defined regions have also been frequent;
- conflicts among very differently developed regions for resources have been intensified by adding interethnic rivalries through the ethnic definition of regions;
- members of larger ethnic groups – especially the largest, the Oromo – are so diverse that many of them feel more closely identified with neighbours belonging to another ethnic group than with distant members of their own group; and
- ethnic federalism may encourage ethnic separatism.

These problems are ironically most severe for the formerly dominant Amhara, who identified with the state more than with being an ethnic group, and whose assimilationist proclivities have created particularly unclear group boundaries; their ethnicization would be likely to increase conflict with other groups, and perhaps to recreate their dominance, given their educational advantages. A federal scheme that identified regions territorially rather than ethnically would have substantially less severe problems of these types.

Conclusion

In this paper, we have identified a number of structural, historical and political factors that combine in distinct ways across space and time to support the rise of successful territorial autonomy demands. We have also shown that, in contemporary Africa, these factors combine in different ways to militate against the rise of successful demands for territorial autonomy. Even when specific factors create supportive conditions for such demands, other factors distinctive to Africa reduce their impact. We conclude by discussing the theoretical implications of our analysis.

The conventional view of the relationship between identity and territorial autonomy posits that the existence of a substantial population with an acknowledged ethnic identity precedes demands for territorial autonomy. This view is simplistic because it is based on the unwarranted assumption of an isomorphic relationship between identity and territory. It is also logically flawed because it does not leave open the possibility that the pursuit of territorial autonomy demands could precipitate the articulation, development and crystallization of ethnic identity. Moreover, it derives from a reflexive primordialism in its treatment of ethnic identity as immutably inscribed in human nature, Finally, the conventional view reflects a crude historicism in its rejection of agency in the construction of ethnic identity and its mobilization to organize and advance group interests.

Our analysis derives from a more complex and nuanced view of the interaction of history, structure and agency in mediating the relationship between identity and territory. It acknowledges the importance of history in shaping the structural conditions that facilitate the emergence of ethnic identity and the rise of territorial demands. But history and structure are neither determinants nor explanations. Agency matters in both the construction and politicization of ethnic identity. Agency means to make choices and agents make choices in contexts defined by historically configured structures.

The historical development of social processes is only interpretatively uniform and that also in retrospect. On the ground, historical processes evolve unevenly and incrementally and produce contradictory outcomes. This is the crucial theoretical implication of the impact of colonial rule on both the territorial basis of political authority and the prevailing social structures in contemporary Africa. The introduction of the modern state with its territorial basis of political authority in Africa under colonialism established the initial conditions for encouraging the occasional territorial demands by ethnonationalists as well as militating against their success. The exigencies of colonial rule established administrative divisions and invested potential ethnic groups with political authority in them, thus creating a historical basis for territorial autonomy demands after independence. These demands, however, clashed with the juridical sovereignty of the state, also a colonial innovation in Africa. The institutionalization of the latter principle in international law and the OAU Charter and the ethnic diversity of successor postcolonial states engendered the combined opposition of African leaders and the international community to territorial autonomy demands, severely curtailing their prospects for success.

The incremental expansion of colonial rule also established the distinctive social structural configuration of contemporary Africa. On the one hand, the assimilative effects of social and economic modernization engendered by colonial policies merged, but without eroding, the varied and exclusive local identities into more encompassing and inclusive ethnic identities. On the other hand, the strategic utility of these larger ethnic identities in demonstrating and securing the power of competing emergent African élites in the waning days of colonial rule led to their political entrenchment after independence. The successor African élites, despite their rhetorical commitment to national integration and legal proscriptions of ethnicity in politics, routinely deployed ethnicity to organize and advance group interests. Hence, the prevalence of communal contention among large numbers of culturally similar ethnic groups in contemporary Africa. By retaining their group's separate existence, each group's leaders hope to maximize payoffs through competitive bargaining with governing and opposition coalitions seeking its support. Communal contention provides no incentives to exaggerate cultural differences, but it does provide incentives to maintain a strong group identity. This identity links ethnic leaders and followers in a mutually beneficial relationship that is sustained by the leaders' participating in multiethnic coalitions and thereby securing valued goods and opportunities for their followers.

The combination of historically contingent social structures and agency thus helps to account for the continued salience of ethnicity in African politics and especially its role in sustaining communal contention at the expense of territorial autonomy demands. Crucial to this account is the combined impact of political regimes and group morphology. Thus polyarchies with multiparty competition, and even hegemonial-exchange regimes with constrained competition in single-party systems, have relied heavily on multiethnic coalitions as a mode of governance. Both regime types have thus encouraged ethnopolitical groups to engage in protest when accommodative routines have broken down. Repressive hegemonial-control regimes, on the other hand, have almost routinely precipitated ethnonationalism and territorial autonomy demands. The virtually uniform failure of the latter demands, moreover, highlight the critically supportive role of ethnopolitical group morphology in privileging and sustaining communal contention as the organized expression of ethnopolitical conflicts. Thus the modal characteristics of African ethnopolitical groups – many small groups that are not sharply divided by highly correlated cultural, economic and political differences, multiple levels of ethnopolitical identity, and significant changes in the ethnopolitical landscape – seriously diminish the prospects of territorial autonomy demands. And as the troubled experiment of Ethiopian ethnic federalism shows, the combination of sharp intra-group and intra-regional diversity seriously threaten the sustainability of even deliberately designed territorial autonomy for ethnopolitical groups.

In sum, the analysis presented in this chapter contains four important theoretical lessons. First, there is a reciprocal relationship between the development of ethnic identity and demands for territorial autonomy. Second, ethnic identity will conduce to such demands only if the supportive historical and structural conditions are present. Third, however, even if countries approximate to these conditions, the contingent politicization of ethnic identity due to the specific conjuncture of history, structure and agency may foster different patterns of ethnopolitics (e.g., communal contention) that severely curtail prospects of territorial autonomy. Finally, and most significantly, politics remains the single most important determinant of the strategic construction and assertion of ethnic identity and whether ethnic identity, once constructed and asserted, will lead to communal contention or territorial autonomy.

ACKNOWLEDGEMENTS

The National Science Foundation (SBER 95-154391) provided financial support for the larger project on democratization in Africa from which this paper is drawn. The views expressed in the paper are solely those of the authors and not those of NSF or USAID. Mozaffar thanks the Boston University African Studies Center for continued research support. Lydie Ultimo at Bridgewater State College and Glen Galaich, Adrian Hull, Michelle Camou, and Eitan Schiffman at the University of Colorado, Boulder, provided invaluable research assistance.

NOTES

1. John Coakley, 'Introduction: The Territorial Management of Ethnic Conflict', in John Coakley (ed.), *The Territorial Management of Ethnic Conflict* (London: Frank Cass, 1993), pp.12–18.
2. Richard W. Flournoy, Jr. and Manley O. Hudson (eds), *A Collection of Nationality Laws of Various Countries as Contained in Constitutions, Statutes and Treaties* (Oxford: Oxford University Press, 1929) cited in Coakley, pp.1–22. The discussion here and in the next two paragraphs relies on Coakley's very useful analysis.
3. Paul Brass, *Ethnicity and Nationalism: Theory and Comparison* (Newbury Park, CA: Sage Publications, 1991), p.20.
4. John A. Armstrong, *Nations before Nationalism* (Chapel Hill, NC: University of North Carolina Press, 1982).
5. Donald Horowitz, *Ethnic Groups in Conflict* (Berkeley, CA: University of California Press, 1985), pp.71–3; Nelson Kasfir, 'Explaining Ethnic Political Participation', *World Politics*, Vol.31 (1979), pp.373–5; Victor T. Le Vine, 'Conceptualizing 'Ethnicity' and 'Ethnic Conflict': A Controversy Revisited', *Studies in Comparative International Development*, Vol.32, No.2, (1997), pp.45–55. We adopt what is designated as empiricist/positivist constructivism in Paris Yeros, 'Introduction: On the Uses and Implications of Constructivism', in Paris Yeros (ed.), *Ethnicity and Nationalism in Africa: Constructivist Reflections and Contemporary Politics* (London: Macmillan, 1999), p.6.
6. 'Institutional completeness' refers to the extent to which the set of prescriptive rules and ascriptive markers that distinguish an ethnic group make the group the exclusive source of its members' social and economic needs. *Ceteris paribus*, the greater the institutional completeness of the group the greater the dependence of social actors on it for their life chances. For explication of the concept of institutional completeness, see Raymond Breton, 'Institutional Completeness of Ethnic Groups and the Personal Relationship of Immigrants', *American Journal of Sociology*, Vol.70 (1964), pp.193–208, and Arthur L. Stinchcombe, 'Social Structure and Politics', in Fred I. Greenstein and Nelson Polsby (eds), *Handbook of Political Science*, Vol.5: *Macropolitical Theory* (Reading, MA: Addison-Wesley, 1975), pp.601–6. For the broader historical link between the rise of the modern state and ethnic identity, see Michael Hannan, 'The Dynamic of Ethnic Boundaries in Modern States', in John W. Meyer and Michael T. Hannan (eds), *National Development and the World System: Education, Economic, and Political Changes, 1950–1970* (Chicago,IL: University of Chicago Press, 1979), pp.253–75.
7. Arend Lijphart, 'Political Theories and the Explanation of Ethnic Conflict in the Western

World: Falsified Predictions and Plausible Postdictions', in Milton Esman (ed.), *Ethnic Conflict in the Western World* (Ithaca, NY: Cornell University Press, 1977), p.48.

8. See, among others, Paul R. Brass, *Language, Religion, and Politics in Northern India* (New York: Cambridge University Press, 1974); James Smoot Coleman, *Nigeria: Background to Nationalism* (Berkeley, CA: University of California Press, 1959); Abner Cohen, *Custom and Politics in Urban Africa: A Study of Hausa Migrants in Yoruba Towns* (Berkeley, CA: University of California Press, 1969); Cynthia Enloe, *Ethnic Conflict and Political Development* (Boston, MA: Little, Brown, 1973); Robert Melson and Howard Wolpe, 'Modernization and the Politics of Communalism', *American Political Science Review*, Vol.64, No.4 (December 1970), pp.1112–30; Saul Newman, 'Does Modernization Breed Ethnic Conflict?', *World Politics* Vol.43, No.3 (April 1991), pp.451–78; Francois Nielsen, 'Toward a Theory of Ethnic Solidarity in Modern Societies', *American Sociological Review* Vol.50 (1985), pp.133–49.

9. Michael Hechter and Margaret Levi, 'The Comparative Analysis of Ethnoregional Movements', *Ethnic and Racial Studies*, Vol.3 (1979), pp.260–74.

10. On the Third World, see, 'Donald L. Horowitz, 'Patterns of Ethnic Separatism', *Comparative Studies in Society and History* Vol.23, No.1 (1981), pp.165–95; Jeffrey G. Williams, 'Regional Inequality and the Process of National Development', *Economic Development and Cultural Change* Vol.13 (1965), pp.3–84. On western Europe, see Milton J. Esman (ed.), *Ethnic Conflict in the Western World* (Ithaca, NY: Cornell University Press, 1977); Saul Newman, *Ethnoregional Conflict in Democracies: Mostly Ballots, Rarely Bullets* (Westport, CT: Greenwood Press, 1996); Joseph R. Rudolph, Jr. and Robert J. Thompson (eds), *Ethnoterritorial Politics, Policy, and the Western World* (Boulder, CO: Lynne Rienner 1989).

11. The prototype of this process in the post-World War Two period is Bangladesh. For the politics surrounding the escalation of the initial demand for regional parity through regional autonomy to eventual secession that led to the break-up of Pakistan and the creation of Bangladesh, see Rounaq Jahan, *Pakistan: Failure in National Integration* (New York: Columbia University Press, 1972).

12. Newman, 'Does Modernization Breed Ethnic Conflict?', p.468.

13. Newman, *Ethnoregional Conflicts in Democracies*; Philip G. Roeder, 'Soviet Federalism and Ethnic Mobilization', *World Politics*, Vol.43, No.1 (1991), pp.196–232; Hurst Hannum, *Autonomy, Sovereignty, and Self-Determination: The Accommodation of Conflicting Rights* (Philadelphia, PA: University of Pennsylvania Press, 1990), esp. pp.458–68.

14. John Middleton, 'Ethnic and Identity Groups', pp.477–563 in John Middleton (ed.), *Encyclopedia of Africa South of the Sahara*, Vol. 4 (New York: Simon & Schuster Macmillan, 1997); James R. Scarritt, 'Communal Conflict and Contention for Power in Africa South of the Sahara', in Ted Robert Gurr *et al.* (eds), *Minorities at Risk: A Global View of Ethnopolitical Conflict* (Washington, DC: United States Institute of Peace Press, 1993), pp.254–5.

15. See the data presented in the following: Gurr *et al.*; Ted Robert Gurr, 'Why Minorities Rebel: A Global Analysis of Communal Mobilization and Conflict Since 1945, *International Political Science Review*, Vol.14, No.1 (1993), pp.161–201; James R. Scarritt and Shaheen Mozaffar, 'The Specification of Ethnic Cleavages and Ethnopolitical Groups for the Analysis of Democratic Competition in Contemporary Africa', *Nationalism and Ethnic Politics* Vol.5, No.1 (Spring 1999), pp.82–117.

16. On the Hausa, see William F.S. Miles, *Hausaland Divided: Colonialism and Independence in Nigeria and Niger* (Ithaca: Cornell University Press, 1994). On the Yoruba, see A.I. Asiwaju, *Western Yorubaland Under European Rule, 1889–1945* (Atlantic Highlands, NJ: Humanities Press, 1976). On the Ewe, see Claude E. Welch, *Dream of Unity: Pan-Africanism and Political Unification in West Africa* (Ithaca: Cornell University Press, 1966), pp.37–147. On other groups, see A.I. Asiwaju (ed.), *Partitioned Africans: Ethnic Relations Across Africa's International Boundaries, 1885–1984* (Lagos: University of Lagos Press, 1989).

17. Jeffrey Herbst, 'The Creation and Maintenance of National Boundaries in Africa', *International Organization*, Vol.43 (1989), pp.673–92; John M. MacKenzie, *The Partition of Africa, 1880–1900: European Imperialism in the Nineteenth Century* (New York: Methuen, 1983).

252   IDENTITY AND TERRITORIAL AUTONOMY IN PLURAL SOCIETIES

18. On multilingualism in Africa, see Bernd Heine, *Status and Use of African Lingua Francas* (Munich: Weltforum, 1970). On language policy in Africa, see Bernd Heine, 'Language Policy in Africa', in Brian Weinstein (ed.), *Language Policy and Political Development* (Norwood, NJ: Ablex, 1990), pp.167–84. For an excellent study of the relationship of multilingualism and state construction in Africa, see David Laitin, *Language Repertoires and State Construction in Africa* (New York: Cambridge University Press, 1992).
19. On the Shari'a debate, see David Laitin, 'Shari'a Debate and the Origins of Nigeria's Second Republic', *Journal of Modern African Studies*, Vol.20 (1982), pp.411–30. For opposing views on the OIC debate, see Rotimi T. Suberu, 'Religion and Politics: A View from the South', and Omar Farouk Ibrahim, 'Religion and Politics: A View from the North', both in Larry Diamond *et al.* (eds), *Transition Without End: Nigerian Politics and Civil Society Under Babangida* (Boulder, CO: Lynne Rienner, 1997), pp.401–25 and 427–47, respectively.
20. For a theoretically rigorous analysis of the institutionalization of ancestral birthplaces as defining social identities at the expense of religious divisions under colonial rule and their critical role in moderating religious conflicts in postcolonial Nigeria, see David Laitin, *Hegemony and Culture: Politics and Religious Change Among the Yoruba* (Chicago, IL: University of Chicago Press, 1986).
21. On the concept of invented tradition, see Eric Hobsbawm and Terence Ranger (eds), *The Invention of Tradition* (New York: Cambridge University Press, 1983).
22. On the concept of social capital, see James Samuel Coleman, *Foundations of Social Theory* (Cambridge, MA: Harvard University Press, 1990), pp.300–21, and Robert Putnam, *Making Democracy Work: Civic Traditions in Modern Italy* (Princeton, NJ: Princeton University Press, 1993), pp.163–85.
23. On the concept of syncretistic inclusivity, see Nielsen, p.145.
24. For theoretical elaboration and empirical support of the social processes described in this paragraph, see, among others: Robert Bates, *Beyond the Miracle of the Market* (New York: Cambridge University Press, 1989); Robert Bates, 'Capital, Kinship, and Conflict: The Structuring Influence of Capital in Kinship Societies', *Canadian Journal of African Studies*, Vol.24 (1990), pp.151–64; Sara Berry, *No Condition is Permanent: The Social Dynamics of Agrarian Change in Sub-Saharan Africa* (Madison, WI: University of Wisconsin Press, 1993); Jean Ensminger, *Making a Market: The Institutional Transformation of an African Society* (New York: Cambridge University Press, 1992); Leroy Vail (ed.), *The Creation of Tribalism in Southern Africa* (Berkeley, CA: University of California Press, 1991).
25. The distinctive historical conjuncture of politics, economics and culture described in this paragraph created distinct ethnic identities not only among African populations, but among European (e.g., Afrikaner identity) and 'mixed' (e.g. coloured, mestizo) populations as well. See the contributions by Hemann Giliomee, Jeffrey Butler, and Ian Goldin in Vail, *The Creation of Tribalism*. See also, Ian Goldin, *Making Race: The Politics and Economics of Coloured Identity in South Africa* (London: Longman, 1987).
26. For theoretical elaboration and empirical support of the discussion in this paragraph, see, among others, Robert Bates, *Markets and States in Tropical Africa: The Political Basis of Agricultural Policies* (Berkeley, CA: University of California Press, 1981); Richard Sklar, 'The Nature of Class Domination in Africa', *Journal of Modern African Studies*, Vol.17 (1979), pp.531–52; Robert Bates, 'Modernization, Ethnic Competition, and the Rationality of Politics in Contemporary Africa', in Donald Rothchild and Victor Olorunsola (eds), *State versus Ethnic Claims: African Policy Dilemmas* (Boulder, CO: Westview Press, 1983), pp.152–71. On the strategic role of ethnic identity in organizing and sustaining collective action and in linking ethnic élites and followers in mutually beneficial relationship, see Russell Hardin, *One For All: The Logic of Group Conflict* (Princeton, NJ: Princeton University Press, 1995), and Shaheen Mozaffar, 'The Institutional Logic of Ethnic Politics: A Prolegomenon', in Harvey Glickman (ed.) *Ethnic Conflict and Democratization in Africa* (Atlanta, GA: African Studies Assoication Press) pp.56–62.
27. Donald Rothchild, 'State-Ethnic Relations', in Gwendolen M. Carter and Patrick O'Meara (eds), *African Independence: The First Twenty-Five Years* (Bloomington, IN: Indiana University Press, 1985), pp.71–96; Donald Rothchild, 'Hegemonial Exchange: An Alternative Model for Managing Conflict in Africa', in Dennis L. Thompson and Dov Ronen

(eds), *Ethnicity, Politics, and Development* (Boulder, CO: Lynne Rienner, 1986); Donald Rothchild, 'An Interactive Model of State-Ethnic Relations', in Francis M. Deng and I. William Zartman (eds), *Conflict Resolution in Africa* (Washington, DC: Brookings Institution, 1991), pp.190–215.

28. James R. Scarritt and Susan McMillan, 'Protest and Rebellion in Africa: Explaining Conflicts Between Ethnic Minorities and the State in the 1980s', *Comparative Political Studies*, Vol.28 (1995), pp.323–49. Their analysis uses Polity II data rather than Rothchild's regime types, but the two sources are very similar in their conceptualization.

29. Donald Rothchild and Michael W. Foley, 'African States and the Politics of Inclusive Coalitions', in Naomi Chazan and Donald Rothchild (eds), *The Precarious Balance: State and Society in Africa* (Boulder, CO: Westview Press, 1988), pp.233–64.

30. Scarritt and McMillan.

31. Larry W. Bowman, *Mauritius: Democracy and Development in the Indian Ocean* (Boulder, CO: Westview Press, 1991).

32. On the difference between negotiable interest-based demands and non-negotiable identity-based demands, see Donald Rothchild, 'Collective Demands for Improved Distributions', in Rothchild and Olorunsola, pp.172–98.

33. Gurr *et al.*; Scarritt, pp.252–89; Scarritt and McMillan; James R. Scarritt, Susan McMillan and Shaheen Mozaffar, 'The Interaction Between Democracy and Ethnopolitical Protest and Rebellion in Africa', manuscript, University of Colorado at Boulder, 1998.

34. See especially Scarritt and McMillan. Group grievances concern demands for economic rights, social rights, political rights and political autonomy.

35. Scarritt and Mozaffar.

36. Ruth Iyob, *The Eritrean Struggle for Independence* (Cambridge: Cambridge University Press, 1995), and Tekle M. Woldemikael, 'The Cultural Construction of Eritrean Nationalist Movements', in Crawford Young (ed.), *The Rising Tide of Cultural Pluralism* (Madison, WI: University of Wisconsin Press, 1993), pp.179–99.

37. Kassahun Berhanu, 'Democracy, State-Building, and 'Nations' in Ethiopia', in Jean-Germain Gros (ed.), *Democratization in Late Twentieth-Century Africa* (Westport, CT: Greenwood Press, 1998), pp.77–96; Walle Engedayehu, 'Ethiopia: Democracy and the Politics of Ethnicity', *Africa Today*, Vol.40, No.2 (1993), pp.29–52; Sandra Fullerton Joireman, 'Opposition Politics and Ethnicity in Ethiopia: We Will All Go Down Together', *Journal of Modern African Studies*, Vol.35, No.3 (1997), pp.387–407; Eva Poluha, 'Ethnicity and Democracy – A Viable Alliance', in M. A. Mohamed Salih and John Markakis (eds), *Ethnicity and the State in Eastern Africa* (Uppsala: Nordiska Afrikainstitutet, 1998), pp.30–41; Tegegne Teka, 'Amhara Ethnicity in the Making', in ibid., pp.116–26; and John Young, 'Regionalism and Democracy in Ethiopia', *Third World Quarterly*, Vol.19, No.2 (1998), pp.191–204. For a defence of Ethiopia's ethnic federalism see Kidane Mengisteab, 'New Approaches to State Building in Africa: The Case of Ethiopia's Ethnic-Based Federalism', *African Studies Review*, Vol.40, No.3 (1997), pp.111–32.

Security in Deeply Divided Societies:
The Role of Territorial Autonomy

DONALD ROTHCHILD and
CAROLINE A. HARTZELL

Genocide in Rwanda. The killing fields of Cambodia. Ethnic cleansing in Bosnia and Kosovo. The media are full of chilling accounts and troubling images of violence in societies that have experienced a breakdown in inter-group relations. Fearful of seeing the violence spread and wrestling with the humanitarian impact of these and other civil wars, policy-makers and analysts are seeking means to end such conflicts and help produce a stable peace. As they attempt to construct civil war settlements, the élite representatives of warring groups, members of the policy-making community and scholars find themselves grappling with the following types of questions: Is it possible to provide for the safety of former antagonists without long-term intervention by outsiders and while still maintaining the state's territorial integrity? How can one reassure antagonists in deeply divided societies that once they settle a conflict some group will not seize state power and use it to the detriment of other groups? And how does one go about convincing groups who not only face concerns regarding the survival of group identities but whose very group membership may make them distinguishable from others and thus place them at greater risk of the abuse of central power?

This study focuses on one solution that has been suggested to the problems outlined above: the use of some type of territorial autonomy arrangement in deeply divided societies to spread decision-making power between the state and sub-regional units, thereby creating moderate incentives for cooperation and producing stable inter-group relations.[1] Territorial autonomy can serve to maintain a state's external borders, thus preserving its sovereignty, and may even help give expression to institutional pluralism. But is this dispersion of power sufficient to overcome the problem of group uncertainty and to mitigate group feelings regarding threats to security? In the wake of recent events in Bosnia, Kosovo, and other countries experiencing civil war, serious consideration is

Donald Rothchild, University of California, Davis; Caroline Hartzell, Gettysburg College being given to this and related questions. Some analysts are encouraged by the fact that territorial autonomy can help to empower groups with political and administrative authority and allay group concerns about inclusion in the state. Others question how much impact territorial autonomy can have, given its potential for dynamic and shifting relations over time and the multidimensional nature of the security threats groups may face in divided societies.[2]

To try to gain some insight into the capacity of territorial autonomy to reassure groups about their security in a deeply divided society, we will start by examining the strategic interactions taking place in these contexts. Second, we look at the use of institutions of territorial autonomy as a means of reconciling demands for state control and group self-determination. What types of territorial autonomy solutions are available to those engaged in post-civil war peacebuilding and why do some social scientists regard them as an effective means for creating or re-establishing stable routines of inter-group relations? Third, we examine data on the use of territorial autonomy drawn from experiences with 35 settlements that have been negotiated to end civil wars in the 1945 to 1999 period. We use these data to test the effects of territorial autonomy as well as to examine alternative explanations for settlement stability, namely the impact of the issues at stake in a conflict, the duration of a conflict, whether or not a negotiated settlement includes rules regarding the use of coercive force by the state, and the impact of superpower relations.

Strategic Interactions in Deeply Divided Societies: The Sources of Insecurity

The intensity of conflict in divided societies largely reflects prevailing levels of individual and group insecurity. Although this is true both in societies divided along identity lines (i.e., ethnic, religious, racial or linguistic) and those in which the fault lines are of a politico-economic nature (i.e., class-based or ideological), as we discuss below, the insecurity may be even more pronounced in the former societies than in the latter. In many settings, differentiated communities have lived side by side in relative amity, feeling secure about their future and holding pragmatic perceptions about each other's intentions. With institutions in place that promote cooperative behaviour, it is not unusual to have incentive structures available that favour constructive behaviour.[3] Not surprisingly, as James Fearon and David Laitin's data indicate, interethnic cooperation is commonplace and incidences of ethnic violence relatively low.[4]

However, where ambitious or predatory political élites come to power and mobilize their constituents for aggressive purposes, these outlooks can undergo a marked shift from pragmatic to essentialist perceptions.[5] Thus Tutsi and Hutu and Serb and Croat peoples long lived side by side in peace, until mobilized along ethnic lines by leaders who played on their latent grievances and fears of the future. By manipulating the norms of inclusion within the group or threat of exclusion from the group, political spokespersons can bring about a conformity among threatened members that can be menacing towards outsiders. In contrast to conflicts over economic distributions or opportunities, where there is an overriding need for cooperation to achieve common goals, ethnic conflicts (which involve psychological hurts and feelings as well as material interests) can be deeply divisive and possibly destructive. Thus, the existence of diffuse fears for the survival of group cultures or physical existence or over the possibility of downward mobility and a denial of respect are not easily negotiable. Where ethnic communities become deeply anxious over their subordination or survival, conflict becomes intense and the transethnic ties of the past may be overlooked for the time being. In these circumstances, leaders can manipulate symbols and organize their members for repressive, and sometimes violent, actions against their adversaries. The result is a deeply divided society whose members may withdraw temporarily into their communal containers for life support. Again, there is nothing inevitable about zero-sum interethnic relations. However, in circumstances where leaders hold 'essentialist' views, group members are fearful for their future and determined upon inclusion within the group, and the state is unable to enforce the peace, ethnic polarization and hostility have all too often become manifest.

The role and capacity of the state is clearly a critical element in the strategic interactions between collectivities. The cumulative effects of poverty, unemployment, land pressures, an inadequate basis for taxation, lack of education, insufficient available human skills and environmental degradation act as constraints on the state's capacity to regulate and oversee the compliance of individuals and groups with societal rules. 'A society with weak political institutions,' observes Samuel Huntington, 'lacks the ability to curb the excesses of personal and parochial desires.'[6] State weakness involves two interrelated scenarios, both of which can be highly destabilizing in their consequences. First, when the state is dominated by a single group or coalition of groups and acts aggressively towards out-group interests, exploiting and repressing their politically disadvantaged peoples, it can combine the hardness of military and police strength with the softness of illegitimacy. In this event, the state itself can become the source of manifest grievances and opposition. Second, a state's general inability to offer sustained leadership to the society as a whole is also likely to result in conflict-creating outcomes. State weakness heightens insecurity because there is no effective agency present that is capable of ensuring that that society's agreed-upon rules are implemented. With no administrative or juridical body willing and able to oversee the rules in a fair manner, groups are largely left to their own devices. Incentives to engage in joint problem-solving decline and, instead, collective self-help becomes the order of the day. Either way, the opportunistic, overbearing state or the ineffective weak state results in a political environment where the rules are inequitably or ineffectively enforced and societal actors feel compelled to take action to rectify an unsatisfactory situation. More than likely, new perceptions of insecurity and vulnerability will emerge from such encounters.

The exclusion of a minority group from critical decision-making processes at the political centre can gravely heighten that community's sense of exposure and vulnerability to other powerful elements in the society. Exclusion is potentially costly to a group's well-being, because it often involves a limitation on important information and access to those in positions of power and influence in determining policies and priorities. Prevented from participating in a full and effective manner, group leaders feel denied the power necessary to advance the interests of their membership. More basically, exclusion from seats of influence at the political centre also creates unease, real or imagined, over the likelihood of aggressive intentions on the part of adversary interests. The exclusion of significant group interests, in brief, undermines confidence about the intentions of a dominant state élite towards political minorities in their midst. Once this confidence is replaced with suspicion about the goodwill of competing interests, it becomes quite possible that arbitrary actions will be blown out of proportion and increased insecurities will come to undermine cooperative behaviour.

Another factor undermining minority confidence regarding the intentions of dominant state élites is inadequate or misleading information about their purposes. Where details about their strategies and actions are readily available to all group leaders, the resulting transparency is reassuring to those who feel uncertain about their future security. Contrariwise, where knowledge about adversary élite purposes is tightly controlled and misrepresents reality, political minorities are likely to be distrustful of an adversary, causing them to be wary of making commitments and cooperating in joint problem-solving activities. Certainly, bargaining parties have every reason to misrepresent their situation during negotiations where they seek to extract concessions from a rival party, but, if repeated too often, this tactic can backfire and undermine the deceiver's reputation in the process. Unreliable information increases distrust on the part of the deceiver and the deceived, increasing fears on both sides regarding a cooperative solution and widening the social distance between them. To prevent the mass media from being used to provoke hostility and violence, as in Rwanda and Serbia, international intervention may be necessary to ensure that accurate information is available to the public at large. Following the murder of Hamas bomb-maker Muhyiaddin al-Sharif in March 1998, the sharing of factual intelligence data between the Israeli security agency and the Palestinian Authority may have precluded new terrorist attacks against Israeli civilians – and against the peace process itself.[7] As the Israeli/Palestinian example indicates, if private information is a cause of mistrust and escalating tensions, then one possible means of coping with this course of conflict may be for the state involved or for external actors to attempt to ensure that reliable data on the purposes and behaviour of adversaries are broadcast widely.[8]

If state fragility, group exclusion, and low information contribute to an understanding of why the public's preference for cooperation is sometimes thwarted, the central element that combines or takes advantage of these factors is opportunistic actions on the part of the political élite. Where the political élite has an incentive to mobilize its constituents along group lines and to strive to realize parochial objectives, the result may be to polarize the communities and intensify the struggle for particular (as opposed to general) purposes. When structured along societal fault lines, this élite-organized struggle is likely to draw in marginal as well as committed group members because of the membership's strong desire both to advance self-interest and to avoid exclusion from the community.[9]

While the political élite may itself feel reasonably safe from political harm, it draws support on the basis of appeals to political memories of past collective hurt (whether accurate or inaccurate), the desire to avenge the deprivation of lost lands and opportunities, and the perceived possibility of future material and physical harm. The role of political leaders in drawing conclusions about comparable experiences in other countries, mobilizing ethnic-based constituencies for action, organizing and triggering violent encounters, and negotiating and implementing peace is critical. Michael Brown is not overstating the case when he concludes that '[m]ost major internal conflicts are triggered by internal, élite-level actors. ... Mass-level forces are important, but mainly in terms of creating the underlying conditions that make conflict possible. Bad leaders are usually the catalysts that turn potentially viable situations into open warfare.'[10] In the way that political leaders structure strategic interactions they play a critically important role in organizing their communities for cooperative or destructive encounters. Should they generate extreme demands or engage in efforts to 'outbid' moderate politicians within their own community, the results can be escalating fears, the collapse of networks of reciprocity, the hardening of essentialist perceptions, and an increase in the problem of making or implementing commitments.[11] What seems paradoxical in all this is the fact that *long*-term group interests are often served by policies and actions that promote general as opposed to parochial interests. However, given the needs and appeals of economic opportunities and the all-too-often legitimate fears of living alongside others in the present, it is not surprising that long-term interests remain obscured by the pressures of the here and now.

Territorial Autonomy

As the foregoing discussion suggests, conditions of state softness, incomplete information and group exclusion may hamper the ability of institutions to foster cooperative inter-group relations. The insecurity that facilitates the arming and triggering of violence and civil war reinforces enemy perceptions. The effect is to frustrate reciprocity and bargaining and to complicate the establishment of moderate, brokerage institutions that provide incentives for accommodative politics. Under these conditions, are some institutions better able than others to stabilize inter-group conflict? As a first cut at answering this question, we probe the ability of one type of institution – territorial autonomy – to 'shape' the contents of compromise, and thereby to help ease the fears of groups in deeply divided societies.[12]

We define territorial autonomy as an institutional arrangement that delimits a regionally-based, self-administering entity or entities within a state as having explicit policy-making responsibilities in one or more political, economic or cultural spheres. The relevance of territorial autonomy institutions where the security fears of groups are concerned arises from their capacity to recognize and empower spatially separated groups with political and administrative authority. (As the case of Nicaragua discussed below makes clear, groups that are not initially separated can, through the use of territorial autonomy, be granted their own space, which in turn can be used to recognize and empower them.) Territorial devices that ensure that identity and other groups are included in the central government, for example, provide these interests with policy-making influence at the political centre and a means of blocking other groups from capturing the state.[13] In addition, by diffusing political power to sub-state interests, territorial autonomy can reassure minority groups about their ability to control social, cultural, and economic matters that are important to the maintenance of communal identities and interests. If issues such as language, education, access to governmental civil service positions and social services are considered by a community to be essential to the guarantee of its survival, its leaders and members should find their ability to exercise control over these issues reassuring.

The aim of territorial autonomy is to cede responsibilities over specified subjects, and in some cases a certain degree of self-determination, to a group that constitutes the majority in a specific region.[14] Because the extent of local authority differs from case to case, various forms of autonomy can be utilized. Examples of territorial autonomy arrangements include confederalism, federalism, regional autonomy and cantonization.[15] We focus in this study on the two most common forms of territorial protection for communal and other interests, regional autonomy and federalism. In addition, in an effort to distinguish between spatially decentralized and centralized political systems within the state, we differentiate centralized federalism from decentralized federalism.

Seeking to manage inter-group relations, states may give regions with a minority population a special status of regional autonomy. In some cases these autonomous regions may have their own constitutions and be empowered to enact their own legislation. In other cases, the autonomous power of regions may lie in their control over matters of education, culture, local industry, and social welfare. 'The constitutional legal core of local autonomy is the authority to decide about the law of the region,' observes Hans-Joachim Heintze, noting that this 'is generally different and separate from legislation that applies in the rest of the country'.[16] It may be this very difference which accounts for the fact that central government officials often harbour suspicions regarding autonomous regions, fearful that these sub-state units may be one step away from secession.[17]

Despite regional autonomy's potential for instability, a number of such territorial arrangements have been arrived at as part of negotiated civil war settlements. One recent example involves the government of the Philippines and the Muslim secessionist Moro National Liberation Front, which signed a settlement in 1996 ending 24 years of conflict on the southern island of Mindanao. The agreement established a special zone for peace and development (SZPD) and a Southern Philippines Council for Peace and Development, the latter authorized to operate the SZPD. The settlement also provided that after three years a referendum is to be held to determine which of 14 out of 26 Mindanao provinces would join the autonomous region. In the interim, the autonomous region is to control its own special budget as well as a 20,000-strong special security force.[18] And in Nicaragua, on 30 May 1990, the government of Violeta Chamorro and the Contras signed a protocol on disarmament, one in a series of agreements designed to end the civil war in that country. The Nicaraguan civil war, which was primarily a politico-economic conflict, did not involve territorial issues *per se*. Nevertheless, in an effort to reassure the Contras who were concerned about their vulnerability once they had disarmed, the Chamorro government agreed to create 23 self-governing development zones (for a total of 25,000 square kilometres, or nearly 20 per cent of the country) in which the former Contras would settle with government help. These zones were chosen not because the Contras controlled that territory or represented a majority group within those areas, but because the land was available for settlement.

Federalism differs from regional autonomy in recognizing two levels of government which are considered to have separate constitutional responsibilities. Each of these levels of government possesses separate domains of authority, although they may also have concurrent powers. Other characteristics of federal systems are bicameral legislatures and codified and written constitutions. Because federalism allows for regional self-government and thus a certain degree of sub-state autonomy, it may help manage group security concerns by facilitating the identification of minority groups with state and sub-state institutions.[19]

Although we do not deal with the concept of asymmetrical federalism (in which some sub-state units have greater self-governing powers than others) in this study, we do distinguish between centralized and decentralized federalism. In the former, the state holds most of the power at the political centre and allows the sub-state units to exercise only narrow responsibilities over essentially local matters. An example of centralized federalism can be found in the case of South Africa's interim constitution. This constitution assigned concurrent, but not exclusive, powers to the country's four provinces in such areas as education, health, welfare and policing, gave the provincial assemblies the power to write their own provincial constitutions, and provided that disputes between the central and provincial governments be mediated by the Constitutional Court. Several years later, the interim constitution was overtaken by a new constitution, which was even more explicit about the country's political unification.

Significantly greater power is assigned to the sub-units in a decentralized relationship. The 1995 Dayton Peace Accords which officially ended the conflict in Bosnia, for example, call for a single nation of Bosnia-Herzegovina, loosely governed by a multiethnic, Sarajevo-based federal government responsible for foreign and economic policy, citizenship, immigration, and other issues, and composed of two multiethnic provinces which wield significant powers: the Muslim-Croat federation and the Republika Srpska.

What is striking, then, is the presence of a wide range of choices as to autonomy schemes open to constitutional drafters and peacemakers. Constitution-makers can select between regional autonomy for a region or regions or centralized and decentralized federalism. Whether or not provision is made for a territorial autonomy arrangement in a negotiated settlement and, if so, what shape territorial autonomy takes is likely to be the outcome of two factors – the contending groups' reading of the causes of the conflict and their respective bargaining power.[20] In those instances in which minority groups consider the state's behaviour to have been particularly predatory or repressive, we might expect group leaders to press for regional autonomy. In those cases in which the political centre retains a considerable degree of bargaining capacity, state élites, while countenancing some form of territorial autonomy, are likely to press for a more centralized federalism.

Data

Territorial autonomy arrangements have been proposed as a means of helping to prevent or manage conflict between the state and identity or politico-economic groups. In this project we limit ourselves to examining the relationship between territorial autonomy and civil wars fought in the post-World War Two era. More specifically, we seek to examine what role, if any, territorial autonomy plays in stabilizing settlements negotiated to end civil wars during this period.

Civil conflicts that erupted between 1945 and 1997 were classified as civil wars if they met the four criteria employed by Melvin Small and J. David Singer in the Correlates of War project. These are: that the conflict generated at least one thousand battle deaths per year; that the national government was one of the parties to the conflict; that there was effective resistance on the part of both the government and its adversaries during the course of the conflict; and that the conflict occurred within a defined political unit.[21] Between 1945 and 1999, 102 conflicts meeting these criteria broke out.

The civil war cases were next coded on the basis of the means by which they were resolved.[22] Seventeen of the 102 conflicts were still ongoing in 1999, and 47 ended in a military victory by one side. Thirty-eight civil wars were ended through negotiated settlement. The stability of these settlements, the dependent variable, was coded as either stable or unstable. Peace agreements were coded as stable if civil war did not break out again for at least five years. The logic of using a five-year period to measure stability is that during this time countries might typically be expected to hold their first set of post-settlement elections; countries that make it through these elections peacefully are judged to have reached a milestone as far as stability is concerned. The five-year time requirement disqualifies those settlements reached after 1994 (it is still too early to tell whether they have proved stable or not). This eliminates nine of the 38 negotiated settlements.

A negotiated settlement was considered to have taken place if representatives from the opposing sides of a conflict met, in face-to-face

TABLE 1
CIVIL WAR SETTLEMENTS AND TERRITORIAL AUTONOMY, 1945–99

Civil war	Does settlement provide for territorial autonomy?	Centralized federalism	Decentralized federalism	Regional autonomy	Settlement stability
Angola: 1975–89	no				unstable
Angola: 1989–91	no				unstable
Angola: 1992–94	yes		+		unstable
Azerb (N–K): 1989–94	yes			+	stable
Bosnia: 1992–95	yes		+		1
Cambodia: 1970–91	no				stable
Chad: 1979	no				unstable
Chad: 1989–96	no				1
Chechnya: 1994–96	yes			+	1
Colombia: 1948–57	no				stable
Croatia: 1991	no				unstable
Croatia: 19955	no				1
Dominican Rep: 1965	no				stable
El Salvador: 1979–91	no				stable
Georgia (S-O): 1989–92	yes			+	stable
Georgia (Abk): 1992–94	yes		+		stable
Guatemala: 1968–1996	yes	+			1
India: 1946–48	yes	+			unstable
Iraq: 1961–70	yes		+		unstable
Laos: 1959–73	no				unstable
Lebanon: 1958	no				stable
Lebanon: 1975–89	no				stable
Liberia: 1989–96	no				1
Malaysia: 1948–56	yes	+			stable
Moldova: 1992	yes			+	stable
Mozambique: 1982–92	yes		+		stable
Nicaragua: 1981–89	yes			+	stable
Philippines: 1972–96	yes			+	1
Rwanda: 1990–93	no				unstable
Sierra Leone: 1991–96	no				1
South Africa: 1983–91	yes	+			stable
Sudan: 1963–72	yes		+		stable
Tajikistan: 1992–97	no				1
Yemen: 1962–70	yes		+		stable
Zimbabwe: 1972–79	no				stable

Note
1= Case is ineligible for analysis as a result of not yet having met the five-year criterion for judging settlement stability.

talks, to discuss issues and conditions they believed relevant to ending the war. In order to qualify as a negotiated settlement the antagonists themselves had to participate in the bargaining process and agree to any concessions, compromises or substantive agreements, although third-party actors might actively be involved in the negotiation process. We have eliminated three of the agreements listed in Table 1 because the adversaries did not act as bargaining parties, leaving a total of 26 settlements for analysis. Although the two conflicts in Cyprus and the Korean war can be considered stable settlements in the sense that fighting did not break out (or has not broken out) for years, the absence of civil war in these three cases is not the product of a settlement directly agreed to by the adversaries themselves. Rather, in these cases, third party actors have imposed a settlement that depends on the continued presence of foreign troops in order to separate the warring parties and enforce the peace. Those civil wars which were ended on the basis of negotiated settlements are listed in Table 1.

The coding for two of the independent variables, territorial autonomy and rules regarding the coercive use of force by the state, was done, wherever possible, on the basis of the texts of the negotiated agreements themselves. In those instances in which copies of the settlements were not available, material from the annual yearbook of the Stockholm International Peace Research Institute (SIPRI), *Keesing's Contemporary Archives* and case-studies of the conflicts and their resolution were used for the coding. The independent variable 'territorial autonomy' was scored '1' if a negotiated settlement called for either of the following: allowing one (or more) sub-units of the country to exercise control over local issues, without extending those powers to other sub-units of the country; or providing that all sub-state units have similar internal governance structures and wield powers separate from those possessed by the central government. If the agreement does not provide for any such arrangement, territorial autonomy was scored '0'. Seventeen of the 35 settlements negotiated to end civil wars during the period in question provided for some form of territorial autonomy. Of the 26 settlements whose stability we attempt to analyse, fully half included a territorial autonomy arrangement. The negotiated civil war settlements are identified in Table 1.

Data Analysis

In this section we use probit analysis to examine the effects of territorial autonomy arrangements on settlement stability while controlling for the influence of four other independent variables: institutional protections regarding the coercive use of force by the state; the issues at stake in a civil war; the duration of a conflict; and the impact of superpower relations. The dependent variable, settlement stability, is scored '1' if fighting was terminated for at least five years, and '0' otherwise.

Although identity and politico-economic groups may find territorial autonomy a useful and reassuring means by which to maintain collective identities and self-determination, if they are to be induced to abide by the terms of a negotiated settlement they may require other arrangements that more directly address their security fears, particularly those regarding their physical safety. As they contemplate negotiating an end to a conflict, contending parties seek reassurance that, once they disarm, a rival will not be able to take advantage of the settlement and score a victory it was unable to achieve on the battlefield. Antagonists also seek some guarantee that the national army and police forces, particularly if controlled by an opposing group, will not be used against them once a peace is struck.[23] If adversaries are to be reassured on this point, the coercive forces of the state must somehow be neutralized or balanced through the presence of competing groups. According to this line of thought, if stability is to be achieved settlements must be constructed to include institutional safeguards regarding the coercive use of force by the state. The independent variable, 'coercive force rules', was scored '1' if a negotiated settlement called for any of the following four actions: creating the state's security forces by integrating the antagonists' armed forces on the basis of a formula representative of the size of the armed factions; creating the state's security forces on the basis of a strict balance in troop numbers drawn from the antagonists' armed forces; appointing members of the weaker armed factions to key leadership positions in the state's security forces; allowing antagonists to keep their weapons and retain their own armies.[24] A negotiated settlement was scored '0' otherwise. Fifteen of the 26 negotiated settlements whose stability we can assess included rules regarding the state's coercive forces.

We also explore the possibility that certain types of civil wars are more amenable to stable settlement than others. Some scholars have suggested that accommodation may be more difficult to reach and sustain in the case of identity-based civil wars than politico-economic conflicts. Reasoning that the stakes, defined in terms of physical safety and survival, are greater in the former type of conflict than the latter and also less divisible, analysts of conflict resolution have hypothesized that the settlements negotiated to end identity conflicts are less likely to prove stable than settlements crafted to resolve politico-economic conflicts.[25] The independent variable, 'conflict issue', is based on the motivating concern of the actors involved in the civil war. This variable was scored '1' if the interests at stake were ethnic, religious, racial, or linguistic, and '0' otherwise. Sixteen of the 26 civil wars were identity-based conflicts.

Third, we examine the impact of the duration of a conflict on settlement stability. T. David Mason and Patrick M. Fett suggest that the longer a civil war lasts, the more likely participants are to believe that it will continue for an even longer time, and thus the greater the likelihood that they will be willing to negotiate a solution rather than continue the conflict. Mason and Fett also observe that 'the longer the war has lasted without either side being able to subdue its rival, the lower both parties' estimates of the probability of ever defeating their rival will be'.[26] Based on this assessment we might expect that parties to lengthy conflicts will have the greatest incentive to commit to a stable, negotiated peace. Opponents who negotiate a settlement to a conflict of shorter duration, on the other hand, might still believe it possible to best their rivals, and thereby lessen their commitment to a stable peace. The independent variable, 'conflict duration', was scored on the basis of the number of years each conflict endured, with conflicts lasting less than one year scored '1'.

Finally, the end of the Cold War and the demise of the Soviet Union has focused attention on the effect that superpower conflict might have had on whether settlements proved to be durable or not.[27] The crux of this argument is that a key obstacle to the stability of settlements has been removed with the end of the East-West struggle. Whereas the competition between the United States and the Soviet Union once led the superpowers to funnel resources to client groups in what amounted to a war by proxy, now that the Cold War is over these competing groups can no longer count on such patronage. In the face of funding and resource scarcity and lacking other options, some observers anticipate that antagonists will now commit themselves to a stable peace.[28] The independent variable, 'superpower conflict', was coded on the basis of whether settlements were constructed during the Cold War years 1945–89, or the post-Cold War period from 1990–4.[29] (Settlements constructed after 1994 are not considered because they do not meet the five year period necessary to judge settlement stability.) Settlements negotiated during the post-Cold War years were scored '1' and those constructed during the Cold War were coded '0'. Twelve of the 26 conflicts were negotiated between 1990 and 1994.

The multivariate analysis in Table 2 indicates that there is a statistically significant, albeit rather weak, relationship between territorial autonomy and settlement stability.[30] Controlling for the effects of other explanatory variables, the coefficient for territorial autonomy is significant at the .10 level. In addition, the model, which correctly classified 76.92 per cent of the cases, reveals two other significant explanatory variables. Another institutional variable, rules regarding the coercive use of force by the state, is also significant at the .10 level. Finally, the conflict issue variable is also significant, this time at the .05 level. The results of the analysis thus provide some support for the hypotheses that negotiated settlements that are constructed to include territorial autonomy arrangements and those that include rules that serve to neutralize or balance the coercive forces of the state are the ones most likely to prove stable. They give yet stronger support

TABLE 2
PROBIT ANALYSIS OF NEGOTIATED SETTLEMENT STABILITY

Independent variables	Coefficient	z
Territorial autonomy	1.006	1.501*
Coercive force rules	1.233	1.610*
Conflict issue	−1.464	−1.717**
Conflict duration	.007	0.101
Superpower conflict	−.663	−0.800

**p < .05 (one-tailed test); Ip < .10 (one-tailed test)

Number of observations	26
Log-likelihood	−11.579
Chi-squared	10.38
% correctly categorized	76.92
Pseudo R-squared	.31
Prob. > Chi-squared	.0651

TABLE 3
EFFECTS OF INDIVIDUAL VARIABLES ON PROBABILITY OF SETTLEMENT
STABILITY, HOLDING ALL OTHER VARIABLES CONSTANT

Variable	Probability of success
Territorial autonomy	.316
Coercive force rules	.403
Conflict issue	−.404
Conflict duration	.002
Superpower conflict	−.215

for the hypothesis that settlements negotiated to end identity civil wars are the most likely to prove fragile.

Table 3 reports the substantive impact of the independent variables. The table displays the effect of a one-unit change in each variable on the probability that a negotiated settlement will prove stable when holding all other variables at their mean values. For example, holding all else constant, the probability that a negotiated settlement will prove stable increases by 31.7 per cent when a settlement includes a provision for territorial autonomy and 40.3 per cent when it incorporates rules regarding the coercive use of force by the state. The conflict issue is the variable that, at 40.4 per cent, has the single largest impact on the probability that a settlement will prove stable.

Discussion

The fact that fully half of the cases of negotiated civil war settlements in our data set include provisions for territorial autonomy appears to indicate that contending parties to a conflict do put some stock in the utility of this institution for conflict management. Seeking a means by which to provide for their security and perhaps maintain group identities and self-determination, minority groups may find some reassurance and protection in rules that assign powers to sub-state units and limit the potential for what they feel may be the arbitrary or unjust exercise of power by the political centre. Although the results of our analysis do not speak directly to the ability of territorial autonomy to provide such protections for minority groups, they do reveal that including territorial autonomy in a settlement is more likely to ensure its stability. Because our coding focused on whether or not a territorial autonomy arrangement was included in a negotiated settlement, rather than on whether territorial autonomy was actually implemented or what form it took over time, we cannot say whether it is the institution itself, or the mere fact that contending parties agree to include such an institution in a settlement, that proves reassuring to groups in deeply divided societies.

One central issue we did not address in this study is whether certain forms of territorial autonomy may better serve to promote settlement stability than others. The limited number of cases, as well as the fact that many settlements have not yet had the opportunity to meet the five-year test for stability, make it difficult to test hypotheses regarding the relationship between settlement stability and particular types of territorial autonomy. We note, however, that of the three forms of territorial autonomy discussed in this work – centralized federalism, decentralized federalism, and regional autonomy – only one, regional autonomy, has been consistently related with stable settlement outcomes. It may be that this particular institutional arrangement, because it goes furthest in granting autonomy to the sub-state units, proves particularly reassuring to minority groups and thus serves to persuade them not to defect from negotiated agreements. Although the logic of the argument regarding the stabilizing effects of regional autonomy may be sound, we would be remiss if we did not recognize that three of the four stable negotiated settlements that employed regional autonomy – Azerbaijan (Nagorno-Karabakh), Georgia (South Ossetia), and Nicaragua – also contained rules regarding the use of coercive force that placed considerable security-related powers in the hands of the sub-state units. Therefore, in these cases it is not clear which of these two institutional arrangements may have proved most reassuring to sub-state units.

The finding of an inverse relationship between identity conflicts and settlement stability is an interesting result, in part because there is increasingly mixed evidence regarding this issue. Although many of the works of a theoretical nature cited earlier support the notion that civil wars in which identity issues are at stake are less likely to result in stable settlements, empirical studies have been mixed in their support for this hypothesis. Some works have found that identity conflicts are no less likely than politico-economic conflicts to produce stable settlements;[31] others have found that stability is adversely affected by identity conflicts.[32] Although ultimate resolution of this issue awaits further research, it is worth noting that the empirical studies that support the hypothesis are based on tests of larger numbers of negotiated settlements than previous studies.

Finally, our study shows that neither the duration of a conflict nor the status of relations between the superpowers is significantly related to the stability of a negotiated settlement. In the case of conflict duration, it may well be that the effect of a long conflict is to heighten distrust and resentment among adversaries rather than to convince them of the difficulty of ever defeating their rivals. In such an atmosphere, one might expect that any suspicious move on the part of one set of antagonists is more likely to provoke a reaction on the part of others. As for the larger international environment, although this variable was not statistically significant, our results indicate that, if anything, the post-Cold War system has proved to be a more difficult one for settlement stability. This may reflect a post-Cold War tendency on the part of the United States and Russia to disengage from regional issues, including those of conflict resolution and external intervention.

Conclusion

With civil wars the deadliest form of combat in the current international system, increased attention has been devoted to means of managing conflict in deeply divided societies. Those in search of means of achieving this end may find some encouragement in this study's findings regarding the effects of territorial autonomy on the stability of negotiated civil war settlements. Territorial autonomy, by itself, is not likely to be sufficient to secure the stability of negotiated civil war settlements. Given the multifaceted security concerns of groups in deeply divided societies, this is hardly surprising. However, this study indicates that territorial autonomy can be used as part of a creative and constructive approach to conflict management. If territorial autonomy is combined with other safeguards and can be used to reassure groups in deeply divided societies about their security and ability to exercise a limited authority, then these arrangements may help to lay the foundation for a stable, accommodative politics.

270   IDENTITY AND TERRITORIAL AUTONOMY IN PLURAL SOCIETIES

ACKNOWLEDGEMENTS

We would like to thank David Lewis and Roger Rose for their comments and advice.

NOTES

1. Donald Rothchild, *Managing Ethnic Conflict in Africa: Pressures and Incentives for Cooperation* (Washington, DC: Brookings Institution Press, 1997).
2. Carl J. Friedrich, *Trends of Federalism in Theory and Practice* (New York: Frederick A. Praeger, 1968); and David A. Lake and Donald Rothchild, 'Political Decentralization and the Durability of Civil War Settlements', paper presented at the IGCC Conference on Durable Peace Settlements, La Jolla, CA, 7–8 May 1999.
3. Russell Hardin, *One for All: The Logic of Group Conflict* (Princeton, NJ: Princeton University Press, 1995).
4. James D. Fearon and David D. Laitin, 'Explaining Interethnic Cooperation', *American Political Science Review*, Vol.90, No.4 (1996), pp.715–6.
5. This discussion is drawn from Rothchild, *Managing Ethnic Conflict in Africa*, Ch.2.
6. Samuel Huntington, *Political Order in Changing Societies* (New Haven, CT: Yale University Press, 1968), p.24.
7. Serge Schmemann, 'Palestinians and Hamas Feud Over Killing of a Bomb Maker', *New York Times*, 11 Apr. 1998, p.A3.
8. David A. Lake and Donald Rothchild (eds), *The International Spread of Ethnic Conflict: Fear, Diffusion, and Escalation* (Princeton, NJ: Princeton University Press, 1998).
9. Hardin.
10. Michael E. Brown, 'The Causes and Regional Dimensions of Internal Conflict', in Michael E. Brown (ed.), *The International Dimensions of Internal Conflict* (Cambridge, MA: MIT Press, 1996), p.571.
11. Alvin Rabushka and Kenneth A. Shepsle, *Politics in Plural Societies: A Theory of Democratic Instability* (Columbus, OH: Charles E. Merrill Publishing Company, 1972); Donald L. Horowitz, *Ethnic Groups in Conflict* (Berkeley, CA: University of California Press, 1985); and Timothy D. Sisk, *Power Sharing and International Mediation in Ethnic Conflicts* (Washington, DC: US Institute of Peace Press, 1996).
12. Ruth Lapidoth, *Autonomy: Flexible Solutions to Ethnic Conflicts* (Washington, D.C.: US Institute of Peace Press, 1996).
13. Caroline A. Hartzell, 'Explaining the Stability of Negotiated Settlements to Intrastate Wars', *Journal of Conflict Resolution*, Vol.43, No.1 (1999), p.10.
14. Hans-Joachim Heintze, 'Autonomy and Protection of Minorities under International Law' in Gunther Bachler (ed.), *Federalism against Ethnicity? Institutional, Legal and Democratic Instruments to Prevent Violent Minority Conflicts* (Zurich: Verlag Ruegger, 1997).
15. Ted Robert Gurr, 'Why do Minorities Rebel? The Worldwide Geography of Ethnopolitical Conflicts and Their Challenge to Global Security', in Bachler (ed.).
16. Heintze, p.88.
17. Walter Kalin, 'Federalism and the Resolution of Minority Conflicts', in Bachler (ed.).
18. Government of the Philippines, Executive Order No. 371 (2 Oct. 1996), http://www.philippines.gcinfo/spcpd/exec371.html
19. Kalin.
20. In some cases, the provisions of a negotiated settlement may reflect the influence of third parties in the negotiation process. See, for example, Stephen J. Stedman's discussion of the role Britain played in the Lancaster House negotiations to end the civil war in Zimbabwe. Stedman, *Peacemaking in Civil War: International Mediation in Zimbabwe, 1974–1980* (Boulder, CO: Lynne Rienner, 1991).
21. Melvin Small and J. David Singer, *Resort to Arms: International and Civil Wars, 1816–1980* (Beverly Hills, CA: Sage Publications, 1982).
22. The discussion of the data and coding rules draws upon Hartzell.
23. Stephen John Stedman, 'Negotiation and Mediation in Internal Conflict', in Brown (ed.), *The*

International Dimensions of Internal Conflict; and Barbara F. Walter, 'The Critical Barrier to Civil War Settlement', *International Organization*, Vol.51, No.3 (1997), pp.338–9.
24. Hartzell, p.14.
25. Roy Licklider, 'How Civil Wars End: Questions and Methods', in Roy Licklider (ed.), *Stopping the Killing: How Civil Wars End* (New York: New York University Press, 1993); David A. Lake and Donald Rothchild, 'Containing Fear: The Origins and Management of Ethnic Conflict', *International Security*, Vol.21 (1996); and Caroline Hartzell and Donald Rothchild, 'Political Pacts as Negotiated Agreements: Comparing Ethnic and Non-Ethnic Cases', *International Negotiation*, Vol.2 (1997), p.152.
26. T. David Mason and Patrick J. Fett, 'How Civil Wars End: A Rational Choice Approach', *Journal of Conflict Resolution*, Vol.40, No.4 (1996), p.552.
27. Fen Osler Hampson, *Nurturing Peace: Why Peace Settlements Succeed or Fail* (Washington, DC: US Institute of Peace Press, 1996).
28. Peter Wallensteen and Margareta Sollenberg, 'Armed Conflicts, Conflict Termination and Peace Agreements, 1989–96', *Journal of Peace Research*, Vol.32 (1997).
29. Hartzell, p.16.
30. The weakness of the results for the 'territorial autonomy' and 'coercive force rules' variables is marked in light of the fact that the p-values are for one-way tests, rather than two-way tests.
31. Roy Licklider, 'The Consequences of Negotiated Settlements in Civil Wars, 1945–1993', *American Political Science Review* Vol.89, No.3 (1995); Mason and Fett; Walter; and Hartzell.
32. Caroline Hartzell, Donald Rothchild and Matthew Hoddie, 'Civil Wars and the Security Dilemma: Can Territorial Autonomy Stabilize the Peace?', unpublished manuscript, 1999.

Abstracts

Spatial and Functional Dimensions of Autonomy: Cross-national and Theoretical Perspectives *by William Safran*
This essay discusses the different meanings and types of autonomy and their relationship to the culture and identity of ethnic or religious minorities. Referring to selected historical experiences, it deals with the impact of autonomy on the political system and on society as a whole. Finally it raises questions and advances a number of hypotheses about the conditions under which autonomy, whether territorial or functional, is or should be granted and about its consequences for the integrity and stability of the state.

Democracy, Federalism, and Nationalism in Multinational States *by Ramón Máiz*
This contribution examines some normative fundamentals of multinational states, specifically those containing minorities coexisting with a national majority that has historically been the backbone of the state. The crises in traditionally unitary states and post-communist ones that pursue compulsory policies of national homogenization have forced a re-examination of the conditions conducive to the coexistence of several nationalities within one state. The present study contains a constructivist critique of the organic concept of nation and suggests a cooperative reformulation of federalism as an asymmetric means to institutionalize democratic pluralism

Local and Global: Mesogovernments and Territorial Identities *by Luis Moreno*
New telecommunications are shaping social life worldwide and are bringing with them elements of rapid social change and uncertainty. This contribution reflects on the conjunction of both dimensions of the local and the global, and offers a prescription for the progressive consolidation of a new *cosmopolitan localism* within the meso-level of community life. References made to the European context seek to illustrate how the interaction of multiple identities makes possible effective access for civil society to political decision-making.

Identity, Ethnicity and State in Spain: 19th and 20th Centuries *by Justo G. Beramendi*
The development of various national and regional identities in Spain has been a long paradoxical process spanning at least the nineteenth and twentieth centuries: while the Spanish state is one of very few European states that has remained territorially intact throughout this period, it has undergone an acute national and identity conflict. This unique case can be explained by a specific combination of factors: the prior existence of a highly consolidated state and pre-national Spanish identity, the relative weakness of political and socio-economic developments, the consequent strength and capacity for reaction of anti-modern social groups, the survival of ethnic identities which are susceptible to political activation, the lack of correspondence between the centres of political power and the centres of emerging economic power, and the loss of the old empire along with an inability to construct a new one.

Basque Polarization: Between Autonomy and Independence *by Francisco J. Llera*
The political behaviour of élites and citizens, the party system, and the standards of

governability in Spain cannot be understood without adequate attention to the splits of identity between citizens and territories in that country. The Basque case is the most critical of those splits, because the relationship between the national government and the Basque region reflects a cleavage of the first order in Spanish politics. The present study of Basque polarized pluralism includes political attitudes, ethnic identity, and the support of terrorism.

Autonomist Regionalism within the Spanish State of the Autonomous Communities: An Interpretation by Xosé-Manoel Núñez

Minority nationalism in the Basque country, Catalonia and Galicia has been a constant feature of twentieth-century Spanish politics. Nevertheless, a new phenomenon added to it has been the emergence of regionalist parties in several of the 17 Spanish autonomous communities created by the 1978 constitution, as well as its consolidation during the 1980s and first half of the 1990s. By examining the political evolution of Spanish regionalisms over the last two decades, an attempt is made at establishing the differences existing between regionalism and minority nationalism.

National Identity and Self-government in Spain: The Galician Case by Antón Losada

This contribution reviews the recent evolution of Galicia (Spain) as a region with very high levels of autonomy. The main idea is that the regional institutional setting developed to administer these levels of autonomy and resources is playing a very important role in the process of national identification and nation construction in Galicia. This new institutional setting is one of the relevant variables that explain recent economic, political and social changes in Galicia.

Autonomy of the Sacred: The Endgame in Kosovo by Steven Majstorovic

Serbia's southern province of Kosovo presents a unique context for the study of autonomy and identity in plural societies in which two sides, Albanians and Serbs, have made maximal demands. This contribution presents a conflict resolution arrangement than can be best described as mixed autonomy. In this arrangement, the issues of Albanian territorial aspirations will be balanced with the powerful ethnic identity markers that Kosovo and certain areas within Kosovo symbolize for Serbs. This mixed autonomy solution might satisfy the bulk of Albanian territorial and demographic demands and can also reassure the cultural identity needs of the Serbs.

Internal Unit Demarcation and National Identity: India, Pakistan and Sri Lanka by Swarna Rajagopalan

What is the relationship between 'internal unit demarcation' and 'national identity'? National (state) identity is defined by the external borders of the national state and expressed by its *internal* units, as is that of sub-state and trans-state collectivities. Negotiation over the demarcation of (their) space within the state is also a negotiation of place and thus of identity. In this contribution, the experiences of India, Pakistan, and Sri Lanka are recalled to amplify and qualify this argument.

The Political Demands of Isolated Indian Bands in British Columbia by Dennis L. Thomson

Canadian Indian policy is examined in the light of the efforts of isolated Indian bands in British Columbia to maintain their culture by staying outside governmental structures. It shows that while promoting a policy of multiculturalism for the mainstream population, Canada's policy has only recently begun to recognize the rights of isolated minorities. The isolated Indians, in turn, have had to seek territorial autonomy, contrary to their concept of territory, in order to allow them to obtain functional autonomy.

Why Territorial Autonomy Is Not a Viable Option for Managing Ethnic Conflict in African Plural Societies by Shaheen Mozaffar and James R. Scarritt
Territorial autonomy is not a viable option for managing ethnic conflict in Africa. The structural, historical and political conditions that have traditionally favoured the use of territorial autonomy elsewhere are nonexistent or occur only infrequently in Africa. Moreover, across the continent, varied combinations of distinctive group morphology, territoriality, changing bases of ethnic identity, and regime types and responses to ethnopolitical mobilization encourage communal contention and increase the strategic utility of multiethnic coalitions as a more effective alternative than the quest for autonomy for resolving ethnopolitical conflicts.

Security in Deeply Divided Societies: The Role of Territorial Autonomy by Donald Rothchild and Caroline A. Hartzell
Territorial autonomy is increasingly being advocated as a means of stabilizing inter-group conflict. Can territorial autonomy successfully mitigate group feelings of insecurity in deeply divided societies? In addressing this question, this study examines data on the use of territorial autonomy drawn from 26 settlements negotiated to end civil wars in the 1945–99 period. We find that when used in conjunction with other institutional safeguards, territorial autonomy can contribute to the stability of such negotiated settlements.

Notes on Contributors

William Safran is professor of Political Science at the University of Colorado, Boulder. He is the author of numerous books, chapters and articles on European and comparative politics as well as on ethnic politics. Among his books are *Veto-Group Politics* (1967), *Ideology and Politics* (1979) and *The French Polity* (5th ed., 1998). He is the editor of *Nationalism and Ethnic Politics*, and is currently serving as president of the Research Committee on Politics and Ethnicity, International Political Science Association.

Ramón Máiz is professor of Political Science at the University of Santiago de Compostela, Spain. He has researched and written on political theory, comparative nationalism and federalism. He is the author of *A Idea de nacion* (1997), editor of *Nacionalismo y Movilización política* (1997) and co-editor of *Nationalism in Europe: Past and Present* (1994).

Luis Moreno is Senior Fellow at the Spanish National Research Council in Madrid. Among his publications in the field of nationalism, federalism, and territorial politics, he is author of *Decentralisation in Britain and Spain: The Cases of Scotland and Catalonia* (1986), *Multiple Ethnoterritorial Concurrence in Spain* (1995), *Federalism: The Spanish Experience* (1997)' and *The Federalization of Spain* (forthcoming).

Justo G. Beramendi is professor of modern history at the University of Santiago de Compostela. His research interests focus on nationalism, particularly in Spain, political ideologies and, recently, on urban social history. Among his books are: *Miseria de la Economía* (1974), *El nacionalismo gallego* (1997), and the edited volumes *Los nacionalismos en la España de la Segunda República* (1991) and *Nationalism in Europe. Past and Present* (1994).

Francisco J. Llera is professor of political science and director of the Department of Political Science at the Basque Country University (Bilbao). He is also vice-president of the Spanish Political Science Association (AECPA). He received a doctorate in political science and sociology from the Universidad de Deusto (Bilbao). His publications include *Postfranquismo y fuerzas políticas en Euskadi* (1985) and *Los vascos y la política* (1994).

Xosé-Manoel Núñez obtained his Ph.D. from the European University Institute of Florence, and is currently professor of contemporary history at the University of Santiago de Compostela. His fields of interest are comparative nationalism, the nationality question in inter-war Europe and the history of migration. Recent publications are *Movimientos nacionalistas en Europa. Siglo XX* (1998) and *Los nacionalismos en la España contemporánea, siglos XIX y XX* (1999).

Antón Losada is assistant professor of political science in the political science faculty and researcher at the University of Compostela's department of sociology and political science. He holds a European doctorate in law from the University of Compostela and a master's in public administration from the Universitat Autónoma de Barcelona (UAB).

Steven Majstorovic is an assistant professor of political science at the University of Wisconsin – Eau Claire. He teaches comparative politics and his research interests include ethnic conflict and conflict resolution. He has published work on ethnicity in Eastern and Western Europe as well as Asia, and is currently at work on a book project that addresses ethnicity in a cross-national context.

Swarna Rajagopalan received her Ph.D. in political science from the University of Illinois at Urbana-Champaign. She currently holds a post-doctoral appointment at Michigan State University's James Madison College.

Dennis L. Thomson is professor of political science at Brigham Young University.

Shaheen Mozaffar is currently AAAS Science, Engineering and Diplomacy Fellow at the United States Agency for International Development. He is an associate professor of political science at Bridgewater State College (on leave) and a research fellow at Boston University's African Studies Center.

James R. Scarritt is professor of political science and faculty associate of the Institute of Behavioral Science at the University of Colorado, Boulder.

Donald Rothchild is professor of political science at the University of California, Davis. His recent books include: co-author, *Sovereignty as Responsibility: Conflict Management in Africa* (1996); *Managing Ethnic Conflict in Africa: Pressures and Incentives for Cooperation* (1997); and co-editor, *The International Spread of Ethnic Conflict:Fear, Diffusion, and Escalation* (1998).

Caroline Hartzell is assistant professor of political science at Gettysburg College. She has written articles and chapters in books on the negotiated settlement of civil wars.

Index

Abkhazians, 21, 23
Aboriginal Peoples, Royal Commission on (Canada), 226
Aborigines, 18, 19, 212, 228 n1
Afghani, Jamaluddin, 201
Africa, sub-Saharan, 5–6, 20, 230
ethnic group morphology in, 235–7
ethnopolitical conflict in, 243–7
ethnopolitical identity in, 236, 238, 239–42, 243–6, 248, 249, 252 n25
history of rule in, 237–8
postindependence regimes in, 242–7
and territorial autonomy, 20, 230, 235, 244, 248, 249
Aga Khan, 202
Agricultural sector. *See* Rural sector
Alava, 129–30
Alava's Union (Unidad Alavesa) (UA; Basque), 112 (table), 113 (table), 114, 115, 116 (table), 117, 129–30, 139 n22
Albania, 22, 177, 178, 179, 182, 185
Albanians, Kosovar, 30, 31
and ethnonational claims on Kosovo, 172, 175–6, 177–8
and future in Kosovo, 15, 22, 170, 182–7
and 20th c. events in Kosovo, 168–71, 177–81
Albor, Fernández, 143
Ali, Rahmat, 202
Alianza Popular (AP)
in Basque country, 112 (table), 113 (table)
in Galicia, 143, 153, 154 (figure)
Alli, Juan-Cruz, 134, 135, 141 n38
Álvarez Junco, José, 80
Ambedkar, B. R., 196
American Indians. *See* Indians, Canadian
Amish, 12, 28, 214
Anderson, B., 137
Angola, 239, 263 (table)
AP. *See* Alianza Popular
Apartheid, 6, 239, 241, 242
Arabs. *See* Palestinian Arabs
Aragon, 81, 128, 130, 132 (table), 133–4
Aragonese Party (Partido Aragonés; PAR), 128, 130, 133–4
Arana, Sabino, 90, 101, 118 n5
Arévalo, M. Clavero, 133
Armenians, 27
Arrow, Kenneth, 55
Assimilation, 40, 48, 65
of Canadian Indians, 223, 224–5, 226

Asturias, 131
Austrian Empire, 175, 176, 178
Authoritarianism, 64, 74 n12
Autonomía model. *See* Autonomous communities, in Spain
Autonomous communities, in Spain, 93, 101, 125–6, 153
distribution of powers in, 126–8, 139 n16
inter-community relations of, 124, 127–8, 129, 130, 131, 132, 133, 136, 139 n20
and invented tradition, 132, 140 n30
and national government, 126, 127, 128, 129, 130, 132, 133, 136
nationalism in, 133, 134, 135, 136, 138
See also Aragon; Asturias; Basque country; Canary Islands; Cantabria; Catalonia; Galicia; La Rioja; Navarre; Valencia
Autonomy, 11, 30, 38, 39
See also Cultural autonomy; Ethnic autonomy; Functional autonomy; Personal autonomy; Self-determination; Self-government; Territorial autonomy
Azerbaijan, 263 (table), 268
Aziz, K.K., 201

Bachelard, Gaston, 192
Baltic republics, 26
Baluchistan, 200, 202, 203
Bandaranaike, S. W. R. D., 205
Bandaranaike-Chelvanayagam Pact (1956), 206
Bangladesh, Bangladeshis, 193, 204, 251 n11
Barreiro, Xose Luis, 143
Basi, D. D., 196
Basque country, Basques, 3, 17, 86, 118 n1
and government institutions, 101, 104–7, 109, 110
identity formation of, 72 n4, 73 n9, 81, 82–3, 84–5, 88, 99 n7, 101–4, 107, 109, 117
and independence, 104–5, 117–8
and language, 102, 103, 104, 107, 117
name of, 102, 119 n8
nationalism of, 82, 87, 89–90, 93, 94, 101, 109–10, 118, 121, 125, 126, 136, 153
parties of, 105, 106–7, 108, 109–10, 111–17, 129
and public/private expression, 102, 103
and violence, 107–12, 113, 118
See also Autonomous communities, in Spain

281

Hamas, 29, 258
HB. *See* Herri Batasuna
HB/EH. *See* Herri Batasuna/Euskal Herritarrok
Heartland, 200, 211 n17
Hegemonic-control regimes, and
  ethnopolitical demands, 242, 244, 245, 249
Hegemonic-exchange regimes, and
  ethnopolitical demands, 242–3, 245, 249
Heintze, Hans-Joachim, 260
Herri Batasuna (HB; Basque), 105, 106, 107,
  109, 110 (table), 112, 115, 117
Herri Batasuna/Euskal Herritarrok (HB/EH;
  Basque), 112 (table), 113, 114
Hindus, 200, 201
Historical memory, 109, 171–2, 178, 186
Hobbes, Thomas, 51
Holbrooke, Richard, 169
Homeland, 192, 231, 242, 246
Hoxha, Enver, 179
Hroch, M., 121
Human rights. *See* Individual rights
Huntington, Samuel, 256
Hutterites, 214
Hutus, 245, 256

Ibos, 30
Identity
  dual, 63–4, 73 n8, n9
  functional, 74 n28
  and modernization, 62–3, 64, 73 n10
  project, 70, 75 n30
  See also Ethnic identity; Territorial
  identity
Immigration, 19, 71, 103
India, 7, 263 (table)
  and Tamils, 26, 191, 207, 208
  territorial unit demarcation in, 4, 192,
  195–200, 209, 210 n7, n10
Indian acts (1876, 1880, 1911, 1951;
  Canada), 224–5, 227
Indian and Northern Affairs, Department of
  (DINA; Canada), 218, 219, 220, 226
Indians, Canadian, 5, 12, 212, 213–14, 228
  n1
  and cultural preservation, 213–14, 215–21,
  226–8
  as defined by government, 215–16
  and government interaction, 218–19, 220–21
  government treatment of, 221–6, 228 n10
  populations of, 216–21, 223, 226
  and self-government, 218, 220, 224, 227
  See also Land rights
Indigenous groups, 18, 19, 212, 228 n1
Individualist pluralism, 44
Individual rights, 20, 25, 32, 41–2, 45, 130,
  183, 184

in monocultural nation, 48
Indo-Sri Lanka Accord (1987), 208
Industrial development. *See* Economy
Information technology, 61, 64, 66–7, 70,
  161 (table)
Institutional completeness, 233, 250 n6
Institutionalism, institutionalization, 15, 25
  See also Neoinstitutionalism; *Under*
  Federalism
Institutional mimicry, 131, 140 n28
Intelligentsia, in Spain, 85, 86, 89, 137
Internet, 66–7
Inuit, 25
Iqbal, 202
Iraq, 263 (table)
Ireland, 23, 97
Irredentism, 25, 26
Islam
  in Balkans, 175, 177
  in sub-Saharan Africa, 240
Israel, 16, 19, 20, 21–2, 25–6, 29, 30, 34 n22
Italy, 15, 70
IU. *See* United Left

Jacobinism, 2, 17, 19, 20, 25, 122
Jayawardene, Junius, 208
Jews, 12, 13, 24, 25, 27, 28, 184

Karachi, 191–2, 203, 204–5
Karadjordjevic (Serbian leader), 176
Kashmir, 194, 202, 203
Kastrioti, Gjergi, 175
Kastrioti, John, 175
Keesing's Contemporary Archives, 264
Khuhro, Hamida, 195
KLA. *See* Kosovo Liberation Army
Kluskus Band, Carrier, 217, 219–21
Kosovo, Kosova, 182–3, 186
Kosovo, Kosovars, 180, 187 n1
  Albanian ethnonational claims on, 172,
  175–6, 177–8
  mixed autonomy as proposal in, 170, 183–7
  populations in, 167, 179, 182, 184
  present issues for, 7, 15, 17, 18, 19, 22, 23,
  30, 31
  Serb ethnonational claims on, 4, 172–7,
  181, 184, 186
  20th c. events in, 168–71, 177–81, 182
Kosovo Liberation Army (KLA), 168, 169,
  170, 182
  and PLO, 182
Kosovo Polje, battle of (Field of the
  Blackbirds; 1389), 173–5, 178, 181, 184,
  186, 187
Krasniqi, Jakup, 182
Kraus, Peter 124

Books of Related Interest

Politics and Policy in Democratic Spain

No Longer Different?

Paul Heywood, *University of Nottingham* (Ed)

> *'This assessment of Spain's transition from forty years of stagnation to a dynamic and successful democracy provides much insight into exactly how this was accomplished and what it portends for the future'*
>
> **Contemporary Review**

'Spain is different' was a favourite tourist board slogan of the Franco dictatorship. But is Spain still different? Spain's 1978 Constitution marked the formal establishment of democracy, following nearly 40 years of dictatorial rule, but what shape has Spanish democracy taken? This volume provides an original series of analyses of the development of politics in Spain since the remarkable success of the transition to democracy. Drawing on the latest research by both established and younger scholars, most of them Spainish, the book offers an up-to-date assessment of democracy in the least studied of Europe's major states. It will be essential reading for those who want to understand politics in contemporary Spain.

248 pages 1999
0 7146 4910 4 cloth
0 7146 4467 6 paper
A special issue of the journal West European Politics

FRANK CASS PUBLISHERS
Newbury House, 900 Eastern Avenue, Ilford, Essex, IG2 7HH
Tel: +44 020 8599 8866 Fax: +44 020 8599 0984 E-mail: info@frankcass.com
NORTH AMERICA
5804 NE Hassalo Street, Portland, OR 97213 3644, USA
Tel: 800 944 6190 Fax: 503 280 8832 E-mail: cass@isbs.com
Website: www.frankcass.com

The Political Economy of Regionalism

Michael Keating, *University of Aberdeen and European University Institute*, and **John Loughlin**, *Cardiff University* (Eds)

> 'This is a very welcome addition to the literature. It comes at a time of confusion and uncertainty where the basic notions and concepts about power, legitimacy, allegiance and institutions are challenged by the redefinition of their territorial dimension. This book brings new insights and effectively blends theoretical considerations with empirical case studies.'
>
> **Yves Mény, European University Institute, Florence**

This book examines the effects of economic and political restructuring on regions in Europe and North America. The main theses are: international economic restructuring and its impact on regions; political realignments at the regional level; questions of territorial identity and their connection with class, gender and neighbourhood identity; policy choices and policy conflicts in regional development.

504 pages 1997
0 7146 4658 X cloth
0 7146 4187 1 paper
Regional & Federal Studies Series Volume 1

FRANK CASS PUBLISHERS
Newbury House, 900 Eastern Avenue, Ilford, Essex, IG2 7HH
Tel: +44 020 8599 8866 Fax: +44 020 8599 0984 E-mail: info@frankcass.com
NORTH AMERICA
5804 NE Hassalo Street, Portland, OR 97213 3644, USA
Tel: 800 944 6190 Fax: 503 280 8832 E-mail: cass@isbs.com
Website: www.frankcass.com

Boundaries, Territory and Postmodernity

David Newman, *Ben Gurion University of the Negev* (Ed)

' ... adds important pieces to the puzzle which makes up global politics.'
Millennium: Journal of International Studies

As the world undergoes rapid technological and economic change, so also the role and functions of the State are challenged. There are those who argue that the nation state has come to an end and that we are entering a new phase in the territorial ordering of the world system. Others hold that boundaries have disappeared and that a globalised world has no need or use for artificial, man-made territorial boundaries. This book seeks to determine the extent to which states and boundaries have in fact disappeared, or are simply changing their functions as we move from an area of fixed territories into a post-Westphalian territorial system. A group of international political geographers and political scientists examine the changing nature of the state, pointing to significant changes on the one hand but equally noting the continued importance of territory and boundaries in determining the political ordering of the postmodern world.

Contributors: *David Newman, Gearóid Ó Tuathial, Fabrizio Eva, Mathias Albert, Anssi Paasi, Alan Hudson, Stanley D Brunn, Simon Dalby, Vladimir Kolossov, John O'Loughlin and Mira Sucharov.*

164 pages 1999
0 7146 4973 2 cloth
0 7146 8033 8 paper
A special issue of the journal Geopolitics

FRANK CASS PUBLISHERS
Newbury House, 900 Eastern Avenue, Ilford, Essex, IG2 7HH
Tel: +44 020 8599 8866 Fax: +44 020 8599 0984 E-mail: info@frankcass.com
NORTH AMERICA
5804 NE Hassalo Street, Portland, OR 97213 3644, USA
Tel: 800 944 6190 Fax: 503 280 8832 E-mail: cass@isbs.com
Website: www.frankcass.com

The Territorial Management of Ethnic Conflict

John Coakley, *University College, Dublin* (Ed)

Recent history has thrown up vivid examples of the renewed capacity of ethnic differences to lead to deep tensions within states, tensions which frequently find expression in some form of inter-territorial conflict. One of the most characteristic approaches to resolve disputes of this kind, or at least to reduce their destructive capacities to a minimum, is to seek an accommodation between the competing groups through some form of territorial restructuring. The object of this book is to look at the very topical issue of the manner in which states attempt to cope with ethnic conflict through such territorial approaches.

Three entirely new chapters Northern Ireland, South Africa, and Yugoslavia – have been commissioned for the revised edition of this highly successful book Several other contributors have provided major revisions, and the editor has written a conclusion to bring the book up to date.

248 pages 2000 (Second Edition)
0 7146 4988 0 cloth
0 7146 8051 6 paper
A special issue of the journal Regional & Federal Studies
Regional & Federal Studies Series

FRANK CASS PUBLISHERS
Newbury House, 900 Eastern Avenue, Ilford, Essex, IG2 7HH
Tel: +44 020 8599 8866 Fax: +44 020 8599 0984 E-mail: info@frankcass.com
NORTH AMERICA
5804 NE Hassalo Street, Portland, OR 97213 3644, USA
Tel: 800 944 6190 Fax: 503 280 8832 E-mail: cass@isbs.com
Website: www.frankcass.com